The Cognitive Neuroscience
of Consciousness

COGNITION Special Issues

The titles in this series are paperback, readily accessible special issues of *COGNITION: An International Journal of Cognitive Science*, edited by Jacques Mehler and produced by special agreement with Elsevier Science Publishers B.V.

Published by The MIT Press:

Visual Cognition
Steven Pinker, guest editor

The Onset of Literacy: Cognitive Processes in Reading Acquisition
Paul Bertelson, guest editor

Spoken Word Recognition
Uli H. Frauenfelder and Lorraine Komisarjevsky Tyler, guest editors

Connections and Symbols
Steven Pinker and Jacques Mehler, guest editors

Neurobiology of Cognition
Peter D. Eimas and Albert M. Galaburda, guest editors

Animal Cognition
C. R. Gallistel, guest editor

COGNITION *on Cognition*
Jacques Mehler and Susana Franck, guest editors

Computational Approaches to Language Acquisition
Michael R. Brent, guest editor

Similarity and Symbols in Human Thinking
Steven A. Sloman and Lance J. Rips, guest editors

Object Recognition in Man, Monkey, and Machine
Michael J. Tarr and Heinrich H. Bülthoff, guest editors

The Cognitive Neuroscience of Consciousness
Stanislas Dehaene, guest editor

Published by Blackwell:

Numerical Cognition
S. Dehaene, guest editor

Lexical and Conceptual Semantics
Beth Levin and Steven Pinker, guest editors

Reasoning and Decision Making
P. N. Johnson-Laird and Eldar Shafir, guest editors

The Cognitive Neuroscience of Consciousness

edited by Stanislas Dehaene

A Bradford Book

The MIT Press
Cambridge, Massachusetts
London, England

Reprinted from COGNITION: *International Journal of Cognitive Science,* Volume 79, Numbers 1–2, April 2001. The MIT Press has exclusive license to sell this English-language book edition throughout the world.

Library of Congress Cataloging-in-Publication Data

The cognitive neuroscience of consciousness / edited by Stanislas Dehaene.
    p.   ; cm. — (Cognition special issues)
"A Bradford book."
"Reprinted from Cognition: international journal of cognitive science, volume 79, numbers 1–2, April 2001"—T.p. verso.
Includes bibliographical references and index.
ISBN 0-262-54131-9 (pbk. : alk. paper)
1. Consciousness 2. Perception 3. Cognitive neuroscience. I. Dehaene, Stanislas. II. Series.
[DNLM: 1. Consciousness—physiology. 2. Cognitive Science. 3. Neuropsychology. BF 311 C676345 2001]
QP411 .C564 2001
153—dc21
  ISBN-13: 978-0-262-54131-2 (pbk. : alk. paper)   2001055864

10 9 8 7 6 5 4 3 2

Contents

Towards a cognitive neuroscience of consciousness: basic evidence and a workspace framework

Stanislas Dehaene[*], Lionel Naccache

Unité INSERM 334, Service Hospitalier Frédéric Joliot, CEA/DRM/DSV, 4, Place du Général Leclerc, 91401 Orsay Cedex, France

Abstract

This introductory chapter attempts to clarify the philosophical, empirical, and theoretical bases on which a cognitive neuroscience approach to consciousness can be founded. We isolate three major empirical observations that any theory of consciousness should incorporate, namely (1) a considerable amount of processing is possible without consciousness, (2) attention is a prerequisite of consciousness, and (3) consciousness is required for some specific cognitive tasks, including those that require durable information maintenance, novel combinations of operations, or the spontaneous generation of intentional behavior. We then propose a theoretical framework that synthesizes those facts: the hypothesis of a global neuronal workspace. This framework postulates that, at any given time, many modular cerebral networks are active in parallel and process information in an unconscious manner. An information becomes conscious, however, if the neural population that represents it is mobilized by top-down attentional amplification into a brain-scale state of coherent activity that involves many neurons distributed throughout the brain. The long-distance connectivity of these 'workspace neurons' can, when they are active for a minimal duration, make the information available to a variety of processes including perceptual categorization, long-term memorization, evaluation, and intentional action. We postulate that this global availability of information through the workspace is what we subjectively experience as a conscious state. A complete theory of consciousness should explain why some cognitive and cerebral representations can be permanently or temporarily inaccessible to consciousness, what is the range of possible conscious contents, how they map onto specific cerebral circuits, and whether a generic neuronal mechanism underlies all of them. We confront the workspace model with those issues and identify novel experimental predictions. Neurophysiological, anatomical, and brain-imaging data strongly argue for a major role of prefrontal cortex,

* Corresponding author. Tel.: +33-1-69-86-78-73; fax: +33-1-69-86-78-16.
 E-mail address: dehaene@shfj.cea.fr (S. Dehaene).

anterior cingulate, and the areas that connect to them, in creating the postulated brain-scale workspace. © 2001 Elsevier Science B.V. All rights reserved.

Keywords: Consciousness; Awareness; Attention; Priming

---

1. Introduction

The goal of this volume is to provide readers with a perspective on the latest contributions of cognitive psychology, neuropsychology, and brain imaging to our understanding of consciousness. For a long time, the word 'consciousness' was used only reluctantly by most psychologists and neuroscientists. This reluctance is now largely overturned, and consciousness has become an exciting and quickly moving field of research. Thanks largely to advances in neuropsychology and brain imaging, but also to a new reading of the psychological and neuropsychological research of the last decades in domains such as attention, working memory, novelty detection, or the body schema, a new comprehension of the neural underpinnings of consciousness is emerging. In parallel, a variety of models, pitched at various levels in neural and/or cognitive science, are now available for some of its key elements.

Within this fresh perspective, firmly grounded in empirical research, the problem of consciousness no longer seems intractable. Yet no convincing synthesis of the recent literature is available to date. Nor do we know yet whether the elements of a solution that we currently have will suffice to solve the problem, or whether key ingredients are still missing. By grouping some of the most innovative approaches together in a single volume, this special issue aims at providing the readers with a new opportunity to see for themselves whether a synthesis is now possible.

In this introduction, we set the grounds for subsequent papers by first clarifying what we think should be the aim of a cognitive neuroscience approach to consciousness. We isolate three major findings that are explored in greater detail in several chapters of this volume. Finally, we propose a synthesis that integrates them into what we view as a promising theoretical framework: the hypothesis of a global neuronal workspace. With this framework in mind, we look back at some of the remaining empirical and conceptual difficulties of consciousness research, and examine whether a clarification is in sight.

2. Nature of the problem and range of possible solutions

Let us begin by clarifying the nature of the problem that a cognitive neuroscience of consciousness should address. In our opinion, this problem, though empirically challenging, is conceptually simple. Human subjects routinely refer to a variety of conscious states. In various daily life and psychophysical testing situations, they use phrases such as 'I was not conscious of X', 'I suddenly realized that Y', or 'I knew that Z, therefore I decided to do X'. In other words, they use a vocabulary of psychological attitudes such as believing, pretending, knowing, etc., that all involve to various extents the concept of 'being conscious'. In any given situation, such conscious phenomenological reports can be very consistent both within and across subjects. The task of cognitive neuroscience is to identify which mental representations and, ultimately, which brain states are associated with such reports. Within a materialistic framework, each instance of mental activity is also a physical brain state.[1] The cognitive neuroscience of consciousness aims at determining whether there is a systematic form of information processing and a reproducible class of neuronal activation patterns that systematically distinguish mental states that subjects label as 'conscious' from other states.[2]

From this perspective, the problem of the cognitive neuroscience of consciousness does not seem to pose any greater conceptual difficulty than identifying the cognitive and cerebral architectures for, say, motor action (identifying what categories of neural and/or information-processing states are systematically associated with moving a limb). What is specific to consciousness, however, is that the object of our study is an introspective phenomenon, not an objectively measurable response. Thus, the scientific body of consciousness calls for a specific attitude which departs from the 'objectivist' or 'behaviorist' perspective often adopted in behavioral and neural experimentation. In order to cross-correlate subjective reports of consciousness with neuronal or information-processing states, the first crucial step is to take seriously introspective phenomenological reports. Subjective reports are the key phenomena that a cognitive neuroscience of consciousness purport to study. As such, they constitute primary data that need to be measured and recorded along with other psychophysiological observations (Dennett, 1992; Weiskrantz, 1997; see also Merikle, Smilek, & Eastwood, this volume).

The idea that introspective reports must be considered as serious data in search of a model does not imply that introspection is a privileged mode of access to the inner workings of the mind. Introspection can be wrong, as is clearly demonstrated, for instance, in split-brain subjects whose left-hemispheric verbal 'interpreter' invents a plausible but clearly false explanation for the behavior caused by their right hemisphere (Gazzaniga, LeDoux, & Wilson, 1977). We need to find a scientific explanation for subjective reports, but we must not assume that they always constitute accurate descriptions of reality. This distinction is clearest in the case of hallucinations. If someone claims to have visual hallucinations of floating faces, or 'out-of-body' experiences, for instance, it would be wrong to take these reports as unequi-

---

[1] We use the word 'state' in the present context to mean any configuration of neural activity, whether stable (a fixed point) or dynamic (a trajectory in neural space). It is an open question as to whether neural states require stability over a minimal duration to become conscious, although the workspace model would predict that some degree of stable amplification over a period of at least about 100 ms is required.

[2] One should also bear in mind the possibility that what naive subjects call 'consciousness' will ultimately be parceled into distinct theoretical constructs, each with its own neural substrate, just like the naive concept of 'warmth' was ultimately split into two distinct physical parameters, temperature and heat.

vocal evidence for parapsychology, but it would be equally wrong to dismiss them as unverifiable subjective phenomena. The correct approach is to try to explain how such conscious states can arise, for instance by appealing to an inappropriate activation of face processing or vestibular neural circuits, as can indeed be observed by brain-imaging methods during hallucinations (Ffytche et al., 1998; Silbersweig et al., 1995).

The emphasis on subjective reports as data does not mean that the resulting body of knowledge will be inherently subjective and therefore non-scientific. As noted by Searle (1998), a body of knowledge is scientific ('epistemically objective') inasmuch as it can be verified independently of the attitudes or preferences of the experimenters, but there is nothing in this definition that prevents a genuinely scientific approach of domains that are inherently subjective because they exist only in the experience of the subject ('ontologically subjective' phenomena). "The requirement that science be objective does not prevent us from getting an epistemically objective science of a domain that is ontologically subjective." (Searle, 1998, p. 1937).

One major hurdle in realizing this program, however, is that "we are still in the grip of a residual dualism" (Searle, 1998, p. 1939). Many scientists and philosophers still adhere to an essentialist view of consciousness, according to which conscious states are ineffable experiences of a distinct nature that may never be amenable to a physical explanation. Such a view, which amounts to a Cartesian dualism of substance, has led some to search for the bases of consciousness in a different form of physics (Penrose, 1990). Others make the radical claim that two human brains can be identical, atom for atom, and yet one can be conscious while the other is a mere 'zombie' without consciousness (Chalmers, 1996).

Contrary to those extreme statements, contributors to the present volume share the belief that the tools of cognitive psychology and neuroscience may suffice to analyze consciousness. This need not imply a return to an extreme form of direct psychoneural reductionism. Rather, research on the cognitive neuroscience of consciousness should clearly take into account the many levels of organization at which the nervous system can be studied, from molecules to synapses, neurons, local circuits, large scale networks, and the hierarchy of mental representations that they support (Changeux & Dehaene, 1989). In our opinion, it would be inappropriate, and a form of 'category error', to attempt to reduce consciousness to a low level of neural organization, such as the firing of neurons in thalamocortical circuits or the properties of NMDA receptors, without specifying in functional terms the consequences of this neural organization at the cognitive level. While characterization of such neural bases will clearly be indispensable to our understanding of consciousness, it cannot suffice. A full theory will require many more 'bridging laws' to explain how these neural events organize into larger-scale active circuits, how those circuits themselves support specific representations and forms of information processing, and how these processes are ultimately associated with conscious reports. Hence, this entire volume privileges cognitive neuroscientific approaches to consciousness that seem capable of addressing both the cognitive architecture of mental representations and their neural implementation.

3. Three fundamental empirical findings on consciousness

In this section, we begin by providing a short review of empirical observations that we consider as particularly relevant to the cognitive neuroscience of consciousness. We focus on three findings: the depth of unconscious processing; the attention-dependence of conscious perception; and the necessity of consciousness for some integrative mental operations.

3.1. Cognitive processing is possible without consciousness

Our first general observation is that a considerable amount of processing can occur without consciousness. Such unconscious processing is open to scientific investigation using behavioral, neuropsychological and brain-imaging methods. By increasing the range of cognitive processes that do not require consciousness, studies of unconscious processing contribute to narrowing down the cognitive bases of consciousness. The current evidence indicates that many perceptual, motor, semantic, emotional and context-dependent processes can occur unconsciously.

A first line of evidence comes from studies of brain-lesioned patients. Pöppel, Held, and Frost (1973) demonstrated that four patients with a partial blindness due to a lesion in visual cortical areas (hemianopsic scotoma) remained able to detect visual stimuli presented in their blind field. Although the patients claimed that they could not see the stimuli, indicating a lack of phenomenal consciousness, they nevertheless performed above chance when directing a visual saccade to them. This 'blindsight' phenomenon was subsequently replicated and extended in numerous studies (Weiskrantz, 1997). Importantly, some patients performed at the same level as control subjects, for instance in motor pointing tasks. Thus, unconscious processing is not limited to situations in which information is degraded or partially available. Rather, an entire stream of processing may unfold outside of consciousness.

Dissociations between accurate performance and lack of consciousness were subsequently identified in many categories of neuropsychological impairments such as visual agnosia, prosopagnosia, achromatopsia, callosal disconnection, aphasia, alexia, amnesia, and hemineglect (for reviews, see Köhler & Moscovitch, 1997; Schacter, Buckner, & Koutstaal, 1998; see also Driver & Vuilleumier, this volume). The current evidence suggests that, in many of these cases, unconscious processing is possible at a perceptual, but also a semantic level. For instance, Renault, Signoret, Debruille, Breton, and Bolgert (1989) recorded event-related potentials to familiar and unknown faces in a prosopagnosic patient. Although the patient denied any recognition of the familiar faces, an electrical waveform indexing perceptual processing, the P300, was significantly shorter and more intense for the familiar faces. Similar results were obtained by recording the electrodermal response, an index of vegetative processing of emotional stimuli, in prosopagnosic patients (Bauer, 1984; Tranel & Damasio, 1985). Even clearer evidence for semantic-level processing comes from studies of picture–word priming in neglect patients (McGlinchey-Berroth, Milberg, Verfaellie, Alexander, & Kilduff, 1993). When two images are presented simultaneously in the left and right visual fields, neglect patients deny seeing the one on the left, and indeed cannot report it beyond chance level. Nevertheless, when having to perform a lexical decision task on a subsequent foveal word, which can be related or unrelated to the previous image, they show the same amount of semantic priming from both hemifields, indicating that even the unreportable left-side image was processed to a semantic level.

Similar priming studies indicate that a considerable amount of unconscious processing also occurs in normal subjects. Even a very brief visual stimulus can be perceived consciously when presented in isolation. However, the same brief stimulus can fail to reach consciousness when it is surrounded in time by other stimuli that serve as masks. This lack of consciousness can be assessed objectively using signal detection theory (for discussion, see Holender, 1986; Merikle, 1992; see also Merikle et al.).[3] Crucially, the masked stimulus can still have a measurable influence on the processing of subsequent stimuli, a phenomenon known as masked priming. There are now multiple demonstrations of perceptual, semantic, and motor processing of masked stimuli. For instance, in various tasks, processing of a conscious target stimulus can be facilitated by the prior masked presentation of the same stimulus (repetition priming; e.g. Bar & Biederman, 1999). Furthermore, masked priming also occurs when the relation between prime and target is a purely semantic one, such as between two related words (Dehaene, Naccache et al., 1998; Klinger & Greenwald, 1995; Marcel, 1983; see also Merikle et al.). We studied semantic priming with numerical stimuli (Dehaene, Naccache et al., 1998; Koechlin, Naccache, Block, & Dehaene, 1999). When subjects had to decide whether target numbers were larger or smaller than five, the prior presentation of another masked number accelerated the response in direct proportion to its amount of similarity with the target, as measured by numerical distance (Koechlin et al., 1999). Furthermore, the same number-comparison experiment also provided evidence that processing of the prime occurs even beyond this semantic stage to reach motor preparation systems (Dehaene, Naccache et al., 1998). When the instruction specified that targets larger than five should be responded to with the right hand, for instance, primes that were larger than five facilitated a right-hand response, and measures of brain activation demonstrated a significant covert activation of motor cortex prior to the main overt response (see also Eimer & Schlaghecken, 1998; Neumann & Klotz, 1994). Thus, an entire stream of perceptual, semantic and motor processes, specified by giving arbitrary verbal instructions to a normal subject, can occur outside of consciousness.

The number priming experiment also illustrates that it is now feasible to visualize

---

[3] Unfortunately, signal detection theory provides an imperfect criterion for consciousness. If subjects exhibit a d' measure that does not differ significantly from zero in a forced-choice stimulus detection or discrimination task, one may conclude that no information about the stimulus was available for conscious processing. Conversely, however, a non-zero d' measure need not imply consciousness, but may result from both conscious and unconscious influences. Experimental paradigms that partially go beyond this limitation have been proposed (e.g. Jacoby, 1991; Klinger & Greenwald, 1995). We concur with Merikle et al. (this volume), however, in thinking that subjective reports remain the crucial measure when assessing the degree of consciousness (see also Weiskrantz, 1997).

directly the brain areas involved in unconscious processing, without having to rely exclusively on indirect priming measures (Dehaene, Naccache et al., 1998; Morris, Öhman, & Dolan, 1998; Sahraie et al., 1997; Whalen et al., 1998; see also Driver & Vuilleumier and Kanwisher, this volume). In the Whalen et al. (1998) experiment, for instance, subjects were passively looking at emotionally neutral faces throughout. Yet the brief, unconscious presentation of masked faces bearing an emotional expression of fear, relative to neutral masked faces, yielded an increased activation of the amygdala, a brain structure known to be involved in emotional processing. We expect such brain-imaging studies to play an important role in mapping the cerebral networks implicated in unconscious processing, and therefore isolating the neural substrates of consciousness.

3.2. Attention is a prerequisite of consciousness

Experiments with masked primes indicate that some minimal duration and clarity of stimulus presentation are necessary for it to become conscious. However, are these conditions also sufficient? Do all stimuli with sufficient intensity and duration automatically gain access to consciousness? Evidence from brain-lesioned patients as well as normal subjects provides a negative answer. Conditions of stimulation, by themselves, do not suffice to determine whether a given stimulus is or is not perceived consciously. Rather, conscious perception seems to result from an interaction of these stimulation factors with the attentional state of the observer. The radical claim was even made that "there seems to be no conscious perception without attention" (Mack & Rock, 1998, p. ix).

Brain-lesioned patients suffering from hemineglect provide a striking illustration of the role of attentional factors in consciousness (Driver & Mattingley, 1998; see also Driver & Vuilleumier, 2001, this issue). Hemineglect frequently results from lesions of the right parietal region, which is thought to be involved in the orientation of attention towards locations and objects. Neglect patients fail to attend to stimuli located in contralesional space, regardless of their modality of their presentation. The focus of attention seems permanently biased toward the right half of space, and patients behave as if the left half had become unavailable to consciousness. This is seen most clearly in the extinction phenomenon: when two visual stimuli are presented side by side left and right of fixation, the patients report only seeing the stimulus on the right, and appear completely unconscious of the identity or even the presence of a stimulus on the left. Nevertheless, the very same left-hemifield stimulus, when presented in isolation at the same retinal location, is perceived normally. Furthermore, even during extinction, priming measures indicate a considerable amount of covert processing of the neglected stimulus at both perceptual and semantic levels (e.g. McGlinchey-Berroth et al., 1993). Hence, although the cortical machinery for bottom-up processing of left-lateralized stimuli seems to be largely intact and activated during extinction, this is clearly not sufficient to produce a conscious experience; a concomitant attentional signal seems compulsory.

In normal subjects, the role of attention in conscious perception has been the subject of considerable research (see Merikle et al., 1995). While there remains controversy concerning the depth of processing of unattended stimuli, there is no doubt that attention serves as a filter prior to conscious perception (see Driver & Vuilleumier, 2001, this issue). Visual search experiments indicate that, given an array of items, the orienting of attention plays a critical role in determining whether a given item gains access to consciousness (Sperling, 1960; Treisman & Gelade, 1980). Objects that do not fall in an attended region of the visual field cannot be consciously reported. Furthermore, there are systematic parallels between the fate of unattended stimuli and the processing of masked primes. Merikle and Joordens (1997) describe three phenomena (Stroop priming, false recognition, and exclusion failure) in which qualitatively similar patterns of performance are observed in divided attention and in masked priming experiments. They conclude that "perception with and without awareness, and perception with and without attention, are equivalent ways of describing the same underlying process distinction" (p. 219).

Mack and Rock (1998) have investigated a phenomenon called inattentional blindness that clearly illustrates this point. They asked normal subjects to engage in a demanding visual discrimination task at a specific location in their visual field. Then on a single trial, another visual stimulus appeared at a different location. This stimulus clearly had sufficient contrast and duration (typically 200 ms) to be perceptible in isolation, yet the use of a single critical trial and of a distracting task ensured that it was completely unattended and unexpected. Under these conditions a large percentage of subjects failed to report the critical stimulus and continued to deny its presence when explicitly questioned about it. In some experimental conditions, even a large black circle presented for 700 ms in the fovea failed to be consciously perceived! Yet priming measures again indicated that the unseen stimulus was processed covertly. For instance, a word extinguished by inattentional blindness yielded strong priming in a subsequent stem completion task. Such evidence, together with similar observations that supra-threshold visual stimuli fail to be reported during the 'attentional blink' (Luck, Vogel, & Shapiro, 1996; Raymond, Shapiro, & Arnell, 1992; Vogel, Luck, & Shapiro, 1998), and that large changes in a complex visual display fail to be noticed unless they are attended ('change blindness'; e.g. O'Regan, Rensink, & Clark, 1999), support the hypothesis that attention is a necessary prerequisite for conscious perception.[4]

3.3. Consciousness is required for specific mental operations

Given that a considerable amount of mental processing seems to occur uncon-

---

[4] The notion that attention is required for conscious perception seems to raise a potential paradox: if we can only perceive what we attend to, how do we ever become aware of unexpected information? In visual search experiments, for instance, a vertical line 'pops out' of the display and is immediately detected regardless of display size. How is this possible if that location did not receive prior attention? Much of this paradox dissolves, however, once it is recognized that some stimuli can automatically and unconsciously capture attention (Yantis & Jonides, 1984, 1996). Although we can consciously orient our attention, for instance to search through a display, orienting of attention is also determined by unconscious bottom-up mechanisms that have been attuned by evolution to quickly orient us to salient new features of our environment. Pop-out experiments can be reinterpreted as revealing a fast attraction of attention to salient features.

sciously, one is led to ask what are the computational benefits associated with consciousness. Are there any specific mental operations that are feasible only when one is conscious of performing them? Are there sharp limits on the style and amount of unconscious computation? This issue is obviously crucial if one is to understand the computational nature and the evolutionary advantages associated with consciousness. Yet little empirical research to date bears on this topic. In this section, which is clearly more speculative than previous ones, we tentatively identify at least three classes of computations that seem to require consciousness: durable and explicit information maintenance, novel combinations of operations, and intentional behavior (see also Jack & Shallice, this volume for a similar attempt to identify 'Type-C' processes specifically associated with consciousness).

3.3.1. Durable and explicit information maintenance

The classical experiment by Sperling (1960) on iconic memory demonstrates that, in the absence of conscious amplification, the visual representation of an array of letters quickly decays to an undetectable level. After a few seconds or less, only the letters that have been consciously attended remain accessible. We suggest that, in many cases, the ability to maintain representations in an active state for a durable period of time in the absence of stimulation seems to require consciousness. By 'in an active state', we mean that the information is encoded in the firing patterns of active populations of neurons and is therefore immediately available to influence the systems they connect with. Although sensory and motor information can be temporarily maintained by passive domain-specific buffers such as Sperling's iconic store, with a half-life varying from a few hundreds of milliseconds to a few seconds (auditory information being possibly held for a longer duration than visual information), exponential decay seems to be the rule whenever information is not attended (e.g. Cohen & Dehaene, 1998; Tiitinen, May, Reinikainen, & Naatanen, 1994).

Priming studies nicely illustrate the short-lived nature of unconscious representations. In successful masked priming experiments, the stimulus onset asynchrony (SOA) between prime and target is typically quite short, in the order of 50–150 ms. Experiments that have systematically varied this parameter indicate that the amount of priming drops sharply to a non-significant value within a few hundreds of milliseconds (Greenwald, 1996). Thus, the influence of an unconscious prime decays very quickly, suggesting that its mental representation vanishes dramatically as time passes.[5] This interpretation is supported by single-unit recordings in the monkey infero-temporal (IT) cortex during masked and unmasked presentations of faces (Rolls & Tovee, 1994; Rolls, Tovee, & Panzeri, 1999). A very short and masked visual presentation yields a short-lasting burst of firing (~50 ms) in face-

---

[5] Some incidental learning and mere exposure experiments have reported unconscious priming effects at a long duration (e.g. Bar & Biederman, 1999; Bornstein & D'Agostino, 1992; Elliott & Dolan, 1998). We interpret these findings as suggesting that even unseen, short-lived stimuli may leave long-lasting latent traces, for instance in the form of alterations in synaptic weights in the processing network. This is not incompatible, however, with our postulate that no active, explicit representation of a prime can remain beyond a few hundred milliseconds in the absence of conscious attentional amplification.

selective cells. However, an unmasked face presented for the same short duration yields a long burst whose duration (up to 350 ms) far exceeds the stimulation period. Physiological and behavioral studies in both humans and monkeys suggest that this ability to maintain information on-line independently of the stimulus presence depends on a working memory system associated with dorsolateral prefrontal regions (Fuster, 1989; Goldman-Rakic, 1987). By this argument, then, the working memory system made available by prefrontal circuitry must be tightly related to the durable maintenance of information in consciousness (e.g. Fuster, 1989; Kosslyn & Koenig, 1992; Posner, 1994; see below).

Another remarkable illustration of the effect of time delays on the ability to maintain active and accurate unconscious representation is provided by studies of the impact of visual illusions on reaching behavior (Aglioti, DeSouza, & Goodale, 1995; Daprati & Gentilucci, 1997; Gentilucci, Chieffi, Deprati, Saetti, & Toni, 1996; Hu, Eagleson, & Goodale, 1999). In the Müller-Lyer and Tichener illusions, although two objects have the same objective length, one of them is perceived as looking shorter due to the influence of contextual cues. Nevertheless, when subjects make a fast reaching movement toward the objects, their finger grip size is essentially unaffected by the illusion and is therefore close to objective size. Hence, the motor system is informed of an objective size parameter which is not available to consciousness, providing yet another instance of unconscious visuo-motor processing. Crucially, however, when one introduces a short delay between the offset of stimuli and the onset of the motor response, grip size becomes less and less accurate and is now influenced by the subjective illusion (Gentilucci et al., 1996). In this situation, subjects have to bridge the gap between stimulus and response by maintaining an internal representation of target size. The fact that they now misreach indicates that the accurate but unconscious information cannot be maintained across a time delay. Again, active information survives a temporal gap only if it is conscious.

3.3.2. Novel combinations of operations

The ability to combine several mental operations to perform a novel or unusual task is a second type of computation that seems to require consciousness. Conflict situations, in which a routine behavior must be inhibited and superseded by a non-automatized strategy, nicely illustrate this point. Merikle, Joordens, and Stolz (1995) studied subjects' ability to control inhibition in a Stroop-like task as a function of the conscious perceptibility of the conflicting information. Subjects had to classify a colored target string as green or red. Each target was preceded by a prime which could be the word GREEN or RED. In this situation, the classical Stroop effect was obtained: responses were faster when the word and color were congruent than when they were incongruent. However, when the prime–target relations were manipulated by presenting 75% of incongruent trials, subjects could strategically take advantage of the predictability of the target from the prime, and became faster on incongruent trials than on congruent trials, thus inverting the Stroop effect. Crucially, this strategic inversion only occurred when the prime was consciously perceptible. No strategic effect was observed when the word prime was masked (Merikle et al.,

1995) or fell outside the focus of attention (Merikle & Joordens, 1997). In this situation, only the classical, automatic Stroop effect prevailed. Thus, the ability to inhibit an automatic stream of processes and to deploy a novel strategy depended crucially on the conscious availability of information.

We tentatively suggest, as a generalization, that the strategic operations which are associated with planning a novel strategy, evaluating it, controlling its execution, and correcting possible errors cannot be accomplished unconsciously. It is noteworthy that such processes are always associated with a subjective feeling of 'mental effort', which is absent during automatized or unconscious processing and may therefore serve as a selective marker of conscious processing (Dehaene, Kerszberg, & Changeux, 1998).[6]

3.3.3. Intentional behavior

A third type of mental activity that may be specifically associated with consciousness is the spontaneous generation of intentional behavior. Consider the case of blindsight patients. Some of these patients, even though they claim to be blind, show such an excellent performance in pointing to objects that some have suggested them as a paradigmatic example of the philosopher's 'zombie' (a hypothetical human being who would behave normally, but lacks consciousness). As noted by Dennett (1992) and Weiskrantz (1997), however, this interpretation fails to take into account a fundamental difference with normal subjects: blindsight patients never spontaneously initiate any visually-guided behavior in their impaired field. Good performance can be elicited only by forcing them to respond to stimulation.

All patients with preserved implicit processing seem to have a similar impairment in using the preserved information to generate intentional behavior. The experimental paradigms that reveal above-chance performance in these patients systematically rely on automatizable tasks (stimulus–response associations or procedural learning) with forced-choice instructions. This is also true for normal subjects in subliminal processing tasks. As noted above, masked priming experiments reveal the impossibility for subjects to strategically use the unconscious information demonstrated by priming effects. Given the large amount of information that has been demonstrated to be available with consciousness, this limitation on subliminal processing is not trivial. Intentionally driven behaviors may constitute an important class of processes accessible only to conscious information.

Introspective speech acts, in which the subject uses language to describe his/her mental life, constitute a particular category of intentional behaviors that relate to conscious processing. Consciousness is systematically associated with the potential ability for the subject to report on his/her mental state. This property of reportability is so exclusive to conscious information that it is commonly used as an empirical

---

[6] An important qualification is that even tasks that involve complex series of operations and that initially require conscious effort may become progressively automatized after some practice (e.g. driving a car). At this point, such tasks may proceed effortlessly and without conscious control. Indeed, many demonstrations of unconscious priming involve acquired strategies that required a long training period, such as word reading.

criterion to assess the conscious or unconscious status of an information or a mental
state (Gazzaniga et al., 1977; Weiskrantz, 1997).

4. A theoretical framework for consciousness

Once those three basic empirical properties of conscious processing have been
identified, can a theoretical framework be proposed for them? Current accounts of
consciousness are founded on extraordinarily diverse and seemingly incommensu-
rate principles, ranging from cellular properties such as thalamocortical rhythms to
purely cognitive constructions such as the concept of a 'central executive'. Instead
of attempting a synthesis of those diverse proposals, we isolate in this section three
theoretical postulates that are largely shared, even if they are not always explicitly
recognized. We then try to show how these postulates, taken together, converge onto
a coherent framework for consciousness: the hypothesis of a global neuronal workspace.

4.1. The modularity of mind

A first widely shared hypothesis is that automatic or unconscious cognitive
processing rests on multiple dedicated processors or 'modules' (Baars, 1989;
Fodor, 1983; Shallice, 1988). There are both functional and neurobiological definitions of modularity. In cognitive psychology, modules have been characterized by
their information encapsulation, domain specificity, and automatic processing. In
neuroscience, specialized neural circuits that process only specific types of inputs
have been identified at various spatial scales, from orientation-selective cortical
columns to face-selective areas. The breakdown of brain circuits into functionally
specialized subsystems can be evidenced by various methods including brain
imaging, neuropsychological dissociation, and cell recording.

We shall not discuss here the debated issue of whether each postulated psychological module can be identified with a specific neural circuit. We note, however,
that the properties of automaticity and information encapsulation postulated in
psychology are partially reflected in modular brain circuits. Specialized neural
responses, such as face-selective cells, can be recorded in both awake and anesthetized animals, thus reflecting an automatic computation that can proceed without
attention. Increasingly refined analyses of anatomical connectivity reveal a channel-
ing of information to specific targeted circuits and areas, thus supporting a form of
information encapsulation (Felleman & Van Essen, 1991; Young et al., 1995).

As a tentative theoretical generalization, we propose that a given process, involving several mental operations, can proceed unconsciously only if a set of
adequately interconnected modular systems is available to perform each of the
required operations. For instance, a masked fearful face may cause unconscious
emotional priming because there are dedicated neural systems in the superior colliculus, pulvinar, and right amygdala associated with the attribution of emotional
valence to faces (Morris, Öhman, & Dolan, 1999). Our hypothesis implies that
multiple unconscious operations can proceed in parallel, as long as they do not

simultaneously appeal to the same modular systems in contradictory ways. Note that unconscious processing may not be limited to low-level or computationally simple operations. High-level processes may operate unconsciously, as long as they are associated with functional neural pathways either established by evolution, laid down during development, or automatized by learning. Hence, there is no systematic relation between the objective complexity of a computation and the possibility of its proceeding unconsciously. For instance, face processing, word reading, and postural control all require complex computations, yet there is considerable evidence that they can proceed without attention based on specialized neural subsystems. Conversely, computationally trivial but non-automatized operations, such as solving 21 − 8, require conscious effort.

4.2. The apparent non-modularity of the conscious mind

It was recognized early on that several mental activities cannot be explained easily by the modularity hypothesis (Fodor, 1983). During decision making or discourse production, subjects bring to mind information conveyed by many different sources in a seemingly non-modular fashion. Furthermore, during the performance of effortful tasks, they can temporarily inhibit the automatic activation of some processors and enter into a strategic or 'controlled' mode of processing (Posner, 1994; Schneider & Shiffrin, 1977; Shallice, 1988). Many cognitive theories share the hypothesis that controlled processing requires a distinct functional architecture which goes beyond modularity and can establish flexible links amongst existing processors. It has been called the central executive (Baddeley, 1986), the supervisory attentional system (Shallice, 1988), the anterior attention system (Posner, 1994; Posner & Dehaene, 1994), the global workspace (Baars, 1989; Dehaene, Kerszberg, & Changeux, 1998) or the dynamic core (Tononi & Edelman, 1998).

Here we synthesize those ideas by postulating that, besides specialized processors, the architecture of the human brain also comprises a distributed neural system or 'workspace' with long-distance connectivity that can potentially interconnect multiple specialized brain areas in a coordinated, though variable manner (Dehaene, Kerszberg, & Changeux, 1998). Through the workspace, modular systems that do not directly exchange information in an automatic mode can nevertheless gain access to each other's content. The global workspace thus provides a common 'communication protocol' through which a particularly large potential for the combination of multiple input, output, and internal systems becomes available (Baars, 1989).

If the workspace hypothesis is correct, it becomes an empirical issue to determine which modular systems make their contents globally available to others through the workspace. Computations performed by modules that are not interconnected through the workspace would never be able to participate in a conscious content, regardless of the amount of introspective effort (examples may include the brainstem systems for blood pressure control, or the superior colliculus circuitry for gaze control). The vast amounts of information that we can consciously process suggests that at least five main categories of neural systems must participate in the work-space: perceptual circuits that inform about the present state of the environment; motor circuits that allow the preparation and controlled execution of actions; long-term memory circuits that can reinstate past workspace states; evaluation circuits that attribute them a valence in relation to previous experience; and attentional or top-down circuits that selectively gate the focus of interest. The global interconnec-tion of those five systems can explain the subjective unitary nature of consciousness and the feeling that conscious information can be manipulated mentally in a largely unconstrained fashion. In particular, connections to the motor and language systems allow any workspace content to be described verbally or non-verbally ('reportabil-ity'; Weiskrantz, 1997).

4.3. Attentional amplification and dynamic mobilization

A third widely shared theoretical postulate concerns the role of attention in gating access to consciousness. As reviewed earlier, empirical data indicate that consider-able processing is possible without attention, but that attention is required for infor-mation to enter consciousness (Mack & Rock, 1998). This is compatible with Michael Posner's hypothesis of an attentional amplification (Posner, 1994; Posner & Dehaene, 1994), according to which the orienting of attention causes increased cerebral activation in attended areas and a transient increase in their efficiency.

Dehaene, Kerszberg, and Changeux (1998) have integrated this notion within the workspace model by postulating that top-down attentional amplification is the mechanism by which modular processes can be temporarily mobilized and made available to the global workspace, and therefore to consciousness. According to this theory, the same cerebral processes may, at different times, contribute to the content of consciousness or not. To enter consciousness, it is not sufficient for a process to have on-going activity; this activity must also be amplified and maintained over a sufficient duration for it to become accessible to multiple other processes. Without such 'dynamic mobilization', a process may still contribute to cognitive perfor-mance, but only unconsciously.

A consequence of this hypothesis is the absence of a sharp anatomical delineation of the workspace system. In time, the contours of the workspace fluctuate as differ-ent brain circuits are temporarily mobilized, then demobilized. It would therefore be incorrect to identify the workspace, and therefore consciousness, with a fixed set of brain areas. Rather, many brain areas contain workspace neurons with the appro-priate long-distance and widespread connectivity, and at any given time only a fraction of these neurons constitute the mobilized workspace. As discussed below, workspace neurons seem to be particularly dense in prefrontal cortices (PFCs) and anterior cingulate (AC), thus conferring those areas a dominant role. However, we see no need to postulate that any single brain area is systematically activated in all conscious states, regardless of their content. It is the style of activation (dynamic long-distance mobilization), rather than its cerebral localization, which charac-terizes consciousness. This hypothesis therefore departs radically from the notion of a single central 'Cartesian theater' in which conscious information is displayed

(Dennett, 1992). In particular, information that is already available within a modular process does not need to be re-represented elsewhere for a 'conscious audience': dynamic mobilization makes it directly available in its original format to all other workspace processes.

The term 'mobilization' may be misinterpreted as implying the existence of an internal homunculus who decides to successively amplify and then suppress the relevant processes at will. Our view, however, considers this mobilization as a collective dynamic phenomenon that does not require any supervision, but rather results from the spontaneous generation of stochastic activity patterns in workspace neurons and their selection according to their adequacy to the current context (Dehaene, Kerszberg, & Changeux, 1998). Stochastic fluctuations in workspace neurons would result, at the collective neuronal assembly level, in the spontaneous activation, in a sudden, coherent, exclusive and 'auto-catalytic' (self-amplifying) manner, of a subset of workspace neurons, the rest being inhibited. This active workspace state is not completely random, but is heavily constrained and selected by the activation of surrounding processors that encode the behavioral context, goals, and rewards of the organism. In the resulting dynamics, transient self-sustained workspace states follow one another in a constant stream, without requiring any external supervision. Explicit, though still elementary, computer simulations of such 'neuronal Darwinism' are available, illustrating its computational feasibility (Changeux & Dehaene, 1989; Dehaene & Changeux, 1997; Dehaene, Kerszberg, & Changeux, 1998; Friston, Tononi, Reeke, Sporns, & Edelman, 1994).

5. Empirical consequences, reinterpretations, and predictions

The remainder of this paper is devoted to an exploration of the empirical consequences of this theoretical framework. We first examine the predicted structural and dynamical conditions under which information may become conscious. We then consider the consequences of our views for the exploration of the neural substrates of consciousness and its clinical or experimental disruption.

5.1. Structural constraints on the contents of consciousness

An important scientific goal regarding consciousness is to explain why some representations that are encoded in the nervous system are permanently impervious to consciousness. In the present framework, the conscious availability of information is postulated to be determined by two structural criteria which are ultimately grounded in brain anatomy. First, the information must be represented in an active manner in the firing of one or several neuronal assemblies. Second, bidirectional connections must exist between these assemblies and the set of workspace neurons, so that a sustained amplification loop can be established. Cerebral representations that violate either criteria are predicted to be permanently inaccessible to consciousness.

The first criterion – active representation – excludes from the contents of consciousness the enormous wealth of information which is present in the nervous system only in latent form, for instance in the patterns of anatomical connections or in strengthened memory traces. As an example, consider the wiring of the auditory system. We can consciously attend to the spatial location of a sound, but we are oblivious to the cues that our nervous system uses to compute it. One such cue is the small time difference between the time of arrival of sound in the two ears (interaural delay). Interaural delay is coded in a very straightforward manner by the neural connection lengths of the medial superior olive (Smith, Joris, & Yin, 1993). Yet such connectivity information, by hypothesis, cannot reach consciousness.

More generally, the 'active representation' criterion may explain the observation that we can never be conscious of the inner workings of our cerebral processes, but only of their outputs. A classical example is syntax: we can become conscious that a sentence is not grammatical, but we have no introspection on the inner workings of the syntactical apparatus that underlies this judgment, and which is presumably encoded in connection weights within temporal and frontal language areas.

There is, however, one interesting exception to this limit on introspection. Subjects' verbal reports do provide a reliable source of information on a restricted class of processes that are slow, serial, and controlled, such as those involved in solving complex arithmetic problems or the Tower of Hanoi task (Ericcson & Simon, 1993). We propose that what distinguishes such processes is that they are not encoded in hardwired connectivity, but rather are generated dynamically through the serial organization of active representations of current goals, intentions, decisions, intermediate results, or errors. The firing of many prefrontal neurons in the monkey encodes information about the animal's current goals, behavioral plans, errors and successes (e.g. Fuster, 1989). According to the workspace model, such active representations of on-going performance can become available for conscious amplification and communication to other workspace components, explaining, for instance, that we can consciously report the strategic steps that we adopted. The model implies that this is the only situation where we can have reliable conscious access to our mental algorithms. Even then, such access is predicted to be limited. Indeed, when multiplying 32 by 47, we are conscious of our goals, subgoals, main steps (multiplying 2 by 7, then 3 by 7, etc.), and possible errors, but we have no introspection as to how we solve each individual problem.

Our second criterion – bidirectional connectivity with the workspace – implies that some representations, even though they are encoded by an active neuronal assembly, may permanently evade consciousness. This may occur if the connectivity needed to establish a reverberating loop with workspace units is absent or damaged. Consider, for example, the minimal contrast between patients with visual neglect, patients with a retinal scotoma, and normal subjects who all have a blind spot in their retina. Superficially, these conditions have much in common. In all of them, subjects fail to consciously perceive visual stimuli presented at a certain location. Yet the objective processing abilities and subjective reports associated with those visual impairments are strikingly different (see Table 1). Patients with visual neglect typically cannot see stimuli in the neglected part of space, but are not conscious that they are lacking this information. Patients with a retinal scotoma also cannot see in a specific region of their visual field, but they are conscious of their

Table 1

Three classical perceptual conditions in which conscious vision is affected, and their proposed theoretical interpretation. A plus sign indicates an available ability, while a minus sign indicates an absent or deteriorated ability

Condition	Symptoms			Theoretical interpretation	
	Consciousness of visual stimulus	Consciousness of visual impairment	Capacity for unconscious processing	Conscious amplification	Modular processing
Visual neglect	−	−	+	−	+
Retinal scotoma	−	+	−	+	−
Blind spot in normal subjects	−	−	−	−	−

blindness in this region. Finally, all of us have a blind region devoid of photoreceptors in the middle of our retinas, the blind spot, yet we are not conscious of having a hole in our vision.

Table 1 shows how the hypothesis of a conscious mobilization of visual processes through top-down amplification can explain these phenomena. In the case of parietal neglect patients, it has been shown that considerable information about the neglected stimulus is still being actively processed (cf. supra). The lesion, however, is thought to affect parietal circuits involved in spatial attention. According to our framework, this may have the effect of disrupting a crucial component in the top-down amplification of visual information, and therefore preventing this information from being mobilized into the workspace. This predicts that recordings of activity evoked by a neglected stimulus in the intact occipito-temporal visual pathway would reveal a significant short-lived activation (sufficient to underlie residual unconscious processing), but without attentional amplification and with an absence of cross-correlation with other distant areas (correlating with the subjects' inability to bring this information to consciousness). Very recently, data compatible with those predictions have been described (Rees et al., 2000; see also Driver & Vuilleumier, 2001, this issue).

The case of retinal scotomas is essentially symmetrical:[7] subjects lack peripheral visual input, but they have an intact network of cortical areas supporting the attentional amplification of visual information into consciousness. Thus, the information

---

[7] We do not attempt here a full theoretical treatment of visual scotomas of cortical origin, which are more complex than those of retinal origin. In both types of pathologies, patients are conscious of their visual impairment, presumably because their intact attentional system allows them to detect the absence of visual inputs. However, patients with cortical scotomas sometimes exhibit residual unconscious processing abilities in their blind field (blindsight). One possibility is that those residual abilities rely on subcortical circuits such as the superior colliculus (Sahraie et al., 1997) which, for lack of workspace neurons, would remain permanently inaccessible to consciousness. Alternatively, they may be supported by cortical activity (e.g. in area V5; Zeki & Ffytche, 1998), but of a weakened and transient nature insufficient to establish a sustained closed loop with the workspace and therefore to enter consciousness.

that visual inputs are no longer available in their scotoma can be made available to the workspace and, from there, contact long-term memory and motor intention circuits. Retinal patients can therefore recognize that they are impaired relative to an earlier time period, and they can report it verbally or non-verbally. According to this account, becoming conscious that one is blind occurs when a discrepancy is detected, within the preserved cortical visual representations, between the activity elicited when attending to long-term memory circuits, and the absence of activity elicited when attempting to attend to the outside world. (Note that this would predict that a person blinded from birth would not experience blindness in the same form; being unable to elicit memories of prior seeing, he/she would have a more 'intellectual' or verbal understanding of blindness, perhaps similar to the one that sighted people have.)

Finally, normal subjects' lack of consciousness of their blind spot can be explained by the lack of both perceptual and attentional resources for this part of the visual field (Dennett, 1992). Our visual cortex receives no retinal information from the blind spot, but then, neither can we orient attention to this absence of information. We therefore remain permanently unaware of it. It is noteworthy that the presence of the blind spot can only be demonstrated indirectly: closing one eye, we attend to a small object and move it on the retina until we suddenly see it disappear as it passes over the blind spot. In this situation, object-oriented attention is used to detect an anomalous object disappearance. Spatial attention, however, is permanently unable to let us perceive the blind spot as a hole in our visual field.[8]

As should be clear from the above discussion, whether or not a given category of information is accessible to consciousness cannot be decided a priori, but must be submitted to an empirical investigation. Indeed, recent research has begun to reveal brain circuits that seem to be permanently inaccessible to consciousness. For instance, psychophysical experiments indicate that some information about visual gratings, though extracted by V1 neurons, cannot be consciously perceived (He, Cavanagh, & Intriligator, 1996). Likewise, the dorsal occipito-parietal route involved in guiding hand and eye movements makes accurate use of information about object size and shape, of which subjects can be completely unaware (Aglioti et al., 1995; Daprati & Gentilucci, 1997; Gentilucci et al., 1996; Hu et al., 1999). Although such experiments bear on the contents, rather than on the mechanisms, of consciousness, they may provide crucial tests of theories of consciousness (Crick & Koch, 1995). If the present hypothesis is correct, they should always reveal that the unconscious information is either not explicitly encoded in neural firing, or is encoded by neural populations that lack bidirectional connectivity with the workspace.

5.2. Dynamical constraints on consciousness

The previous section dealt with permanently inaccessible information. However, information can also be temporarily inaccessible to consciousness for purely dynamical reasons, as seen in masking paradigms. A masked stimulus presented for a very short duration, even if subject to considerable scrutiny, cannot be brought to consciousness; a slightly longer duration of presentation, however, is sufficient to render the prime easily visible.

According to workspace theory, conscious access requires the temporary dynamical mobilization of an active processor into a self-sustained loop of activation: active workspace neurons send top-down amplification signals that boost the currently active processor neurons, whose bottom-up signals in turn help maintain workspace activity. Establishment of this closed loop requires a minimal duration, thus imposing a temporal 'granularity' to the successive neural states that form the stream of consciousness. This dynamical constraint suggests the existence of two thresholds in human information processing, one that corresponds to the minimal stimulus duration needed to cause any differentiated neural activity at all, and another, the 'consciousness threshold', which corresponds to the significantly longer duration needed for such a neural representation to be mobilized in the workspace through a self-sustained long-distance loop. Stimuli that fall in between those two thresholds cause transient changes in neuronal firing and can propagate through multiple circuits (subliminal processing), but cannot take part in a conscious state.

Fig. 1 shows an elementary neural network that illustrates this idea (though it is obviously too simplistic to represent more than a mere aid to intuition). A cascading series of feed-forward networks initially receives a short burst of firing, similar to the phasic response that can be recorded from IT neurons in response to a masked face (Rolls & Tovee, 1994). As seen in Fig. 1, this burst can then propagate through a large number of successive stages, which might be associated with a transformation of the information into semantic, mnemonic or motor codes. At all these levels, however, only a short-lived burst of activity is seen. Although a closed loop involving a distant workspace network is present in the circuit, it takes a longer or stronger stimulus to reliably activate it and to place the network in a long-lasting self-sustained state. Short stimuli cause only a weak, transient and variable activation of the workspace. It is tempting to view such transient firing as a potential neuronal basis for the complex phenomenology of masking paradigms. At intermediate prime durations (40–50 ms), subjects never characterize their perception of the masked prime as 'conscious', but many of them report that they occasionally experience a glimpse of the stimulus that seems to immediately recede from their grasp, thus leaving them unable to describe what they saw.

In a more realistic situation, the chain of subliminal processing need not be as rigid as suggested in Fig. 1. In humans at least, verbal instructions can induce a rapid reorganization of existing processors into a novel chain through top-down amplification and selection (Fig. 2). Could such a dynamic chain also be traversed by unconscious information? The model leads us to answer positively as long as the instruction or context stimulus used to guide top-down selection itself is conscious.

---

[8] A more thorough discussion of unawareness of the blind spot would require mention of filling-in experiments (e.g. Ramachandran, 1992). The parts of objects or textures that fall in the blind spot seem to be partially reconstructed or 'filled in' further on in the visual system, and the results of this reconstruction process can then be consciously attended. None of those experiments, however, refute the basic fact that we are not conscious of having a hole in our retinas.

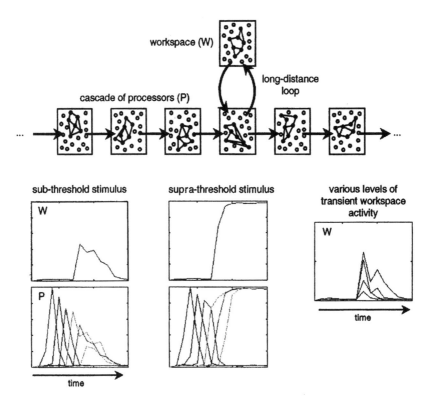

Fig. 1. A simple neural network exhibits dynamical activation patterns analogous to the processing of visual stimuli below and above the consciousness threshold in human subjects. In this minimal scheme, a series of processors are organized in a feed-forward cascade. One of them can also enter in a self-sustained reciprocal loop with a distant workspace network. For simplicity, the evolution of the activation of each assembly (processors and workspace) is modeled by a single McCulloch–Pitts equation, which assumes that activation grows as a non-linear sigmoidal function of the sum of inputs to the assembly, including a small self-connection term, a noise term, and a threshold. Across a wide range of parameters, the same basic findings are reproduced. A short, transient input burst propagates through the processors while causing only a minimal, transient workspace activation (bottom left panels, plots of activation as a function of time). This illustrates how a masked prime, which causes only a transient burst of activation in perceptual neurons of the ventral visual stream (Rolls & Tovee, 1994), can launch an entire stream of visual, semantic and motor processes (Dehaene, Naccache et al., 1998) while failing to establish the sustained coherent workspace activation necessary for consciousness. A slightly more prolonged input causes a sharp transition in activation, with the sudden establishment of a long-lasting activation of both workspace and processor units (middle panels). Thus, the system exhibits a perceptual threshold that stimuli must exceed in order to evoke sustained workspace activation. The right panel illustrates how the very same subthreshold stimulus, on different trials, can evoke transient workspace activity of variable intensity and duration. Similarly, subjects presented with masked primes report a variable phenomenology that ranges from total blindness to a transient feeling that the prime may be on the brink of reportability.

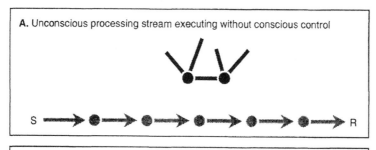

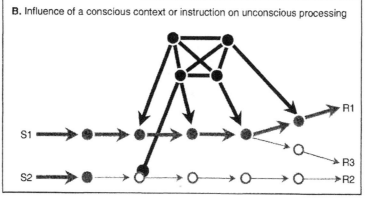

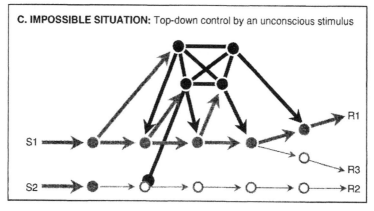

Fig. 2. Which tasks may or may not proceed unconsciously? In these schemas, the gray lines represent the propagation of neural activation associated with the unconscious processing of some information, and the black lines the activation elicited by the presently active conscious workspace neurons. The workspace model predicts that one or several automated stimulus–response chains can be executed unconsciously while the workspace is occupied elsewhere (A). Even tasks that require stimulus and processor selection may be executed unconsciously once the appropriate circuit has been set up by a conscious instruction or context (B). However, it should be impossible for an unconscious stimulus to modify processing on a trial-by-trial basis through top-down control (C). A stimulus that contacts the workspace for a duration sufficient to alter top-down control should always be globally reportable.

Thus, the workspace model makes the counter-intuitive prediction that even a complex task that calls for the setting up of a novel non-automatized pathway, once prepared consciously, can be applied unconsciously. Support for this prediction comes from the above-cited masked priming experiments, which indicate that a novel and arbitrary task instruction can be applied to masked primes (Dehaene, Naccache et al., 1998), even when the instruction changes on every trial (Neumann & Klotz, 1994). The same argument leads us to expect that neglect and blindsight patients should be able to selectively attend to stimuli in their blind field and even to react differentially to them as a function of experimenter instructions, all the while denying seeing them.

What should not be possible, however, is for an unconscious stimulus itself to control top-down circuit selection (Fig. 2C). Thus, tasks in which the instruction stimulus itself is masked, or is presented in the blind field of a neglect or blindsight patient, should not be applicable unconsciously. Although this prediction has not been tested explicitly, the finding that normal subjects cannot perform exclusion and strategic inversion tasks with masked primes (Merikle et al., 1995) fits with this idea, since those tasks require an active inhibition that varies on a trial-by-trial basis.

5.3. Neural substrates of the contents of consciousness

The new tools of cognitive neuroscience, particularly brain-imaging methods, now make it possible to explore empirically the neural substrates of consciousness. Rather than attempting a exhaustive review of this fast-growing literature, we use the workspace framework to help organize existing results and derive new predictions. The framework predicts that multiple processors encode the various possible contents of consciousness, but that all of them share a common mechanism of coherent brain-scale mobilization. Accordingly, brain-imaging studies of consciousness can be coarsely divided into two categories: studies of the various contents of consciousness, and studies of its shared mechanisms.

We first examine studies of the cerebral substrates of specific contents of consciousness. Brain-imaging studies provide striking illustrations of a one-to-one mapping between specific brain circuits and categories of conscious contents. For instance, Kanwisher (this volume) describes an area, the fusiform face area (FFA), that seems to be active whenever subjects report a conscious visual percept of a face. This includes non-trivial cases, such as rivalry and hallucinations. When subjects are presented with a constant stimulus consisting of a face in one eye and a house in the other, they report alternatively seeing a face, then a house, but not both (binocular rivalry). Likewise, the FFA does not maintain a constant level of activity, but oscillates between high and low levels of activation in tight synchrony with the subjective reports (Tong, Nakayama, Vaughan, & Kanwisher, 1998). Furthermore, when patients hallucinate faces, the FFA activates precisely when subjects report seeing the hallucination (Ffytche et al., 1998). Although the FFA may not be entirely specific for faces, as suggested by its involvement in visual expertise for cars or birds

(Gauthier, Skudlarski, Gore, & Anderson, 2000), its activation certainly correlates tightly with conscious face perception.[9]

Another classical example is motion perception. The activation of the human area V5 (or MT) correlates systematically with the conscious perception of motion (Watson et al., 1993), even in non-trivial cases such as visual illusions. For instance, V5 is active when subjects are presented with static paintings of 'kinetic art' that elicit a purely subjective impression of motion (Zeki, Watson, & Frackowiak, 1993). V5 is also active when subjects report experiencing a motion-aftereffect to a static stimulus, and the duration of the activation matches the duration of the illusion (Tootell et al., 1995).

Such experiments indicate a tight correlation between the activation of a specific neural circuit (say, V5) and the subjective report of a conscious content (motion). However, correlation does not imply causation. To establish that a given brain state represents the causal substrate of a specific conscious content, rather than a mere correlate of consciousness, causality must be established by demonstrating that alterations of this brain state systematically alter subjects' consciousness. In the case of face or motion perception, this can be verified with several methods. Some patients happen to suffer from brain lesions encompassing the FFA or area V5. As predicted, they selectively lose the conscious visual perception of faces or motion (for review, see Young, 1992; Zeki, 1993). Transcranial magnetic stimulation can also be used to temporarily disrupt brain circuits. When applied to area V5, it prevents the conscious perception of motion (Beckers & Zeki, 1995; Walsh, Ellison, Battelli, & Cowey, 1998). Finally, implanted electrodes can be used, not only to disrupt consciousness, but even to change its contents. In the monkey, microstimulation of small populations of neurons in area V5 biases the perception of motion towards the neurons' preferred direction (Salzman, Britten, & Newsome, 1990). While the interpretation of this particular study raises the difficult issue of animal consciousness, similar experiments can also be performed in conscious humans in whom electrodes are implanted for therapeutic purposes. It is known since Penfield that human brain stimulation can elicit a rich conscious phenomenology, including dream-like states. Stimulation can even induce highly specific conscious contents such as feelings of profound depression (Bejjani et al., 1999) or hilarity (Fried, Wilson, MacDonald, & Behnke, 1998). Such experiments, together with the others reported in this section, begin to provide evidence for a form of 'type–type physicalism', in which the major categories of contents of consciousness are causally related, in a systematic manner, to categories of physical brain states that can be reproducibly identified in each subject.

---

[9] The workspace theory predicts that the same modular processors are involved in both conscious and unconscious processing. Hence, the systematic correlation between FFA activation and conscious face perception is predicted to break down under conditions of subliminal face perception or inattentional blindness for faces. In those situations, there should be a small but significant FFA activation (relative to non-face stimuli) without consciousness. Driver and Vuilleumier (this volume) report results compatible with this prediction (see Rees et al., 2000).

5.4. Neural substrates of the mechanisms of consciousness: prefrontal cortex (PFC), anterior cingulate (AC), and the workspace hypothesis

While the various contents of consciousness map onto numerous, widely distributed brain circuits, the workspace model predicts that all of these conscious states share a common mechanism. The mobilization of any information into consciousness should be characterized by the simultaneous, coherent activation of multiple distant areas to form a single, brain-scale workspace. Areas rich in workspace neurons should be seen as 'active' with brain-imaging methods whenever subjects perform a task which is feasible only in a conscious state, such as one requiring a novel combination of mental operations. Finally, conscious processing should be accompanied by a temporary top-down amplification of activity in neural circuits encoding the current content of consciousness. The cognitive neuroscience literature contains numerous illustrations of these principles, and many of them point to PFC and AC as playing a crucial role in the conscious workspace (Posner, 1994).

5.4.1. Brain imaging of conscious effort

Although this was not their goal, many early brain-imaging experiments studied complex, effortful tasks that presumably cannot be performed without conscious guidance. A common feature of those tasks is the presence of intense PFC and AC activation (Cohen et al., 1997; Pardo, Pardo, Janer, & Raichle, 1990; Paus, Koski, Caramanos, & Westbury, 1998). Importantly, PFC and AC activations do not seem needed for automatized tasks, but appear suddenly whenever an automatized task suddenly calls for conscious control. In the verb generation task, for instance, Raichle et al. (1994) demonstrated that PFC and AC activation is present during initial task performance, vanishes after the task has become automatized, but immediately recovers when novel items are presented. Furthermore, in a variety of tasks, AC activates immediately after errors and, more generally, whenever conflicts must be resolved (Carter et al., 1998; Dehaene, Posner, & Tucker, 1994). In the Wisconsin card sorting test, PFC activates suddenly when subjects have to invent a new behavioral rule (Konishi et al., 1998). Both PFC and AC possess the ability to remain active in the absence of external stimulation, such as during the delay period of a delayed-response task (Cohen et al., 1997), or during internally driven activities such as mental calculation (Chochon, Cohen, van de Moortele, & Dehaene, 1999; Rueckert et al., 1996). Finally, concomitant to PFC and AC activation, a selective attentional amplification is seen in relevant posterior areas during focused-attention tasks (Corbetta, Miezin, Dobmeyer, Smulman, & Petersen, 1991; Posner & Dehaene, 1994).

In those experiments, whose goal was not to study consciousness, conscious control is correlated with a variety of factors such as attention, difficulty, and effort. A stronger test of the neural substrates of consciousness requires contrasting two experimental conditions that differ minimally in all respects except for the subjects' state of consciousness (Baars, 1989). In the last few years, many such paradigms have been developed, contrasting, for instance, levels of anesthesia (Fiset et al., 1999) or implicit versus explicit memory tasks (Rugg et al., 1998). Here we discuss only two examples (but see Frith, Perry, & Lumer, 1999, for review).

5.4.2. Contrasting conscious and unconscious subjects

An elegant approach consists of using exactly the same stimuli and tasks, but in separating a posteriori subjects who became conscious of an aspect of the experimental situation and subjects who did not. Using this method, McIntosh, Rajah, and Lobaugh (1999) showed an increased activation in left PFC (and, to a lesser degree, in bilateral occipital cortices and left thalamus) only in subjects who became aware of a systematic relation between auditory and visual stimuli. Importantly, this activation was accompanied by a major increase in the functional correlation of left PFC with other distant brain regions including the contralateral PFC, sensory association cortices, and cerebellum. This long-distance coherence pattern appeared precisely when subjects became conscious and started to use their conscious knowledge to guide behavior. Using a sequence learning task, Grafton, Hazeltine, and Ivry (1995) also identified a large-scale circuit with a strong focus in the right PFC, which was only observed in subjects who became aware of the presence of a repeated sequence in the stimuli.

5.4.3. Binocular rivalry

In binocular rivalry, subjects are presented with two dissimilar images, one in each eye, and report seeing only one of them at a time. The dominant image, however, alternates with a period of a few seconds. This paradigm is ideal for the study of consciousness because the conscious content changes while the stimulus remains constant. One can therefore study the cerebral activity caused by the dominant image and, a few seconds later, contrast it with the activity when the very same image has become unconscious. Neuronal recordings in awake monkeys trained to report their perception of two rivaling stimuli indicate that early on in visual pathways (e.g. areas V1, V2, V4, and V5), many cells maintain a constant level of firing, indicating that they respond to the constant stimulus rather than to the variable percept (Leopold & Logothetis, 1999). As one moves up in the visual hierarchy, however, an increasing proportion of cells modulate their firing with the reported perceptual alternations. In IT, as many as 90% of the cells respond only to the perceptually dominant image. Brain imaging in humans indicates that IT activity evoked by the dominant image of a rivaling stimulus is indistinguishable from that evoked when the same image is presented alone in a non-rivaling situation (Tong et al., 1998). Importantly, however, IT activity is accompanied by a concomitant widespread increase in AC, prefrontal, and parietal activation (Lumer, Friston, & Rees, 1998). Thus, the point in time when a given image becomes dominant is characterized by a major brain-scale switch in many areas including AC and PFC. This is not merely a coincidental activation of several unrelated neural systems. Rather, posterior and anterior areas appear to transiently form a single large-scale coherent state, as revealed by increases in functional correlation in fMRI (Lumer & Rees, 1999), high-frequency coherences over distances greater than 10 cm in MEG (Srinivasan, Russell, Edelman, & Tononi, 1999), and transient synchronous neuronal firing in V1 neurons (Fries, Roelfsema, Engel, Konig, & Singer, 1997).

In humans, similar increases in coherence and phase synchrony in the EEG and MEG gamma band (30–80 Hz) have been evidenced in a variety of conscious perception paradigms besides rivalry (Rodriguez et al., 1999; Tallon-Baudry & Bertrand, 1999). According to the workspace model, such a long-range coherence should be systematically observed whenever distant areas are mobilized into the conscious workspace. Conversely, however, it cannot be excluded that temporal coding by synchrony is also used by modular processors during non-conscious processing. Thus, increased high-frequency coherence and synchrony are predicted to be a necessary but not sufficient neural precondition for consciousness.

5.4.4. Anatomy and neurophysiology of the conscious workspace

Is the workspace hypothesis compatible with finer-grained brain anatomy and physiology? The requirements of the workspace model are simple. Neurons contributing to this workspace should be distributed in at least five categories of circuits (high-level perceptual, motor, long-term memory, evaluative and attentional networks). During conscious tasks, they should, for a minimal duration, enter into coherent self-sustained activation patterns in spite of their spatial separation. Therefore, they must be tightly interconnected through long axons. Again, all three criteria point to PFC, AC, and areas interconnected with them as playing a major role in the conscious workspace (Fuster, 1989; Posner, 1994; Shallice, 1988).

Consider first the requirement for long-distance connectivity. Dehaene, Kerszberg, and Changeux (1998) noted that long-range cortico-cortical tangential connections, including interhemispheric connections, mostly originate from the pyramidal cells of layers 2 and 3. This suggests that the extent to which an area contributes to the global workspace might be simply related to the fraction of its pyramidal neurons that belong to layers 2 and 3. Those layers, though present throughout the cortex, are particularly thick in dorsolateral prefrontal and inferior parietal cortical structures. A simple prediction, then, is that the activity of those layers may be tightly correlated with consciousness. This could be tested using auto-radiography and other future high-resolution functional imaging methods in primates and in humans, for instance in binocular rivalry tasks.

In monkeys, Goldman-Rakic (1988) and her collaborators have described a dense network of long-distance reciprocal connections linking dorsolateral PFC with premotor, superior temporal, inferior parietal, anterior and posterior cingulate cortices as well as deeper structures including the neostriatum, parahippocampal formation, and thalamus (Fig. 3). This connectivity pattern, which is probably also present in humans, provides a plausible substrate for fast communication amongst the five categories of processors that we postulated contribute primarily to the conscious workspace.[10] Temporal and parietal circuits provide a variety of high-level perceptual categorizations of the outside world. Premotor, supplementary

---

[10] For her studies of monkey anatomy, Goldman-Rakic (1988) proposes a strictly modular view of PFC, according to which multiple such circuits run in parallel, each of them specialized for a stimulus attribute. The non-modularity of the workspace, however, leads us to postulate that humans may differ from monkeys in showing greater cross-circuit convergence towards common prefrontal and cingulate projection sites as well as heavier reciprocal projections between various sectors of PFC. The degree of cross-circuit convergence in the monkey PFC might also be greater than was initially envisaged (e.g. Rao, Rainer & Miller, 1997)

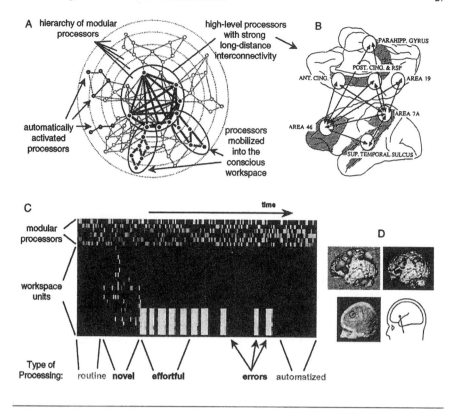

Fig. 3. Neural substrates of the proposed conscious workspace. (A) Symbolic representation of the hierarchy of connections between brain processors (each symbolized by a circle) (after Dehaene, Kerszberg, & Changeux, 1998). Higher levels of this hierarchy are assumed to be widely interconnected by long-distance interconnections, thus forming a global neuronal workspace. An amplified state of workspace activity, bringing together several peripheral processors in a coherent brain-scale activation pattern (black circles), can coexist with the automatic activation of multiple local chains of processors outside the workspace (gray circles). (B) Possible anatomical substrate of the proposed workspace: long-distance network identified in the monkey and linking dorsolateral prefrontal, parietal, temporal, and AC areas with other subcortical targets (from Goldman-Rakic, 1988). (C) Neural dynamics of the workspace, as observed in a neural simulation of a connectivity pattern simplified from (A) (see Dehaene et al., 1998 for details). The matrix shows the activation level of various processor units (top lines) and workspace units (bottom lines) as a function of time. Increased workspace unit activity is seen whenever a novel effortful task is introduced and after errors. Although processor unit activity is continuously present, selective amplification can also be seen when workspace activity is present. (D) Examples of functional neuroimaging tasks activating the postulated workspace network: generation of a novel sequence of random numbers (top left, from Artiges et al., 2000), effortful arithmetic (Chochon et al., 1999), and error processing (left, fMRI data from Carter et al., 1998; right, ERP dipole from Dehaene et al., 1994).

motor and posterior parietal cortices, together with the basal ganglia (notably the caudate nucleus), the cerebellum, and the speech production circuits of the left inferior frontal lobe, allow for the intentional guidance of actions, including verbal reports, from workspace contents. The hippocampal region provides an ability to store and retrieve information over the long term. Direct or indirect connections with orbitofrontal cortex, AC, hypothalamus, amygdala, striatum, and mesencephalic neuromodulatory nuclei may be involved in computing the value or relevance of current representations in relation to previous experience. Finally, parietal and cingulate areas contribute to the attentional gating and shifting of the focus of interest. Although each of these systems, in isolation, can probably be activated without consciousness, we postulate that their coherent activity, supported by their strong interconnectivity, coincides with the mobilization of a conscious content into the workspace.[11]

Physiologically, the neural dynamics of those areas are compatible with the role of consciousness in the durable and explicit maintenance of information over time. The dynamics of prefrontal activity are characterized by periods of long-lasting self-sustained firing, particularly obvious when the animal is engaged in a delayed response task (Fuster, 1989). Sustained firing can also be observed in most cortical regions belonging to the above-mentioned circuit, and prefrontal cooling abolishes those distant sustained responses, suggesting that self-sustained states are a functional property of the integral circuit (Chelazzi, Duncan, Miller, & Desimone, 1998; Fuster, Bauer, & Jervey, 1985; Miller, Erickson, & Desimone, 1996). Lesion studies in monkeys and humans indicate that prefrontal lesions often have little effect on the performance of automatized tasks, but strongly impact on exactly the three types of tasks that were listed earlier as crucially dependent on consciousness: the durable maintenance of explicit information (frontal patients suffer from impairments in delayed response and other working memory tests); the elaboration of novel combinations of operations (frontal patients show perseveration and impaired performance in tasks that call for the invention of novel strategies, such as the Tower of London test; Shallice, 1982); and the spontaneous generation of intentional behavior (patients with frontal or cingulate lesions may perform unintended actions that are induced by the experimenter or the context, as seen in utilization and imitation behavior; Lhermitte, 1983; Shallice, Burgess, Schon, & Baxter, 1989).

Given that workspace neurons must be distributed in widespread brain areas, it should not be surprising that prefrontal lesions do not altogether suppress consciousness, but merely interfere, with variable severity, with some of its functions. However, workspace neurons must be specifically targeted by diffuse neuromodulator systems involved in arousal, the sleep/wake cycle, and reward (Dehaene,

---

[11] Some have postulated that the hippocampus plays a central role in consciousness (e.g. Clark & Squire, 1998). However, recent evidence suggests that the hippocampus also contributes to implicit learning (Chun & Phelps, 1999) and can be activated by subliminal stimuli such as novel faces (Elliott & Dolan, 1998). Thus, it seems more likely that the hippocampus and surrounding cortices support a modular system that at any given time may or may not be mobilized into the workspace. Gray (1994) proposes that one possible role for the hippocampus, in relation to consciousness, is to serve as a 'novelty detector' that automatically draws attention when the organism is confronted with an unpredicted situation.

Kerszberg, & Changeux, 1998). Impairments of those ascending systems may thus cause a global alteration of conscious workspace activity. For instance, upper brainstem lesions affecting reticular ascending systems frequently cause vigilance impairments or coma (see Parvizi & Damasio, this volume). Interestingly, brain imaging of patients in this vegetative state has revealed a partial preservation of cortical activation, for instance to speech stimuli (de Jong, Willemsen, & Paans, 1997; Menon et al., 1998), indicating that modular processors may still be partially functional at a subliminal level.

6. Final remarks

The present chapter was aimed at introducing the cognitive neuroscience of consciousness and proposing a few testable hypotheses about its cerebral substrates. While we think that a promising synthesis is now emerging, based on the concepts of global workspace, dynamic mobilization, attentional amplification, and frontal circuitry, some readers may feel that those ideas hardly scratch the surface. What about the so-called 'hard problems' posed by concepts such as voluntary action, free will, qualia, the sense of self, or the evolution of consciousness? Our personal view is that, in the present state of our methods, trying to address those problems head-on can actually impede rather than facilitate progress (but see Block, this volume, for a different view). We believe that many of these problems will be found to dissolve once a satisfactory framework for consciousness is achieved. In this conclusion, we examine how such a dissolution might proceed.

6.1. Voluntary action and free will

The hypothesis of an attentional control of behavior by supervisory circuits including AC and PFC, above and beyond other more automatized sensorimotor pathways, may ultimately provide a neural substrate for the concepts of voluntary action and free will (Posner, 1994). One may hypothesize that subjects label an action or a decision as 'voluntary' whenever its onset and realization are controlled by higher-level circuitry and are therefore easily modified or withheld, and as 'automatic' or 'involuntary' if it involves a more direct or hardwired command pathway (Passingham, 1993). One particular type of voluntary decision, mostly found in humans, involves the setting of a goal and the selection of a course of action through the serial examination of various alternatives and the internal evaluation of their possible outcomes. This conscious decision process, which has been partially simulated in neural network models (Dehaene & Changeux, 1991, 1997), may correspond to what subjects refer to as 'exercising one's free will'. Note that under this hypothesis free will characterizes a certain type of decision-making algorithm and is therefore a property that applies at the cognitive or systems level, not at the neural or implementation level. This approach may begin to address the old philosophical issue of free will and determinism. Under our interpretation, a physical system whose successive states unfold according to a deterministic rule can still be described as having free will, if it is able to represent a goal and to estimate the outcomes of its actions before initiating them.[12]

6.2. Qualia and phenomenal consciousness

According to the workspace hypothesis, a large variety of perceptual areas can be mobilized into consciousness. At a microscopic scale, each area in turn contains a complex anatomical circuitry that can support a diversity of activity patterns. The repertoire of possible contents of consciousness is thus characterized by an enormous combinatorial diversity: each workspace state is 'highly differentiated' and of 'high complexity', in the terminology of Tononi and Edelman (1998). Thus, the flux of neuronal workspace states associated with a perceptual experience is vastly beyond accurate verbal description or long-term memory storage. Furthermore, although the major organization of this repertoire is shared by all members of the species, its details result from a developmental process of epigenesis and are therefore specific to each individual. Thus, the contents of perceptual awareness are complex, dynamic, multi-faceted neural states that cannot be memorized or transmitted to others in their entirety. These biological properties seem potentially capable of substantiating philosophers' intuitions about the 'qualia' of conscious experience, although considerable neuroscientific research will be needed before they are thoroughly understood.

To put this argument in a slightly different form, the workspace model leads to a distinction between three levels of accessibility. Some information encoded in the nervous system is permanently inaccessible (set I_1). Other information is in contact with the workspace and could be consciously amplified if it was attended to (set I_2). However, at any given time, only a subset of the latter is mobilized into the workspace (set I_3). We wonder whether these distinctions may suffice to capture the intuitions behind Ned Block's (Block, 1995; see also Block, this volume) definitions of phenomenal (P) and access (A) consciousness. What Block sees as a difference in essence could merely be a qualitative difference due to the discrepancy between the size of the potentially accessible information (I_2) and the paucity of information that can actually be reported at any given time (I_3). Think, for instance, of Sperling's experiment in which a large visual array of letters seems to be fully visible, yet only a very small subset can be reported. The former may give rise to the intuition of a rich phenomenological world – Block's P-consciousness – while the latter corresponds to what can be selected, amplified, and passed on to other processes (A-consciousness). Both, however, would be facets of the same underlying phenomenon.

6.3. Sense of self and reflexive consciousness

Among the brain's modular processors, some do not extract and process signals

---

[12] This argument goes back to Spinoza: "men are mistaken in thinking themselves free; their opinion is made up of consciousness of their own actions, and ignorance of the causes by which they are conditioned. Their idea of freedom, therefore, is simply their ignorance of any cause for their actions." (Ethics, II, 35).

from the environment, but rather from the subject's own body and brain. Each brain thus contains multiple representations of itself and its body at several levels (Damasio, 1999). The physical location of our body is encoded in continuously updated somatic, kinesthetic, and motor maps. Its biochemical homeostasis is represented in various subcortical and cortical circuits controlling our drives and emotions. We also represent ourselves as a person with an identity (presumably involving face and person-processing circuits of the inferior and anterior temporal lobes) and an autobiography encoded in episodic memory. Finally, at a higher cognitive level, the action perception, verbal reasoning, and 'theory of mind' modules that we apply to interpret and predict other people's actions may also help us make sense of our own behavior (Fletcher et al., 1995; Gallese, Fadiga, Fogassi, & Rizzolatti, 1996; Weiskrantz, 1997). All of those systems are modular, and their selective impairment may cause a wide range of neuropsychological deficits involving misperception of oneself and others (e.g. delusions of control, Capgras and Fregoli syndrome, autism). We envisage that the bringing together of these modules into the conscious workspace may suffice to account for the subjective sense of self. Once mobilized into the conscious workspace, the activity of those 'self-coding' circuits would be available for inspection by many other processes, thus providing a putative basis for reflexive or higher-order consciousness.

6.4. The evolution of consciousness

Any theory of consciousness must address its emergence in the course of phylogenesis. The present view associates consciousness with a unified neural workspace through which many processes can communicate. The evolutionary advantages that this system confers to the organism may be related to the increased independence that it affords. The more an organism can rely on mental simulation and internal evaluation to select a course of action, instead of acting out in the open world, the lower are the risks and the expenditure of energy. By allowing more sources of knowledge to bear on this internal decision process, the neural workspace may represent an additional step in a general trend towards an increasing internalization of representations in the course of evolution, whose main advantage is the freeing of the organism from its immediate environment.

This evolutionary argument implies that 'having consciousness' is not an all-or-none property. The biological substrates of consciousness in human adults are probably also present, but probably in partial form in other species (or in young children or brain-lesioned patients). It is therefore a partially arbitrary question as to whether we want to extend the use of the term 'consciousness' to them. For instance, several mammals, and possibly even young human children, exhibit greater brain modularity than human adults (Cheng & Gallistel, 1986; Hermer & Spelke, 1994). Yet they also show intentional behavior, partially reportable mental states, some working memory ability – but perhaps no theory of mind. Do they have consciousness, then? Our hope is that once a detailed cognitive and neural theory of the various aspects of consciousness is available, the vacuity of this question will become obvious.

References

Aglioti, S., DeSouza, J. F., & Goodale, M. A. (1995). Size-contrast illusions deceive the eye but not the hand. Current Biology, 5 (6), 679–685.

Artiges, E., Salame, P, Recasens, C., Poline, J. B., Attar-Levy, D., De La Raillere, A., Pailere-Martinot, M. L., Danion, J. M., & Martinot, J. L. (2000). Working memory control in patients with schizophrenia: a PET study during a random number generation task. American Journal of Psychiatry, 157 (9), 1517–1519.

Baars, B. J. (1989). A cognitive theory of consciousness. Cambridge: Cambridge University Press.

Baddeley, A. D. (1986). Working memory. Oxford: Clarendon Press.

Bar, M., & Biederman, I. (1999). Localizing the cortical region mediating visual awareness of object identity. Proceedings of the National Academy of Sciences USA, 96 (4), 1790–1793.

Bauer, R. M. (1984). Autonomic recognition of names and faces in prosopagnosia: a neuropsychological application of the Guilty Knowledge Test. Neuropsychologia, 22 (4), 457–469.

Beckers, G., & Zeki, S. (1995). The consequences of inactivating areas V1 and V5 on visual motion perception. Brain, 118 (Pt. 1), 49–60.

Bejjani, B. P., Damier, P., Arnulf, I., Thivard, L., Bonnet, A. M., Dormont, D., Cornu, P., Pidoux, B., Samson, Y., & Agid, Y. (1999). Transient acute depression induced by high-frequency deep-brain stimulation. New England Journal of Medicine, 340 (19), 1476–1480.

Block, N. (1995). On a confusion about a function of consciousness. Behavioral and Brain Sciences, 18 (2), 227–287.

Bornstein, R. F., & D'Agostino, P. R. (1992). Stimulus recognition and the mere exposure effect. Journal of Personality and Social Psychology, 63 (4), 545–552.

Carter, C. S., Braver, T. S., Barch, D., Botvinick, M. M., Noll, D., & Cohen, J. D. (1998). Anterior cingulate cortex, error detection, and the online monitoring of performance. Science, 280, 747–749.

Chalmers, D. (1996). The conscious mind. New York: Oxford University Press.

Changeux, J. P., & Dehaene, S. (1989). Neuronal models of cognitive functions. Cognition, 33, 63–109.

Chelazzi, L., Duncan, J., Miller, E. K., & Desimone, R. (1998). Responses of neurons in inferior temporal cortex during memory-guided visual search. Journal of Neurophysiology, 80 (6), 2918–2940.

Cheng, K., & Gallistel, C. R. (1986). A purely geometric module in the rat's spatial representation. Cognition, 23, 149–178.

Chochon, F., Cohen, L., van de Moortele, P. F., & Dehaene, S. (1999). Differential contributions of the left and right inferior parietal lobules to number processing. Journal of Cognitive Neuroscience, 11, 617–630.

Chun, M. M., & Phelps, E. A. (1999). Memory deficits for implicit contextual information in amnesic subjects with hippocampal damage. Nature Neuroscience, 2 (9), 844–847.

Clark, R. E., & Squire, L. R. (1998). Classical conditioning and brain systems: the role of awareness. Science, 280 (5360), 77–81.

Cohen, J. D., Perlstein, W. M., Braver, T. S., Nystrom, L. E., Noll, D. C., Jonides, J., & Smith, E. E. (1997). Temporal dynamics of brain activation during a working memory task. Nature, 386, 604–608.

Cohen, L., & Dehaene, S. (1998). Competition between past and present. Assessing and explaining verbal perseverations. Brain, 121, 1641–1659.

Corbetta, M., Miezin, F. M., Dobmeyer, S., Smulman, G. L., & Petersen, S. E. (1991). Selective and divided attention during visual discriminations of shape color and speed: functional anatomy by positron emission tomography. Journal of Neuroscience, 11, 2383–2402.

Crick, F., & Koch, C. (1995). Are we aware of neural activity in primary visual cortex? Nature, 375, 121–123.

Damasio, A. (1999). The feeling of what happens. New York: Harcourt Brace.

Daprati, E., & Gentilucci, M. (1997). Grasping an illusion. Neuropsychologia, 35 (12), 1577–1582.

Dehaene, S., & Changeux, J. P. (1991). The Wisconsin Card Sorting Test: theoretical analysis and modelling in a neuronal network. Cerebral Cortex, 1, 62–79.

Dehaene, S., & Changeux, J. P. (1997). A hierarchical neuronal network for planning behavior. Proceedings of the National Academy of Sciences USA, 94, 13293–13298.

Dehaene, S., Kerszberg, M., & Changeux, J. P. (1998). A neuronal model of a global workspace in effortful cognitive tasks. Proceedings of the National Academy of Sciences USA, 95, 14529–14534.

Dehaene, S., Naccache, L., Le Clec'H, G., Koechlin, E., Mueller, M., Dehaene-Lambertz, G., van de Moortele, P. F., & Le Bihan, D. (1998). Imaging unconscious semantic priming. Nature, 395, 597–600.

Dehaene, S., Posner, M. I., & Tucker, D. M. (1994). Localization of a neural system for error detection and compensation. Psychological Science, 5, 303–305.

de Jong, B. M., Willemsen, A. T., & Paans, A. M. (1997). Regional cerebral blood flow changes related to affective speech presentation in persistent vegetative state. Clinical Neurology and Neurosurgery, 99 (3), 213–216.

Dennett, D. C. (1992). Consciousness explained. London: Penguin.

Driver, J., & Mattingley, J. B. (1998). Parietal neglect and visual awareness. Nature Neuroscience, 1 (1), 17–22.

Driver, J., & Vuilleumier, P. (2001 this issue). Perceptual awareness and its loss in unilateral neglect and extinction. Cognition, 79, 39–88.

Eimer, M., & Schlaghecken, F. (1998). Effects of masked stimuli on motor activation: behavioral and electrophysiological evidence. Journal of Experimental Psychology: Human Perception and Performance, 24 (6), 1737–1747.

Elliott, R., & Dolan, R. J. (1998). Neural response during preference and memory judgments for subliminally presented stimuli: a functional neuroimaging study. Journal of Neuroscience, 18 (12), 4697–4704.

Ericcson, K. A., & Simon, H. A. (1993). Protocol analysis: verbal reports as data. Cambridge, MA: MIT Press.

Felleman, D. J., & Van Essen, D. C. (1991). Distributed hierarchical processing in the primate cerebral cortex. Cerebral Cortex, 1 (1), 1–47.

Ffytche, D. H., Howard, R. J., Brammer, M. J., David, A., Woodruff, P., & Williams, S. (1998). The anatomy of conscious vision: an fMRI study of visual hallucinations. Nature Neuroscience, 1 (8), 738–742.

Fiset, P., Paus, T., Daloze, T., Plourde, G., Meuret, P., Bonhomme, V., Hajj-Ali, N., Backman, S. B., & Evans, A. C. (1999). Brain mechanisms of propofol-induced loss of consciousness in humans: a positron emission tomographic study. Journal of Neuroscience, 19 (13), 5506–5513.

Fletcher, P. C., Happé, F., Frith, U., Baker, S. C., Donlan, R. J., Frackowiak, R. S. J., & Frith, C. D. (1995). Other minds in the brain: a functional imaging study of theory of mind in story comprehension. Cognition, 57, 109–128.

Fodor, J. A. (1983). The modularity of mind. Cambridge, MA: MIT Press.

Fried, I., Wilson, C. L., MacDonald, K. A., & Behnke, E. J. (1998). Electric current stimulates laughter. Nature, 391 (6668), 650.

Fries, P., Roelfsema, P. R., Engel, A. K., Konig, P., & Singer, W. (1997). Synchronization of oscillatory responses in visual cortex correlates with perception in interocular rivalry. Proceedings of the National Academy of Sciences USA, 94 (23), 12699–12704.

Friston, K. J., Tononi, G., Reeke, G. N., Sporns, O., & Edelman, G. M. (1994). Value-dependent selection in the brain: simulation in a synthetic neural model. Neuroscience, 59, 229–243.

Frith, C., Perry, R., & Lumer, E. (1999). The neural correlates of conscious experience: an experimental framework. Trends in Cognitive Science, 3, 105–114.

Fuster, J. M. (1989). The prefrontal cortex. New York: Raven Press.

Fuster, J. M., Bauer, R. H., & Jervey, J. P. (1985). Functional interactions between inferotemporal and prefrontal cortex in a cognitive task. Brain Research, 330 (2), 299–307.

Gallese, V., Fadiga, L., Fogassi, L., & Rizzolatti, G. (1996). Action recognition in the premotor cortex. Brain, 119 (Pt. 2), 593–609.

Gauthier, I., Skudlarski, P., Gore, J. C., & Anderson, A. W. (2000). Expertise for cars and birds recruits brain areas involved in face recognition. Nature Neuroscience, 3 (2), 191–197.

Gazzaniga, M. S., LeDoux, J. E., & Wilson, D. H. (1977). Language, praxis, and the right hemisphere: clues to some mechanisms of consciousness. Neurology, 27 (12), 1144–1147.

Gentilucci, M., Chieffi, S., Deprati, E., Saetti, M. C., & Toni, I. (1996). Visual illusion and action. Neuropsychologia, 34 (5), 369–376.

Goldman-Rakic, P. S. (1987). Circuitry of primate prefrontal cortex and regulation of behavior by representational knowledge. In F. Plum, & V. Mountcastle (Eds.), Handbook of physiology (Vol. 5, pp. 373–417). Bethesda, MD: American Physiological Society.

Goldman-Rakic, P. S. (1988). Topography of cognition: parallel distributed networks in primate association cortex. Annual Review of Neuroscience, 11, 137–156.

Grafton, S. T., Hazeltine, E., & Ivry, R. (1995). Functional mapping of sequence learning in normal humans. Journal of Cognitive Neuroscience, 7, 497–510.

Gray, J. A. (1994). The contents of consciousness: a neuropsychological conjecture. Behavioral and Brain Sciences, 18, 659–722.

Greenwald, A. G. (1996). Three cognitive markers of unconscious semantic activation. Science, 273 (5282), 1699–1702.

He, S., Cavanagh, P., & Intriligator, J. (1996). Attentional resolution and the locus of visual awareness. Nature, 383 (6598), 334–337.

Hermer, L., & Spelke, E. S. (1994). A geometric process for spatial reorientation in young children. Nature, 370, 57–59.

Holender, D. (1986). Semantic activation without conscious identification in dichotic listening, parafoveal vision and visual masking: a survey and appraisal. Behavioral and Brain Sciences, 9, 1–23.

Hu, Y., Eagleson, R., & Goodale, M. A. (1999). The effects of delay on the kinematics of grasping. Experimental Brain Research, 126 (1), 109–116.

Jacoby, L. L. (1991). A process dissociation framework: separating automatic from intentional uses of memory. Journal of Memory and Language, 30, 513–541.

Klinger, M. R., & Greenwald, A. G. (1995). Unconscious priming of association judgments. Journal of Experimental Psychology: Learning, Memory and Cognition, 21 (3), 569–581.

Koechlin, E., Naccache, L., Block, E., & Dehaene, S. (1999). Primed numbers: exploring the modularity of numerical representations with masked and unmasked semantic priming. Journal of Experimental Psychology: Human Perception and Performance, 25, 1882–1905.

Köhler, S., & Moscovitch, M. (1997). Unconscious visual processing in neuropsychological syndromes: a survey of the literature and evaluation of models of consciousness. In M. D. Rugg (Ed.), Cognitive neuroscience (pp. 305–373). Hove: Psychology Press.

Konishi, S., Nakajima, K., Uchida, I., Kameyama, M., Nakahara, K., Sekihara, K., & Miyashita, Y. (1998). Transient activation of inferior prefrontal cortex during cognitive set shifting. Nature Neuroscience, 1, 80–84.

Kosslyn, S. M., & Koenig, O. (1992). Wet mind: the new cognitive neuroscience. New York: Macmillan.

Leopold, D. A., & Logothetis, N. K. (1999). Multistable phenomena: changing views in perception. Trends in Cognitive Science, 3, 254–264.

Lhermitte, F. (1983). "Utilization behaviour" and its relation to lesions of the frontal lobe. Brain, 106, 237–255.

Luck, S. J., Vogel, E. K., & Shapiro, K. L. (1996). Word meanings can be accessed but not reported during the attentional blink. Nature, 383 (6601), 616–618.

Lumer, E. D., Friston, K. J., & Rees, G. (1998). Neural correlates of perceptual rivalry in the human brain. Science, 280, 1930–1934.

Lumer, E. D., & Rees, G. (1999). Covariation of activity in visual and prefrontal cortex associated with subjective visual perception. Proceedings of the National Academy of Sciences USA, 96 (4), 1669–1673.

Mack, A., & Rock, I. (1998). Inattentional blindness. Cambridge, MA: MIT Press.

Marcel, A. J. (1983). Conscious and unconscious perception: experiments on visual masking and word recognition. Cognitive Psychology, 15, 197–237.

McGlinchey-Berroth, R., Milberg, W. P., Verfaellie, M., Alexander, M., & Kilduff, P. (1993). Semantic priming in the neglected field: evidence from a lexical decision task. Cognitive Neuropsychology, 10, 79–108.

McIntosh, A. R., Rajah, M. N., & Lobaugh, N. J. (1999). Interactions of prefrontal cortex in relation to awareness in sensory learning. Science, 284 (5419), 1531–1533.

Menon, D. K., Owen, A. M., Williams, E. J., Minhas, P. S., Allen, C. M., Boniface, S. J., & Pickard, J. D. (1998). Cortical processing in persistent vegetative state. Lancet, 352 (9123), 200.

Merikle, P. M. (1992). Perception without awareness: critical issues. American Psychologist, 47, 792–796.

Merikle, P. M., & Joordens, S. (1997). Parallels between perception without attention and perception without awareness. Consciousness and Cognition, 6 (2–3), 219–236.

Merikle, P. M., Joordens, S., & Stolz, J. A. (1995). Measuring the relative magnitude of unconscious influences. Consciousness and Cognition, 4, 422–439.

Miller, E. K., Erickson, C. A., & Desimone, R. (1996). Neural mechanisms of visual working memory in prefrontal cortex of the macaque. Journal of Neuroscience, 16 (16), 5154–5167.

Morris, J. S., Öhman, A., & Dolan, R. J. (1998). Conscious and unconscious emotional learning in the human amygdala. Nature, 393, 467–470.

Morris, J. S., Öhman, A., & Dolan, R. J. (1999). A subcortical pathway to the right amygdala mediating "unseen" fear. Proceedings of the National Academy of Sciences USA, 96 (4), 1680–1685.

Neumann, O., & Klotz, W. (1994). Motor responses to non-reportable, masked stimuli: where is the limit of direct motor specification. In C. Umiltà, & M. Moscovitch (Eds.), Conscious and non-conscious information processingAttention and performance (Vol. XV, pp. 123–150). Cambridge, MA: MIT Press.

O'Regan, J. K., Rensink, R. A., & Clark, J. J. (1999). Change-blindness as a result of 'mudsplashes'. Nature, 398 (6722), 34.

Pardo, J. V., Pardo, P. J., Janer, K. W., & Raichle, M. E. (1990). The anterior cingulate cortex mediates processing selection in the Stroop attentional conflict paradigm. Proceedings of the National Academy of Sciences USA, 87, 256–259.

Passingham, R. (1993). The frontal lobes and voluntary action (Vol. 21). New York: Oxford University Press.

Paus, T., Koski, L., Caramanos, Z., & Westbury, C. (1998). Regional differences in the effects of task difficulty and motor output on blood flow response in the human anterior cingulate cortex: a review of 107 PET activation studies. NeuroReport, 9, R37–R47.

Penrose, R. (1990). The emperor's new mind. Concerning computers, minds, and the laws of physics. London: Vintage Books.

Pöppel, E., Held, R., & Frost, D. (1973). Residual visual function after brain wounds involving the central visual pathways in man. Nature, 243 (405), 295–296.

Posner, M. I. (1994). Attention: the mechanisms of consciousness. Proceedings of the National Academy of Sciences USA, 91, 7398–7403.

Posner, M. I., & Dehaene, S. (1994). Attentional networks. Trends in Neuroscience, 17, 75–79.

Raichle, M. E., Fiez, J. A., Videen, T. O., MacLeod, A. K., Pardo, J. V., Fox, P. T., & Petersen, S. E. (1994). Practice-related changes in human brain functional anatomy during non-motor learning. Cerebral Cortex, 4, 8–26.

Ramachandran, V. S. (1992). Filling in the blind spot. Nature, 356 (6365), 115.

Rao, S. C., Rainer, G., & Miller, E. K. (1997). Intergration of what and where in the primate prefrontal cortex. Science, 276 (5313), 821–824.

Raymond, J. E., Shapiro, K. L., & Arnell, K. M. (1992). Temporary suppression of visual processing in an RSVP task: an attentional blink? Journal of Experimental Psychology: Human Perception and Performance, 18 (3), 849–860.

Rees, G., Wojciulik, E., Clarke, K., Husain, M., Frith, C., & Driver, J. (2000). Unconscious activation of visual cortex in the damaged right hemisphere of a parietal patient with extinction. Brain, 123 (Pt. 8), 1624–1633.

Renault, B., Signoret, J. L., Debruille, B., Breton, F., & Bolgert, F. (1989). Brain potentials reveal covert facial recognition in prosopagnosia. Neuropsychologia, 27 (7), 905–912.

Rodriguez, E., George, N., Lachaux, J. P., Martinerie, J., Renault, B., & Varela, F. J. (1999). Perception's shadow: long-distance synchronization of human brain activity. Nature, 397 (6718), 430–433.

Rolls, E. T., & Tovee, M. J. (1994). Processing speed in the cerebral cortex and the neurophysiology of visual masking. Proceedings of the Royal Society of London, Series B, Biological Sciences, 257 (1348), 9–15.

Rolls, E. T., Tovee, M. J., & Panzeri, S. (1999). The neurophysiology of backward visual masking: information analysis. Journal of Cognitive Neuroscience, 11 (3), 300–311.

Rueckert, L., Lange, N., Partiot, A., Appollonio, I., Litvar, I., Le Bihan, D., & Grafman, J. (1996). Visualizing cortical activation during mental calculation with functional MRI. NeuroImage, 3, 97–103.

Rugg, M. D., Mark, R. E., Walla, P., Schloerscheidt, A. M., Birch, C. S., & Allan, K. (1998). Dissociation of the neural correlates of implicit and explicit memory. Nature, 392 (6676), 595–598.

Sahraie, A., Weiskrantz, L., Barbur, J. L., Simmons, A., Williams, S. C. R., & Brammer, M. J. (1997). Pattern of neuronal activity associated with conscious and unconscious processing of visual signals. Proceedings of the National Academy of Sciences USA, 94, 9406–9411.

Salzman, C. D., Britten, K. H., & Newsome, W. T. (1990). Cortical microstimulation influences perceptual judgements of motion direction. Nature, 346 (6280), 174–177.

Schacter, D. L., Buckner, R. L., & Koutstaal, W. (1998). Memory, consciousness and neuroimaging. Philosophical Transactions of the Royal Society of London, Series B, Biological Sciences, 353 (1377), 1861–1878.

Schneider, W., & Shiffrin, R. M. (1977). Controlled and automatic human information processing. 1. Detection, search, and attention. Psychological Review, 84, 1–66.

Searle, J. R. (1998). How to study consciousness scientifically. Philosophical Transactions of the Royal Society of London, Series B, 353, 1935–1942.

Shallice, T. (1982). Specific impairments of planning. Philosophical Transactions of the Royal Society of London, Series B, 298, 199–209.

Shallice, T. (1988). From neuropsychology to mental structure. Cambridge: Cambridge University Press.

Shallice, T., Burgess, P. W., Schon, F., & Baxter, D. M. (1989). The origins of utilization behaviour. Brain, 112, 1587–1598.

Silbersweig, D. A., Stern, E., Frith, C. D., Cahill, C., Holmes, A., Grootoonk, S., Seaward, J., McKenna, P., Chua, S. E., Schnoor, L., Jones, T., & Frackowiak, R. S. J. (1995). A functional neuroanatomy of hallucinations in schizophrenia. Nature, 378, 176–179.

Smith, P. H., Joris, P. X., & Yin, T. C. (1993). Projections of physiologically characterized spherical bushy cell axons from the cochlear nucleus of the cat: evidence for delay lines to the medial superior olive. Journal of Comparative Neurology, 331 (2), 245–260.

Sperling, G. (1960). The information available in brief visual presentation. Psychological Monographs, 74, 1–29.

Srinivasan, R., Russell, D. P., Edelman, G. M., & Tononi, G. (1999). Increased synchronization of neuromagnetic responses during conscious perception. Journal of Neuroscience, 19 (13), 5435–5448.

Tallon-Baudry, C., & Bertrand, O. (1999). Oscillatory gamma activity in humans and its role in object representation. Trends in Cognitive Science, 3, 151–162.

Tiitinen, H., May, P., Reinikainen, K., & Naatanen, R. (1994). Attentive novelty detection in humans is governed by pre-attentive sensory memory. Nature, 372 (6501), 90–92.

Tong, F., Nakayama, K., Vaughan, J. T., & Kanwisher, N. (1998). Binocular rivalry and visual awareness in human extrastriate cortex. Neuron, 21 (4), 753–759.

Tononi, G., & Edelman, G. M. (1998). Consciousness and complexity. Science, 282 (5395), 1846–1851.

Tootell, R. B. H., Reppas, J. B., Dale, A. M., Look, R. B., Sereno, M. I., Malach, R., Brady, T. J., & Rosen, B. R. (1995). Visual motion aftereffect in human cortical area MT revealed by functional magnetic resonance imaging. Nature, 375, 139–141.

Tranel, D., & Damasio, A. R. (1985). Knowledge without awareness: an autonomic index of facial recognition by prosopagnosics. Science, 228 (4706), 1453–1454.

Treisman, A., & Gelade, G. (1980). A feature-integration theory of attention. Cognitive Psychology, 12, 97–136.

Vogel, E. K., Luck, S. J., & Shapiro, K. L. (1998). Electrophysiological evidence for a postperceptual locus of suppression during the attentional blink. Journal of Experimental Psychology: Human Perception and Performance, 24 (6), 1656–1674.

Walsh, V., Ellison, A., Battelli, L., & Cowey, A. (1998). Task-specific impairments and enhancements induced by magnetic stimulation of human visual area V5. Proceedings of the Royal Society of London, Series B, Biological Sciences, 265 (1395), 537–543.

Watson, J. D. G., Myers, R., Frackowiak, R. S. J., Hajnal, J. V., Woods, R. P., Mazziotta, J. C., Shipp, S., & Zeki, S. (1993). Area V5 of the human brain: evidence from a combined study using positron emission tomography and magnetic resonance imaging. Cerebral Cortex, 3, 79–94.

Weiskrantz, L. (1997). Consciousness lost and found: a neuropsychological exploration. New York: Oxford University Press.

Whalen, P. J., Rauch, S. L., Etcoff, N. L., McInerney, S. C., Lee, M. B., & Jenike, M. A. (1998). Masked presentations of emotional facial expressions modulate amygdala activity without explicit knowledge. Journal of Neuroscience, 18, 411–418.

Yantis, S., & Jonides, J. (1984). Abrupt visual onsets and selective attention: evidence from visual search. Journal of Experimental Psychology: Human Perception and Performance, 10 (5), 601–621.

Yantis, S., & Jonides, J. (1996). Attentional capture by abrupt onsets: new perceptual objects or visual masking? Journal of Experimental Psychology: Human Perception and Performance, 22 (6), 1505–1513.

Young, A. W. (1992). Face recognition impairments. Philosophical Transactions of the Royal Society of London, Series B, Biological Sciences, 335 (1273), 47–54.

Young, M. P., Scannell, J. W., O'Neill, M. A., Hilgetag, C. C., Burns, G., & Blakemore, C. (1995). Non-metric multidimensional scaling in the analysis of neuroanatomical connection data and the organization of the primate cortical visual system. Philosophical Transactions of the Royal Society of London, Series B, Biological Sciences, 348 (1325), 281–308.

Zeki, S. (1993). A vision of the brain. London: Blackwell.

Zeki, S., & Ffytche, D. H. (1998). The Riddoch syndrome: insights into the neurobiology of conscious vision. Brain, 121 (Pt. 1), 25–45.

Zeki, S., Watson, J. D., & Frackowiak, R. S. (1993). Going beyond the information given: the relation of illusory visual motion to brain activity. Proceedings of the Royal Society of London, Series B, Biological Sciences, 252 (1335), 215–222.

2

Perceptual awareness and its loss in unilateral neglect and extinction

Jon Driver*, Patrik Vuilleumier

Institute of Cognitive Neuroscience, University College London, 17 Queen Square,
London WC1N 3AR, UK

Abstract

We review recent evidence from studies of patients with unilateral neglect and/or extinction, who suffer from a loss of awareness for stimuli towards the affected side of space. We contrast their deficit with the effects of damage to primary sensory areas, noting that such areas can remain structurally intact in neglect, with lesions typically centred on the right inferior parietal lobe. In keeping with preservation of initial sensory pathways, many recent studies have shown that considerable residual processing can still take place for neglected or extinguished stimuli, yet without reaching the patient's awareness. This ranges from preserved visual grouping processes through to activation of identity, semantics and emotional significance. Similarly to 'preattentive' processing in normals, such residual processing can modulate what will enter the patient's awareness. Recent studies have used measures such as ERPs and fMRI to determine the neural correlates of conscious versus unconscious perception in the patients, which in turn can be related to the anatomy of their lesions. We relate the patient findings to neurophysiological data from areas in the monkey parietal lobe, which indicate that these serve as cross-modal and sensorimotor interfaces highlighting currently relevant locations as targets for intentional action. We speculate on the special role such brain regions may play in perceptual awareness, seeking to explain how damage to a system which appears primarily to code space could eliminate awareness even for non-spatial stimulus properties at affected locations. This may relate to the extreme nature of 'winner-takes-all' functions within the parietal lobe, and their correspondingly strong influence on other brain areas. © 2001 Elsevier Science B.V. All rights reserved.

Keywords: Spatial neglect; Extinction; Awareness; Parietal cortex; Attention

* Corresponding author. Fax: +44-20-7916-8517.
 E-mail addresses: j.driver@ucl.ac.uk (J. Driver), p.vuilleumier@ucl.ac.uk (P. Vuilleumier).

1. Introduction

Unilateral spatial neglect is a relatively common and disabling neurological disorder after unilateral brain damage. It is characterized by a lack of awareness for sensory events located towards the contralesional side of space (e.g. towards the left following a right lesion), together with a loss of the orienting behaviours, exploratory search and other actions that would normally be directed toward that side. Neglect patients often behave as if half of their world no longer exists. In daily life, they may be oblivious to objects and people on the neglected side of the room, may eat from only one side of their plate, read from only one end of a newspaper page, and make-up or shave only one side of their face. The spatial bias towards one side can also be apparent in many simple paper-and-pencil tests. When required to search for and mark all target shapes on a page, the patients may cancel only those towards the ipsilesional side. When bisecting a horizontal line, they may err towards that side, and when drawing from memory, or copying a picture, they may omit details from the contralesional side (Fig. 1).

The characteristic spatial bias of neglect patients has been observed in some form for all of the sensory modalities (vision, audition, touch, proprioception, even smell; see Bellas, Novelly, Eskenazi, & Wasserstein, 1988; Heilman, Watson, & Valenstein, 1993; Mesulam, 1981; Vallar, Guariglia, Nico, & Bisiach, 1995). Analogous spatial biases may also be apparent in motor-output systems, as we discuss later (e.g. with eye or hand movements being biased towards the 'good' ipsilesional side; see Bisiach, Geminiani, Berti, & Rusconi, 1990; Coslett, Bowers, Fitzpatrick, Haws, & Heilman, 1990; Heilman, Boweres, Coslett, Whelan, & Watson, 1985). Some patients may neglect their own contralesional limbs, attempting to climb out of bed without moving these, even though they have no primary motor weakness on that side. Others may be paralyzed on the contralesional side, yet remain unaware of this. In general, neglect patients often have little insight into their deficits for the affected side, especially in the acute stage. In the longer term, they may acknowledge that they can 'miss things' on the affected side, yet continue to do so.

Thus, neglect ostensibly involves a dramatic loss of awareness, and of appropriate action, for sensory events towards the affected side. The paradox is that this can arise even though the primary sensory pathways for processing the neglected information may all still be intact. That is, patients may show profound neglect for sights, sounds and touches towards the affected side, even though they are by no means blind, deaf or insensitive on this side. Here we will argue, in keeping with recent advances in neglect research, that this paradox can be resolved to some extent by relating the plight of neglect patients to particular aspects of normal cognition. Even neurologically healthy people can fail to see, hear or feel salient stimuli, provided that their selective attention is engaged elsewhere, as we shall describe (see also Merikle, Smilek, & Eastwood in this volume). Perceptual awareness is not determined solely by the stimuli impinging on our senses, but also by which of these stimuli we choose to attend. This choice seems pathologically restricted in neglect patients, with their attention strongly biased towards events on the ipsilesional side.

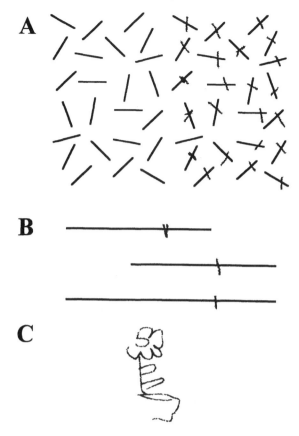

Fig. 1. Examples of deficits found in patients with left spatial neglect on typical clinical tasks. (A) Line cancellation task. The patient has to mark each of many small lines that are spread out on a sheet of paper presented in front of them. Typically, the patient fails to detect some lines on the contralesional side, even when given considerable time to complete the task. More sensitive cancellation tasks may involve the marking of a target letter or shape among distractors. (B) Line bisection task. The patient is asked to mark the midpoint of long horizontal lines and deviates towards the right ipsilesional side, as if neglecting the left contralesional extent. Such an ipsilesional bias is often greater when the lines are positioned more to the left side. It can be partly alleviated when the patient is cued to the contralesional end of the line, for instance by reporting a letter there. (C) Neglect in drawing is characterized by the omissions of all or parts of the elements on the contralesional side. This can occur when the patient is required to draw an object from memory (as here, a flower in a pot) or to copy a drawing template.

2. Basic anatomy of neglect, and multiple components to the clinical syndrome

Unilateral spatial neglect can be observed in some form after various unilateral brain lesions, but is most common and long-lasting in humans when the damage involves the inferior parietal lobe, particularly in the right hemisphere. Studies seeking to determine the critical cortical areas, by looking for overlap in the lesions of different cases, have pointed to the angular and supramarginal gyri (Fig. 2A), corresponding to Brodmann areas 39 and 40 (Heilman et al., 1993; Leibovitch et al.,

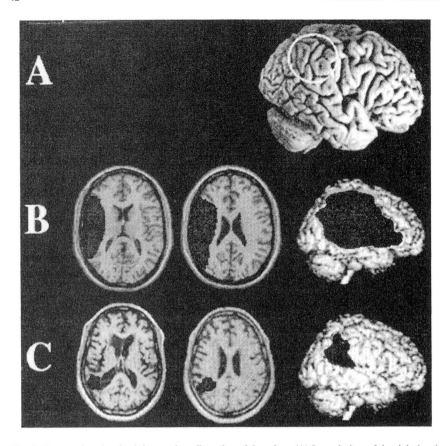

Fig. 2. Topography of parietal damage in unilateral spatial neglect. (A) Lateral view of the right hemisphere in the human brain. The supramarginal and angular gyri in the inferior parietal lobe (circled) are most often involved in severe chronic cases of neglect. Early visual areas in the posterior part of the brain and anterior motor areas are typically spared. Individual patients may have varying extent of damage to other cortical or subcortical regions outside the parietal lobe. While a large lesion in the territory of the middle cerebral artery is very common (B, patient SD), a smaller focal lesion may be sufficient to produce marked visual extinction and neglect (C, patient KG). It is likely that such differences in lesion size may lead to significant differences in clinical signs of neglect, though it is still largely unknown which differences.

1998; Perenin, 1997; Vallar, 1993; Vallar & Perani, 1986). Concomitant damage to white-matter fibre-bundles beneath the parieto-temporo-occipital junction is also common (Leibovitch et al., 1998; Samuelsson, Jensen, Ekholm, Naver, & Blomstrand, 1997), and may result in a larger functional lesion than that implied by considering only the grey-matter damage (e.g. see Gaffan & Hornak, 1997).

It is controversial whether parietal damage in monkeys can produce an equivalent syndrome to spatial neglect in humans. The exact homology between particular human parietal areas and monkey parietal areas is also debated. Architectonic studies suggest that human areas 39 and 40 may correspond to monkey areas 7a and 7b, respectively located caudally and rostrally below the intraparietal sulcus (Eidelberg & Galaburda, 1984). However, while unilateral excision of these areas in the monkey can produce some spatial biases in perception and behaviour (Deuel & Regan, 1985; Heilman, Pandya, & Geschwind, 1970; Mesulam, 1981), these deficits are usually considered milder and more transient than human neglect. It has been argued that more inferior excisions, extending into the superior temporal sulcus, produce a stronger spatial bias in monkeys (Luh, Butter, & Buchtel, 1986; Watson, Day, Valenstein, & Heilman, 1994), as does complete parietal ablation combined with hemispheric disconnection (Gaffan & Hornak, 1997). One difficulty in any monkey–human comparison for neglect is that comparable tasks have rarely been used across the species. It seems clear that spatial biases towards the ipsilesional side can be produced by several lesions in the monkey, including those brain areas implicated in human neglect, but these deficits are usually more specific and transient than for human neglect. Moreover, the right-hemisphere specialization so apparent in humans is not evident in monkeys.

The lesions in human neglect patients are typically much larger and more diffuse than the focal surgical lesions used in monkey studies, being caused by natural accidents such as strokes. Although it has become common to refer to 'parietal patients' in the neglect literature, in fact severe cases often have a very extensive lesion that will encompasses part of the frontal and temporal lobes, plus subcortical structures, in addition to the parietal lobe (e.g. see Fig. 2B). Patients with lesions of this kind will clearly suffer from more than one problem. Clinical neglect often involves a combination of deficits, each of which may exacerbate the others. Since the anatomical extent of brain damage varies from one case to another, different patients can also exhibit somewhat different combinations of deficits. As noted earlier, neglect can involve not only spatial biases in perceptual awareness, but also in motor output (Bisiach et al., 1990; Coslett et al., 1990; Heilman et al., 1985; Mattingley, Bradshaw, & Phillips, 1992; Mattingley, Husain, Rorden, Kennard, & Driver, 1997). Famously, spatial neglect can also be apparent in visual imagery and memory for some patients (Bisiach & Luzzatti, 1978; Meador, Loring, Bowers, & Heilman, 1987). Recent studies suggest that imaginal neglect can dissociate from perceptual neglect, and may have a more anterior anatomical substrate (Coslett, 1997; Guariglia, Padovani, Pantano, & Pizzamiglio, 1993).

The spatial biases towards one side that are the primary cause of neglect may also be exacerbated by some further deficits which do affect both sides of space. For instance, cortical damage around the right temporal-parietal junction biases visual perception towards fine local details of visual scenes, rather than the more global properties apparent at larger spatial scales (Lamb, Robertson, & Knight, 1990; Robertson, Lamb, & Knight, 1988). Since this particular brain area is typically included in the large strokes that produce neglect (e.g. see Fig. 2B), many neglect patients will have a local bias in addition to their bias towards one side. This may be an important element in some aspects of the neglect syndrome (Halligan & Marshall, 1991a, 1993), and in the clinical tests used to diagnose it. For instance, both drawing and cancellation tests may reflect the patients' tendency to lock onto small details (see Fig. 1).

Neglect may also be exacerbated by sensory loss or paralysis in those patients who suffer from these additional deficits. While blindness and paralysis are not primary causes of neglect (see below), a field cut which completely wipes out input from the left visual field may exaggerate any existing tendency to neglect that side of space (e.g. Doricchi & Angelelli, 1999); similarly, an inability to move the left of the body may exaggerate any tendency to respond only to right events.

Thus, each patient will have a particular constellation of deficits and anatomical damage. Nevertheless, there are many commonalities between neglect patients, as we emphasize here. Likewise, we shall tend to focus anatomically on the effects of (right) inferior parietal damage, as this is the most common denominator across patients with severe neglect. Human neglect can occasionally be seen after lesions restricted to subcortical (Bogousslavsky et al., 1988; Rafal & Posner, 1987; Vallar, 1993; Vallar & Perani, 1987; Watson & Heilman, 1979) or frontal areas (Damasio, Damasio, & Chui, 1987; Heilman & Valenstein, 1972; Husain & Kennard, 1996, 1997), with the latter apparently involving ventral lateral cortex (Husain & Kennard, 1996) rather than dorsal superior regions as formerly thought (Mesulam, 1981). However, such neglect is usually more transient than that following inferior parietal damage, and may involve remote metabolic effects on parietal structures in the chronic state (Perani, Vallar, Cappa, Massa, & Fazio, 1987). The full anatomical picture that emerges for neglect is thus of an extended network (Heilman et al., 1993; Mesulam, 1981), involving subcortical, frontal, cingulate and superior temporal structures, but with the inferior parietal lobe as the major hub. Although many neglect patients have large lesions, severe and prolonged neglect can still be observed in cases with a more focal lesion centred on the right inferior parietal lobe (e.g. Fig. 2C).

3. Neglect as a window on the neural basis of awareness, and the contrast with blindsight

Clinical descriptions of neglect were documented by German neurologists a century ago (e.g. Loeb, 1885; Oppenheim, 1885; Poppelreuter, 1917; Zingerle, 1913). However, the syndrome subsequently received less systematic attention than other classical neurological syndromes (such as aphasia or agnosia), perhaps because of the paucity of suitable theoretical ideas or analogies for grappling with it. Moreover, despite the dramatic loss of awareness for one side, neglect was rarely considered in discussions of the neural basis of conscious perceptual experience until recently. Most discussions tended to focus on the neuropsychological syndrome of 'blindsight' instead. We shall contrast neglect with blindsight here. While some similar issues arise, there are fundamental differences.

The excitement about blindsight stemmed from reports of unconscious residual vision (Pöppel, Held, & Frost, 1973; Weiskrantz, 1986; Weiskrantz, Warrington, Sanders, & Marshall, 1974) in patients who were consciously blind for a region of the visual field, following a lesion to a corresponding part of primary visual cortex in the occipital lobe. This area provides a complete retinotopic map of the visual field (as do many subsequent areas of visual cortex). It has been known since early this century that damage to parts of this map leads to blindness for corresponding parts of the visual field (a 'field cut' or 'hemianopia'). So nobody was surprised by the loss of conscious vision in the Pöppel et al. (1973) or Weiskrantz et al. (1974) patients. What was surprising was the report that some visual functions (e.g. the direction of eye movements or pointing) could still take place for stimuli presented within the retinotopically blind region, in an apparently unconscious fashion. The challenge of blindsight ever since has been to explain this residual function, not the loss of awareness. It was simply taken as read that removing primary visual cortex (and thus the input to many subsequent visual cortical areas also) would remove visual awareness.

Some similar issues arise for neglect, in the sense that there is a spatially-specific loss of awareness, and also (as we will show) considerable residual but unconscious processing for the information which escapes awareness. However, in other respects the situation could not be more different. The challenge in neglect is very much to explain the loss of awareness itself, rather than the residual processing, because so many of the neural pathways conventionally associated with conscious perception (including primary sensory areas) remain intact in many neglect patients. For instance, some neglect patients have no visual field cut whatsoever. Unlike an occipital blindsight patient, they are able consciously to report an isolated light, wherever it appears. Yet they still show severe visual neglect in daily life, where visual events can occur on all sides at once, as we emphasize below. Conversely, many patients with field cuts on one side, due to damage in primary visual cortex for one hemisphere, will exhibit no visual neglect whatsoever, even though they are consciously blind for isolated lights presented on one side of their retinae. Clearly, neglect is not equivalent to retinotopic blindness, and the effects of parietal damage are very different from those of occipital damage, even though we have no reason to doubt the parietal neglect patient's insistence that they do not consciously see the information they neglect, any more than for the occipital blindsight patient's reports of seeing nothing in their field cut.

4. The spatial nature of neglect, and further contrasts with primary sensory loss

The loss of awareness in neglect differs from that in blindsight in its spatial nature also. The visual field cut of an occipital patient is absolutely tied to a region on the retina, in accordance with the damage to the retinotopic map in primary visual cortex. Usually there is a fairly sharp demarcation between the affected region and the intact region, often corresponding to one sensory hemifield versus the other in patients with unilateral damage.

This is very different from the spatial nature of the loss in conscious perception for neglect patients. First, there is rarely a sharp divide in performance at some anatomical midline. Instead, there is more typically a gradient of impairment, with performance gradually declining for stimulus locations that are further in the affected direction (Kinsbourne, 1987; Ladavas, Petronio, & Umilta, 1990; Smania et al., 1998). Second, in neglect patients, performance for a given stimulus at the eye, ear or skin can depend strongly on whether any other stimulation is provided at the same time. An occipital patient with a left visual field cut will not consciously detect a light on the left even if presented in complete isolation, in an otherwise dark room. But many patients with left neglect would detect such a light with relative ease. Their deficit would only become apparent if two lights were presented simultaneously, in which case they would typically miss whichever light was presented further to the left (Bender & Teuber, 1946; Critchley, 1953; Loeb, 1885; Oppenheim, 1885; Wortis, Bender, & Teuber, 1948). This deficit during double simultaneous stimulation is known as 'extinction', as the right event is said to 'extinguish' the other event from awareness. We later discuss this phenomenon and its boundary conditions at length.

A further difference between primary sensory loss and neglect is that the spatial deficit in neglect can depend strongly on the current posture of the patient, because it reflects an impairment at a higher level of spatial representation than provided in primary sensory areas. In patients with damage to primary visual cortex, a blind retinal hemifield will remain blind irrespective of current eye-in-orbit posture, moving with any change in gaze direction. But in neglect patients, the same visual stimulus at a fixed retinal position may be neglected or detected depending on the current orbital position of the eye (Kooistra & Heilman, 1989; Vuilleumier, Valenza, Perrig, Mayer, & Landis, 1999), or of the head on the neck (Karnath, Schenkel, & Fischer, 1991; Vuilleumier et al., 1999). For instance, a left visual field stimulus that was neglected with the head and eyes directed forwards may be detected when presented at the same point on the retina but with the eyes and/or head turned right (see Fig. 3). Passively twisting the trunk towards the left, while leaving the eyes and head facing straight ahead, can also bring an otherwise neglected left visual field stimulus back into awareness (Karnath et al., 1991), again suggesting that extraretinal factors can influence visual neglect. This is a remarkable finding; whether the patient sees a stimulus depends not only on the visual information entering the eyes, but on body posture also.

Neglect within touch can also be affected by postural changes that would have no influence on a primary (somatotopic) loss. Tactile stimuli that are not felt on the contralesional arm may eventually be perceived if the arm is placed further towards the ipsilesional side of the trunk (Aglioti, Smania, & Peru, 1999; Smania & Aglioti, 1995). By contrast, damage to primary somatosensory cortex would cause a loss of sensation for the corresponding body part no matter where it is placed. .

When facing forwards in a standard upright posture (as in many clinical examinations and experiments), numerous potential frames of reference are usually aligned, and thus potentially confounded (e.g. egocentric co-ordinate systems such as those centred on the retina, head, or trunk are all aligned, along with more allocentric co-ordinates such as those centred on the computer screen or testing page, the objects appearing upon these, the table and the room, etc). A number of neglect studies have now attempted to uncouple some of these spatial frames of reference by various manipulations such as tilting the patient or the display (e.g. see Bisiach, 1997, for a review) in a complex literature that we cannot describe fully

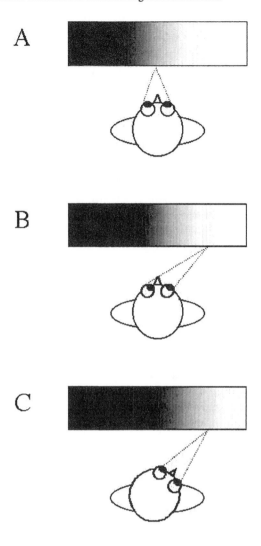

Fig. 3. Schematic illustration of varying spatial co-ordinates in unilateral neglect and effects of posture. A hypothetical patient with right-brain damage and left spatial neglect is depicted as seen from above the head when facing a hypothetical visual scene. Perception of visual stimuli generally improves as a gradient from the contralesional side (black area, complete unawareness) to the ipsilesional side (white area, normal awareness). This spatial gradient could in principle be defined with respect to the retina (line of gaze, depicted by dashed lines), head, or body, which are often aligned in experiments. If the patient keeps his gaze straight ahead (A), he may fail to detect stimuli falling on the contralesional hemiretina. But if the patient directs his gaze to the right while keeping the head straight (B), or if he turns both gaze and head to the right (C), stimuli falling on the contralateral hemiretina may now be perceived. Such effects demonstrate that spatial neglect differs from hemianopic visual field cuts. Also, they indicate that neglect is partly determined by the head and/or trunk position in addition to the primary retinal afferents, and that posture signals can modulate awareness of contralesional stimuli. Adapted from Vuilleumier et al. (1999).

here. Suffice to say that these studies demonstrate there is more to the spatial nature of neglect than mere primary sensory loss within fixed retinal or somatotopic co-ordinates. They imply that neglect can arise at higher levels of spatial representation, some of which involve the integration of different sources of spatial information (e.g. retinal location together with postural signals about the current dispositions of the eye in its orbit, and/or the head on the neck, etc; see Pouget, Fisher, & Sejnovski, 1993; Pouget & Sejnovski, 1997). In a later section, we try to relate this aspect of neglect to current findings on such spatial integration at the level of single neurons in the monkey parietal lobe.

Another complexity to the spatial nature of neglect, which again differentiates it from primary sensory loss, is that visual neglect for one side of far space (well out of the patient's reach) has been reported to dissociate from neglect for one side of **near** space (within reach). This was in fact predicted for humans on the basis of pioneer-ing monkey-lesion studies (Rizzolatti & Camarda, 1987; Rizzolatti, Matelli, & Pavesi, 1983). After an initial report of one patient who exhibited neglect in near but not far space (Halligan & Marshall, 1991b), a further case was described who showed the opposite pattern, neglecting visual stimuli in far-left space but not near-left space, even when retinal visual angles and response requirements were closely matched (Vuilleumier, Valenza, Mayer, Réverdin, & Landis, 1998). However, it is probably more common to observe similar neglect in near and far space for most patients (Cowey, Small, & Ellis, 1994; Pizzamiglio et al., 1989).

A final difference between neglect and primary sensory loss is that neglect patients more frequently lack insight into their deficit. Patients with visual field cuts may realize that their vision is restricted, and can compensate with eye move-ments. Neglect patients are typically more disabled, in effect 'neglecting' their own contralesional deficit.

5. Attentional perspectives on neglect

By now we hope to have convinced the reader that there is more to neglect than primary sensory loss. Neglect patients can be unaware of sights, sounds, touches and body parts towards their left in daily life, even though they are not blind, deaf or insensitive on that side. As we foreshadowed earlier, this seeming paradox may be resolved by considering that, in some circumstances, this applies to neurologically healthy individuals also, when their attention is engaged elsewhere. We can fail to see something, even when a perfectly clear image is available on our retina, if attending elsewhere (e.g. Mack & Rock, 1998; Rees, Russell, Frith, & Driver, 1999; Rensink, O'Regan, & Clark, 1997; see also Merikle et al. in this volume), or fail to hear something which is no quieter at the ear than the conversation we are currently following. Our perceptual awareness thus depends not only on stimulation of our senses, and on the projection of this information to primary sensory areas of cortex, but also on what we choose to attend.

Of course there are some limits on our freedom of choice here; a particularly intrusive, painful or emotive stimulus can be hard to ignore, as documented in the extensive literature on normal selective attention (for recent reviews see Egeth & Yantis, 1997; Wells & Matthews, 1994; see also Merikle et al. in this volume). Nevertheless, this literature contains countless examples of the dramatic phenomenal and objective effects that selective attention can exert on perception. Classic experiments on selective listening (Broadbent, 1958; Cherry, 1953) show that when presented with two spoken messages (e.g. one on the left, one on the right) we can choose to follow one or the other, resulting in a rich awareness of the contents for that attended message, but very restricted awareness for the other. Similar phenomena have long been established in vision (e.g. Neisser & Becklen, 1975) even for constant retinal inputs (Rock & Guttman, 1981). There is currently renewed interest in such phenomena under the heading of 'inattentional blindness' (e.g. Mack & Rock, 1998; Rensink et al., 1997; see also Merikle et al. in this volume).

In addition to these textbook effects of selective attention on phenomenology and report, attention can affect many objective psychophysical measures of perceptual performance, including thresholds to detect a stimulus (e.g. Muller & Humphreys, 1991). Finally, data from many different methods in neuroscience (e.g. single-cell recording, ERPs, functional imaging) converge to show that the brain response to a given stimulus can vary substantially, depending on the current attentional state of the observer (see Parasuraman, 1998, for reviews). Thus, a stimulus which is optimal for driving a particular visual neuron will produce greatly attenuated firing if a behaving monkey is instructed to attend elsewhere (Chelazzi, Duncan, Miller, & Desimone, 1998; Gottlieb, Kusunoki, & Goldberg, 1998; Moran & Desimone, 1985; Treue & Maunsell, 1997).

Against the backdrop of these findings on normal selective attention, the dilemma of a neglect patient who remains unaware of sensory information, even though primary sensory projections are demonstrably intact, may seem less paradoxical. It is tempting to suggest that such patients may neglect left-sided information because their attention is pathologically locked onto right-sided information. Proposals of this kind have become increasingly frequent in recent years (e.g. Humphreys & Riddoch, 1993; Posner, Walker, Friedrich, & Rafal, 1984; Rafal, 1994), and can be traced back to suggestions by Kleist (1923) and others (Brain, 1941; Critchley, 1953; Heilman & Valenstein, 1979; Mesulam, 1981) that neglect involves 'inattention'. However, attentional accounts for neglect are not universally popular. Sceptics point out that little explanation is offered until the concept of attention is fleshed out in mechanistic terms. Fortunately, there is now a vast body of knowledge on normal attentional mechanisms within both psychology (e.g. see Pashler, 1998) and neuroscience (e.g. Parasuraman, 1998).

For many years it was conventional to contrast attentional accounts for neglect with those positing a failure to construct internal representations of contralesional space (e.g. Battersby, Bender, Pollack, & Kahn, 1956; Bisiach & Berti, 1987; Bisiach, Luzzatti, & Perani, 1979; Denny-Brown & Banker, 1954; Hécaen, 1972; Paterson & Zangwill, 1944; Scheller & Seidemann, 1931). In our view, this is rather a false dichotomy. On the one hand, many aspects of selective attention operate spatially (e.g. Tsal & Lavie, 1993); hence, attention has spatially-selective representational consequences. On the other hand, the ultimate cause of neglect is the loss of neurons which selectively represent certain parts of space for specific functions.

The lesion in many neglect patients is so large (see Fig. 2B) that one may doubt whether it could correspond to a surgical removal of just 'selective attention' and nothing else. As we emphasized earlier, most patients have several concurrent deficits. Nevertheless, it remains useful to think of one primary component of neglect as involving 'inattention', and we justify this later in relation to the damaged neural systems. For now, the usefulness of the analogy between neglect in patients and inattention in normals can be judged by the new questions and answers it has provoked in recent years, as described below.

6. Extinction as a difficulty in attending to multiple targets

The analogy with normal attention seems particularly apt for one aspect of the neglect syndrome that we mentioned earlier, namely extinction during double simultaneous stimulation. Recall that many neglect patients can detect a single left-sided event in isolation, missing this only when presented in combination with another event further to its right. Such extinction can actually be found within hemifields as well as between them, but for simplicity we will stick to the example of two events in different fields. Extinction can be observed within vision, hearing or touch, and even between two events in separate sensory modalities (e.g. Mattingley, Driver, Beschin, & Robertson, 1997), as we describe later. The phenomenon suggests that the patients' spatial bias is most detrimental when multiple events compete for attention at the same time, as will usually be the case in the cluttered scenes of daily life.

Although extinction can be seen in some form after various lesions (Vallar, Rusconi, Bignamini, Geminiani, & Perani, 1994), and may represent only one aspect of the heterogeneous neglect syndrome (Liu, Bolton, Price, & Weintraub, 1992), it is often present in patients with focal parietal lesions that leave primary sensory pathways intact (e.g. Fig. 2C). Moreover, a recent study found that neglect as measured clinically (by conventional cancellation scores; see Fig. 1A) correlated directly with the rate of extinction by distracting ipsilesional shapes in a computerized test (Vuilleumier & Rafal, 2000; see also Morrow & Ratcliff, 1987). We take the position that while extinction is by no means the whole story for neglect, it encapsulates a critical general principle that applies for most aspects of neglect, namely that the patients' spatial deficit is most apparent in competitive situations, where information further towards the 'good' ipsilesional side comes to dominate information that would otherwise be acknowledged towards the contralesional side (see Dennett in this volume for further discussion about competition in relation to awareness).

Other authors (e.g. Milner, 1997) have argued that extinction may reflect a separable 'attentional' component of neglect, associated with a more superior lesion. However, the anatomical aspect of this argument was based on a single study (Posner et al., 1984), and more recent studies suggest a critical lesion that resembles the typical anatomy of neglect (see Driver, Mattingley, Rorden, & Davis, 1997;

Friedrich, Egly, Rafal, & Beck, 1998, for further discussion). In any case, extinction is one aspect of the neglect syndrome that clearly involves a loss of perceptual awareness, and so is particularly relevant to the theme of this volume.

Extinction may relate to a well-established but often overlooked attentional limitation in neurologically healthy people (Duncan, 1980; Eriksen & Spencer, 1969; Shiffrin & Gardner, 1972). In many situations, we are able to monitor several streams of information for a specified target as efficiently as one stream. This apparently implies that our sensory systems can transduce all the incoming information at once. Yet if several streams happen to each contain a target at the same time (or close together in time, as in so-called 'attentional blink' paradigms; e.g. Raymond, Shapiro, & Arnell, 1992), people will typically miss some of these targets. This shows that we cannot become aware of multiple targets all at once, even if our sensory systems have transduced them. As we have argued at length elsewhere (e.g. Driver et al., 1997; Vuilleumier & Rafal, 2000), this seems analogous to the plight of a patient suffering from extinction, who is able to detect a single target in any location, with a deficit only for multiple concurrent targets. There are of course a few obvious differences between the normal observer and the patient. One can usually predict which target the patient will miss (the one further towards the contralesional side, presumably because the lesion has reduced its competitive strength). Second, the patient has this difficulty even with just two salient supra-threshold stimuli, whereas the normal attentional limitation with multiple targets arises only for very brief or masked stimuli in more cluttered displays. This suggests a non-spatial restriction in capacity for the patients (Duncan et al., in press; Husain, Shapiro, Martin, & Kennard, 1997; Robertson, 1989; Vuilleumier & Rafal, 2000) in addition to their spatial bias. Indeed, 'simultanagnosia' (a restriction in the number of objects than can be concurrently seen; Holmes & Horax, 1919; Rafal, 1997) may be a critical component of the deficit, over and above any bias to one side. Extinction can be regarded as a pathological, spatially-specific exaggeration of the normal difficulty in distributing attention to multiple targets. This leads to several testable new predictions, as described below.

7. Preserved 'preattentive' processing in extinction: grouping effects

Recent patient studies show that considerable processing can still take place prior to the level at which extinction arises. As a first approximation, such processing typically corresponds well with that considered to take place 'preattentively' in the normal system (see Merikle et al. in this volume). As in normals, this processing can determine which information will attract attention and reach awareness in the patients, and which will escape awareness.

In normal vision, the limitation in attending to multiple concurrent targets can be reduced if these are linked into a single object or group by Gestalt principles such as good continuation, closure, and so on (e.g. Baylis & Driver, 1993; Duncan, 1984). This suggests that the retinal image may initially be segmented into separate groups or objects, so that competition for attention acts on the resulting segmented perceptual units (Duncan, 1984). If extinction is indeed a pathological exaggeration of the normal difficulty with multiple concurrent targets, then we can predict that it too should be reduced if the two competing events could be grouped together. Several recent findings from right-parietal patients with left extinction confirm this prediction (e.g. Gilchrist, Humphreys, & Riddoch, 1996; Mattingley, Davis, & Driver, 1997; Ward, Goodrich, & Driver, 1994), suggesting that 'preattentive' grouping mechanisms may still operate despite the pathological spatial bias of the patient to influence whether a particular stimulus will reach the patient's awareness.

Kanizsa subjective figures (Kanizsa, 1976) provide one interesting stimulus for addressing this issue. They comprise spatially discontinuous elements that can nevertheless yield the subjective percept of a single object, due to modal surface completion (e.g. see the bright white rectangle in Fig. 4B). Moreover, their neural basis is relatively well understood. Neurophysiological work in monkeys indicates that neurons in early cortical visual areas of the occipital lobe (e.g. V2) respond to the illusory contours in Kanizsa stimuli as for real contrast-defined contours (Von Der Heydt, Peterhans, & Baumgartner, 1984). Furthermore, psychological evidence in normal observers suggests that grouping of elements into Kanizsa figures can arise 'preattentively' (i.e. without any need to attend to each set of inducers in turn; see Davis & Driver, 1998).

Mattingley, Davis, and Driver (1997) used Kanizsa rectangles in an extinction study with a patient suffering from an extensive lesion centred on the right inferior parietal lobe, which spared early visual areas (similar to Fig. 2B). The patient had to report[1] whether she saw quarter-segments being removed from four black circles on the right, left, or both sides of central fixation (see illustrative display sequences for bilateral trials in Fig. 4). She extinguished most left-sided events in bilateral trials when narrow arcs on the circles prevented the formation of a connecting subjective surface (Fig. 4A). However, her extinction was virtually abolished when such arcs were removed, as the bilateral events then yielded a single subjective object (a bright white rectangle, apparently superimposed on the black circles) due to modal surface completion (Fig. 4B). This suggests that extinction is reduced when the concurrent target events can be linked into a single subjective object, becoming allies rather than competitors in the bid to attract attention. It also implies that the visual segmentation processes generating subjective figures were still intact in the patient, despite her extensive lesion and associated spatial bias. The latter conclusion was also reached in a study of three neglect patients, which again used Kanizsa stimuli, but now in the task of bisecting 'real' or subjective figures (Vuilleumier & Landis, 1998). The subjective figures produced performance like that for real (physically complete) figures, and unlike control stimuli that did not support grouping into a subjective figure.

---

[1] As with other investigations of awareness in normal people, we have to rely on such reports as indices of phenomenal awareness (though see Block in this volume). As emphasized later, the conclusions from the patient studies agree well with those from studies of normal attention. For the latter studies, a sceptical but neurologically-healthy reader can confirm the phenomenology of most attentional demonstrations for themselves!

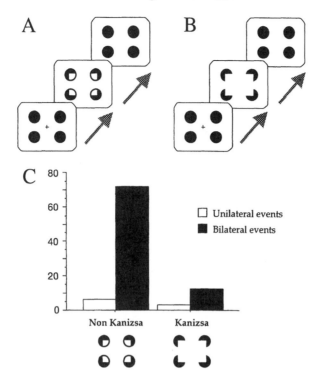

Fig. 4. Reduction of extinction by illusory surface completion in Kanizsa figures. Example sequence of events in one trial when bilateral events did not form (A) or did form (B) a single object bounded by illusory contours (bright white rectangle in B). Arrows depict time between successive frames. In each trial, four black circles were first presented around a central fixation cross; then quarter-segments could be briefly removed from all four black circles (bilateral trials) as shown here, or just from two circles on one side (right or left), or not at all. These displays were used to test a patient with right-hemisphere damage and left extinction. Her task was to detect and report the side(s) of the brief offsets. The percentage of contralesional (left) events missed in each condition is shown below (C). The patient exhibited little extinction when removals from both sides produced a subjective Kanizsa rectangle (as in B), although there was a marked extinction when small arcs remained on the circles so as to prevent the formation of an illusory surface (as in A). Unilateral left events were correctly detected on most trials in both situations. Adapted from Mattingley, Davis, and Driver (1997).

Visual extinction is now known to be modulated by other forms of grouping, including connectedness, collinearity of edges, and similarity of contrast polarity, with less extinction in all cases when the two events can be grouped together (Driver et al., 1997; Gilchrist et al., 1996; Ward et al., 1994). Pavlovskaya, Sagi, Soroker, and Ring (1997) showed a similar phenomenon using formal psychophysical threshold measures and gabor-patch stimuli (which have well-characterized physical properties and are thought to drive highly selective subsets of visual neurons in occipital cortex). Extinction was reduced when two patches in different hemifields were co-oriented and coaxial. Moreover, this depended on the distance between the gratings in a manner consistent with known lateral interactions between neurons at relatively early stages of cortical visual processing, possibly within primary visual cortex.

In summary, these recent studies show that visual extinction can be modulated by grouping processes, consistent with the prediction derived from the analogy with normal attentional limitations. This implies that 'preattentive' grouping processes still take place on contralesional inputs despite the lesion and associated spatial bias of the patients, and that visual extinction reflects 'attentional' competition between segmented objects, not just between particular points on the retina. The preserved segmentation processes can have a dramatic influence on whether or not the patient will become aware of a stimulus at a particular point on the retina. The extensive literature on so-called 'object-based' neglect, which we do not have space to review in full here, makes very similar points (e.g. see Buxbaum & Farah, 1997; Driver, 1999, for reviews).

8. Task effects on extinction

In standard visual extinction studies, the patient is asked to report whether anything is seen on the left, the right, on both sides, or not at all. A seemingly minor change to this task can have a dramatic effect on what the patient reports seeing. Vuilleumier and Rafal (1999) presented stimuli in one, two, or four possible locations across hemifields (Fig. 5). When asked to report where the shapes appeared (i.e. on the left, right or both sides), as usually required, three right-parietal patients consistently extinguished left-sided stimuli in bilateral displays. However, when shown the same stimuli but now asked to enumerate them (i.e. one, two, or four), these patients had no difficulty reporting 'two' or 'four' shapes in bilateral displays; extinction was eliminated. This remarkable change in outcome seems consistent with evidence in normals that enumerating a few (≤ 4) visual elements may exploit special 'subitizing' mechanisms (Dehaene & Cohen, 1994; Mandler & Shebo, 1982), which allow individual elements to be processed together 'preattentively' as a single numerable group (Trick & Pylshyn, 1993), rather than each being attended in a serial manner, as for the counting of larger sets.

In this situation, the reduction in extinction was produced by a change in task-set, not in the stimuli. Nevertheless, the general principle may be similar to that for the grouping experiments described above; extinction is reduced when the concurrent events can be attended as a single perceptual unit, becoming allies rather than competitors in the bid to attract attention.

9. The fate of extinguished stimuli

The previous section focused on factors determining whether a stimulus will be extinguished from awareness in the patients. The results implied some preserved processing for contralesional events, with this (preattentive) processing determining which perceptual units will go on to act as competitors (for attention), and thus which will reach awareness. We turn now to consider the fate of those contralesional

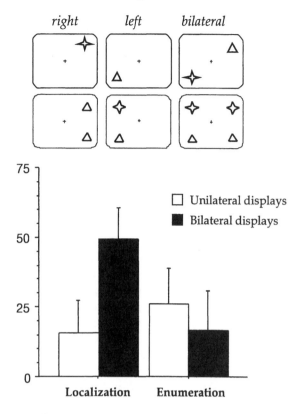

Fig. 5. Subitizing. (Top) Example of visual displays used for comparing extinction in enumeration and localization. One, two, or four shapes were presented on each trial in a random order, with an equal probability for unilateral and bilateral displays. (Bottom) Percentage of stimuli extinguished on the contralesional (left) side in each task (mean ± SD for four patients). Extinction was severe when the patients had to locate the stimuli but not significant when they had to count them. Adapted from Vuilleumier and Rafal (1999).

stimuli which are extinguished, losing the competition and thus escaping awareness. Many recent studies have found residual unconscious processing for extinguished stimuli in right-parietal patients (see Driver, 1996, for review). Most such studies adapted methods that were initially developed to study unattended processing in normals (see Merikle et al. in this volume); the two fields of study have become complementary.

Unconscious residual processing of extinguished visual stimuli can be revealed by reaction times in the patients. Marzi et al. (1996) had patients with left extinction press a button whenever a visual stimulus appeared, immediately followed by verbal report of what they saw. Like normals, the patients were faster to respond to bilateral trials than unilateral right trials, even though the patients were not aware of any visual difference between the two types of trials, reporting that they saw only the right stimulus. In another study where the task required target localization (on the right, left, or both sides), responses were significantly slower on bilateral trials when a left target was extinguished than on unilateral right trials, even though the patients reported the same subjective percept (Vuilleumier & Rafal, 1999).

Other studies have found that reaction times can show unconscious influences not only from the presence of an extinguished stimulus, but also from more complex properties such as its colour, shape, or even identity and semantics. Using a flanker-interference procedure adapted from the normal literature, Audet, Bub, and Lecours (1991) found that the identity of an extinguished letter could affect the speed of response to a concurrent target letter presented centrally. Similar flanker effects have been obtained on the basis of shape and colour (Cohen, Ivry, Rafal, & Kohn, 1995; Di Pellegrino & De Renzi, 1995). In a related vein, Baylis, Rafal, and Driver (1993) observed that similarity in the colour or shape of two bilateral stimuli could modulate the rate of contralesional extinction, in keeping with 'repetition blindness' effects found in normals (Kanwisher, Driver, & Machado, 1995). As with the normal effect, this occurred only for similarity on the currently attended dimension (i.e. shape when reporting shapes, colour when reporting colours).

Further observations suggest unconscious processing of object category or semantics level in patients with extinction. An early study by Volpe, Ledoux, and Gazzaniga (1979) used pairs of pictured objects. Parietal patients who apparently extinguished the contralesional picture were nevertheless able to make above-chance guesses as to whether objects in the pair were the same or different. This study has since been criticized and extended (Berti et al., 1992; Farah, Monheit, Brunn, & Wallace, 1991). Berti and Rizzolatti (1992) found category effects from extinguished stimuli in a classification task (fruit/animal), with faster categorizations for ipsilesional objects when an object from the same category was presented on the contralesional side. McGlinchey-Berroth, Milberg, Verfaellie, Alexander, and Kilduff (1993) reported semantic priming in a lexical decision task. An extinguished picture on the contralesional side speeded response to subsequent semantically-related words at central fixation (see also Ladavas, Paladini, & Cubelli, 1993). Further studies have reported Stroop effects, similar to those seen in normals (Logan, 1980; MacLeod, 1991), from neglected incongruent colour-words in tasks requiring an ink-colour to be named (Berti, Frassinetti, & Umilta, 1994; Sharon, Henik, & Nachum, 1999).

One can quibble with the measure of awareness in some of these studies (e.g. see Driver, 1996), but when taken together, they provide impressive evidence for unconscious processing of remarkably complex properties for extinguished and neglected stimuli, even up to a level where the common semantics of words and pictured objects can apparently have some influence. Moreover, this conclusion accords naturally with similar conclusions for unattended processing in normals for some situations (see Driver, 1996; see also Merikle et al. in this volume).

It should be emphasized that the evidence for considerable unconscious processing in the patients by no means implies that such processing is as full as for consciously perceived events, nor that it must be equivalent in all respects to unattended processing in normals. Fuentes and Humphreys (1996) and Kim and Ivry (1998) found that flanking stimuli which produce negative priming effects on reaction times to subsequent central targets in normals (Tipper & Driver, 1988) actually produce positive priming effects in the patients, perhaps because activated representations for extinguished stimuli in the patients do not need to be suppressed in order to be ignored. A further caveat is that the extent of residual processing for extinguished or neglected stimuli can vary from one patient to another, depending on the exact extent of their lesion, as we elaborate below.

The examples of residual unconscious processing so far all concern the visual modality. Evidence is starting to emerge that similar effects may exist for extinguished tactile stimuli (Aglioti, Smania, Moro, & Peru, 1998; Berti et al., 1999; Maravita, 1997), and we predict that they may be found in audition also.

10. Anatomy of conscious and unconscious perception in relation to neglect and extinction

The accumulating evidence for considerable unconscious processing in neglect patients has now reached the point where it raises specific questions about the underlying anatomical substrates. Here again our discussion will concentrate mostly on vision, as this is best understood, though similar principles may apply to other modalities. The visual system of primates includes many distinct cortical areas, organized hierarchically in both parallel and serial pathways (Felleman & Van Essen, 1991). Long established in animal studies, such areas can now be mapped non-invasively for humans via functional imaging (see Fig. 6). One major pathway from the retina projects via subcortical relays in the thalamus into the primary visual cortex (V1), destruction of which is associated with field cuts and blindsight, and then from V1 into several extrastriate areas within the occipital lobe (Fig. 6). Neurophysiology indicates that striate and early extrastriate areas subserve basic visual operations, such as analysis by spatial frequency and orientation, extraction of contours, figure-ground segmentation, plus some forms of grouping (e.g. Peterhans & Von Der Heydt, 1991). Extraction of colour and of motion parameters has also been associated with particular extrastriate areas (Tootell, Hadjikhani, Mendola, Marrett, & Dale, 1998; Zeki, 1993).

Subsequent stages of visual processing are broadly considered in terms of two major parallel pathways: a ventral stream of successive areas along occipito-temporal cortex encoding object attributes such as shape, colour or identity for the purpose of recognition by contact with long-term memories in the temporal lobe; and a dorsal stream into the parietal cortex encoding spatial parameters (Unge-leider & Mishkin, 1982) for the on-line control of spatial action (Milner & Goodale, 1995). A role of dorsal pathways in unconscious residual vision (plus subcortical thalamo-collicular circuits and their cortical projections bypassing primary visual cortex) has been emphasized by past studies of patients with blindsight, given their ability to point or saccade towards unseen stimuli presented within a field cut (e.g. Cowey & Stoerig, 1991; Rossetti, 1998; Weiskrantz, 1986). Dorsal pathways have also been implicated in the preserved visuomotor function in a patient with a severe loss of conscious form vision after extensive ventral damage (Milner et al., 1991).

This has led to a common view that the dorsal stream may operate unconsciously, with only the ventral stream producing conscious visual awareness.

However, a compelling hypothesis to explain the behavioural results we have described from patients with neglect and extinction is that considerable unconscious processing may take place not only within early visual areas of the occipital lobe, but also along the ventral pathway into the temporal lobe. Neglect patients typically suffer from parietal lesions which can leave posterior occipital and inferior temporal

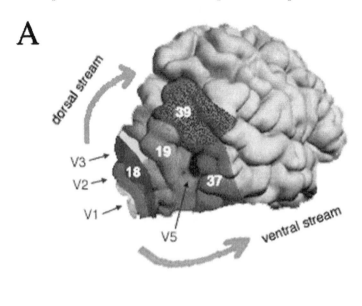

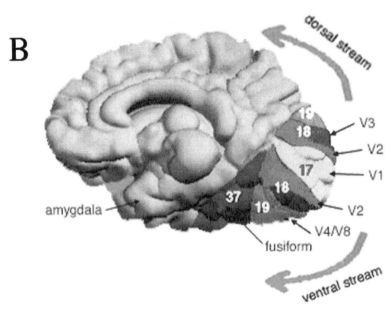

cortices relatively intact (e.g. Fig. 2C). These brain areas may still receive sufficient input from contralesional stimuli to support the preserved grouping processes and unconscious activation of representations for identity and semantics, which we have described.

This anatomical perspective predicts that the extent of unconscious residual processing in neglect should depend on how far the parietal lesion extends towards the occipital or temporal cortex in a given patient. Consistent with this, a recent study of 12 neglect patients found that effects of grouping into Kanizsa subjective figures occurred only in some cases (Vuilleumier, Valenza, & Landis, submitted for publication), depending closely on the lesion. Patients with a preserved influence of subjective figures had focal brain damage centred in parietal or subcortical regions, sparing the occipital lobe (Fig. 7A, top row). The subjective-figure influence was absent in patients whose damage extended posteriorly into lateral occipital cortex (Fig. 7B, bottom row). This accords with the fact that areas in monkey lateral occipital cortex (e.g. V2) contain neurons responding to Kanizsa subjective contours (Von Der Heydt et al., 1984). Moreover, similar occipital extrastriate regions can be activated by illusory Kanizsa figures during functional neuroimaging in normal humans (Ffytche & Zeki, 1996).

Other behavioural effects in neglect patients, such as those implying extraction of identity, category or semantics for extinguished visual objects (e.g. Audet et al., 1991; McGlinchey-Berroth et al., 1993), presumably implicate ventral temporal areas (Driver, 1996). Such brain areas have long been associated with visual shape recognition and object identification (Grüsser & Landis, 1991; Milner & Goodale, 1995), as lesions there produce various deficits in visual recognition, termed 'agnosia'. This association has been supported by functional imaging evidence for activation in ventral brain areas by seen objects, words or faces,

---

Fig. 6. Pathways of cortical visual processing. (A) Three-quarter view of the posterior lateral side of the human brain. (B) View of the medial side of the human brain. Distinct areas of the occipital lobe are indicated with shades of grey. In most cases, each shaded area corresponds to a Brodmann area (numbered in white), as traditionally defined by cytoarchitecture. In a few cases (specifically for those marked V2, V3 and V5) the shaded areas shown were defined by mapping of functionally distinct areas with fMRI in humans (see Tootell et al., 1998). The geniculate pathway from the retina projects to primary striate visual cortex (V1, Brodmann's area 17), and then from V1 to several extrastriate areas in the occipital lobe (e.g. V2, V3, and V3A, Brodmann's area 18). These early occipital areas appear concerned with the analysis of spatial frequency and orientation, and some forms of grouping and surface-extraction. Later extrastriate areas may be associated with more specific visual properties (e.g. colour in V4 and V8, or motion in V5). Two streams of forward projection from the occipital lobe can be broadly distinguished: a 'dorsal' stream into the parietal lobe, and a 'ventral' stream into the temporal lobe (see thick arrows). Areas in ventral temporal cortex subserve discrimination of object shape, identity and semantics, in relation to long-term memory. For instance, the fusiform gyrus (area 37) may be specialized in the recognition of faces, while distinct adjacent areas are more important for objects or letter strings. The amygdala is implicated in the recognition and learning of emotional cues. By contrast, areas in dorsal parietal pathways encode spatial location of stimuli and parameters for directing action towards them, including hand, or eye movements. Lesions associated with neglect involve the right inferior parietal cortex (Brodmann's areas 39–40, see speckled area in A) and may therefore leave many occipito-temporal areas intact (at least in some patients; see Fig. 7 for comparison). Adapted from Tootell et al. (1998).

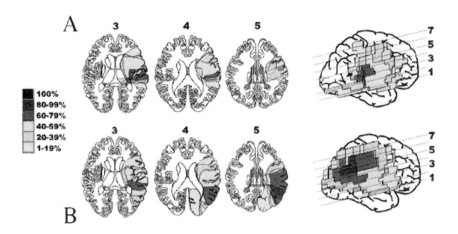

Fig. 7. Average overlap of brain lesions in patients with unilateral left neglect who either showed preserved grouping effects with illusory Kanizsa figures (A: Group + , n = 6) or did not show preserved grouping effects (B: Group − , n = 6). Lesions were reconstructed from CT or MRI scans in each patient. Three axial slices and the lateral aspect of the right hemisphere are shown. The grey shade scale indicates the percentage of overlapping lesions. Grouping into illusory figures was revealed in a bisection task where all patients in Group + produced midpoint judgements similar for Kanizsa stimuli and figures with real contours, but different from other discontinuous displays. The two groups of patients did not differ in the severity of neglect in standard line bisection and cancellation tasks. However, there was a clear difference in the extent of cortical damage. Patients in Group + had damage overlapping in the inferior posterior parietal lobe (Brodmann's area 40) or in the thalamus, with posterior lateral occipital areas always spared. By contrast, patients in Group − had larger lesions extending from the inferior parietal cortex to the lateral occipital lobe (Brodmann's areas 18–19). The latter might include human areas homologous to monkey V2, where neurons have been found to code similarly for real contrast-defined contours and illusory contours of the Kanizsa type (compare with Fig. 6). Adapted from Vuilleumier et al. (2000).

with different areas activated most strongly by each stimulus class (Farah & Aguirre, 1999). For instance, some areas along the fusiform gyrus appear to respond particularly strongly to seen faces (Kanwisher, McDermott, & Chun, 1996).

A recent study (Vuilleumier, 2000) found suggestive behavioural support for preserved activation of such structures by contralesional stimuli in extinction patients, observing that schematic faces show less extinction than other types of stimuli (e.g. scrambled faces, letter strings, or ring shapes, all of which should produces less activation of the 'fusiform face area' than intact faces). With a constant stimulus on the ipsilesional side during bilateral trials, less extinction was suffered by a contralesional intact face than by the other classes of stimuli (Fig. 8A,B), although faces could still be extinguished to some extent. Conversely, a face on the right side produced more extinction of a constant left stimulus than other types of right stimuli. Both aspects of the results suggest a competitive advantage for face stimuli, which may relate both to their biological significance and to the existence of many specialized neurons responding to them in the fusiform cortex.

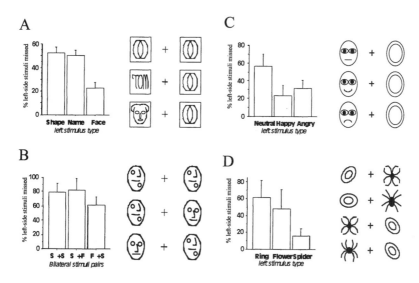

Fig. 8. Stimulus-dependent effects on the severity of extinction. For each experiment, stimulus examples are shown in the right-hand panel and the percentage of contralesional (left) stimuli extinguished on bilateral trials is shown in the left-hand panel (mean ± SD in three patients). Unilateral stimuli (data not shown) were most often correctly detected and identified on either side. (A) In one experiment, a schematic face, a familiar name, or a symmetrical shape could be briefly presented on either side. On bilateral trials where there was a constant competing shape ipsilesionally (e.g. circles, as shown), a face in the contralesional hemifield was much less extinguished than other types of visual stimuli. Adapted from Vuilleumier (2000). (B) In a similar experiment, either schematic faces or scrambled faces were briefly presented. On bilateral trials, the intact faces were again less extinguished, now compared to the scrambled ones. (C) In a further experiment, a schematic face or a shape was presented in either hemifield, with the face having one of three possible emotional expressions: neutral, happy, or angry. On bilateral trials, when there was always the same competing shape on the ipsilesional side, contralesional faces with a happy or angry expression were less extinguished than neutral faces. There was no significant difference between happy and angry faces. Adapted from Vuilleumier and Schwartz (in press). (D) In this experiment, the stimuli included schematic spiders, flowers, or meaningless ring shapes that were presented bilaterally or unilaterally on either side. On bilateral trials, contralesional spiders were extinguished much less often than flowers or rings, while both flowers and meaningless rings were extinguished to the same degree. Data for left-sided rings are collapsed across two possible bilateral pairs with either flowers or spiders on the right, since extinction in these two conditions did not differ. Adapted from Vuilleumier and Schwartz (2000).

These extinction results also accord with claims that some perceptual organization of facial features may occur 'preattentively' in normal vision (Suzuki & Cavanagh, 1995).

The modulation of extinction by face stimuli provides yet another example of preserved processing (presumably activation of category-specific ventral regions, such as the fusiform) affecting what reaches awareness, similar to Merikle et al.'s (this volume) description of how preattentive processes modulate what reaches awareness in normals. It makes adaptive sense that the limited contents of awareness should be determined to some extent by the biological significance of the competing inputs. Further extinction findings suggest that emotional significance can exert a similar influence. Vuilleumier and Schwartz (in press) found not only less extinction for contralesional faces than other shapes, but also for schematic faces with a happy or angry facial expression versus those with a neutral expression (Fig. 8C). This may relate to similar observations on the capture of normal attention by emotional faces (Mack & Rock, 1998). Such effects may also have a neural basis in the activation of anterior temporal structures, including the amygdala.

Amygdala activation has been reported when viewing emotional facial expressions in both humans (Breiter et al., 1996; Morris, Öhman, & Dolan, 1998b) and monkeys (Brothers, Ring, & Kling, 1990). This may feedback to enhance fusiform responses to face stimuli (Morris et al., 1998a; Sugase, Yamane, Ueno, & Kawano, 1999). Such amygdala activations have been reported in normals even for subliminal stimuli (Whalen et al., 1998), in particular when previously associated with fear (e.g. Morris, et al., 1998b). As for emotional faces, parietal patients also show less extinction for contralesional pictures of spiders, known to elicit consistent fear responses even in non-phobic individuals (e.g. Öhman, 1986), than for pictures of flowers made from similar visual features (Fig. 8D) (Vuilleumier & Schwartz, 2000). Emotionally salient contralesional stimuli may thus tend to capture attention and awareness. Here again, the results seem to imply considerable processing of contralesional stimuli (here, concerning their biological or affective significance) despite the patient's lesion and associated spatial bias.

11. The neural fate of extinguished stimuli: neurophysiological measures

In the previous sections, we speculatively related the modulation of extinction by factors such as grouping or emotional salience, and the preserved unconscious processing for extinguished stimuli, to activation of known neural pathways. More direct evidence for such activation would be provided by measuring neural activity directly in the patients, with functional imaging or event-related potentials. Such methods have been widely used to study normal attention (e.g. Corbetta, Meizin, Dobmeyer, Shulman, & Petersen, 1990; Mangun, 1995), and have been applied to neurological deficits of awareness in occipital blindsight patients (Sahraie et al., 1997; Shefrin, Goodin, & Aminoff, 1988). But apart from a few pioneering studies (Spinelli, Burr, & Morrone, 1994; Vallar, Sandroni, Rusconi, & Barbieri, 1991; Viggiano, Spinelli, & Mecacci, 1995), they have only been applied to neglect and extinction very recently.

Rees et al. (2000) used event-related fMRI to study a patient (GK) with left extinction and neglect after a focal inferior parietal lesion (shown in Fig. 3C). Pictures of faces and houses were briefly presented in either the right, left, or both hemifields, with stimulus parameters chosen such that even faces were extinguished. Comparing bilateral trials on which the left stimulus was extinguished with unilateral right trials (for which the patient's conscious report was identical) revealed that extinguished contralesional stimuli significantly activated primary visual cortex and early extrastriate visual areas in the damaged right hemisphere (Fig. 9) in a similar

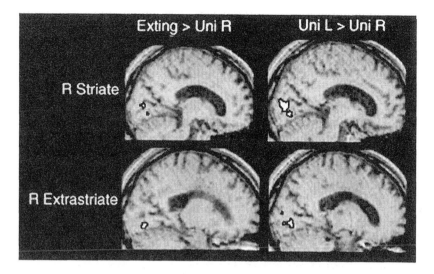

Fig. 9. Functional magnetic resonance imaging of seen and extinguished stimuli in the contralesional visual hemifield of a patient with right-parietal damage. Compared to the activation produced by unilateral right events, bilateral events in which the patient extinguished the left-side stimulus (left column) produced more activation in both striate and extrastriate visual areas of the damaged right hemisphere (Exting > UniR), although the patient's conscious report was identical in these two conditions. The location of such activation by unseen contralesional events in extinguished trials (left column) was similar to that associated with seen contralesional events in unilateral trials (UniL > UniR). Adapted from Rees et al. (2000).

manner to that found for consciously seen unilateral left stimuli. This confirms for the first time our prediction that early visual areas in the occipital lobe, including those lesioned in blindsight patients, can be activated in an unconscious manner in parietal patients.

Furthermore, comparing extinguished faces to extinguished houses (Rees et al., 2000) revealed weak but reliable activation in a right-hemisphere fusiform region, whose anatomical co-ordinates corresponded to face-selective regions in normal subjects (Kanwisher et al., 1996), and to the response to faces versus houses when consciously seen (and fixated) in the patient. A similar event-related fMRI study was independently carried out by Vuilleumier et al. (2000) on another right-parietal patient (CW), who showed extinction for only a proportion of bilateral trials. Their results agree with Rees et al. (2000), showing some preserved occipito-temporal response for extinguished stimuli. They further suggest that those contralesional stimuli which are consciously perceived on bilateral trials may produce stronger activity within occipital and ventral regions, and activate additional structures also, including parietal and frontal areas in the intact (left) hemisphere. Moreover, analysis of trial-specific 'coupling' between areas showed increased coupling between right striate cortex and left parietal and frontal areas on those bilateral trials where the left stimulus was detected.

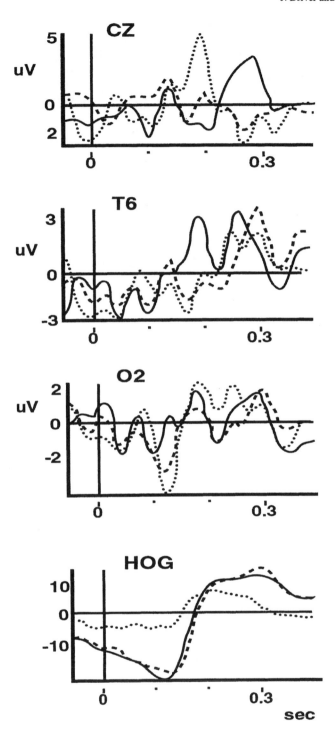

Event-related potential (ERP) scalp recordings have also recently been employed in the same two parietal patients (Eimer, pers. commun.; Sagiv, Vuilleumier, & Swick, 2000). The same stimuli were used as in the fMRI experiments to exploit the fact that face stimuli can evoke specific ERP components around 170–200 ms after stimulus onset (Bentin, Allison, Puce, Perez, & McCarthy, 1996; Eimer, 1998), in addition to earlier activity that is not category-specific (around 100 ms). In patient CW (Sagiv et al., 2000), stimulus duration was titrated to produce extinction on approximately 50% of bilateral trials. In comparison with perceived contralesional faces, extinguished faces evoked similar early visual responses at electrodes over the occipital regions, though slightly decreased in amplitude, plus a similar face-specific component (the 'N170') around 170 ms after stimulus onset at posterior temporal electrodes (see Fig. 10). This suggests that some category-specific face activity was triggered even for an extinguished face, in agreement with the fMRI data.

There were some differences in the ERPs for extinguished versus perceived contralesional stimuli in patient CW. In particular, only perceived faces evoked a positive potential over midline and anterior sites at a later latency (around 200 ms). Another recent ERP study of extinction (Marzi, Girelli, Miniussi, Smania, & Maravita, in press) found considerable differences between the ERPs for extinguished versus perceived contralesional stimuli, even for quite early occipito-parietal components (P100-N100). The stimuli used in this study were small peripheral LEDs, which seem unlikely to drive the ventral activity observed in the recent fMRI studies of extinction (Rees et al., 2000; Vuilleumier et al., 2000). Finally, Hämäläinen, Pirilä, Lahtinen, Lindroos, and Salmelin (1999) reported reduced or absent early potentials (N100) at occipital sites in a series of 20 patients with neglect who failed to detect unilateral stimuli, although distinct ERP responses to occasional deviant stimuli (mismatch negativity components) revealed that some residual processing still took place for the neglected events (but see also Deouell, Bentin, & Soroker, 2000).

Fig. 10. Evoked potentials in a patient with right focal parietal damage and left visual extinction. Stimuli consisted of schematic faces or symmetrical shapes that could be briefly presented in the left, right, or both hemifields. The critical bilateral trials were those with a face on the left side and a shape on the right side. Stimuli duration was titrated so that in roughly half of bilateral trials, left faces were extinguished, while in the other half they were perceived. Average potentials are shown for occipital (O2) and posterior temporal (T6) electrodes, as well as a midline electrode (CZ) over a period of 300 ms after stimulus onset. Horizontal eye saccades are also shown below (HOG). In bilateral trials, left-side faces that were perceived (dotted lines) evoked early visual components around 100 ms at the occipital electrode (O2) and face-specific negative components around 170 ms (N170) at the temporal electrode (T6) in the contralateral damaged hemisphere. Both occipital visual and temporal facial components were still present when left-side faces were extinguished (dashed line) but not when there was only a right-side shape (continuous line), although the patient's conscious perception and eye movements were similar in these two latter conditions. Another face-specific component was observed around 200 ms at the midline electrode only when left-side faces were consciously perceived in bilateral trials (dotted line), and in unilateral trials with left-side faces as well (data not shown). Although oculographic differences (see HOG) may arise for bilateral trials with perceived left faces, note the similarity in eye movements for extinguished faces in bilateral displays versus unilateral right trials. Adapted from Sagiv et al. (2000).

It is heartening when fMRI data and ERP data converge, as for the residual processing for extinguished stimuli revealed in the studies of Rees et al. (2000), Sagiv et al. (2000) and Vuilleumier et al. (2000). However, these two methods of indexing neural activity measure very different things, and so need not always agree. In particular, ERP measures of neural activity, via voltage fluctuations at the scalp, depend heavily on the synchronous firing of many neurons at a fine temporal scale. By contrast, fMRI is much less dependent on the fine time-scale of neural events. One consequence is that a neural activation (e.g. of striate cortex, in response to a contralateral extinguished stimulus) which looks relatively normal with fMRI could in principle look quite abnormal with ERP if the synchrony of firing was somehow disrupted by the parietal lesion. Preliminary ERP data in patient GK (Eimer, pers. commun.) suggest just this.

Given recent suggestions that conscious perception may depend in a large part on the exact timing of neural events (Engel, Konig, Kreiter, & Singer, 1991; von der Malsburg, 1994), it should be interesting to compare fMRI and ERP measures further in future studies of extinction. It should also be informative to look with these methods at extinction in non-visual modalities (Beversdorf et al., 1999; Remy et al., 1999), and at cross-modal extinction (Di Pellegrino, Ladavas, & Farne, 1997; Ladavas, Di Pellegrino, Farne, & Zeloni, 1998; Mattingley, Driver, Beschin, & Robertson, 1997). For the moment, the recent evidence provides initial, tentative steps in delineating the neural correlates for conscious and unconscious perception in extinction patients. Overall, the results converge with the prediction derived from behavioural experiments that extinguished visual events may still activate visual areas of occipital and ventral temporal cortex, without awareness. This may differ from blindsight after occipital damage (Cowey & Stoerig, 1991; Weiskrantz, 1990), where unconscious residual vision has typically been attributed to pathways which bypass occipital cortex, projecting subcortically and into the dorsal stream. Moreover, as mentioned earlier, while the challenge in the study of blindsight has always been to explain the unconscious residual processing with primary visual cortex destroyed, a major challenge in the study of neglect and extinction is to explain the loss of awareness itself, given that many visual afferents are spared. As we have seen, projections into primary visual cortex, and thence to the ventral stream, can still be intact in neglect patients, and the recent fMRI studies show that these areas can still be activated for extinguished stimuli. How then can the patient remain unaware of a contralesional stimulus, even when it can still activate the pathways that are most often considered to support conscious experience?

It is tempting to suppose that some interaction between the (damaged) parietal areas and occipito-temporal areas is involved, with the occipito-temporal activations being insufficient to generate awareness in the absence of appropriate parietal acti-vation or feedback. It remains to be determined exactly how comparable the residual occipito-temporal processing is for extinguished stimuli versus consciously seen stimuli, and exactly how far along the ventral pathway extinguished stimuli can proceed (e.g. can they influence the formation of new learning in temporal or amygdala structures?). In recent unpublished work, we have found that extinguished stimuli can produce implicit learning effects lasting tens of minutes, but no explicit memory.[2]

In the normal visual system, it is already known that spatial attention can modulate the activity of ventral temporal cortical areas, as well as early occipital areas right back to primary visual cortex (e.g. Corbetta et al., 1990; Martinez et al., 1999). Conceivably, such modulation in normals might reflect some interaction of these visual areas with parietal and/or frontal areas that is critical for awareness, and which goes pathologically awry following the unilateral lesions which produce neglect and extinction. The dramatic effect of parietal damage on awareness in neglect patients certainly suggests that interaction of this kind must exist between parietal areas and other parts of the visual system. New methods of analysis are currently being developed in functional imaging (e.g. Friston, 1994; Lumer & Rees, 1999) and event-related potential research (Rodriguez et al., 1999), which should allow researchers to investigate how activity in different brain areas dynamically interacts. For instance, in this way one might determine whether occipital visual areas or the fusiform correlate differentially with other brain areas (e.g. in the parietal or frontal lobe) when a particular stimulus is consciously experienced versus extinguished in the patients (see Lumer & Rees, 1999, for a related finding in normals). Vuilleumier et al. (2000) provide initial evidence for this in a right-parietal extinction patient.

The recent findings that ventral occipito-temporal structures can be activated unconsciously in neglect patients do not fit the simplistic dichotomy sometimes implied in the literature on the neuropsychology of visual awareness between conscious ventral processing versus unconscious dorsal processing. However, Milner and Goodale (1995) had already argued that the inferior parietal areas which are damaged in most neglect patients may be hard to pigeonhole as exclusively dorsal or ventral (Milner, 1997; Milner & Goodale, 1995). Patients with superior parietal lesions typically show the classic 'dorsal' visuomotor impairments in reaching and grasping, but no neglect (Perenin, 1997). Furthermore, one inferior parietal patient with neglect has been reported to show normal scaling of hand grip when reaching for objects in the contralesional space, despite gross perceptual underestimation of size for the same objects, implying some preserved function in dorsal visuomotor pathways in the superior parietal lobe, even in the presence of inferior parietal neglect (Pritchard, Milner, & Harvey, 1997).

Driver (1996) and Heilman, Watson, and Valenstein (1997) have speculated that the inferior parietal lobe areas impaired in most neglect patients may serve as an interface between dorsal and ventral streams, allowing dorsal spatial properties to be linked with ventral non-spatial properties, such as object identity. Watson et al. (1994) made a related suggestion based on monkey studies, but emphasizing areas in the superior temporal sulcus, which can also be affected in many neglect patients. It may be that we cannot become consciously aware of an identified object

---

[2] A recent study (Bisiach, Ricci, Silani, Cossa, & Crespi, 1999) made the striking claim that neglected visual objects may resurface at a later time in explicit memory (see also Block in this volume for philosophical discussion of such a possibility). However, the existing evidence for this can be criticized on methodological and statistical grounds.

when there is no awareness of its location, as following the lesion in neglect patients. A failure to develop appropriate representations for contralesional locations may also preclude intentional actions towards the affected region of space, which in turn may also have implications for awareness. We return to discuss whether spatial location and the parietal lobe may play a special role in awareness after a brief consideration of some of the potentially relevant properties of single neurons in monkey parietal cortex.

12. Cellular properties of the parietal lobe in relation to neglect and extinction

Single-cell recording in awake behaving monkeys has provided dramatic insights into the computational properties of neurons in the parietal lobe and related structures (e.g. see Andersen, Snyder, Bradley, & Xing, 1997, for review). Much of this evidence comes from recordings in posterior parietal cortex, in and around the intraparietal sulcus, though explorations continue into further parietal areas, and similar cellular properties have even been reported in a few of the other brain areas associated with neglect (e.g. premotor and prefrontal regions). We cannot provide a comprehensive review of the complex neurophysiological literature here, but will give some overview of salient features which may relate to human neglect and extinction.

As noted earlier, the spatial deficit in neglect and extinction patients is typically graded in nature, with performance gradually declining for stimulus locations that are further towards the contralesional side (Kinsbourne, 1993; Ladavas, 1990; Smania et al., 1998). Moreover, there is often an off-centre peak in performance for the patients. For instance, many visual tasks are performed best at the centre of the visual field in normals, yet neglect patients often do better within the right visual field than centrally (e.g. for detection RTs and accuracy; Smania et al., 1998). This is quite unlike the impairments seen after lesions to primary sensory cortex, which typically produce deficits with sharp borders, without any off-centre peak within intact parts of the field. The graded impairments that characterize neglect might correspond to a pathological gradient in the number of neurons remaining for particular regions of space within the parietal lobe after the lesion (Pouget & Driver, in press; Pouget & Sejnovski, 1997; see also Rizzolatti & Berti, 1990).

Physiological studies in monkey show that, unlike earlier visual areas, parietal regions include some neurons with ipsilateral receptive fields, so that while the representation within one hemisphere emphasizes contralateral space overall, some ipsilateral representation is present also. More specifically (see Fig. 11), the number of left-hemisphere neurons with visual receptive fields at a particular location decreases monotonically as one considers increasingly peripheral locations in the left visual field, and vice versa in the right hemisphere (Andersen, Asanuma, Essick, & Siegel, 1990; Ben-Hamed and Duhamel, pers. commun.). The number of neurons for different lateral positions within parietal areas for one monkey hemisphere thus resembles (see Fig. 11) the graded performance of neglect patients with

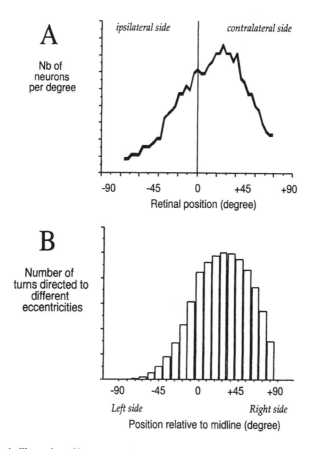

Fig. 11. Schematic illustration of how neuronal representation for a parietal area within one hemisphere may relate to the graded deficits seen in neglect patients. (A) Neurophysiological recordings in the monkey (here from area VIP in the left hemisphere; Ben-Hamed & Duhamel, pers. commun.) show a graded profile in the number of neurons which have receptive fields at particular locations on the retina, with an off-centre peak in the contralateral field (i.e. right field for the left hemisphere), and then a gradual decline for more eccentric locations in the ipsilateral field (left). This is very different from the distribution of receptive fields in the early visual areas of occipital cortex, where neurons have strictly contralateral retinotopic responses and maximally represent the central region near the fovea. Adapted from Andersen et al. (1990) and Ben-Hamed and Duhamel (pers. commun.). (B) After lesions affecting parietal neurons in the right hemisphere, patients with left neglect typically exhibit a spatially graded deficit in their performance, which may relate to the number of remaining neurons (mainly within the intact hemisphere) representing particular points in space. For instance, the number of spontaneous eye and head movements to particular locations in space is pathologically biased towards the ipsilesional side with an off-centre peak, as shown schematically here. Adapted from Karnath et al. (1998). The resemblance to the neural gradient shown above, which might correspond to that within the intact hemisphere, is striking, although it remains to be specified exactly how cellular activity would be read out into overt behaviour.

only one hemisphere intact (Behrmann, Ghiselli-Crippa, Sweeney, Dimatteo, & Kass, 2000; Karnath, Niemeier, & Dichgans, 1998; Ladavas, 1990; Smania et al., 1998). Both show a gradual decline against lateral position, rather than a step-function centred on anatomical midlines, together with an off-centre peak (Fig. 11A,B). Of course, without a computational model that relates single neurons to performance (see Pouget & Sejnovski, 1997), this is just an analogy, plus there may be some differences in the exact neural distribution between humans and monkeys. For instance, while the gradients within the two hemispheres are mirror images of each other in monkeys, these may be asymmetric in humans (Anderson, 1996; Heilman & Van Den Abell, 1980), such that the gradient in the human right hemisphere is shallower (perhaps because this hemisphere has become specialized for representing both sides of space, as the converse of the left hemisphere becoming specialized for language). This might go some way towards explaining why neglect is more severe after right-hemisphere lesions in people, leaving the patient with just the steep gradient of the intact left hemisphere.

The properties of parietal neurons may relate to other aspects of neglect also, beyond its graded nature. As noted earlier, further spatial properties of neglect also distinguish it from primary sensory losses. In particular, whether or not a particular stimulus reaches awareness can depend on current posture, rather than just location on the receptor surface. Thus, a previously neglected left visual field stimulus may become detectable with eyes and/or head deviated to the right (Kooistra & Heilman, 1989; Vuilleumier et al., 1999), or with the trunk deviated towards the left (Karnath et al., 1991) even though the retinal input remains unchanged. The response of neurons in the monkey parietal lobe is also influenced by posture. For instance, although most neurons in parietal areas LIP and 7a have retinotopic receptive fields, the amplitude (or 'gain') of their retinal response is modulated by postural factors such as eye position (Andersen, Essick, & Siegel, 1985). Hence such cells effectively responds to a specific combination of sensory input and posture, thus potentially representing stimulus location in more complex spatial co-ordinates than purely retinal (e.g. the head-centred position of a stimulus could in principle be extracted from such cells). Such 'gain modulation' by non-retinal factors (see Fig. 12) can explain why neglect typically arises in a mixture of egocentric co-ordinates after losses of such cells, with effects of posture in addition to retinal location (Pouget & Sejnovski, 1997). Recent physiological evidence shows that the gain-modulation principle extends to many different types of information (e.g. proprioceptive, vestibular) that are each combined with retinal information in particular areas of parietal cortex (e.g. Snyder, Grieve, Brotchie, & Andersen, 1998). These types of information are also known to influence neglect (e.g. Vallar, 1998). Indeed, neurons that integrate retinal information with vestibular information may conceivably be responsible for the dramatic effects that vestibular interventions (e.g. caloric stimulation via iced water in the left ear) can have in ameliorating the deficit of awareness in neglect (e.g. Rubens, 1985).

As discussed extensively in our sections on extinction, the pathology in the patients typically becomes most evident when several stimuli are presented simultaneously, and this again may relate to recent findings on monkey parietal neurons. Interestingly, extinction in the patients can be determined less by the absolute location of a stimulus within the left or right hemifield than by its position relative

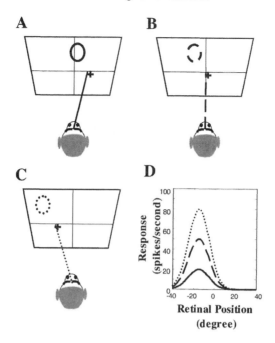

Fig. 12. Schematic showing modulation of visual response by gaze direction in parietal neurons. When a visual stimulus is presented near the receptive field (see circles depicted in A–C) of a given neuron in cortical area LIP of the monkey, the neuron's response (depicted for an idealized neuron in D) depends not only on retinal position of the stimulus, but also on the current eye-in-orbit position (see fixation lines in A–C). While the receptive field remains fixed on the retina (so that its Gaussian profile moves with the eyes), the amplitude of the response increases with gaze directed to the left (C, dotted lines in D) and decreases with gaze to the right (A, continuous lines in D), as compared to the response with eyes central (B, dashed line in D). The gain of visual responses is thus modulated by extraretinal information about posture (see D). In principle, such gain modulation could be used to transform retinal location into visual location with respect to the head or other frameworks. Adapted from Andersen et al. (1985).

to other competing stimuli (Kinsbourne, 1993; Pouget & Driver, in press). Thus, visual extinction can be observed for the leftmost of two stimuli even when both are presented within the right visual field, not just when one is in the left visual field. Whichever stimulus is further to the ipsilesional side will typically capture attention, as if the suggested gradient in the strength of remaining representations in parietal cortex (see Fig. 11A) has some winner-takes-all outcome.

This may relate to the fact that, even in the normal brain, parietal neurons provide a highly selective representation of current sensory input, as compared with earlier visual areas. For instance, neurons in parietal area LIP of the monkey effectively respond only to the most salient (or attended) stimulus in the current visual array (Gottlieb et al., 1998), or to that which the animal currently intends to respond to (Snyder, Batista, & Andersen, 1997). Although many brain areas are now known to show some modulation of visual responses by attention (e.g. Desimone & Duncan, 1995; Moran & Desimone, 1985), these effects are particularly marked in parietal areas (and in other brain regions associated with neglect, such as premotor and prefrontal regions), where a winner-takes-all principle may operate spatially across the entire visual field, so that only a single stimulus becomes dominant. This may relate to the attentional bias associated with neglect, since a lesion in such a population of neurons would bias the suggested winner-takes-all process; in competitive situations the winner will inevitably be a stimulus towards the ipsilesional side of space. Thus, one might think of the gradient depicted in Fig. 11A not only as the number of neurons for particular lateral positions in space, but perhaps also as corresponding to the competitive strength, or 'attentional weight' (Desimone & Duncan, 1995; Moran & Desimone, 1985) of stimuli at these different locations.

A further aspect of neurons in the parietal lobe and related areas is that many have been shown to respond to stimuli in several modalities. For instance, visuo-auditory cells have been reported in parietal areas LIP (Linden, Grunewald, & Andersen, 1999) and MIP (Cohen & Andersen, 1998), and visuo-tactile cells have been found in VIP (Duhamel, Colby, & Goldberg, 1998). Trimodal neurons responding to visual, tactile, and auditory stimuli have also been observed (Graziano & Gross, 1998). These cells typically have spatially congruent receptive fields in the different modalities which can stimulate them. Such convergence of multimodal spatial inputs in posterior parietal cortex seems consistent with the fact that neglect can arise cross-modally (Vallar, 1998). Moreover, several recent studies (e.g. Ladavas et al., 1998; Mattingley, Driver, Beschin, & Robertson, 1997) have shown that an ipsilesional event in one sensory modality can extinguish the patients' awareness of a contralesional event in a separate modality. Ladavas and colleagues (Di Pellegrino et al., 1997; Ladavas et al., 1998) found in right-hemisphere patients that a visual event in the right hemifield extinguishes aware-ness of a touch on the left hand more strongly when placed closer to the (unsti-mulated) right hand. It is tempting to relate such cross-modal interactions to those found at a cellular level in neurons with spatially congruent receptive fields in vision and touch. Such neurons have recently been studied in parietal area VIP as well as in prefrontal cortex, and their visual receptive field is found to follow the tactile receptive field in space as the corresponding body part is moved (Duhamel et al., 1998; Graziano, Yap, & Gross, 1994).

Finally, recent single-cell studies in monkeys reveal that parietal neurons are involved not only in multimodal spatial integration of sensory input, but also in the early stages of planning intentional spatial movements. Area LIP seems to be intimately linked to saccadic eye movements (e.g. Li, Mazzoni, & Andersen, 1999), whereas other parts of the parietal lobe appear to be involved in the control of reaching rather than saccades. For instance, Snyder et al. (1997) found that parietal neurons in LIP respond strongest when their receptive field is the target for an upcoming eye movement (but not for a hand movement), whereas other, anatomi-cally-segregated neurons (in the 'parietal reach region') show the reverse motoric preference. Parietal neurons may thus represent not only the location of a particular stimulus that has been selected for attention, but also some aspects of the decision to make a particular intentional response to it.

This recent evidence that some parietal areas serve as sensorimotor interfaces is consistent with findings that human neglect can involve both perceptual and motor components. It has long been suspected that human neglect may include motor deficits, although any such components were traditionally attributed to frontal rather than parietal damage (Bisiach et al., 1990; Mesulam, 1981; Tegner & Levander, 1991). Recent studies suggest that even neglect patients with focal parietal damage can have deficits in initiating movements towards the affected side, in addition to their perceptual impairments. For instance, they may be slow to direct their 'good' ipsilesional hand in the affected contralesional direction over and above their perceptual deficit for that side (Husain, Mattingley, Rorden, Kennard, & Driver, in press; Mattingley, Husain, Rorden, Kennard, & Driver, 1997), and may show saccadic biases also (Ro, Rorden, Driver, & Rafal, 2000).

13. Do parietal spatial circuits play a special role in perceptual awareness?

Early studies of blindsight (Weiskrantz, 1986) led to suggestions that visual awareness may depend on early visual areas of cortex. More recently, Crick and Koch (1995) sceptically asked 'Are we aware of neural activity in primary visual cortex?', to which we can now reply 'Not in the absence of coupled parietal activity' (see Rees et al., 2000; Vuilleumier et al., 2000). The evidence from neglect and extinction indicates that considerable sensory processing in the occipito-temporal visual system may take place, yet it may not be sufficient for conscious vision. This suggests that spatial circuits within the posterior parietal cortex may make some special contribution to perceptual awareness. We do not wish to imply that neurons here provide the sole neural correlate of perceptual awareness. We doubt that awareness depends on just a single critical brain region, but rather on the interplay between many brain areas in an extended network (Baars, 1997; Dehaene, Kerszberg, & Changeux, 1998; Lumer & Rees, 1999; see also Dehaene & Naccahe, Dennett, and Kanwisher in this volume). The sceptical reader may note that, even within this volume, different authors tend to stress the special role in awareness of those brain areas in which they themselves happen to specialize (be these in the parietal lobe, as here, or the frontal lobe, the hippocampus, the occipital lobe, the cingulate cortex, etc). Perhaps the more important point is the distinctive contributions which these different brain regions may make, and the interplay between them.

Inferior parietal cortex lies in a strategic position within a distributed neural network that interconnects different sensory and motor areas at the cortical and subcortical level (Mesulam, 1981). The recent monkey physiology indicates that posterior parietal areas serve as cross-modal and sensorimotor interfaces which highlight currently relevant locations as targets for intentional action. Parietal areas receive converging inputs from all sensory modalities, including not only vision, audition or touch, but also proprioceptive and vestibular signals about the position of the limbs, head, and eyes. All this information is required to compute stable representations of the location of external stimuli relative to the observer (e.g.

representations which are more stable than the purely retinal inputs to the occipital lobe, which shift every time an eye movement is made, as often as five times per second in daily life). Such disparate sources of spatial information are also required in order to compute how to respond spatially to external stimuli with the eye, head or hand. Neurons within individual parietal areas provide a highly selective representation of current sensory input, effectively responding only to the stimulus that has been selected as the current target for attention or for a particular spatial action. Moreover, they show 'intentional' activity in addition to sensory activity, corresponding to the earliest cortical stages of spatial motor planning, and projecting to various motor-output structures cortically and subcortically.[3]

Given all this evidence for the representation of currently relevant location information within the parietal lobe, perhaps the most intriguing aspect of the human neglect syndrome is that the patient does not lose awareness solely for the location of neglected stimuli, but for their other properties also, and indeed even for the very existence of the neglected information. This is despite the considerable evidence we have reviewed suggesting that the presence and nature of neglected stimuli may still be unconsciously processed in many patients. While the textbook neural pathways for, say, visual face perception and recognition (i.e. from the occipital lobe down into the fusiform gyrus and later temporal areas) may be structurally intact in many patients, under the appropriate conditions these patients can remain entirely unaware of the presence of a face on the left (even though it demonstrably still activates the appropriate occipital and temporal structures to some extent, as in the fMRI studies of extinction). It thus appears that when the appropriate representation of stimulus location is lost or degraded, as in neglect after parietal damage, then awareness of other stimulus properties (presumably coded elsewhere in the brain) is also lost, as if our internal representations of external space (at the level of multimodal sensorimotor interfaces) provided the basic medium for perceptual experience (see Bisiach & Berti, 1987; Robertson, Treisman, Friedman-Hill, & Grabowecky, 1997, for related proposals; see also

---

[3] Although there is some homology between monkeys and humans for the relevant brain areas, it should be acknowledged that differences also exist. Humans appear endowed with a particular development of regions in inferior parietal and frontal cortex (Eidelberg & Galaburda, 1984; Watson et al., 1994), and show more hemispheric specialization than monkeys. It is striking that in humans the right-hemisphere network of brain areas associated with neglect has some symmetry with the left-hemisphere network involved in aphasia, not only for inferior parietal areas in the supramarginal-angular gyri (Vallar, 1993; Vallar & Perani, 1986) but also for areas in the inferior frontal cortex (Husain & Kennard, 1996). Could some of those anatomical factors which led to a special role of these structures for spatial cognition within the human right hemisphere (i.e. strategic position for cross-modal links and for perceptual selection serving intentional sensorimotor transformation) apply also to the special role of left-hemisphere structures in human language (Logan & Zbrodoff, 1999; Mesulam, 1998) and numerical cognition (Dehaene, 1999)? One can even speculate about whether the latter cognitive abilities could somehow have evolved from mechanisms suited to selecting and tagging individuated objects as the targets for purposeful action (with acts like pointing serving as primitive communication and enumeration; Lakoff & Johnson, 1999). Moreover, such mechanisms may relate to a stimulus becoming 'reportable', the conventional objective criterion for awareness.

Kanwisher in this volume for related arguments based on a largely independent database, namely functional imaging in normals). We are not suggesting that other properties do not form part of our conscious percepts, but rather that there seems to be a neuropsychological asymmetry. Losing spatial awareness, as in neglect, invariably leads to losses of, say, 'colour awareness' or 'face awareness' in the affected locations for neglected stimuli there. But losing colour or face awareness (as in cerebral achromatopsia or prosopagnosia) apparently never leads to losses of spatial awareness for the affected colours or faces.

From a philosophical perceptive, this may in part reflect a special role for location in the mental representation of what is 'out there' (even this simple way of referring to perceptual experience in everyday language has a remarkably spatial emphasis). From a neurophysiological and mechanistic perspective, we suspect that it may reflect the extreme nature of the 'winner-takes-all' process in parietal cortex, which we alluded to above, as well as its particular position at the interface between sensory and motor processes. Judging by the recent single-cell evidence from monkey physiology, the function of many of the brain areas implicated in neglect is to select just the currently most relevant location, at a suitably abstract, multi-modal and durable level of spatial representation, as the target for a particular type of action. The work in monkeys and other species suggests that the evolutionary origin of such extreme selectivity may lie in the need to select just one location as the target for the next eye, head or hand movement. A major limitation on any motor-output system, such as that for eye movements, is that no matter how big the brain, the eye can only be moved in one direction at a time. Hence, there is a very real need to have just a single 'winning' stimulus become the target for the next eye movement from among the many competitors in the cluttered scenes of daily life. This may be why the winner-takes-all principle seems to apply in such extreme form in parietal cortex and related areas, with perhaps only a single winner across the entire visual scene (e.g. Gottlieb et al., 1998).

An extreme winner-takes-all principle might explain why a lesion which biases the competition within parietal areas can have such dramatic effects on awareness for stimulus properties presumed to be coded in other brain areas (see also Hahn-loser, Douglas, Mahowald, & Hepp, 1999). This point can be made by reference to Desimone and Duncan's (Desimone & Duncan, 1995; Duncan, 1996) 'integrated competition' approach to selective attention, which seeks to explain both physio-logical data and psychological observations. In their framework, multiple concur-rent stimuli always compete to drive neurons and dominate the network (and thus ultimately to dominate awareness and behaviour). The various phenomena of 'attention' are cast as emergent properties of whichever stimuli happen to win this competition (see also Dennett in this volume). Particularly salient stimuli will have a competitive advantage and thus may tend to 'attract attention' (on purely bottom-up grounds), but the particular stimulus you are currently looking or listening out for may likewise possess some advantage (on purely top-down grounds) accrued by biasing the system in its favour, perhaps even by pre-activat-ing the appropriate set of neurons (Chawla, Rees, & Friston, 1999; Kastner, Pinsk, DeWeerd, Desimone, & Ungerleider, 1999). Within this general framework, the effect of a lesion (e.g. to an area representing candidate targets for attention, saccades, or reaches within one side of space) would be to bias the competition pathologically (in favour of the other side of space). Thus, extinction-like phenomena can be readily explained in much the same way as we suggested earlier.

A key feature of Desimone and Duncan's (Desimone & Duncan, 1995; Duncan, 1996) proposals is that they envisage winner-takes-all competitions to arise initially within many separate modules (e.g. in different areas of the visual system), but with some subsequent integration of the outcomes between modules, so that a strong initial winner in one module then becomes more likely to dominate competition within other models also. The system as a whole ultimately tends to settle on the same particular stimulus as the overall winner, producing those phenomena traditionally attributed to limited-capacity attention. This general perspective leads Desimone and Duncan to argue that no single brain area is special for selective attention, which is seen as the emergent property of competition arising initially within all the modules, and subsequently being integrated across all of them.

While we are sympathetic to many aspects of this powerful approach, we are less sympathetic to the implication that all brain areas are equal for selective attention. Although winner-takes-all operations may be a common principle within many different brain areas, as argued above they may take place according to more extreme rules within inferior parietal cortex (and other brain areas associated with neglect), than in, say, the occipital lobe or other primary sensory areas, where competitive interactions seem to arise on a more local scale (e.g. just between neighbouring visual stimuli (e.g. Polat & Sagi, 1994), rather than across the entire visual field) so that there may be several concurrent 'winners' within the occipital lobe. Parietal areas, each concerned with selection of one stimulus location as the target for a particular type of response, may provide a more clear-cut single 'winner' from cluttered sensory input.

If so, then one can begin to see how the integrated competition proposal could lead to a very extended network becoming dominated by whichever stimulus 'wins' in those particular modules that have the most extreme competition (i.e. within areas of parietal cortex, on our argument). Rather like a Presidential election, winning some Primaries may be more critical than others. This might explain why a pathological bias within brain areas that primarily represent just a currently relevant location could spread to produce a corresponding spatial bias in awareness for all forms of information, including those coded in other brain systems. This may correspond to the marked effects of spatial attention on perceptual awareness.

A further reason for a winner within the parietal competition to be spurred by its victory into dominating competition in other modules is that some degree of location coding exists in most visual modules, whereas coding of face and other object properties is restricted to one or a few. Hence, the outright winner in some parietal area coding space, for a specific purpose, may be well placed to communicate its victory to the various front-runners in other modules, as location may be the main communicative medium. The cascading effects of parietal victory on competitions within many other brain areas could in turn relate to ideas that the content of awareness corresponds to that information which becomes available to a widely distributed network of areas (Baars, 1997; Dehaene et al., 1998; Lumer & Rees, 1999; see also Dehaene & Naccache, and Dennett in this volume).[4]

14. Moving beyond intuitions to the neural basis of awareness

There is currently much excitement about the possibility of relating awareness to neural substrates, and studies of neglect and extinction have much to offer this growing field. However, any pronouncements of 'consciousness explained' remain premature. Part of the problem is that neuroscientists wrestling with intriguing neurological or neurophysiological data often have, at best, only intuitive notions of what awareness constitutes in psychological or philosophical terms (see Block in this volume). Philosophy can of course help to sharpen intuitions and challenge preconceptions but we suspect that even the most sophisticated philosophies of mind may have to be revised drastically as the neuroscience progresses. For now, we cannot resist pointing out that many of the prevailing intuitions about (primarily visual) awareness have some clear resonance with current ideas about spatial function in the parietal lobe.

Visual awareness is highly selective with respect to the current retinal input (Rensink et al., 1997); so too is stimulus representation in the posterior parietal lobe (Gottlieb et al., 1998). Our awareness of visual space is more stable than that provided by fleeting retinal images across rapid eye movements (von Helmholtz, 1867); so too for spatial coding in the parietal cortex (Duhamel, Bremmer, Ben-Hamed, & Graf, 1997; Gottlieb et al., 1998). Many authors have suggested that visual awareness may relate to the binding of diverse properties coded in different brain areas (Baars, 1997; Treisman, 1998); speculatively, this could relate to the contribution of the inferior parietal lobe as an interface between dorsal and ventral streams (Driver, 1996; Heilman et al., 1997; Robertson et al., 1997), and between different modalities (Andersen et al., 1997). It may also relate to the knock-on effects of extreme winner-takes-all competitions within parietal areas, as we have proposed. Some authors suggest that visual awareness may depend more on entry into 'working memory' (Baars, 1997; Crick & Koch, 1995) than on less durable sensory activations. Although areas of prefrontal cortex are often invoked in such discussions, in fact parietal neurons also show clear sustained activity in delays periods of working memory tasks, where an animal must withhold a spatial response to a stimulus which has been removed until a go signal is presented (e.g. Andersen et al., 1985, 1997). Indeed, parietal areas may represent the current contents of working memory, with frontal areas instead controlling and manipulating what enters the proposed store (D'Esposito et al., 1998; Ungerleider, Courtney, & Haxby, 1998; Shallice, 1988). Finally, other authors suggest that perceptual awareness may reside in close contact with intentional motor planning and response selection (Allport, 1988; Crick & Koch, 1995; Rizzolatti & Berti, 1990). While such proposals are

---

[4] The combined ideas of more extreme winner-takes-all functions in parietal areas, plus communication between modules primarily via spatial codes, could provide the mechanism for 'wide broadcasting' which Block (this volume) considers to be lacking.

often accompanied by gestures towards the frontal lobes, in fact initial stages of cortical motor planning (or 'intention') seem to arise in the parietal lobe (Snyder et al., 1997), within the same neural populations as those which show extreme winner-takes-all functions, multimodal integration, and delay activity.

We would not suggest that perceptual awareness resides exclusively in the parietal lobe and those interconnected brain structures which are also implicated in neglect. But we would be amazed if these brain areas do not turn out to play a very major role.

Acknowledgements

Thanks to Alan Allport, Stanislas Dehaene, Masud Husain, Nancy Kanwisher, Jason Mattingley, Alex Pouget, Bob Rafal, Geraint Rees, Tim Shallice, Tony Jack, Noam Sagiv, Russ Poldrack, Eliot Hazeltine, Diane Swick, and Sophie Schwartz. The authors' research is supported by grants from the Medical Research Council (UK), Wellcome Trust, Human Frontiers Science Organization, and Swiss National Science Foundation.

References

Aglioti, S., Smania, N., Moro, V., & Peru, A. (1998). Tactile salience influences extinction. Neurology, 50 (4), 1010–1014.

Aglioti, S., Smania, N., & Peru, A. (1999). Frames of reference for mapping tactile stimuli in brain-damaged patients. Journal of Cognitive Neuroscience, 11 (1), 167–179.

Allport, A. (1988). What concept of consciousness? In A. J. Marcel, & E. Bisiach (Eds.), Consciousness in contemporary science. London: Clarendon Press.

Andersen, R. A., Asanuma, C., Essick, G., & Siegel, R. (1990). Corticocortical connections of anatomically and physiologically defined subdivisions within the inferior parietal lobule. Journal of Comparative Neurology, 296 (1), 65–113.

Andersen, R. A., Essick, G. K., & Siegel, R. M. (1985). Encoding of spatial location by posterior parietal neurons. Science, 230, 456–458.

Andersen, R., Snyder, L. H., Bradley, D. C., & Xing, J. (1997). Multimodal representation of space in the posterior parietal cortex and its use in planning movement. Annual Reviews in Neuroscience, 20, 303–330.

Anderson, B. (1996). A mathematical model of line bisection behaviour in neglect. Brain, 119, 841–850.

Audet, T., Bub, D., & Lecours, A. R. (1991). Visual neglect and left-sided context effects. Brain & Cognition, 16 (1), 11–28.

Baars, B. J. (1997). Some essential differences between consciousness and attention, perception, and working memory. Consciousness & Cognition, 6 (2–3), 363–371.

Battersby, W. S., Bender, M. B., Pollack, M., & Kahn, R. L. (1956). Unilateral spatial agnosia ("inattention") in patients with cerebral lesions. Brain, 79, 68–93.

Baylis, G. C., & Driver, J. (1993). Visual attention and objects: evidence for hierarchical coding of location. Journal of Experimental Psychology: Human Perception and Performance, 19, 451–470.

Baylis, G., Rafal, R., & Driver, J. (1993). Visual extinction and stimulus repetition. Journal of Cognitive Neuroscience, 5, 453–466.

Behrmann, M., Ghiselli-Crippa, T., Sweeney, J., Dimatteo, I., & Kass, R. (2000). Gain fields in human parietal cortex as reflected in saccadic reaction time. Gain fields meeting, Monterey, CA.

Bellas, D. N., Novelly, R. A., Eskenazi, B., & Wasserstein, J. (1988). The nature of unilateral neglect in the olfactory system. Neuropsychologia, 26, 45–52.

Bender, M. B., & Teuber, H. L. (1946). Phenomena of fluctuation, extinction, and completion in visual perception. Archives of Neurology and Psychiatry, 55, 627–658.

Bentin, S., Allison, T., Puce, A., Perez, E., & McCarthy, G. (1996). Electrophysiological studies of face perception in humans. Journal of Cognitive Neuroscience, 8 (6), 551–565.

Berti, A., Allport, A., Driver, J., Dienes, Z., Oxbury, J., & Oxbury, S. (1992). Level of processing for stimuli in an "extinguished" visual field. Neuropsychologia, 30, 403–415.

Berti, A., Frassinetti, F., & Umilta, C. (1994). Nonconscious reading? Evidence from neglect dyslexia. Cortex, 30, 181–197.

Berti, A., Oxbury, S., Oxbury, J., Affanni, P., Umilta, C., & Orlandi, L. (1999). Somatosensory extinction for meaningful objects in a patient with right hemispheric stroke. Neuropsychologia, 37 (3), 333–343.

Berti, A., & Rizzolatti, G. (1992). Visual processing without awareness: evidence from unilateral neglect. Journal of Cognitive Neuroscience, 4, 345–351.

Beversdorf, D. Q., Anderson, J. M., Auerbach, E. J., Briggs, R. W., Hughes, J. D., Crosson, B., & Heilman, K. M. (1999). Functional MRI of the primary somatosensory cortex in extinction to simultaneous bilateral tactile stimuli (abstract). Neurology, 52 (Suppl. 2), A232.

Bisiach, E. (1997). The spatial features of unilateral neglect. In P. Thier, & H. O. Karnath (Eds.), Parietal lobe contributions to orientation in 3D space. Berlin: Springer.

Bisiach, E., & Berti, A. (1987). Dyschiria: an attempt at its systematic explanation. In M. Jeannerod, Neurophysiological and neuropsychological aspects of spatial neglect (Vol. 45, pp. 183–202). , 45. Amsterdam: North-Holland.

Bisiach, E., Geminiani, G., Berti, A., & Rusconi, M. L. (1990). Perceptual and premotor factors of unilateral neglect. Neurology, 40, 1278–1281.

Bisiach, E., & Luzzatti, C. (1978). Unilateral neglect of representational space. Cortex, 14, 129–133.

Bisiach, E., Luzzatti, C., & Perani, D. (1979). Unilateral neglect, representational schema and consciousness. Brain, 102, 609–618.

Bisiach, E., Ricci, R., Silani, G., Cossa, F. M., & Crespi, M. G. (1999). Hyperamnesia in unilateral neglect. Cortex, 35, 701–711.

Bogousslavsky, J., Miklossy, J., Regli, F., Deruaz, J. P., Assal, G., & Delaloye, B. (1988). Subcortical neglect: neuropsychological, SPECT, and neuropathological correlations with anterior choroidal artery territory infarction. Annals of Neurology, 23 (5), 448–452.

Brain, W. R. (1941). Visual disorientation with special reference to lesions of the right hemisphere. Brain, 64, 244–272.

Breiter, H. C., Etcoff, N. L., Whalen, P. J., Kennedy, W. A., Rauch, S. L., Buckner, R. L., Strauss, M. M., Hyman, S. E., & Rosen, B. R. (1996). Response and habituation of the human amygdala during visual processing of facial expression. Neuron, 17, 875–887.

Broadbent, D. E. (1958). Perception and communication. London: Pergamon.

Brothers, L., Ring, B., & Kling, A. (1990). Responses of neurons in the macaque amygdala to complex social stimuli. Neurosciences, 41, 199–213.

Buxbaum, L. J., & Farah, M. J. (1997). Object-based attention in visual neglect: conceptual and empirical distinctions. In H. -O. Karnath, & P. Thier (Eds.), Parietal lobe contributions to orientation in 3D space (pp. 384–400). Berlin: Springer.

Chawla, D., Rees, G., & Friston, K. J. (1999). The physiological basis of attentional modulation in extrastriate visual areas. Nature Neuroscience, 2 (7), 671–676.

Chelazzi, L., Duncan, J., Miller, E. K., & Desimone, R. (1998). Responses of neurons in inferior temporal cortex during memory-guided visual search. Journal of Neurophysiology, 80, 2918–2940.

Cherry, E. C. (1953). Some experiments on the recognition of speech, with one and two ears. Journal of the Acoustic Society of America, 25, 975–979.

Cohen, A., Ivry, R., Rafal, R., & Kohn, C. (1995). Response code activation by stimuli in the neglected visual field. Neuropsychology, 9, 165–173.

Cohen, Y. E., & Andersen, R. A. (1998). The parietal reach region (PRR) encodes reaches to auditory targets in an eye-centered reference frame. Society for Neuroscience Abstracts, 24, 106.3.

Corbetta, M., Meizin, F. M., Dobmeyer, S., Shulman, G. L., & Petersen, S. E. (1990). Selective attention modulates neural processing of shape, color and velocity in humans. Science, 248, 1556–1559.

Coslett, H. B. (1997). Neglect in vision and visual imagery: a double dissociation. Brain, 120 (7), 1163–1171.

Coslett, H. B., Bowers, D., Fitzpatrick, E., Haws, B., & Heilman, K. M. (1990). Directional hypokinesia and hemispatial inattention in neglect. Brain, 113, 475–486.

Cowey, A., Small, M., & Ellis, S. (1994). Left visuospatial neglect can be worse in far than in near space. Neuropsychologia, 32, 1059–1066.

Cowey, A., & Stoerig, P. (1991). The neurobiology of blindsight. Trends in Neuroscience, 14 (4), 140–145.

Crick, F., & Koch, C. (1995). Are we aware of neural activity in primary visual cortex? Nature, 375, 121–123.

Critchley, M. (1953). The parietal lobes. New York: Hafner.

Damasio, A. R., Damasio, H., & Chui, H. C. (1987). Neglect following damage to frontal lobe or basal ganglia. Neuropsychologia, 18 (2), 123–132.

Davis, G., & Driver, J. (1998). Kanizsa subjective figures can act as occluding surfaces at parallel stages of visual search. Journal of Experimental Psychology: Human Perception and Performance, 24 (1), 169–184.

Dehaene, S. (1999). The number sense: how the mind creates mathematics. New York: Penguin.

Dehaene, S., & Cohen, L. (1994). Dissociable mechanisms of subitizing and counting: neuropsychological evidence from simultanagnosic patients. Journal of Experimental Psychology: Human Perception and Performance, 20, 958–975.

Dehaene, S., Kerszberg, M., & Changeux, J. P. (1998). A neuronal model of a global workspace in effortful cognitive tasks. Proceedings of the National Academy of Sciences USA, 95 (24), 14529–14534.

Denny-Brown, D., & Banker, B. Q. (1954). Amorphosynthesis from left parietal lesion. Archives of Neurology and Psychiatry, 72, 302–313.

Deouell, L. Y., Bentin, S., & Soroker, N. (2000). Electrophysiological evidence for an early (preattentive) information processing deficit in patients with right hemisphere damage and unilateral neglect. Brain, 123, 353–365.

Desimone, R., & Duncan, J. (1995). Neural mechanisms of selective visual attention. Annual Reviews in Neuroscience, 18, 193–222.

D'Esposito, M., Aguirre, G. K., Zarahn, E., Ballard, D., Shin, R. K., & Lease, J. (1998). Functional MRI studies of spatial and nonspatial working memory. Cognitive Brain Research, 7 (1), 1–13.

Deuel, R. K., & Regan, D. J. (1985). Parietal hemineglect and motor deficits in the monkey. Neuropsychologia, 23, 305–314.

Di Pellegrino, G., & De Renzi, E. (1995). An experimental investigation on the nature of extinction. Neuropsychologia, 33, 153–170.

Di Pellegrino, G., Ladavas, E., & Farne, A. (1997). Seeing where your hands are. Nature, 388, 370.

Doricchi, F., & Angelelli, P. (1999). Misrepresentation of horizontal space in left unilateral neglect: role of hemianopia. Neurology, 52, 1845–1852.

Driver, J. (1996). What can visual neglect and extinction reveal about the extent of "preattentive" processing? In A. F. Kramer, M. G. H. Cole, & G. D. Logan (Eds.), Convergent operations in the study of visual selective attention (193–224). Washington, DC: APA Press.

Driver, J. (1999). Egocentric and object-based visual neglect. In N. K. Burgess, & J. O'Keefe (Eds.), The hippocampal and parietal foundations of spatial cognitionOxford: Oxford University Press.

Driver, J., Mattingley, J. B., Rorden, C., & Davis, G. (1997). Extinction as a paradigm measure of attentional bias and restricted capacity following brain injury. In H.-O. Karnath, & P. Thier (Eds.), Parietal lobe contributions to orientation in 3D space (pp. 401–429). Berlin: Springer.

Duhamel, J. R., Bremmer, F., Ben-Hamed, S., & Graf, W. (1997). Spatial invariance of visual receptive fields in parietal cortex neurons. Nature, 389 (6653), 845–848.

Duhamel, J. R., Colby, C. L., & Goldberg, M. E. (1998). Ventral intraparietal area of the macaque: congruent visual and somatic response properties. Journal of Neurophysiology, 79 (1), 126–136.

Duncan, J. (1980). The locus of interference in the perception of simultaneous stimuli. Psychological Review, 87, 272–300.

Duncan, J. (1984). Selective attention and the organization of visual information. Journal of Experimental Psychology: General, 113, 501–517.

Duncan, J. (1996). Cooperating brain systems in selective perception and action. In T. Inui, & J. L. McClelland (Eds.), Information integration in perception and communication (Vol. XVI, pp. 549–578). MIT Press: Cambridge, MA.

Duncan, J., Bundesen, C., Olson, A., Humphreys, G., Chavda, S., & Shibuya, H. (in press). Systematic analysis of deficits in visual attention. Journal of Experimental Psychology: General.

Egeth, H. E., & Yantis, S. (1997). Visual attention: control, representation, and time course. Annual Review of Psychology, 48, 269–297.

Eidelberg, G., & Galaburda, A. (1984). Inferior parietal lobule: divergent architectonic asymmetries in the human brain. Archives of Neurology, 41 (8), 843–852.

Eimer, M. (1998). Does the face-specific N170 component reflect the activity of a specialized eye processor. NeuroReport, 9 (13), 2945–2948.

Engel, A., Konig, P., Kreiter, A., & Singer, W. (1991). Interhemispheric synchronization of oscillatory neuronal responses in cat visual cortex. Science, 252, 1177–1179.

Eriksen, C. W., & Spencer, T. (1969). Rate of information processing in visual perception: some results and methodological considerations. Journal of Experimental Psychology Monograph, 79 (2), 1–16.

Farah, M., & Aguirre, G. (1999). Imaging visual recognition: PET and fMRI studies of the functional anatomy of human visual recognition. Trends in Cognitive Sciences, 3 (5), 179–186.

Farah, M. J., Monheit, M. A., Brunn, J. L., & Wallace, M. A. (1991). Unconscious perception of "extinguished" visual stimuli: reassessing the evidence. Neuropsychologia, 29, 949–958.

Felleman, D. J., & Van Essen, D. C. (1991). Distributed hierarchical processing in the primate cerebral cortex. Cerebral Cortex, 1, 1–47.

Ffytche, D., & Zeki, S. (1996). Brain activity related to the perception of illusory contours. NeuroImage, 3, 104–108.

Friedrich, F. J., Egly, R., Rafal, R. D., & Beck, D. (1998). Spatial attention deficits in humans: a comparison of superior parietal and temporal-parietal junction lesions. Neuropsychology, 12 (2), 193–207.

Friston, K. (1994). Functional and effective connectivity: a synthesis. Human Brain Mapping, 2, 56–78.

Fuentes, L. J., & Humphreys, G. W. (1996). On the processing of "extinguished" stimuli in unilateral visual neglect: an approach using negative priming. Cognitive Neuropsychology, 13 (1), 111–136.

Gaffan, D., & Hornak, J. (1997). Visual neglect in the monkey: representation and disconnection. Brain, 120 (9), 1647–1657.

Gilchrist, I. D., Humphreys, G. W., & Riddoch, M. J. (1996). Grouping and extinction: evidence for low-level modulation of visual selection. Cognitive Neuropsychology, 13, 1223–1249.

Gottlieb, J. P., Kusunoki, M., & Goldberg, M. E. (1998). The representation of visual salience in monkey parietal cortex. Nature, 391, 481–484.

Graziano, M. S., & Gross, C. G. (1998). Spatial maps for the control of movement. Current Opinion in Neurobiology, 8, 2195–2201.

Graziano, M., Yap, G., & Gross, C. (1994). Coding of visual space by premotor neurons. Science, 266 (5187), 1054–1057.

Grüsser, O. J., & Landis, T. (1991). Visual agnosia and other disturbances of visual perception and cognition, 12. London: Macmillan.

Guariglia, C., Padovani, A., Pantano, P., & Pizzamiglio, L. (1993). Unilateral neglect restricted to visual imagery. Nature, 364, 235–237.

Hahnloser, R., Douglas, R. J., Mahowald, M., & Hepp, K. (1999). Feedback interactions between neuronal pointers and maps for attentional processing. Nature Neuroscience, 2, 746–752.

Halligan, P. W., & Marshall, J. C. (1991a). Figural modulation of visuo-spatial neglect: a case study. Neuropsychologia, 29, 619–628.

Halligan, P. W., & Marshall, J. C. (1991b). Left neglect for near but not far space in man. Nature, 350, 498–500.

Halligan, P. W., & Marshall, J. C. (1993). Homing in on neglect: a case study of visual search. Cortex, 29 (1), 167–174.

Hämäläinen, H., Pirilä, J., Lahtinen, E., Lindroos, J., & Salmelin, R. (1999). Cognitive ERP components in neglect. Journal of Cognitive Neuroscience, 11; Suppl, Abstracts of the Annual Meeting of the Society of Cognitive Neuroscience, 58.

Hécaen, H. (1972). Introduction à la neuropsychologie. Paris: Larousse.

Heilman, K. M., Boweres, D., Coslett, H. B., Whelan, H., & Watson, R. T. (1985). Directional hypokinesia: prolonged reaction times for leftward movements in patients with right hemisphere lesions and neglect. Neurology, 35, 855–859.

Heilman, K. M., Pandya, D. M., & Geschwind, N. (1970). Trimodal inattention following parietal lobe ablations. Transactions of the American Neurology Association, 95, 259–268.

Heilman, K. M., & Valenstein, E. (1972). Frontal lobe neglect in man. Neurology, 22, 660–664.

Heilman, K. M., & Valenstein, E. (1979). Mechanisms underlying hemispacial neglect. Annals of Neurology, 5, 166–170.

Heilman, K. M., & Van Den Abell, T. (1980). Right hemisphere dominance for attention: the mechanisms underlying hemispheric asymmetries of inattention (neglect). Neurology, 30, 327–330.

Heilman, K. M., Watson, R. T., & Valenstein, E. (1993). Neglect and related disorders. In K. M. Heilman, & E. Valenstein (Eds.), Clinical neuropsychology (pp. 279–336). New York: Oxford University Press.

Heilman, K. M., Watson, R. T., & Valenstein, E. (1997). Neglect: clinical and anatomic aspects. In T. E. Feinberg, & M. J. Farah (Eds.), Behavioral neurology and neuropsychology (pp. 309–317). New York: McGraw-Hill.

Holmes, G., & Horax, G. (1919). Disturbances of spatial orientation and visual attention, with loss of stereoscopic vision. Archives of Neurology and Psychiatry, 1, 385–407.

Humphreys, G. W., & Riddoch, M. J. (1993). Interactive attentional systems in unilateral visual neglect. In I. H. Robertson, & J. C. Marshall (Eds.), Unilateral neglect: clinical and experimental studies (pp. 139–168). Hillsdale, NJ: Lawrence Erlbaum Associates.

Husain, M., & Kennard, C. (1996). Visual neglect associated with frontal lobe infarction. Journal of Neurology, 243, 652–657.

Husain, M., & Kennard, C. (1997). Distractor-dependent frontal neglect. Neuropsychologia, 35, 829–841.

Husain, M., Mattingley, J., Rorden, C., Kennard, C., & Driver, J. (in press). Distinguishing sensory and motor biases in parietal and frontal neglect. Brain.

Husain, M., Shapiro, K., Martin, J., & Kennard, C. (1997). Abnormal temporal dynamics of visual attention in spatial neglect patients. Nature, 385, 154–156.

Kanizsa, G. (1976). Subjective contours. Scientific American, 234, 48–52.

Kanwisher, N., Driver, J., & Machado, L. (1995). Spatial repetition blindness is modulated by selective attention to color or shape. Cognitive Neuropsychology, 29, 303–337.

Kanwisher, N., McDermott, J., & Chun, M. M. (1996). A module for the visual representation of faces. Neuroimage, 3, S361.

Karnath, H., Niemeier, M., & Dichgans, J. (1998). Space exploration in neglect. Brain, 121 (12), 2357–2367.

Karnath, H. O., Schenkel, P., & Fischer, B. (1991). Trunk orientation as the determining factor of the 'contralateral' deficit in the neglect syndrome and as the physical anchor of the internal representation of body orientation in space. Brain, 114 (4), 1997–2014.

Kastner, S., Pinsk, M., DeWeerd, P., Desimone, R., & Ungerleider, L. (1999). Increased activity in human visual cortex during directed attention in the absence of visual stimulation. Neuron, 22 (4), 751–761.

Kim, N., & Ivry, R. (1998). Inhibition and activation of neglected visual stimuli. Journal of Cognitive Neuroscience, 10; Suppl, Abstracts of the Annual Meeting of the Society of Cognitive Neuroscience, 70.

Kinsbourne, M. (1987). Mechanisms of unilateral neglect. In M. Jeannerod (Ed.), Neurophysiological and neuropsychological aspects of spatial neglect (pp. 235–258). Amsterdam: North-Holland.

Kinsbourne, M. (1993). Orientational bias model of unilateral neglect: evidence from attentional gradients within hemispace. In I. H. Robertson, & J. C. Marshall (Eds.), Unilateral neglect: clinical and experimental studies (pp. 63–86). Hillsdale, NJ: Lawrence Erlbaum.

Kleist, K. (1923). Kriegsverletzungen des Gehirns in ihrer Bedeutung für die Hirnlokalisation und Hirnpathologie. In O. Schjerning (Ed.), Handbuch des ärtzlichen Erfahrung im Weltkriege 1914-1918 Geistes- und Nervenkrankenheiten: Vol. 4. Leipzig: Barth.

Kooistra, C. A., & Heilman, K. M. (1989). Hemispatial visual inattention masquerading as hemianopia. Neurology, 39, 1125-1172.

Ladavas, E. (1990). Selective spatial attention in patients with visual extinction. Brain, 113, 1527-1538.

Ladavas, E., Di Pellegrino, G., Farne, A., & Zeloni, G. (1998). Neuropsychological evidence of an integrated visuotactile representation of peripersonal space in humans. Journal of Cognitive Neuroscience, 10 (5), 581-589.

Ladavas, E., Paladini, R., & Cubelli, R. (1993). Implicit associative priming in a patient with left visual neglect. Neuropsychologia, 31, 1307-1320.

Ladavas, E., Petronio, A., & Umilta, C. (1990). The deployment of visual attention in the intact field of hemineglect. Cortex, 26, 307-317.

Lakoff, G., & Johnson, M. (1999). Philosophy in the flesh: the embodied mind and its challenge to western thought. New York: Basic Books.

Lamb, M. R., Robertson, L. C., & Knight, R. T. (1990). Component mechanisms underlying the processing of hierarchically organized patterns: inferences from patients with unilateral cortical lesions. Journal of Experimental Psychology: Learning, Memory and Cognition, 16, 471-483.

Leibovitch, F. S., Black, S. E., Caldwell, C. B., Ebert, P. L., Ehrlich, L. E., & Szalai, J. P. (1998). Brain-behavior correlations in hemispatial neglect using CT and SPECT: the Sunnybrook Stroke Study. Neurology, 50 (4), 901-908.

Li, C., Mazzoni, P., & Andersen, R. (1999). Effect of reversible inactivation of macaque lateral intraparietal area on visual and memory saccades. Journal of Neurophysiology, 81 (4), 1827-1838.

Linden, J., Grunewald, A., & Andersen, R. (1999). Responses to auditory stimuli in macaque lateral intraparietal area. II. Behavioral modulation. Neurophysiology, 82 (1), 343-358.

Liu, G. T., Bolton, A. K., Price, B. H., & Weintraub, S. (1992). Dissociated perceptual-sensory and exploratory-motor neglect. Journal of Neurology, Neurosurgery, and Psychiatry, 55, 701-706.

Loeb, J. (1885). Die elementaren Stoerungen einfacher Functionen nach oberflachlicher umschriebener Verletzung des Grosshirns Plugers. Archives Physiologie, 37, 51-56.

Logan, G. D. (1980). Attention and automaticity in Stroop and priming tasks: theory and data. Cognitive Psychology, 12, 523-553.

Logan, G., & Zbrodoff, J. (1999). Selection for cognition: cognitive constraints on visual spatial attention. Visual Cognition, 6 (1), 55-81.

Luh, K. E., Butter, C. M., & Buchtel, H. A. (1986). Impairments in orienting to visual stimuli in monkeys following unilateral lesions of the superior sucal polysensory cortex. Neuropsychologia, 24, 461-470.

Lumer, E., & Rees, G. (1999). Covariation of activity in visual and prefrontal cortex associated with subjective visual perception. Proceedings of the National Academy of Sciences USA, 95, 1669-1673.

Mack, A., & Rock, I. (1998). Inattentional blindness. Cambridge, MA: MIT Press.

MacLeod, C. M. (1991). Half a century of research on the Stroop effect: an integrative review. Psychology Bulletin, 109, 163-203.

Mandler, G., & Shebo, B. (1982). Subitizing: an analysis of its component processes. Journal of Experimental Psychology: General, 111, 1-22.

Mangun, G. R. (1995). Neural mechanisms of visual selective attention. Psychophysiology, 32, 4-18.

Maravita, A. (1997). Implicit processing of somatosensory stimuli disclosed by a perceptual after-effect. NeuroReport, 8 (7), 1671-1674.

Martinez, A., Anllo-Vento, L., Sereno, M. I., Frank, L. R., Buxton, R. B., Dubowitz, D. J., Wong, E. C., Hinrichs, H., Heinze, H. J., & Hillyard, S. A. (1999). Involvement of striate and extrastriate visual cortical areas in spatial attention. Nature Neuroscience, 2 (4), 364-369.

Marzi, C., Girelli, M., Miniussi, C., Smania, N., & Maravita, A. (in press). Electrophysiological correlates of conscious vision: evidence from unilateral extinction. Journal of Cognitive Neuroscience.

Marzi, C. A., Smania, N., Martini, M. C., Gambina, G., Tomelleri, G., Palamara, A., Alessandrini, F., & Prior, M. (1996). Implicit redundant-targets effect in visual extinction. Neuropsychologia, 34, 9-22.

Mattingley, J. B., Bradshaw, J. G., & Phillips, J. G. (1992). Impairments of movement initiation and execution in unilateral neglect: directional hypokinesia and bradykinesia. Brain, 115, 1849-1874.

Mattingley, J. B., Davis, G., & Driver, J. (1997). Preattentive filling-in of visual surfaces in parietal extinction. Science, 275, 671–674.

Mattingley, J. B., Driver, J., Beschin, N., & Robertson, I. H. (1997). Attentional competition between modalities: extinction between touch and vision after right hemisphere damage. Neuropsychologia, 35 (6), 867–880.

Mattingley, J. B., Husain, M., Rorden, C., Kennard, C., & Driver, J. (1997). Motor role of human inferior parietal lobe revealed in unilateral neglect patients. Nature, 392, 179–182.

McGlinchey-Berroth, R., Milberg, W. P., Verfaellie, M., Alexander, M., & Kilduff, P. T. (1993). Semantic processing in the neglected visual field: evidence from a lexical decision task. Cognitive Neuropsychology, 10, 79–108.

Meador, K. J., Loring, D. W., Bowers, D., & Heilman, K. M. (1987). Remote memory and neglect syndrome. Neurology, 37, 522–526.

Mesulam, M. M. (1981). A cortical network for directed attention and unilateral neglect. Annals of Neurology, 4, 309–325.

Mesulam, M. M. (1998). From sensation to cognition. Brain, 121, 1013–1052.

Milner, A. D. (1997). Neglect, extinction, and the cortical streams of visual processing. In H.-O. Karnath, & P. Thier (Eds.), Parietal lobe contributions to orientation in 3D space (pp. 3–22). Berlin: Springer.

Milner, A. D., & Goodale, M. A. (1995). The visual brain in action. Oxford University Press: Oxford.

Milner, A. D., Perret, D. I., Johnston, R. S., Benson, P. J., Jordan, T. R., Heeley, D. W., Bertucci, D., Mortara, F., Mutani, R., Tezazzi, E., & Davidson, D. L. W. (1991). Perception and action in visual form agnosia. Brain, 114, 405–428.

Moran, J., & Desimone, R. (1985). Selective attention gates visual processing in the extrastriate cortex. Science, 229, 782–784.

Morris, J., Friston, K. J., Buchel, C., Frith, C. D., Young, A. W., Calder, A. J., & Dolan, R. J. (1998). A neuromodulatory role for the human amygdala in processing emotional facial expressions. Brain, 121, 47–57.

Morris, J. S., Öhman, A., & Dolan, R. J. (1998b). Conscious and unconscious emotional learning in the human amygdala. Nature, 393, 467–470.

Morrow, L. A., & Ratcliff, G. C. (1987). Attentional mechanisms in clinical neglect. Journal of Clinical & Experimental Neuropsychology, 9, 74–75.

Muller, H. J., & Humphreys, G. W. (1991). Luminance-increment detection: capacity limited or not? Journal of Experimental Psychology: Human Perception and Performance, 17, 107–124.

Neisser, U., & Becklen, P. (1975). Selective looking: attending to visually superimposed events. Cognitive Psychology, 7, 480–494.

Öhman, A. (1986). Face the beast and fear the face: animal and social fears as prototypes for evolutionary analyses of emotion. Psychophysiology, 23 (2), 123–145.

Oppenheim, H. (1885). Ueber eine durch eine klinisch bisher nich verwertete Untersuchungsmethode ermittelte Form der Sensibitatsstoerung bei einsetigen Erkrankunger des Grosshirns. Neurologische Zentralblatt, 4, 529–533.

Parasuraman, R. (1998). The attentive brain. Cambridge, MA: Bradford Book/MIT Press.

Pashler, H. E. (1998). The psychology of attention. Cambridge, MA: MIT Press.

Paterson, A., & Zangwill, O. L. (1944). Disorders of visual space perception associated with lesions of the right cerebral hemisphere. Brain, 67, 331–358.

Pavlovskaya, M., Sagi, D., Soroker, N., & Ring, H. (1997). Visual extinction and cortical connectivity in human vision. Cognitive Brain Research, 6, 159–162.

Perani, D., Vallar, G., Cappa, S., Massa, C., & Fazio, F. (1987). Aphasia and neglect after subcortical stroke: a clinical cerebral perfusion correlation study. Brain, 110, 1211–1229.

Perenin, M.-T. (1997). Optic ataxia and unilateral neglect: clinical evidence for dissociable spatial functions in posterior parietal cortex. In H.-O. Karnath, & P. Thier (Eds.), Parietal lobe contributions to orientation in 3D space (pp. 289–308). Berlin: Springer.

Peterhans, E., & Von Der Heydt, R. (1991). Subjective contours: bridging the gap between psychophysics and physiology. Trends in Neurosciences, 14, 112–119.

Pizzamiglio, L., Cappa, S., Vallar, G., Zoccolotti, P., Bottini, G., Ciurli, P., Guariglia, C., & Antonucci, G. (1989). Visual neglect for far and near extrapersonal space in humans. Cortex, 25, 471–477.

Polat, U., & Sagi, C. (1994). Lateral interactions between spatial channels: suppression and facilitation revealed by lateral masking experiments. Vision Research, 33 (7), 993–999.

Pöppel, E., Held, R., & Frost, D. (1973). Residual visual function after brain wounds involving the central visual pathways in man. Nature, 243, 295–296.

Poppelreuter, W. (1917). Die psychische Schädigungen durch Kopfschuss im Krieg 1914/16. Leipzig: Leopold Voss.

Posner, M. I., Walker, J. A., Friedrich, F. J., & Rafal, R. (1984). Effects of parietal injury on covert orienting of visual attention. Journal of Neuroscience, 4, 1863–1874.

Pouget, A., & Driver, A. (in press). Relating unilateral neglect to the neural coding of space. Current Opinion in Neurobiology.

Pouget, A., Fisher, S. A., & Sejnovski, T. J. (1993). Egocentric spatial representation in early vision. Journal of Cognitive Neuroscience, 5, 150–161.

Pouget, A., & Sejnovski, T. J. (1997). Spatial transformations in the parietal cortex using basis functions. Journal of Cognitive Neuroscience, 9 (2), 222–237.

Pritchard, C. L., Milner, A. D., & Harvey, M. (1997). Visuospatial neglect: veridical coding of size for grasping but not for perception. Neurocase, 3, 437–443.

Rafal, R. D. (1994). Neglect. Current Opinion in Neurobiology, 4, 231–236.

Rafal, R. D. (1997). Balint syndrome. In T. E. Feinberg, & M. J. Farah (Eds.), Behavioral neurology and neuropsychology (pp. 337–356). New York: McGraw-Hill.

Rafal, R. D., & Posner, M. I. (1987). Deficits in human visual spatial attention following thalamic lesions. Proceedings of the National Academy of Sciences USA, 84, 7349–7353.

Raymond, J. E., Shapiro, K. L., & Arnell, K. M. (1992). Temporary suppression of visual processing in an rsvp task: an attentional blink. Journal of Experimental Psychology: Human Perception and Performance, 18 (3), 849–860.

Rees, G., Russell, C., Frith, C., & Driver, J. (1999). Inattentional blindness versus inattentional amnesia for fixated but ignored words. Science, 286 (5449), 2504–2507.

Rees, G., Wojciulik, E., Clarke, K., Husain, M., Frith, C., & Driver, J. (2000). Unconscious activation of visual cortex in the damaged right-hemisphere of a parietal patient with extinction. Brain, 123 (8), 1624–1633.

Remy, P., Zilbovicius, M., Degos, J. D., Bachoud-Levy, A. C., Rancurel, G., Cesaro, P., & Samson, Y. (1999). Somatosensory cortical activations are suppressed in patients with tactile extinction: a PET study. Neurology, 52, 571–577.

Rensink, R. A., O'Regan, J. K., & Clark, J. J. (1997). To see or not to see: the need for attention to perceive changes in visual scenes. Psychological Science, 8, 368–373.

Rizzolatti, G., & Berti, A. (1990). Neglect as a neural representation deficit. Rev Neurol (Paris), 146, 626–634.

Rizzolatti, G., & Camarda, R. (1987). Neural circuits for spatial attention and unilateral neglect. In M. Jeannerod (Ed.), Neurophysiological and neuropsychological aspects of spatial neglect (Vol. 45, pp. 289–314). , 45. Amsterdam: North-Holland.

Rizzolatti, G., Matelli, M., & Pavesi, G. (1983). Deficits in attention and movement following the removal of postarcuate (area 6) and prearcuate (area 8) cortex in macaque monkeys. Brain, 106, 655–673.

Ro, T., Rorden, C., Driver, J., & Rafal, R. (2000). Ipsilesional biases in saccades but not perception after lesions of the human inferior parietal lobule. San Francisco, CA: Cognitive Neuroscience Society. Manuscript submitted for publication.

Robertson, I. (1989). Anomalies in the laterality of omissions in unilateral left visual neglect: implications for an attentional theory of neglect. Neuropsychologia, 27, 157–165.

Robertson, L. C., Lamb, M. R., & Knight, R. T. (1988). Effects of lesions of the temporal-parietal junction on perceptual and attentional processing in humans. Journal of Neuroscience, 8, 3757–3769.

Robertson, L., Treisman, A., Friedman-Hill, S., & Grabowecky, M. (1997). The interaction of spatial and object pathways: evidence from Balint's syndrome. Journal of Cognitive Neuroscience, 9, 295–317.

Rock, I., & Guttman, D. (1981). The effect of inattention on form perception. Journal of Experimental Psychology: Human Perception and Performance, 7, 275–285.

Rodriguez, E., George, N., Lachaux, J. -P., Martinerie, J., Renault, B., & Varela, F. J. (1999). Perception's shadow: long-distance synchronization of human brain activity. Nature, 397, 430–433.

Rossetti, Y. (1998). Implicit short-lived motor representations of space in brain damaged and healthy subjects. Consciousness & Cognition, 7, 520–558.

Rubens, A. B. (1985). Caloric stimulation and unilateral visual neglect. Neurology, 35, 1019–1024.

Sagiv, N., Vuilleumier, P., & Swick, D. (2000). The neural fate of extinguished faces: electrophysiological correlates of conscious and unconscious perception in unilateral spatial neglect. Cognitive Neuroscience Society Meeting, San Francisco. Journal of Cognitive Neuroscience, 12 (Suppl.), 95.

Sahraie, A., Weiskrantz, L., Barbur, J. L., Simmons, A., Williams, S. C. R., & Brammer, M. J. (1997). Pattern of neuronal activity associated with conscious and unconscious processing of visual signals. Proceedings of the National Academy of Sciences USA, 94, 9406–9411.

Samuelsson, H., Jensen, C., Ekholm, S., Naver, H., & Blomstrand, C. (1997). Anatomical and neurological correlates of acute and chronic visuospatial neglect following right hemisphere stroke. Cortex, 33 (2), 271–285.

Scheller, H., & Seidemann, H. (1931). Zur Frage der optisch-räumlichen Agnosie (zugleich ein Beitrag zur Dyslexie). Monatsschrift für Psychiatrie und Neurologie, 81, 97–188.

Shallice, T. (1988). From neuropsychology to mental structure. Cambridge University Press: Cambridge, England.

Sharon, Z., Henik, A., & Nachum, S. (1999). Dissociation between word and color processing in patients with unilateral neglect. Journal of Cognitive Neuroscience, 11; Suppl, Abstracts of the Annual Meeting of the Society of Cognitive Neuroscience, 58.

Shefrin, S. L., Goodin, D. S., & Aminoff, M. J. (1988). Visual evoked potentials in the investigation of "blindsight". Neurology, 38, 104–109.

Shiffrin, R. M., & Gardner, G. T. (1972). Visual processing capacity and attentional control. Journal of Experimental Psychology, 93, 72–83.

Smania, N., & Aglioti, S. (1995). Sensory and spatial components of somaesthetic deficits following right brain-damage. Neurology, 45 (9), 1725–1730.

Smania, N., Martini, M., Gambina, G., Tomelleri, G., Palamara, A., Natale, E., & Marzi, C. (1998). The spatial distribution of visual attention in hemineglect and extinction patients. Brain, 121 (Pt 9), 1759–1770.

Snyder, L. H., Batista, A. P., & Andersen, R. A. (1997). Coding of intention in the parietal posterior cortex. Nature, 386, 167–170.

Snyder, L., Grieve, K., Brotchie, P., & Andersen, R. (1998). Separate body- and world-referenced representations of visual space in parietal cortex. Nature, 394 (6696), 887–891.

Spinelli, D., Burr, D. C., & Morrone, M. C. (1994). Spatial neglect is associated with increased latencies of visual evoked potentials. Visual Neuroscience, 11, 909–918.

Sugase, Y., Yamane, S., Ueno, S., & Kawano, K. (1999). Global and fine information coded by single neurons in the temporal visual cortex. Nature, 400, 869–873.

Suzuki, S., & Cavanagh, P. (1995). Facial organization blocks access to low-level features: an object inferiority effect. Journal of Experimental Psychology: Human Perception and Performance, 21, 901–913.

Tegner, R., & Levander, M. (1991). Through a looking glass: a new technique to demonstrate directional hypokinesia in unilateral neglect. Brain, 113, 1943–1951.

Tipper, S. P., & Driver, J. (1988). Negative priming between pictures and words in a selective attention task: evidence for semantic processing of ignored stimuli. Memory & Cognition, 16, 64–70.

Tootell, R. B. H., Hadjikhani, N. K., Mendola, J. D., Marrett, S., & Dale, A. M. (1998). From retinotopy to recognition: fMRI in human visual cortex. Trends in Cognitive Sciences, 2 (5), 174–183.

Treisman, A. (1998). Feature binding, attention and object perception. Philosophical Transactions of the Royal Society of London, Series B, 353 (1373), 1295–1306.

Treue, S., & Maunsell, J. H. R. (1997). Attentional modulation of visual signal processing in the parietal cortex. In H. -O. Karnath, & P. Thier (Eds.), Parietal lobe contributions to orientation in 3D space (pp. 359–369). Berlin: Springer.

Trick, L. M., & Pylshyn, Z. W. (1993). What enumeration studies can show us about spatial attention: evidence for limited capacity preattentive processing. Journal of Experimental Psychology: Human Perception and Performance, 19 (2), 331–351.

Tsal, Y., & Lavie, N. (1993). Location dominance in attending to color and shape. Journal of Experimental Psychology: Human Perception and Performance, 19, 131–139.

Ungeleider, L. G., & Mishkin, M. (1982). Two cortical visual systems. In D. J. Ingle, M. A. Goodale, & R. J. W. Mansfield (Eds.), Analysis of visual behavior. Cambridge, MA: MIT Press.

Ungerleider, L., Courtney, S., & Haxby, J. (1998). A neural system for human visual working memory. Proceedings of the National Academy of Sciences USA, 95 (3), 883–890.

Vallar, G. (1993). The anatomical basis of spatial neglect in humans. In I. H. Robertson, & J. C. Marshall (Eds.), Unilateral neglect: clinical and experimental studies (pp. 27–62). Hillsdale, NJ: Lawrence Erlbaum Associates.

Vallar, G. (1998). Spatial hemineglect in humans. Trends in Cognitive Sciences, 2 (3), 87–97.

Vallar, G., Guariglia, C., Nico, D., & Bisiach, E. (1995). Spatial hemineglect in back space. Brain, 118 (2), 467–472.

Vallar, G., & Perani, D. (1986). The anatomy of unilateral neglect after right-hemisphere stroke lesions: a clinical/CT correlation study in man. Neuropsychologia, 24, 609–622.

Vallar, G., & Perani, D. (1987). The anatomy of spatial neglect in humans. In M. Jeannerod (Ed.), Neurophysiological and neuropsychological aspects of spatial neglect (pp. 235–258). Amsterdam: North-Holland.

Vallar, G., Rusconi, M. L., Bignamini, L., Geminiani, G., & Perani, D. (1994). Anatomical correlates of visual and tactile extinction in humans: a clinical and CT scan study. Journal of Neurology, Neurosurgery, and Psychiatry, 57, 464–470.

Vallar, G., Sandroni, P., Rusconi, M. L., & Barbieri, S. (1991). Hemianopia, hemianesthesia, and hemispatial neglect: a study with evoked potentials. Neurology, 41, 1918–1922.

Viggiano, M. P., Spinelli, D., & Mecacci, L. (1995). Pattern reversal visual evoked potentials in patients with hemineglect syndrome. Brain & Cognition, 27, 17–35.

Volpe, B. T., Ledoux, J. E., & Gazzaniga, M. S. (1979). Information processing in an "extinguished" visual field. Nature, 282, 722–724.

Von Der Heydt, R., Peterhans, E., & Baumgartner, G. (1984). Illusory contours and cortical neuron responses. Science, 224, 1260–1262.

von der Malsburg, C. (1994). The correlation theory of brain function. In E. Domany, J. L. van Hemmen & K. Schulten (Eds.), Models of neural networks (Vol. 2, pp. 95–119). Berlin: Springer-Verlag.

von Helmholtz, H. (1867). Treatise of physiological optics. (3rd ed.). New York: Dover Translated in 1962 by J. Cottingham, R. Stoothoff, & D. Murdoch.

Vuilleumier, P. (2000). Faces call for attention: evidence from patients with visual extinction. Neuropsychologia, 38 (5), 693–700.

Vuilleumier, P., Hazeltine, E., Poldrack, R., Sagiv, N., Rafal, R., & Gabrieli, J. (2000). The neural fate of neglected stimuli: an event-related fMRI study of visual extinction. Cognitive Neuroscience Society Meeting, San Francisco. Journal of Cognitive Neuroscience, 12 (Suppl.), 97.

Vuilleumier, P., & Landis, T. (1998). Illusory contours and spatial neglect. NeuroReport, 9, 2481–2484.

Vuilleumier, P., & Rafal, R. (1999). Both means more than two: localizing and counting in patients with visuospatial neglect. Nature Neuroscience, 2, 783–784.

Vuilleumier, P., & Rafal, R. (2000). A systematic study of task-dependent visual extinction: between and within field deficits of attention in hemispatial neglect. Brain, 123, 1263–1279.

Vuilleumier, P., & Schwartz, S. (in press). Emotional facial expressions capture attention. Neurology.

Vuilleumier, P., & Schwartz, S. (2000). Spiders, flowers, and other visual things: capture of attention by fear relevant stimuli in patients with unilateral neglect. Manuscript submitted for publication.

Vuilleumier, P., Valenza, N., & Landis, T. (2000). Explicit and implicit perception of illusory contours in unilateral spatial neglect: behavioural and anatomical correlates of preattentive grouping mechanisms. Manuscript submitted for publication.

Vuilleumier, P., Valenza, N., Mayer, E., Réverdin, A., & Landis, T. (1998). Near and far visual space in unilateral neglect. Annals of Neurology, 43, 406–410.

Vuilleumier, P., Valenza, N., Perrig, S., Mayer, E., & Landis, T. (1999). To see better to the left when looking more to the right: effects of gaze direction and frame of spatial coordinates in unilateral neglect. Journal of the International Neuropsychology Society, 5, 75–82.

Ward, R., Goodrich, S., & Driver, J. (1994). Grouping reduces visual extinction: neuropsychological evidence for weight-linkage in visual selection. Visual Cognition, 1, 101–129.

Watson, R. T., Day, A., Valenstein, E., & Heilman, K. M. (1994). Posterior neocortical systems subserving awareness and neglect: neglect associated with superior temporal sulcus but not area lesions. Archives of Neurology, 51, 1014–1021.

Watson, R. T., & Heilman, K. M. (1979). Thalamic neglect. Neurology, 29 (5), 690–694.

Weiskrantz, L. (1986). Blindsight: a case study and implications. Oxford: Oxford University Press.

Weiskrantz, L. (1990). The Ferrier lecture 1989. Outlooks for blindsight: explicit methodologies for implicit processes. Proceedings of the Royal Society of London (Biology), 239 (1296), 247–278.

Weiskrantz, L., Warrington, E. K., Sanders, M. D., & Marshall, J. (1974). Visual capacity in the hemianopic field following a restricted occipital ablation. Brain, 97, 709–728.

Wells, A., & Matthews, G. (1994). Attention and emotion: a clinical perspective. Hove: Lawrence Erlbaum.

Whalen, P. J., Rauch, S. L., Etcoff, N. L., McInerney, S. C., Lee, M. B., & Jenike, M. A. (1998). Masked presentations of emotional facial expressions modulate amygdala activity without explicit knowledge. Journal of Neuroscience, 18, 411–418.

Wortis, S. B., Bender, M. B., & Teuber, H. L. (1948). The significance of the phenomenon of extinction. Journal of Nervous and Mental Disorders, 107, 382–387.

Zeki, S. (1993). A vision of the brain. Oxford: Blackwell.

Zingerle, H. (1913). Ueber Störungen der Wahrnehmung des eigenen Körpers bei organischen Gehirnerkrankungen. Monatschrift für Psychiatrie und Neurologie, 34, 13–36.

3

Neural events and perceptual awareness

Nancy Kanwisher*

Department of Brain and Cognitive Sciences, MIT, Cambridge, MA 02139, USA

Abstract

Neural correlates of perceptual awareness, until very recently an elusive quarry, are now almost commonplace findings. This article first describes a variety of neural correlates of perceptual awareness based on fMRI, ERPs, and single-unit recordings. It is then argued that our quest should ultimately focus not on mere correlates of awareness, but rather on the neural events that are both necessary and sufficient for perceptual awareness. Indeed, preliminary evidence suggests that although many of the neural correlates already reported may be necessary for the corresponding state of awareness, it is unlikely that they are sufficient for it. The final section considers three hypotheses concerning the possible sufficiency conditions for perceptual awareness. © 2001 Elsevier Science B.V. All rights reserved.

Keywords: Neural events; Perceptual awareness; Correlates of awareness

1. Introduction

The quest for the neural correlates of consciousness (Crick & Koch, 1995), or at least the neural correlates of perceptual awareness, has suddenly become wildly successful. A variety of striking correlations have been reported in just the last few years between specific neural signals and perceptual experiences. But the success of this enterprise leads to a much more difficult question: now that we have found a set of neural correlates of perceptual awareness, what are we to do with them? What if anything do they tell us about awareness?

It is helpful to consider what exactly it is that we want to understand about perceptual awareness in the first place. If the scientific investigation of awareness

---

* Fax: +1-617-253-9767.

E-mail address: ngk@psyche.mit.edu (N. Kanwisher).

0010-0277/01/$ - see front matter © 2001 Elsevier Science B.V. All rights reserved.
PII: S0010-0277(00)00125-6

is different from the scientific investigation of perception, then the two phenomena must not be identical. (In keeping with the possibility that they are distinct, the word 'perception' will be used throughout this article to refer to the extraction and/or representation of perceptual information from a stimulus, without any assumption that such information is necessarily experienced consciously.) So the most basic question is whether all perception is accompanied by awareness, or whether the two phenomena can be uncoupled. Extensive evidence from behavioral studies of both normal subjects (see Merikle, Smilek, & Eastwood in this volume) and neurological patients (Farah, 1994; Milner & Rugg, 1992) shows that perceptual information can indeed be represented in the mind/brain without the subject being aware of that information. This fact opens up for exploration a broad landscape of additional questions. What subset of the information that is perceived reaches awareness? More pointedly, what factors determine which information reaches awareness and which information does not? Is awareness of a perceptual representation a simple monotonic increasing function of the strength or quality (Baars, 1988; Farah, 1994) of the underlying representation (the 'activation strength hypothesis')? How is information within awareness represented and processed differently from information that is not within awareness?

In this article a number of recent studies will be reviewed that use neurophysiological techniques (fMRI, ERPs, and single-unit recording) to investigate these questions. Section 2 describes studies demonstrating neural signals that are strongly correlated with the content of the subject's awareness under conditions in which the stimulus itself does not change. These findings then lead to a consideration of whether the neural correlates of awareness are localized in a particular location (or set of locations) in the brain that play some special role in awareness. I hypothesize to the contrary that the neural correlates of awareness of a particular visual attribute are found in the very neural structure that perceptually analyzes that attribute. Section 3 describes several recent studies using fMRI and ERPs that show that many of the same regions that show strong correlations with awareness under some conditions can also be activated in the absence of the subjects' awareness of the stimulus. Results of this kind argue that activations in these regions may not be sufficient for awareness. This raises the question of what is needed beyond the mere existence of a neural representation for that representation to be experienced consciously. In Section 4 several possible answers to this question are considered. I argue – contrary to the activation strength hypothesis – that even a strong neural representation may not be sufficient for awareness unless other parts of the mind/brain have access to the information so represented (see also Baars, 1988). Behavioral evidence is presented that perceptual awareness involves not only activation of the relevant perceptual properties, but the further construction of an organized representation in which these visual properties are attributed to their sources in external objects and events (see also Kahneman & Treisman, 1984; Marcel, 1983).

I hope in this article to show that scientific evidence can bear importantly on a number of questions about the nature of perceptual awareness. However, it probably can not answer all such questions. In particular, I will not tackle the question of why perceptual awareness feels like anything at all (Chalmers, 1995; Nagel, 1974), because it is not clear that even a rich understanding of the cognitive and neural events that constitute perceptual awareness will provide any clues about how to answer it.

2. Neural correlates of perceptual awareness

When we look at an ambiguous stimulus, such as a Necker cube or Rubin's famous face/vase our perceptual experience alternates between two different states. Yet the stimulus itself does not change. What is the difference in the neural response to the same stimulus when it is seen first as one object (e.g. a face) and then a moment later as a completely different object (e.g. a vase)?

2.1. Evidence for neural correlates of awareness

2.1.1. Binocular rivalry

A particularly striking example of perceptual bistability arises in the long-known phenomenon of binocular rivalry (DuTour, 1763; von Helmholtz, 1962), in which a different image is projected to each eye. When human observers view such displays, instead of seeing a blend of the two images, their perceptual experience seems to reflect a dynamic competition between the two inputs. If vertical stripes are presented to the left eye and horizontal stripes to the right eye, the viewer is likely to see not a superimposition of the two patterns (i.e. a crosshatching plaid pattern), but an alternating sequence in which only vertical stripes will be seen for one moment, and only horizontal stripes the next. Although the precise mechanisms underlying binocular rivalry are a matter of some debate (Blake, Yu, Lokey, & Norman, 1998; Leopold & Logothetis, 1999; Wolfe, 1986), it is clear that experience alternates in a bistable fashion between being dominated by the input to one eye and being dominated by the input to the other eye. Because the retinal input remains constant throughout, binocular rivalry provides an excellent domain in which to search for the neural correlates of perceptual awareness unconfounded by variations in the stimulus hitting the retina.

In a series of classic experiments, Logothetis and colleagues recorded from single neurons in visual areas of the monkey brain as the monkey viewed rivalrous displays (Logothetis, 1998). The monkeys were trained to report by pulling on a lever which of two stimuli they saw each moment. Logothetis and colleagues used a variety of stimuli (moving gratings, faces, etc.) that were selected because they either drove a particular neuron very strongly (a 'preferred' stimulus for that neuron), or because they drove that neuron only very weakly (a 'non-preferred' stimulus). Logothetis and colleagues then asked how the neural response to each stimulus varied as a function of the monkey's reported awareness of the stimulus when it was presented in a rivalrous display. They found that while some cells in the visual pathway responded to stimuli in a fashion independent of the monkey's state of awareness, other neurons showed activity correlated with the monkey's reported percept. For example, if a moving stimulus was delivered to one eye and a stationary stimulus to the other, a motion-sensitive neuron might respond more strongly when the monkey reported seeing motion than when he did not. Further, the percentage of neurons showing correlations with awareness varied across different stages in the visual pathway, from about 20% in V1 and V2 to about 90% in inferotemporal cortex. These results suggest that neurons in later stages of the visual pathway are more closely correlated with the monkey's state of awareness than are neurons earlier in the visual pathway.

It seems reasonable to assume that when a monkey reports the presence of a particular stimulus, he is aware of the stimulus in something like the way that a human would be. Nonetheless, it would be reassuring to find similar results in the human brain. Opportunities for direct electrical recording from human brains are very limited (Allison, Puce, Spencer, & McCarthy, 1999; Fried, MacDonald, & Wilson, 1997). However, Tong, Nakayama, Vaughn, and Kanwisher (1998) used fMRI to run an experiment on humans that was modeled after the monkey experiments just described. Instead of recording the response of single neurons to preferred and non-preferred stimuli, we measured the responses from two regions of human visual cortex that have highly selective responses to specific stimulus classes. One region of extrastriate cortex called the fusiform face area (FFA) responds at least twice as strongly to faces as to other classes of non-face stimuli such as hands, objects, and houses (Allison et al., 1999; Ishai, Ungerleider, Martin, Schouten, & Haxby, 1999; Kanwisher, McDermott, & Chun, 1997; McCarthy, Puce, Gore, & Allison, 1997). Another region on the ventral surface of the brain, the parahippocampal place area (PPA), responds strongly to images of places including houses, but only weakly to non-place stimuli, and not at all to faces (Epstein, Harris, Stanley, & Kanwisher, 1999; Epstein & Kanwisher, 1998). Thus, these two cortical regions, which can be found in almost all subjects, have opposite stimulus preferences: faces are preferred and houses are non-preferred for the FFA, and the opposite pattern holds for the PPA. By displaying a face stimulus to one eye and a house stimulus to the other eye, we could therefore simultaneously monitor with fMRI the neural response to each stimulus during binocular rivalry.

In our experiment subjects viewed a single rivalrous face–house stimulus for an entire scan, while reporting with a button press each switch in the content of their awareness. As in numerous previous studies of binocular rivalry, subjects reported that every few seconds their percept flipped, in this case from the face to the house, then back to the face. We then averaged the MR signal from each subject's FFA and PPA across all the face-to-house flips, and (separately) all the house-to-face flips, time-locked to the button press. For each subject we saw a clear rise in neural activity in each of the two cortical regions when the preferred stimulus for that region (i.e. the face for the FFA, and the house for the PPA) popped into awareness. A fall in the activity in each area was found when the preferred stimulus for that area dropped out of awareness. Thus, the activity in these two cortical areas was clearly correlated with the content of the subject's awareness, even though the retinal stimulus remained unchanged throughout the experiment.

We then asked how these neural correlates of awareness in binocular rivalry compared to the neural correlates of a change in the stimulus itself. In scans carried out on the same subjects in the same session, we recreated the same sequence of perceptual states the subject had reported via button presses in a previous rivalry scan, but in this case we changed the stimulus itself (from just a face to just a house and so on). To our surprise, the data obtained from these stimulus alternation scans not only qualitatively resembled the data from the rivalry scans, but were also quantitatively indistinguishable. That is, the magnitude of the neural responses in the FFA and PPA to a rivalrous change in awareness with the stimulus held constant was as great as the corresponding non-rivalrous change when the stimulus itself changed from face to house or vice versa. Our data thus demonstrated not only a neural correlate of awareness, but a neural response that was just as strongly corre-lated with the subjects' state of awareness as it was with the stimulus. These results parallel the earlier work by Logothetis and colleagues (Logothetis, 1998), extending them to humans and further demonstrating even stronger correlations between neural activity and awareness.

But what exactly do these data tell us about the neural basis of perceptual aware-ness? The FFA and PPA were selected for this study not because of any presumed link to awareness, but instead because the strong stimulus selectivity of these regions provided the markers we needed to do the experiment at all. It would therefore be a monumental coincidence if these two areas just happened to play a special role in awareness. Further, it is unlikely that the FFA and PPA play a major role in aware-ness of stimuli that are neither faces nor places because most other stimuli that have been tested produce a similar and relatively low response in these areas (Kanwisher, Downing, Epstein, & Kourtzi, in press). Thus, the more reasonable conjecture would be that if these two areas play any particular role in perceptual awareness, that role is likely to be largely restricted to awareness of faces (for the FFA) and of places (for the PPA).

Is neural activity in other extrastriate areas also correlated with perceptual aware-ness of the stimulus attributes that are processed in that area? Indeed, evidence already exists for correlations between awareness and neural activity in at least two other extrastriate regions, which I discuss next.

2.1.2. Neural correlates of awareness of motion in MT/MST

Area MT/MST is a cortical region known to be involved in the processing of visual motion information in both monkeys and humans (Tootell, Reppas, Kwong et al., 1995). Several fMRI studies have shown strong correlations between neural activity in MT/MST and the perceptual experience of visual motion, unconfounded from stimulus motion. These studies make use of the motion aftereffect, in which adaptation to a stimulus with a constant direction of motion leads to a subsequent illusory percept of motion in the opposite direction. Tootell, Reppas, Dale et al. (1995) found that activity in MT/MST persisted for a longer period following adaptation to a motion stimulus with constant direction than following adaptation to a stimulus that changed direction frequently, consistent with perceptual reports of the subjects that a motion aftereffect was seen in the former but not the latter case.

Two subsequent studies made use of the fact that no motion percept occurs if the motion adaptation period is followed by a period in complete darkness. Instead, the aftereffect can be 'stored' for some period of time, producing a percept of motion only later when a (stationary) stimulus is presented. Culham et al. (1999) demonstrated that activity in MT/MST was low during the storage period, but increased when a stationary stimulus subsequently appeared, exactly tracking the subjects' report of their experience of visual motion. He, Cohen, and Hu (1998) used a different design that exploited the spatial specificity of the motion aftereffect. After a long adaptation period, the investigators caused the aftereffect to alternately appear and disappear by having the subjects move their eyes so as to place a stationary stimulus either inside or outside the adapted region. The signal in MT/MST closely tracked the percept of motion. By unconfounding motion aftereffect storage from the experience of the motion aftereffect, these two studies strengthen the evidence that the neural signal in MT/MST is correlated with the percept of motion.

In a single-unit study of MT in awake behaving monkeys, Bradley, Chang, and Andersen (1998) showed another situation in which the activity of neurons in MT is correlated with changes in awareness that occur in the absence of changes in the stimulus. They used displays in which two sets of interleaved dots (each in a different stereo depth plane) move in opposite directions, producing a percept of a rotating cylinder. When the same display is viewed without stereo information a rotating cylinder is still perceived, but the percept is bistable, oscillating from one state in which one direction of motion is perceived in front and the opposite direction in back, to the other state in which the assignment of motion directions to depth planes is reversed. Some cells in MT preferred motion in one direction in the front plane and the opposite direction of motion in the back plane in unambiguous stereo displays. Of these, half (34/68) responded differently when the monkey reported different percepts in the ambiguous 2D versions of the same displays. Most of these cells (27/34) showed a higher response when the neuron's preferred pattern was perceived. This finding shows that activity in some cells within area MT in the macaque is correlated with the content of awareness.

2.1.3. Perceiving masked objects and letter stimuli

Another cortical area where correlates of awareness have been demonstrated very recently is the 'lateral occipital complex' (LOC), a large region in the ventral visual pathway that responds more strongly to images of objects, whether familiar or novel, than to scrambled images in which the structure of those objects is not discernable (Kanwisher, Woods, Iacoboni, & Mazziotta, 1996; Malach et al., 1995). Does this region play a role in awareness of object identity? Grill-Spector, Kushnir, Itzchak, and Malach (2000) presented photographs of familiar objects for 40 ms (followed by a 460 ms mask), 120 ms (followed by a 380 ms mask), or 500 ms unmasked. The subjects' accuracy in identifying the objects was measured separately for each presentation duration. Grill-Spector et al. also measured the corresponding response in the LOC using fMRI. For each stimulus presentation duration the investigators compared the response to objects followed by masks with the response to control stimuli with the same timing parameters but in which a different mask was presented in the place of the object (i.e. a mask followed by a different mask). The unmasked 500 ms object exposure was used to derive the maximal fMRI response and maximal behavioral performance. Thus, both accuracy and fMRI response in the two shorter duration conditions could be plotted as a percentage of this maximal response, a clever technique enabling fMRI and behavioral functions to be directly compared. Grill-Spector et al. found strikingly similar functions relating object recognition performance to stimulus duration and relating the MR response in the LOC to stimulus duration. On the other hand, because this correlation was derived from comparisons across different stimulus durations, Grill-Spector et al. carried out a further test for a correlation between behavioral and MR response when the stimulus conditions were identical. They trained subjects to recognize briefly-presented objects, and demonstrated that the improvement in behavioral performance after training was paralleled by an increase in the MR signal in the LOC to these images after training (compared to before). Overall, across trained and untrained conditions and across exposure durations, the correlation between object recognition performance and MR signal in the LOC was very high, and indeed higher than in other regions of cortex that were sensitive to object structure.

Several other related results have also been reported recently. Bar et al. (in press) found a strong correlation between degree of success in object recognition and MR signal intensity in a region of the fusiform gyrus about 1 cm anterior to the FFA. In a similar vein, Kleinschmidt, Buchel, Huton, and Frackowiak (1998) presented a letter in a random dot pattern background and gradually ramped the clarity of the letter up and then down by varying the density of dots making up the letter. A hysteresis effect was found for both perception and MR signal intensity in the region of the LOC in which both the subject's performance and the neural responses were higher for a given intermediate level of stimulus information when the letter clarity was being ramped down compared to when it was being ramped up. That is, for these intermediate levels of stimulus clarity the probability of letter recognition and the neural activity in object-related areas were both higher if the subject had already seen the letter clearly than if they had not. Finally, Rees, Russell, Frith, and Driver (1999) displayed stimuli in which line drawing pictures of familiar objects overlapped spatially with letter strings that were either real words or non-word consonant strings. When subjects directed their attention to the letter stimuli, Rees et al. found a stronger MR response in several cortical areas to real words compared to non-words. More importantly, this differential response to words versus non-words was abolished when subjects directed their attention to the pictures, consistent with subjects' inability to report the identity of words presented in such displays. Thus, the subjective impression that words are not recognized when unattended was mirrored by the loss of the neural signature of word recognition in this condition.

All of these findings show impressive correlations between the ability to identify an object, letter, or word, and the strength of the neural signal in the relevant cortical area. However, one thing these studies do not yet clearly address is the precise aspect of the stimulus information that is correlated with awareness, which could range from detection of something (rather than nothing), to a mid-level analysis of the shape (or orthography, for the Rees et al., 1999 study) of the item, to an appreciation of the high-level meaning of the stimulus in question. Because awareness of each of these kinds of information is likely to be highly correlated in the studies described above, the observed neural correlations could reflect awareness of information at any (or all) of these levels.

2.1.4. Attention, imagery, etc.

Other phenomena that affect the contents of our perceptual awareness include attention, mental imagery, and changing states of consciousness. For each of these phenomena, neural signals have been shown to covary with perceptual awareness. As described above for the Rees et al. (1999) study, simply focusing visual attention on different aspects of an unchanging stimulus has a strong effect on the content and intensity of perceptual awareness. Closely following the effect of attention on subjective experience, numerous studies using single-unit recordings (Desimone & Duncan, 1995), ERPs (Luck & Girelli, 1998), and brain imaging (Corbetta, Miezin, Dobmeyer, Shulman, & Petersen, 1990; O'Craven, Rosen, Kwong, Treisman, & Savoy, 1997) have shown clear modulations of sensory responses by attention, even for a constant stimulus, and even in primary visual cortex (see Kanwisher & Wojciulik, 2000 for a review). A rather different manipulation of perceptual awareness occurs during mental imagery, in which no stimulus is present at all. Selective activation of MT/MST has been reported during mental imagery of motion (Goebel, Khorram-Sefat, Muckli, Hacker, & Singer, 1998), and selective activation of the FFA and PPA has been reported (O'Craven & Kanwisher, in press) for face and place imagery, respectively. In each of these cases, the activations during mental imagery are weaker than the corresponding stimulus activations.[1] Finally, a recent fMRI study has shown that the response of auditory and language cortex to speech stimuli disappears soon after sleep onset (McDermott, 1996), consistent with the subjective experience that auditory awareness largely ceases at sleep onset.

2.1.5. Microstimulation

The studies described above show that across a wide range of manipulations in which the contents of perceptual awareness vary but the stimulus does not, neural signals exist that follow closely in step with subjective experience. But are these patterns of neural activity sufficient to cause the corresponding percept? Evidence bearing on these questions is scarce, but one technique is particularly informative here. Salzman, Britten, and Newsome (1990) showed that when a monkey performs a motion direction discrimination task, its response can be biased by microstimulation of a small region within cortical area MT where cells respond preferentially to a given direction of motion. Such findings provide unusually strong evidence for the causal connection between neural activity in a given

---

[1] This result was anticipated by Hume, who commented on the relationship between percepts and ideas/ images as follows: "The difference betwixt these consists in the degrees of force and liveliness, with which they strike upon the mind... [Perceptions] enter with most force and violence... By ideas I mean the faint images of these in thinking and reasoning."

extrastriate area and the resulting perceptual experience. Although we cannot exactly ask the monkey what it experiences when electrically stimulated, its performance in a perceptual discrimination task seems a reasonable proxy for such a report. Further, a consistent picture is provided by the few studies of cortical microstimulation in humans where we can ask the subject what they experience. Puce, Allison, and McCarthy (1999) measured responses from electrodes implanted subdurally (for the purposes of presurgical mapping) in ventral extrastriate areas in epileptic patients. Face-selective responses were sometimes found in fusiform electrode sites, and in several cases subsequent stimulation through the same site produced a percept of a face or a face part (see also Penfield & Perot, 1963; Vignal, Chauvel, & Halgren, 2000). These results suggest that neural activity in particular locations within extrastriate cortex can cause specific subjective perceptual experiences, strengthening the evidence for a causal connection between neural activity and awareness (but see Section 3 below).

2.2. Brain loci of the neural correlates of perceptual awareness

The multiplicity of cortical loci where correlations with awareness have been found provides some evidence against one of the oldest ideas about consciousness, that the contents of awareness are represented in a single unitary system (Schacter, McAndrews, & Moscovitch, 1988), variously described as a stage (Taine, quoted in Ellenberger, 1970), workspace (Baars, 1988), 'Cartesian theater' (criticized by Dennett, 1991), or cave wall (Plato). Instead, the data described above seem more consistent with a view in which the contents of current awareness can be represented in many different neural structures. However, one could still argue that the neural correlates described above are not in fact the actual representations that constitute the conscious percept, but merely information that is likely to make it onto the (as-yet-undiscovered) screen of awareness, so the possibility of such a unitary awareness system is not definitively ruled out by these data.

In contrast to the idea of a unitary and content-general Cartesian theater of awareness, the data summarized above fit more naturally with the following simple hypothesis: the neural correlates of awareness of a given perceptual attribute are found in the very neural structure that perceptually analyzes that attribute. This hypothesis accommodates the fact that perceptual awareness is not simply a matter of knowing whether a stimulus was or was not presented, but is a much more multifaceted phenomenon. There are as many ways to be aware of a stimulus as there are kinds of information to register about that stimulus. Thus, perceptual awareness might involve any aspect of the stimulus, from its simple presence (as opposed to absence), to the presence or nature of one or more of its perceptual attributes, to the category of object present in the image, to a fine-grained recognition of the particular exemplar of that category, to the 'gist' of a complex scene. Decentralizing the neural correlates of awareness to the processors where this information is extracted provides a straightforward account of why some aspects of a stimulus can be consciously perceived while other attributes are not.

Are there any constraints at all on the neuroanatomical loci that can participate in awareness? Surely events can occur on the retina, for example, without our becoming aware of them. Which neural systems are likely to hold the contents of awareness and which are not? One possibility is that neural representations become more correlated with awareness at later stages of perceptual processing, as Logothetis (1998) found for the macaque in the case of binocular rivalry. However, a recent fMRI study of binocular rivalry in humans found substantial correlations between visual awareness and neural representations in human V1 (Polonsky, Blank, Braun, & Heeger, 2000), so it is not clear that the neural correlates of human visual awareness will behave in the same way, increasing as one ascends the visual system. Another common speculation is that the contents of awareness are represented only in the cortex, not in subcortical structures. A third possibility is that the ventral (occipitotemporal) visual pathway holds the contents of awareness whereas the dorsal (occipitoparietal) pathway is more involved in a variety of unconscious computations underlying visuomotor coordination (Milner & Goodale, 1995). Below I propose the related but somewhat different hypothesis that the neural correlates of the contents of visual awareness are represented in the ventral pathway, whereas the neural correlates of more general-purpose content-independent processes associated with awareness (attention, binding, etc.) are found primarily in the dorsal pathway. However, this hypothesis is highly speculative and indeed is already known to have at least one exception: the correlations between awareness of visual motion and activity in area MT (a dorsal pathway area) already described in Section 2.1.2.

3. Mere correlation, or causal connection?

As Section 2 of this article makes clear, neural correlates of perceptual experience, an exotic and elusive quarry just a few years ago, have suddenly become almost commonplace findings. Specific neural populations have been found in which neural activity is strongly correlated with subjective experiences of faces, places, objects, and motion. But what exactly do these findings tell us about perceptual awareness? Any deep scientific understanding requires getting beyond mere correlations, to a deeper understanding of the causal structure of the underlying phenomena. In the case of the relationship between neural activity and perceptual awareness, what we really want to know is not what patterns of neural activity are correlated with perceptual awareness, but rather what patterns of neural activity are necessary and/or sufficient for perceptual awareness.

The causal relationship between a particular pattern of neural activity (e.g. in the FFA) and the corresponding state of perceptual awareness (e.g. of a face) can be evaluated by considering the situations represented by each of the four cells in Fig. 1. The findings described in Section 2 of this paper include many cases in which the relevant pattern of neural activity and corresponding state of awareness are either both present (the lower right cell) or both absent (the upper left cell). These examples are consistent with a strong causal connection between the relevant neural activity and the relevant state of awareness. The findings from microstimu-

	Perceptual Awareness -	Perceptual Awareness +
Neural Activity -	√	Potential Evidence Against **Necessity**
Neural Activity +	Potential Evidence Against **Sufficiency**	√

Fig. 1. The possible combinations of a particular pattern of neural activity or its absence, and a corresponding state of perceptual awareness or its absence, and the evidence each case can provide about the causal relationship of the pattern of neural activity to the perceptual state.

lation described in Section 2.1.5 are particularly strong evidence for a causal connection. However, it is the other two cells in this figure that are potentially more informative, as it is only these cases that can in principle provide evidence against a strong causal connection (or identity) between a particular pattern of neural activity and a particular state of perceptual awareness. Specifically, a situation in which a given pattern of neural activity is absent but the relevant state of perceptual awareness is present (i.e. the upper right cell in Fig. 1) would imply that the pattern of neural activity in question is not necessary for that state of awareness. And conversely a situation in which a given pattern of neural activity is present but the relevant state of perceptual awareness is absent (i.e. the lower left cell in Fig. 1) would imply that the pattern of neural activity in question is not sufficient for that state of awareness. Evidence for either of these two situations would therefore refute a strong claim that the neural activity in question is causally related to or identical to the perceptual state in question.

Consider first the question of necessity. If a condition were ever found in which a subject is aware of a face yet a strong response were not found in their FFA, that would show that activity in the FFA is not necessary for awareness of faces (modulo the sensitivity of the measurement technique). I know of little convincing evidence of this kind. However, proving the null hypothesis is notoriously problematic, all the more so when the physiological signal being monitored is very noisy (as in the case of fMRI). This is therefore a particularly difficult condition to test. One possible approach is to turn to neuropsychology, to ask whether awareness of a given perceptual attribute is ever found in the complete absence of the relevant cortical structure. For example, if one lacked an MT, would awareness of visual motion be obliterated? Evidence from one patient suggests that it would be (Zihl, von Cramon, & Mai, 1983). Are the FFA and PPA necessary for awareness of faces and places? Some evidence suggests that patients who lack an FFA can perceive faces as faces, but are very impaired at identifying the individual whose face they are looking at (de Gelder & Kanwisher, 1999). One might therefore argue that the FFA is necessary for awareness of facial identity, though perhaps not for the awareness of faces at all. This kind of investigation has the potential to be very useful in determining the particular cortical regions that are necessary for a subject to experience a particular state of perceptual awareness.

Evidence against the sufficiency of a particular pattern of neural activity for a particular perceptual state would come from a situation in which that neural activity occurs (e.g. activation of the FFA for faces) yet the expected perceptual state (e.g. awareness of faces) does not. Insofar as the relevant neural signal was sufficiently selective, such a case would also provide a demonstration of perception without awareness, a question of interest in its own right. More importantly, any such demonstration that perceptual representations can be decoupled from awareness would set the stage for a research program directed toward determining what else is necessary for perceptual awareness beyond the mere existence of a perceptual representation. We therefore consider the evidence for perceptual representations without awareness in some detail in the next section.

3.1. Evidence for activation of perception representations in the absence of awareness

A long tradition of research in experimental psychology has provided considerable evidence that stimuli can affect behavioral responses even when they are not consciously perceived (Sidis, 1898, reviewed in Merikle, Smilek, & Eastwood in this volume). Another fascinating line of work has demonstrated many cases in which perceptual awareness can be decoupled from perceptual processing in neuropsychological patients (Driver & Vuilleumier, this volume; Milner & Rugg, 1992). Here we will focus on the evidence from on-line measures of neural activity.

If a stimulus is so faint as to be completely invisible, can it nonetheless lead to activation of visual cortex? In a recent study by Tootell, Hadjikhani, and Somers (1999), subjects were scanned with fMRI while they viewed stimuli in which periods of dynamic visual gratings alternated with periods in which a uniform gray field of equal mean luminance was displayed. The grating stimuli were displayed with several different levels of contrast in different scans. Two important results were obtained from this study. First, for all visual areas scanned (including V1, V2, V3, VP, V3A, V4v, and MT/MST), activity increased monotonically with stimulus contrast. Second, for the lowest contrast tested, although at the end of the scan the subjects reported having seen nothing but a uniform field for the entire scan,[2] all retinotopic visual areas tested showed significantly stronger activation to the invisible gratings than to the uniform gray field. These results demonstrate a clear neural response to a stimulus that apparently did not enter awareness. Thus, several different stages of the visual hierarchy, from V1 to V4v, can be activated by stimuli that the subject is not aware of.

Can such visual activations outside of awareness be found for even higher levels of processing? Whalen et al. (1998) asked whether the response of the amygdala to angry compared to happy faces would be found even when subjects were unaware of any emotional expression in the faces at all. They scanned subjects who viewed a series of brief (33 ms) presentations of emotionally expressive faces, each of which was immediately followed by a 167 ms presentation of a neutral face. The neutral faces masked the preceding emotionally expressive faces such that emotional expressions were rarely perceived and at the end of the experiment eight of the ten subjects reported never having seen an emotionally expressive face at all in the entire experiment. Nonetheless, a significant activation of the amygdala was found for the epochs in which masked angry faces were presented, compared to masked happy faces. Thus, even such subtle and high-level visual information as the emotional expression of a face can be represented neurally without the subject reporting any awareness of that information.

Are visual responses to emotional stimuli 'special', or can neural representations of other kinds of high-level information be found for stimuli that are not consciously perceived? In a recent study, Rees et al. (2000) (see also Driver & Vuilleumier, this volume) scanned a patient with right parietal damage and extinction, which is the failure to perceive stimuli presented in the contralesional or 'bad' field when a competing stimulus is presented simultaneously in the ipsilesional or 'good' field. Of interest was the finding that an independently-defined face-selective region in the fusiform gyrus of this patient showed activations for faces that were at least as strong when the faces were not consciously perceived (i.e. in the bilateral presentation extinction condition) as when they were (in the unilateral presentation condition). These activations, though statistically weak, appear to be stimulus-selective as they were not found for house stimuli in the same region.

Is there any evidence that even semantic information can be neurally represented without awareness? Luck, Vogel, and Shapiro (1996) also measured the neural response to an unseen stimulus, but they used a perceptual phenomenon called the 'attentional blink' (Raymond, Shapiro, & Arnell, 1992). In the attentional blink,

---

[2] Note that this study (as well as the study by Whalen et al. (1998) described next) used a 'subjective' measure of lack of awareness, rather than an 'objective' measure. That is, the subjects simply said they did not see anything, but were not required to do a forced-choice discrimination task. One might argue that the finding would be stronger if an objective (forced-choice) measure were used, because we don't know what criterion the subject used to decide they 'did not see' something. However, the subjective measure is closer to the intuitive notion of lack of awareness. The choice of definitions could lead to different results if subjects show above-chance performance on a forced-choice task while reporting zero awareness of the stimulus. To insist that we take their performance rather than their subjective report as the index of awareness assumes that any correct performance is consciously mediated, an assumption that is unlikely to be valid. Given this problem, it is most useful to have both measures of awareness.

subjects view two successive masked target stimuli, separated by a temporal interval of variable duration. If subjects must carry out a task on the first target, then their ability to detect the second target falls dramatically for inter-stimulus intervals of 100–400 ms. However, the second target is accurately detected at shorter or longer intervals, or if subjects need not carry out any task on the first target. Thus, the requirement to analyze the first target leads to a drop in awareness of the second target. Luck et al. presented a rapid sequence of symbol strings to subjects, and asked them to report two targets from each sequence. One string in each sequence was a row of identical digits, and subjects had to report whether the digits were odd or even. The second target was a word, and subjects had to report whether the word was related or unrelated to a context word presented just before the sequence began. In different conditions, zero, two, or six items appeared between the digit string and the word. Consistent with prior findings on the attentional blink, performance identifying the digit string was high for all conditions, but accuracy on the word task was much lower for the intermediate lag than for the zero-lag or six-lag conditions. While subjects performed this task their scalp ERPs were measured. The amplitude of the N400, which is found for words that do not fit semantically in the context compared to words that do, was just as great for unrelated word targets for the intermediate lag (when conscious report of those words was very low) as for the other two lags (when overt report of the words was high). Thus, even though subjects failed to recognize the word targets on most of the intermediate-lag trials, their N400 response to the meaning of the word was undiminished compared to the other lags. This study therefore demonstrates that a neural correlate of accessing word meaning is unaffected by whether the word reaches awareness or does not.

One common intuition is that we can only respond overtly to a stimulus if that stimulus has been consciously perceived. But does the preparation of a motor response to a stimulus in fact require awareness of the stimulus responded to? A study by Dehaene et al. (1998) suggests that it may not. These researchers presented number words to subjects very briefly, followed by a mask, under conditions in which subjects were at chance in discriminating their presence versus absence, and at discriminating the words from nonsense strings. Immediately after the masked number word prime, a suprathreshold target digit was displayed, and subjects had to report whether it was greater or less than five. Behavioral responses to the target digit were slower when the correct response to the suprathreshold target was inconsistent with the response that would have been required for the preceding unseen prime word, compared to when the prime was consistent with the target. This result demonstrates that even though subjects had no task to carry out on the prime word, and even though they were not aware of it, they nonetheless processed it to a high level. To obtain this effect the prime word must have been processed at least to the level of representing the meaning (i.e. the magnitude) of the named number. But was this information processed to an even higher level? To answer this question Dehaene et al. measured both scalp ERPs and fMRI responses from motor cortex from the subjects while they carried out the task. As expected, both measures demonstrated clear responses in motor cortex in the hemisphere contralateral to the hand the subject used to respond on that trial. However, more important was the finding that motor cortex activation was also seen contralateral to the hand that would have produced the correct response to the unseen prime word. Of course, the motor responses to the unseen prime word were smaller in magnitude than those to the suprathreshold target digit. Nonetheless, the fact that a specific effect was found to the prime word in motor cortex demonstrates that processing of an unseen target can proceed all the way to the preparation of a motor response. Similar findings using ERPs were also reported by Eimer and Schlaghecken (1998).

In sum, specific neural responses to unseen stimuli have been observed at a variety of levels from early visual processing in retinotopic cortex to the extraction of structural or emotional information from faces, to accessing the meanings of words and even the preparation of a motor response.

4. What is the difference between a conscious perceptual representation and an unconscious one?

The data summarized in Section 3.1 show that perceptual representations can be activated in the absence of awareness of those representations. Evidently, activation of these representations is not sufficient for awareness. What else is needed? Put another way, what is the difference between a perceptual representation that is consciously experienced and one that is not?

4.1. The activation strength hypothesis

Probably the simplest hypothesis that has been offered in answer to this question, sometimes called the 'quality of representation' (Farah, 1994) or 'activation' (Baars, 1988; Palmer, 1999) hypothesis, is this: the more active a given neural representation, the stronger its representation in awareness. This hypothesis is congenial to the fact that perceptual awareness is not generally an all-or-none affair, but a graded phenomenon which admits many shades of gray. This insight forms the basis of signal detection theory (Green & Swets, 1966), which posits a continuum in the possible amounts of perceptual information that may be extracted from a stimulus. This continuum is then divided into two response categories by a somewhat arbitrary threshold that the subject must impose when forced to make a binary decision about the stimulus. Where exactly the subject places the threshold on that continuum is determined by numerous factors such as the instruction and payoff matrix given to the subject by the experimenter. Thus, the fact that we can obligate subjects to produce a binary response should not fool us into thinking that their internal state itself is binary or that there is anything important or fixed about the particular threshold the subject uses. Indeed, anyone who has been a subject in a psychophysical experiment will be familiar with the uncomfortable feeling of having to force an unclear and inchoate perceptual experience into one of a small number of discrete response categories. The activation hypothesis holds that this continuum of degrees of perceptual awareness is encoded neurally as the strength (or 'quality') of the underlying neural representation.

What do the data reviewed in Section 3.1 have to say concerning the activation strength hypothesis? It would be unsurprising if the function relating activation strength to awareness were not linear, but instead contained a threshold. At the lower end of the curve the strength of the neural representation might be greater than zero but the level of awareness might not. Thus, some cases of neural representations outside of awareness might be explained in terms of subthreshold activations that are strong enough to be detected by ERP or fMRI sensors, but not strong enough to result in awareness. However, this account does not work well for cases in which the strength of the neural signal is very similar when a given stimulus is consciously perceived and when it is not. Both the Luck et al. (1996) study and the Rees et al. (2000) study appear to be cases in which the neural signal is about as strong in the conscious as the non-conscious conditions; Driver and Vuilleumier (this volume) discuss parallel cases in which behavioral markers are just as strong for the conscious as the non-conscious cases. Thus, preliminary indications are that although the activation strength hypothesis may be partly true, it is incomplete. This in turn implies that awareness is dependent on something other than the strength of a given perceptual representation. What other factors might be important? Next I consider two more possibilities.

4.2. The informational access hypothesis

One line of thinking suggests that awareness of perceptual information requires not only a strong representation of the contents of awareness, but access to that information by other parts of the mind/brain (Baars, 1988). The idea that access to the relevant representations is a substantial constraint on perceptual awareness makes sense given the known functional architecture of the mind and brain. First, human neuroanatomy is characterized by wide variation in the degree of connectivity between different brain areas. While some neural path exists that connects any two parts of the brain, these paths will vary greatly in strength and directness. Second, at a functional/cognitive level, one of the key principles underlying the concept of the modularity of the human mind is 'informational encapsulation', the idea that there are substantial constraints on the access to intermediate representations computed within each functional module (Fodor, 1983). Thus, it would not be surprising if perceptual representations existed that failed to enter awareness, not because they were not 'strong' enough, but instead because other parts of the mind could not gain access to them.

Third, to appreciate the idea that the mere existence of a representation is not likely to be sufficient for awareness, consider the following thought experiment. Suppose cortical area MT was surgically removed from a human brain. Suppose further that its interconnections remained intact, and it was kept functional in a dish for some period of time despite the lack of input and output connections to the rest of the brain. Now suppose that a region within MT was microstimulated as described in Section 2.1.5, a manipulation that apparently produces a conscious percept when carried out in an intact animal or person. Surely awareness of motion would not occur for an isolated MT in a dish. (Who would see the motion?!) Thus, common sense suggests that perceptual awareness probably requires not only a strong neural representation in a particular cortical area, but access to that representation by at least some other parts of the system.

But who or what must have access to a given representation for it to reach awareness? According to a common intuition about perceptual awareness (e.g. Baars, 1988), if you perceive something, then you can report on it through any output system (speech, button presses, drawing, American Sign Language, etc.). Perceptual information that could be reported through only one output system and not through another just would not fit with most people's concept of a true conscious percept.[3] Thus, conscious access to perceptual information seems to imply access to most or all output systems. On the other hand, few would argue that perceptual awareness would be affected if temporary paralysis made overt report impossible, so access by output systems per se does not seem necessary for perceptual awareness. Instead, it seems that a core part of the idea of awareness is that not only effector systems, but indeed most parts of the mind have access to the information in question. Thus, in agreement with Baars (1988), it seems reasonable to hypothesize that awareness of a particular element of perceptual information must entail not just a strong enough neural representation of that information, but also access to that information by most of the rest of the mind/brain.

How might a given piece of perceptual information become accessible to most of the mind/brain? A unitary 'conscious awareness system' (Schacter et al., 1988) or 'global workspace' (Baars, 1988) that enabled information to be widely 'broadcast' could in principle accomplish this goal. The idea that the contents of awareness must be represented in a distinct neural locus has been criticized on the grounds that it implies a homunculus that must then look at the information so represented (Dennett, 1991). However, there is no need to posit such a mystical entity. The brain could in principle have a discrete locus where the contents of awareness are represented for the same reason that airlines have hub cities: to facilitate the most efficient transfer of information (or people) between any two points in a large space of possible destinations and points of departure. However, because the format of representations is very different in the different modules of the mind/brain, an important problem for any such unitary system would be how it could have the representational power to accommodate inputs from all of the different modules that would send information to it. In any event, I know of no evidence for a discrete neural structure that has the properties that would be required of a unitary system for awareness. Further, as summarized in Section 2, currently available data suggest that the contents of awareness are represented not in a single neural locus but in multiple different cortical areas.

One might think of the global workspace not as a neuroanatomically localized

---

[3] Of course if one output system is damaged (e.g. in the case of aphasia) such that perceptual information could not be communicated through that output system, but could still be communicated through all other remaining intact output systems (drawing, button presses, etc.), this would be consistent with the intuition about awareness put forth here.

system, but instead as some kind of functional state of the brain. For example, on the Desimone and Duncan (1995) 'interactive competition' model, competitive interactions across cortical areas result in domination of perceptual representations by properties of a single object. This competition can be biased by either bottom-up factors (e.g. stimulus salience) or top-down factors (e.g. endogenous attention). In either case the net result is that the various properties of an object, represented in distinct cortical regions, enhance each other and suppress the representation of competing objects. On this view, attention and awareness are global properties of the entire perceptual system that span multiple cortical areas. Although Desimone and Duncan (1995) offer no mechanism to explain how different cortical areas come to represent attributes of the same object, there is some evidence that this in fact occurs (O'Craven, Downing, & Kanwisher, 1999). To the extent that mechanisms exist that can cause disparate cortical areas to represent perceptual information about the same object, one might expect that the same mechanisms could also cause that information to be widely available to much of the rest of the system. Synchronous firing of neurons across cortical areas could play some role in this process (Singer, 2000), though a full account would have to explain how the synchrony is established and how it is interpreted by subsequent stages of processing.

4.2.1. Changing access to perceptual information

Limits on conscious access to perceptual information may not be immutable. In the most extreme case, brain damage may disrupt neural pathways such that perceptual information represented in one neural structure no longer is accessed by other parts of the system. However, dissociations of perception and awareness are abundant in the neuropsychology literature (Farah, 1994; Milner & Rugg, 1992), and disconnections may not be sufficient to explain all of them. Another possibility is brain damage may disrupt a global state of integration of the entire brain, thereby affecting access even to information represented in sites remote from the damage.

Conscious access to perceptual information may also change over time even in undamaged brains. First, cognitive systems may become more integrated over the normal course of development in infancy and childhood, such that each modular component of the mind gains greater access to information represented in other modules. Indeed, Spelke, Vishton, and Von Hofsten (1995) have argued that "In adults, distinct systems of knowledge may work together, such that a wide range of distinct beliefs can jointly influence our thinking and deliberate action... In infancy, distinct knowledge systems may be less interconnected."

A second situation in which information access and awareness may change in normal brains occurs in perceptual learning. It is a common experience of subjects in psychophysical tasks that as one improves at the task, one becomes aware of stimuli that one did not at first perceive. Perhaps what changes with practice is not simply the quality or strength of the underlying perceptual information, but the ability to 'find' or 'read out' that information by other parts of the system. Several studies have shown that the inclusion of a few suprathreshold trials in a perceptual learning procedure can lead to a sudden drop in the threshold for a perceptual task

(Rubin, Nakayama, & Shapley, 1997), as if the stronger signals available in these suprathreshold trials 'show' the subject where the relevant representations can be found in the nervous system. To the extent that this (highly speculative) 'access' interpretation of perceptual learning is true, then two strong predictions follow. First, in cases where perceptual learning occurs, it should be possible to demonstrate that the relevant perceptual information was actually present (though not consciously perceived) before the learning occurred. Second, in cases where perception without awareness has been demonstrated, it should be possible with sufficient training to become aware of the originally unconscious information. While these strong predictions may ultimately be shown to be wrong, the point being raised here is that perceptual learning may be mediated in part by changes in access to the relevant information, and not only by changes in the quality of the information accessed.

4.3. The type-token hypothesis

The many striking recent findings that relate neural activity to awareness are certainly thought provoking. However, there is no a priori reason to suppose that the neural correlates of awareness are any more likely to result in a deep understanding of perceptual awareness than are the cognitivecorrelates of awareness. Indeed, the behavioral literature has already independently led to the idea discussed above that a strong representation of a given perceptual attribute is not sufficient for awareness of that attribute, but that other processes must be involved.

In earlier papers (Kanwisher, 1987, 1991) I suggested that awareness of a particular perceptual attribute requires not only activation of a representation of that attribute, but also individuation of that perceptual information as a distinct event. Perceptual experience is made up not of free-floating perceptual features (e.g. redness, motion to the left), but instead of discrete objects that appear in particular spatial locations and at specific times (Kahneman & Treisman, 1984; Kanwisher, 1991; Treisman & Gelade, 1980; Treisman & Schmidt, 1982). Thus, activated perceptual attributes must become associated with representations of specific objects and/or events in order to be experienced as fully fledged conscious percepts. In the terminology of Marcel (1983), conscious perception requires the attribution of perceptual information to a spatiotemporal 'source'.

The gist of this idea is best explained by describing a typical subjective experience that occurs in experiments from this research tradition. You are seated in front of a computer monitor, and asked to view a very rapidly-presented sequence of words flashing on the screen. You are then asked to report the identities of the words just presented. But all you saw was a bunch of letters and patterns flash by so quickly that you have no idea what words were presented. If pressed to guess, you are left in an uncomfortable situation. Of course you can think up words to guess at random (and come to think of it the word 'tiger' would be as good a guess as any). But the exercise seems absurd and indeed intrusive. Given that you did not see any words, why should you tell the experimenter that the word 'tiger' just popped into your mind? 'Tiger' is simply a random thought, not a percept. And what right does this experimenter have to the contents of your thoughts? But then, obligated to guess, you just say 'tiger' rather than bothering to make up anything else. Then to your amazement the experimenter tells you that that's right, and 'tiger' was indeed one of the words in the sequence you just viewed.

What's going on here? According to the token individuation hypothesis (Kanwisher, 1987), when perception is pushed beyond its processing capacity by very rapid presentation of stimuli, perceptual attributes ('types') can be activated without necessarily becoming linked to an episodic representation of a distinct perceptual object or event (a 'token'). Because the activated type (e.g. the word 'tiger') does not get attributed to a specific external source (e.g. the flash of light at position x,y on the screen at time t), it feels subjectively more like a thought than a percept. This decoupling of type activation from token individuation occurs in numerous demonstrations of masked priming (Marcel, 1983), and is particularly strong in perceptual phenomena such as repetition blindness (Chun & Cavanagh, 1997; Kanwisher, 1987) and the attentional blink (Raymond et al., 1992). The experiment by Luck et al. (1996) described in Section 3.1 above provides evidence that the meaning of a 'blinked' word is activated even when the subject is unaware of the word. Indeed, Luck et al.'s evidence suggests that activation of the meaning of the word is no weaker when it is blinked than when it is not, consistent with our hypothesis that awareness is not merely a function of the strength of activation of the relevant information. The account proposed here is that the further necessary prerequisite for awareness that fails to occur in the attentional blink (and repetition blindness, masked priming, and presumably other cases of perception without awareness) is the binding of activated perceptual attributes with a representation that specifies the time and place that the word appeared (i.e. a 'token').[4]

What exactly is this process of binding activated types to individuated token? Some evidence (Kanwisher, 1991) suggests that it is the same process that is necessary for conjoining visual features (Treisman & Gelade, 1980). Visual attention is necessary for this binding to occur (Treisman & Gelade, 1980), and hence also for visual awareness. Thus, token individuation and visual attention are likely to be closely linked (if not identical) concepts, and they are likely to involve similar or identical neural substrates. Indeed, extensive evidence suggests that damage to similar structures in the parietal lobe leads to disorders of attention and awareness, explicit feature binding (Friedman-Hill, Robertson, & Treisman, 1995; Wojciulik & Kanwisher, 1998, 1999), and the linking of activated types to individuated perceptual tokens (Baylis, Driver, & Rafal, 1993).

Thus, neural activity in specific regions within the ventral pathway is apparently correlated with the content of perceptual awareness, whereas neural activity in the dorsal pathway may be correlated instead with the occurrence of perceptual awareness in a completely content-independent fashion. Interestingly, Driver and Vuilleumier (this volume) arrive at a very similar conclusion based on largely

---

[4] See Mel and Fiser (2000) for suggestions on how object recognition may be possible without bottom-up feature binding, as implied by the type-token hypothesis.

independent evidence from that considered in this article. Further consistent with this suggestion, recent studies have provided evidence for content-independent activations of parietal structures during both the engagement of visual attention (Wojciulik & Kanwisher, 1999) and during changes in perceptual awareness (Lumer, Friston, & Rees, 1998). Although extensive evidence is not yet available, I will hazard a conjecture that (i) the same cognitive and neural mechanisms are involved in explicit feature binding, perceptual awareness, visual attention, and token individuation, and (ii) each of these processes will require interactions with the ventral pathway, where the relevant perceptual contents are represented. It may take a relatively long time in perceptual terms (between 100 and 200 ms) for these interactions to get established in a stable fashion for each percept. When this process is prevented or incomplete the subject may experience either a complete lack of awareness of the stimulus, or fleeting awareness followed by rapid forgetting (Potter, 1993).

5. Conclusions.

FMRI and ERPs have enabled us to peer into the human brain and observe the neural signatures of the contents of awareness, the shadows on the cave wall of the mind. Although the evidence described above sheds little light on the really difficult question of why awareness feels like anything, it does provide preliminary answers to a number of more scientifically tractable questions. Neural correlates of the contents of perceptual awareness can be found in many different cortical areas, from V1 to MT and the face area. I hypothesize that the contents of awareness are not represented in a single unitary consciousness system, but rather that each conscious perceptual content is represented in the same set of neurons that analyze that perceptual information in the first place. Further, there is now fairly compelling evidence from several different techniques showing that perception without awareness is possible. Thus, a strong neural representation in a given cortical area is not sufficient for awareness of the information so represented, raising the question of which perceptual information will reach awareness. I speculate that in order for a focal neural representation to reach awareness it may have to be accessible to other parts of the brain. Finally, I suggest that a conscious percept is not simply a disorganized soup of activated visual attributes, but rather a spatiotemporally structured representation in which visual attributes are associated with particular objects and events. The construction of a fully conscious percept may involve interactions between domain-specific systems for representing the contents of awareness (primarily in the ventral visual pathway) and domain-general systems (primarily in the dorsal pathway) for organizing those contents into structured percepts.

Acknowledgements

I thank the following people for very useful discussions and comments on the manuscript: Moshe Bar, Ned Block, Francis Crick, Dan Dennett, Russell Epstein,

Kalanit Grill-Spector, Christof Koch, Ken Nakayama, Molly Potter, John Rubin, Miles Shuman, and Frank Tong. This work was supported by a Human Frontiers grant and NIH grant 59150 to N.K.

References

Allison, T., Puce, A., Spencer, D. D., & McCarthy, G. (1999). Electrophysiological studies of human face perception. I. Potentials generated in occipitotemporal cortex by face and non-face stimuli. Cerebral Cortex, 5, 415–430.

Baars, B. (1988). A cognitive theory of consciousness. Cambridge, MA: Cambridge University Press.

Bar, M., Tootell, R. B. H., Schacter, D.L., Greve, D. N., Fischl, B., Mendola, J. D., Rosen, B.R., & Dale, A. M. (in press). Cortical mechanisms specific to explicit visual object recognition. Neuron.

Baylis, G., Driver, J., & Rafal, R. D. (1993). Visual extinction and stimulus repetition. Journal of Cognitive Neuroscience, 5, 453–466.

Blake, R., Yu, K., Lokey, M., & Norman, H. (1998). Binocular rivalry and motion perception. Journal of Cognitive Neuroscience, 10, 46–60.

Bradley, D. C., Chang, G. C., & Andersen, R. A. (1998). Encoding of three-dimensional structure-from-motion by primate area MT neurons. Nature, 392, 714–717.

Chalmers, D. (1995). The conscious mind: in search of a fundamental theory. Oxford: Oxford University Press.

Chun, M. M., & Cavanagh, P. (1997). Seeing two as one: linking apparent motion and repetition blindness. Psychological Science, 8, 74–79.

Corbetta, M., Miezin, F. M., Dobmeyer, S., Shulman, G. L., & Petersen, S. E. (1990). Attentional modulation of neural processing of shape, color, and velocity in humans. Science, 248 (4962), 1556–1559.

Crick, F., & Koch, C. (1995). Are we aware of neural activity in primary visual cortex? Nature, 375, 121–123.

Culham, J. C., Dukelow, S. P., Vilis, T., Hassard, F. A., Gati, J. S., Menon, R. S., & Goodale, M. A. (1999). Recovery of fMRI activation in motion area MT following storage of the motion aftereffect. Journal of Neurophysiology, 81, 388–393.

de Gelder, B., & Kanwisher, N. (1999). Absence of a fusiform face area in a prosopagnosic patient. NeuroImage, 9, S604.

Dehaene, S., Naccache, L., Le Clec, H. G., Koechlin, E., Mueller, M., Dehaene-Lambertz, G., van de Moortele, P. F., & Le Bihan, D. (1998). Imaging unconscious semantic priming. Nature, 395, 597–600.

Desimone, R., & Duncan, J. (1995). Neural mechanisms of selective visual attention. Annual Review of Neuroscience, 18, 193–222.

Dennett, D.C. (1991). Consciousness explained. Boston: Little, Brown and Company.

DuTour, E. -F. (1763). Discussion d'une question d'optique. Memoire de mathematique et de physique presentes par divers savants (Vol. 4, pp. 499–511). Paris: Academie des Sciences.

Eimer, M., & Schlaghecken, F. (1998). Effects of masked stimuli on motor activation: behavioral and electrophysiological evidence. Journal of Experimental Psychology: Human Perception and Performance, 24, 1737–1747.

Ellenberger, H.F. (1970). The discovery of the unconscious: the history and evolution or dynamic psychiatry. New York: Basic Books.

Epstein, R., Harris, A., Stanley, D., & Kanwisher, N. (1999). The parahippocampal place area: recognition, navigation, or encoding? Neuron, 23, 115–125.

Epstein, R., & Kanwisher, N. (1998). A cortical representation of the local visual environment. Nature, 392, 598–601.

Farah, M. J. (1994). Visual perception and visual awareness after brain damage: a tutorial overview. In C. Umilta. & M. Moscovitch, (Eds.) Attention and performance, XV. Cambridge, MA: MIT Press.

Fodor, J. (1983). The modularity of mind. Cambridge, MA: MIT Press.

Fried, I., MacDonald, K., & Wilson, C. (1997). Single neuron activity in human hippocampus and amygdala during recognition of faces and objects. Neuron, 18, 753–765.

Friedman-Hill, S. R., Robertson, L. C., & Treisman, A. (1995). Parietal contributions to visual feature binding: evidence from a patient with bilateral lesions. Science, 269, 853–855.

Goebel, R., Khorram-Sefat, D., Muckli, L., Hacker, H., & Singer, W. (1998). The constructive nature of vision: direct evidence from functional magnetic resonance imaging studies of apparent motion and motion imagery. European Journal of Neuroscience, 10 (5), 1563–1573.

Green, D. M., & Swets, J. (1966). Signal detection theory and psychophysics. New York: Wiley.

Grill-Spector, K., Kushnir, T., Itzchak, Y., & Malach, R. (2000). The dynamics of object-selective activation correlate with recognition performance in humans. Nature Neuroscience, 3, 837–843.

He, S., Cohen, E. R., & Hu, X. (1998). Close correlation between activity in brain area MT/V5 and the perception of a visual motion aftereffect. Current Biology, 5, 1215–1218.

Ishai, A., Ungerleider, L. G., Martin, A., Schouten, J. L., & Haxby, J. V. (1999). Distributed representation of objects in the human ventral visual pathway. Proceedings of the National Academy of Sciences USA, 96, 9379–9384.

Kahneman, D., & Treisman, A. (1984). Changing views of attention and automaticity. In R. Parasuraman, & D. R. Davies (Eds.), Varieties of attention (pp. 29–61). New York: Academic Press.

Kanwisher, N. (1987). Repetition blindness: type recognition without token individuation. Cognition, 27, 117–143.

Kanwisher, N. (1991). Repetition blindness and illusory conjunctions: errors in binding visual types with visual tokens. Journal of Experimental Psychology: Human Perception and Performance, 17, 404–421.

Kanwisher, N., Downing, P., Epstein, R., & Kourtzi, Z. (in press). Functional neuroimaging of human visual recognition. In Kingstone, A., & Cabeza, R. (Eds.), The handbook on functional neuroimaging. Cambridge, MA: MIT Press.

Kanwisher, N., McDermott, J., & Chun, M.M. (1997). The fusiform face area: a module in human extrastriate cortex specialized for face perception. Journal of Neuroscience, 17, 4302–4311.

Kanwisher, N., & Wojciulik, E. (2000). Visual attention: insights from brain imaging. Nature Neuroscience Reviews. Manuscript submitted for publication.

Kanwisher, N., Woods, R., Iacoboni, M., & Mazziotta, J. (1996). A locus in human extrastriate cortex for visual shape analysis. Journal of Cognitive Neuroscience, 91, 133–142.

Kleinschmidt, A., Buchel, C., Huton, C., & Frackowiak, R. S. J. (1998). Hysteresis effects in figure-ground segmentation. NeuroImage, 7, S356.

Leopold, D. A., & Logothetis, N. K. (1999). Multistable phenomena: changing views in perception. Trends in Cognitive Sciences, 3, 254–264.

Logothetis, N. K. (1998). Single units and conscious vision. Proceedings of the Royal Society of London, Series B, 353, 1801–1818.

Luck, S. J., & Girelli, M. (1998). Electrophysiological approaches to the study of selective attention in the human brain. In R. Parasuraman (Ed.), The attentive brain (pp. 71–94). Cambridge, MA: MIT Press.

Luck, S. J., Vogel, E.K. & Shapiro K.L. (1996). Word meanings can be accessed but not reported during the attentional blink. Nature, 383, 616–618.

Lumer, E. D., Friston, K. J., & Rees, G. (1998). Neural correlates of perceptual rivalry in the human brain. Science, 280, 1930–1934.

Malach, R., Reppas, J. B., Benson, R. B., Kwong, K. K., Jiang, H., Kennedy, W. A., Ledden, P. J., Brady, T. J., Rosen, B. R., & Tootell, R. B. H. (1995). Object-related activity revealed by functional magnetic resonance imaging in human occipital cortex. Proceedings of the National Academy of Sciences USA, 92, 8135–8138.

Marcel, A. J. (1983). Conscious and unconscious perception: an approach to the relations between phenomenal experience and perceptual processes. Cognitive Psychology, 15, 238–300.

McCarthy, G., Puce, A., Gore, J., & Allison, T. (1997). Face-specific processing in the human fusiform gyrus. Journal of Cognitive Neuroscience, 9, 605–610.

McDermott, J. (1996, April). Sleep induced changes in auditory processing: an fMRI study. Poster presented at the 3rd annual meeting of the Cognitive Neuroscience Society, San Francisco, CA.

Mel, B. W., & Fiser, J. (2000). Minimizing binding errors using learned conjunctive features. Neural Computation, 12, 731–762.

Milner, A. D., & Goodale, M. A. (1995). The visual brain in action. Oxford: Oxford University Press.

Milner, A. D., & Rugg, M. D. (1992). The neuropsychology of consciousness. London: Academic Press.

Nagel, T. (1974). What is it like to be a bat? Mortal questions (pp. 165–180). Cambridge, MA: Cambridge University Press.

O'Craven, K., & Kanwisher, N. (in press). Mental imagery of faces and places activates corresponding stimulus-specific brain regions. Journal of Cognitive Neuroscience.

O'Craven, K. M., Rosen, B. R., Kwong, K. K., Treisman, A., & Savoy, R. L. (1997). Voluntary attention modulates fMRI activity in human MT-MST. Neuron, 18, 591–598.

O'Craven, K., Downing, P., & Kanwisher, N. (1999). fMRI Evidence for objects as the units of attentional selection. Nature, 401, 584–587.

Palmer, S. (1999). Vision science. Cambridge, MA: MIT Press.

Penfield, W., & Perot, P. (1963). The brain's record of auditory and visual experience. Brain, 86, 595–696.

Polonsky, A., Blank, R., Braun, J., & Heeger, D. (2000). Neuronal activity in human primary visual cortex correlates with perception during binocular rivalry. Manuscript submitted for publication.

Potter, M. C. (1993). Very short-term conceptual memory. Memory & Cognition, 21, 156–161.

Puce, A., Allison, T., & McCarthy, G. (1999). Electrophysiological studies of human face perception. III. Effects of top-down processing on face-specific potentials. Cerebral Cortex, 9, 445–458.

Raymond, J. E., Shapiro, K. L., & Arnell, K. M. (1992). Temporary suppression of visual processing in an RSVP task: an attentional blink? Journal of Experimental Psychology: Human Perception and Performance, 18, 849–860.

Rees, G., Russell, C., Frith, C. D., & Driver, J. (1999). Inattentional blindness versus inattentional amnesia for fixated but ignored words. Science, 286, 2504–2507.

Rees, G., Wojciulik, E., Clarke, K., Husain, M., Frith, C., & Driver, J. (2000). Unconscious activation of visual cortex in the damaged right hemisphere of a parietal patient with extinction. Brain, 123, 1624–1633.

Rubin, N., Nakayama, K., & Shapley, R. (1997). Abrupt learning and retinal size specificity in illusory-contour perception. Current Biology, 7, 461–467.

Salzman, C.D., Britten, K.H., & Newsome, W.T. (1990). Cortical microstimulation influences perceptual judgements of motion direction. Nature, 346, 174–177.

Schacter, D. L., McAndrews, M. P., & Moscovitch, M. (1988). Access to consciousness: dissociations between implicit and explicit knowledge in neuropsychological syndromes. In L. Weiskrantz (Ed.), Thought without language. Oxford: Oxford University Press.

Singer, W. (2000). Response synchronization: a universal coding strategy for the definition of relations. In M. Gazzaniga, The new cognitive neurosciences. Cambridge, MA: MIT Press.

Spelke, E., Vishton, P., & Von Hofsten, C. (1995). Object perception, object-directed action, and physical knowledge in infancy. In M. Gazzaniga (Ed.), The cognitive neurosciences (pp. 165–179). Cambridge, MA: MIT Press.

Tong, F., Nakayama, K., Vaughan, J. T., & Kanwisher, N. (1998). Binocular rivalry and visual awareness in human extrastriate cortex. Neuron, 21, 753–759.

Tootell, R. B. H., Hadjikhani, N., & Somers, D. C. (1999). fMRI reveals subthreshold activation in human visual cortex: implications for consciousness. Talk presented at the 29th annual meeting of the Society for Neuroscience, Miami Beach, FL.

Tootell, R. B., Reppas, J. B., Dale, A. M., Look, R. B., Sereno, M. I., Malach, R., Brady, T. J., & Rosen, B. R. (1995). Visual motion aftereffect in human cortical area MT revealed by functional magnetic resonance imaging. Nature, 375, 139–141.

Tootell, R. B. H., Reppas, J. B., Kwong, K. K., Malach, R., Brady, T., Rosen, B., & Belliveau, J. (1995). Functional analysis of human MT/V5 and related visual cortical areas using magnetic resonance imaging. Journal of Neuroscience, 15 (4), 3215–3230.

Treisman, A. M., & Gelade, G. (1980). A feature-integration theory of attention. Cognitive Psychology, 12, 97–136.

Treisman, A., & Schmidt, H. (1982). Illusory conjunctions in the perception of objects. Cognitive Psychology, 14, 107–141.

Whalen, P.J., Rauch, S.L., Etcoff, N.L., McInerney, S.C., Lee, M.B., & Jenike, M.A. (1998). Masked presentations of emotional facial expressions modulate amygdala activity without explicit knowledge. Journal of Neuroscience, 18, 411–418.

Vignal, J. P., Chauvel, P., & Halgren, E. (2000). Localized face-processing by the human prefrontal cortex: 1. Stimulation-evoked hallucinations of faces. In N. Kanwisher, & M. Moscovitch (Eds.), The cognitive neuroscience of face processing (pp. 281–292). East Sussex: Psychology Press.

von Helmholtz, H. (1962). Helmholtz's treatise on physiological optics (J. P. C. Southall, Trans.). New York: Dover. (Original work published 1866)

Wojciulik, E., & Kanwisher, N. (1999). The generality of parietal involvement visual attention. Neuron, 4, 747–764.

Wojciulik, E., Kanwisher, N., & Driver, J. (1998). Covert visual attention modulates face-specific activity in the human fusiform gyrus: fMRI study. Journal of Neurophysiology, 79, 1574–1578.

Wolfe, J. M. (1986). Stereopsis and binocular rivalry. Psychology Review, 93, 269–282.

Zihl, J., von Cramon, D., & Mai, N. (1983). Selective disturbance of movement vision after bilateral brain damage. Brain, 106, 313–340.

4

Perception without awareness: perspectives from cognitive psychology

Philip M. Merikle[*], Daniel Smilek, John D. Eastwood

Department of Psychology, University of Waterloo, Waterloo, Ontario, N2L 3G1, Canada

Abstract

Four basic approaches that have been used to demonstrate perception without awareness are described. Each approach reflects one of two types of experimental logic and one of two possible methods for controlling awareness. The experimental logic has been either to demonstrate a dissociation between a measure of perception with awareness and a measure that is sensitive to perception without awareness or to demonstrate a qualitative difference between the consequences of perception with and without awareness. Awareness has been controlled either by manipulating the stimulus conditions or by instructing observers on how to distribute their attention. The experimental findings based on all four approaches lead to the same conclusion; namely, stimuli are perceived even when observers are unaware of the stimuli. This conclusion is supported by results of studies in which awareness has been assessed with either objective measures of forced-choice discriminations or measures based on verbalizations of subjective conscious experiences. Given this solid empirical support for the concept of perception without awareness, a direction for future research studies is to assess the functions of information perceived without awareness in determining what is perceived with awareness. The available evidence suggests that information perceived without awareness both biases what stimuli are perceived with awareness and influences how stimuli perceived with awareness are consciously experienced. © 2001 Elsevier Science B.V. All rights reserved.

Keywords: Perception; Awareness; Perspectives; Cognitive psychology

1. Introduction

Questions regarding whether stimulus information is perceived even when there is no awareness of perceiving have been the focus of considerable research and discus-

* Corresponding author. Tel.: +1-519-888-4567, ext. 2629; fax: +1-519-746-8631.
E-mail address: pmerikle@uwaterloo.ca (P.M. Merikle).

sion for many years. One reason for this continual interest in perception without awareness is that the very idea that perception occurs when there is no awareness of perceiving is inconsistent with the conventional belief that the perception of stimulus information capable of influencing feelings, thoughts or actions is always accompanied by an awareness of perceiving. Given this belief, any evidence that perception is not necessarily accompanied by an awareness of perceiving attracts attention because it challenges the idea that perception implies consciousness.

In the first part of this paper, we describe a conceptual framework for classifying studies of visual perception which, contrary to the conventional belief that perception implies consciousness, show that stimulus information can be perceived even when there is no awareness of perceiving. Although many different methods have been used to investigate perception without awareness, the vast majority of studies represent one of the four basic experimental approaches illustrated in Fig. 1. What the figure shows is that the studies can be classified in terms of (a) the experimental logic used to demonstrate perception without awareness and (b) the method used to control or vary awareness. By far the most frequently followed experimental logic has been to demonstrate a dissociation between two different measures of perception. One measure is assumed to assess perception with awareness, whereas the second measure is assumed to be sensitive to perception without awareness. An alternative but less frequently used experimental logic has been to contrast perception with and without awareness. The goal of these studies has been to establish qualitative differences in the consequences of perceiving with and without awareness. In studies based on either experimental logic, awareness of the critical stimuli has been controlled in one of two ways. In some studies, awareness has been controlled by manipulating the stimulus conditions, whereas in other studies, awareness has been controlled by instructing observers on how to distribute their attention. In general, the results of studies in which any of the four approaches have been

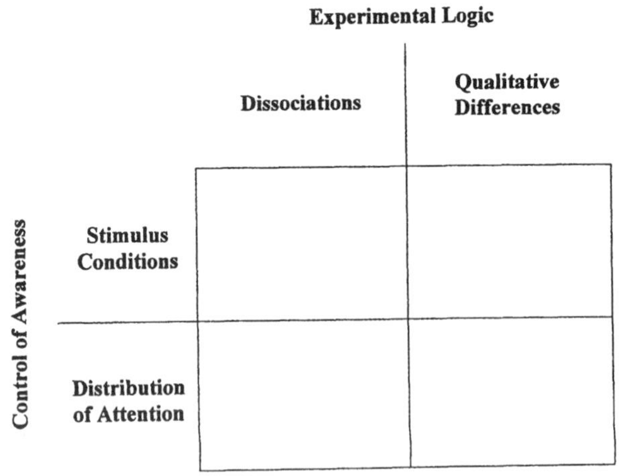

Fig. 1. Classification of studies investigating perception without awareness.

adopted show that observers can perceive critical stimuli even when they are unaware of the stimuli. Taken together, the results of these studies provide considerable evidence that perception without awareness is a valid or useful concept in the sense that it leads to verifiable predictions regarding how people perceive the world.

In the second part of the paper, we consider how information perceived without awareness influences conscious experience. The goal of the vast majority of studies to date has been simply to show that information is perceived without awareness. However, a potentially more interesting and important issue concerns how information perceived without awareness, or in other words unconsciously perceived information, influences conscious experience. We describe a number of studies which assess the influence of stimuli perceived without awareness on the conscious experiences associated with perceiving other visual stimuli. The results of these studies show not only that visual stimuli are perceived when there is no awareness of perceiving but that visual stimuli perceived without awareness can both bias which stimuli are perceived with awareness and influence how stimuli are consciously experienced.

2. Dissociations between measures

In the majority of studies investigating perception without awareness, the basic experimental logic has involved demonstrating a dissociation between two measures of perception. One measure is assumed to assess the stimulus information that is perceived with awareness, or in other words, conscious perception, whereas the second measure is assumed to assess the stimulus information that is perceived without awareness. The logic of using dissociations to demonstrate perception without awareness requires a demonstration of perception even under conditions where the measure of conscious perception indicates that there is no awareness of the critical stimuli.

A classic study by Sidis (1898) provides a good example of how dissociations between measures can be used to demonstrate perception without awareness. In this study, Sidis (1898) showed observers cards, each containing a single printed letter or digit. The distance between the observers and the cards was such that the observers complained that all that they could see on each card was a dim, blurred spot or nothing at all. Sidis assumed that the observers' reports of their subjective experiences when viewing the cards were good measures of conscious perception. Thus, when the observers reported either that they did not 'see' what was on the cards or that they saw nothing but dim blurred spots, Sidis assumed that the observers were unaware of perceiving either letters or digits. However, when Sidis used a second measure, forced-choice guessing, to assess whether the observers may in fact have perceived the critical stimuli that they claimed not to 'see', he found that the observers were able to guess both the category of the stimulus (i.e. letter versus digit) and the identity of the stimulus at a considerably better than chance level of performance. Thus, Sidis demonstrated a dissociation between two measures of perception. The assumed measure of conscious perception, verbal reports of conscious perceptual experiences, indicated that the observers did not 'see' the critical stimuli, whereas his alternative measure of perception, forced-choice guessing, indicated that the observers did in fact perceive the critical stimuli. On the basis of this dissociation between the two measures of perception, Sidis concluded that he had found evidence for perception without awareness.

An important implied assumption whenever a dissociation between measures is interpreted as evidence for perception without awareness is that the measure of conscious perception provides an exhaustive measure of all relevant conscious experiences (Reingold & Merikle, 1990). For example, the study reported by Sidis only provides evidence for perception without awareness if it is assumed that the observers' verbal reports of their conscious perceptual experiences provided an accurate indication of whether the observers were aware of perceiving any aspects of the stimuli that could have possibly influenced their guesses regarding the category and identity of the stimulus items. If the observers' verbal reports of their conscious experiences were not an exhaustive measure of all relevant conscious perceptual experiences, then the dissociation between the observers' verbal reports and their guesses may simply indicate that the two measures of perception were sensitive to different aspects of consciously perceived information.

There has been considerable discussion in recent years regarding whether subjective or objective measures provide the more accurate method for assessing whether stimuli are perceived with or without awareness (for summaries of these discussions see Merikle & Reingold, 1998; Reingold & Merikle, 1990). With subjective measures, awareness is assessed on the basis of the observers' self-reports of their conscious experiences, whereas with objective measures, awareness is assessed on the basis of the observers' forced-choice decisions regarding different stimulus states. When subjective measures are used, as in the study reported by Sidis (1898), if observers report that they 'see' the critical stimuli, it is assumed that the stimuli were perceived with awareness, and if observers report that they do not see the stimuli, it is assumed that the observers were unaware of the critical stimuli. In contrast, when objective measures are used, it is assumed that any ability to discriminate between alternative stimulus states at a better than chance level of performance indicates that the stimuli were perceived with awareness, and that an inability to discriminate between alternative stimulus states indicates that the observers were unaware of any differences between the stimuli.

The primary question addressed in studies based on either subjective or objective measures of awareness is whether observers perceive stimuli even when the measure of awareness indicates that the observers are unaware of the stimuli. In the studies in which awareness has been controlled by varying the stimulus conditions, awareness has been assessed using both subjective and objective measures, whereas in the studies in which awareness has been controlled by instructing the observers on how to distribute their attention, awareness has been assessed primarily by subjective measures. The results of all the studies lead to the same conclusion. Namely, the results are unequivocal in showing that stimulus information is perceived when either subjective or objective measures indicate that the observers were unaware of the critical stimuli. Thus, despite what appear to be considerably different methods for assessing awareness, the results of studies based on either subjective or objective measures of awareness lead to the same conclusion. We suggest that in many contexts subjective measures of awareness based on self-reports and objective measures of awareness based on perceptual discriminations assess the same under-lying conscious experience of perceiving.

2.1. Awareness controlled by varying stimulus conditions

The studies most often associated with the concept of perception without aware-ness are those studies in which the stimulus conditions have been systematically degraded until the perceived quality of the stimulus information is so poor that observers are unaware of the critical stimuli. In these studies, awareness thresholds, or in other words the minimum stimulus conditions needed to experience awareness of the critical stimuli, are first established. The critical stimuli are then presented under stimulus conditions that are even poorer than the stimulus conditions asso-ciated with the awareness thresholds to assess whether stimuli presented below the awareness threshold are perceived. Awareness thresholds in these studies have been based on both subjective and objective measures of awareness, and in the following sections we describe examples of studies which have used each type of measure.

2.1.1. Subjective measures of awareness

Some of the best examples of studies based on subjective measures of awareness come from studies of perception in the absence of awareness conducted during the late 1800s and early 1900s (for reviews and summaries see Adams, 1957; Miller, 1942). The study conducted by Sidis (1898) provides a good example of this general approach. Another good example is a study reported by Williams (1938). In this study, a circle, a triangle, or a square was projected on a screen at an intensity that was near each participant's threshold for awareness. The participants knew that just one of three possible figures would be presented on each trial and they were instructed to name "the first figure that enters your mind" (p. 191). In addition, they were instructed to indicate whether (a) they saw the figure clearly, (b) they saw something but were doubtful of their choice, or (c) they saw nothing at all and their choice was a pure guess. The results of the study showed that the participants' accuracy in naming the figures was considerably better than the chance level of performance even when they indicated they had seen nothing at all. On the basis of these results, Williams concluded "that subliminal stimuli are effective in evoking a correct response" (p. 195).

Over the years there have been many studies of perception without awareness in which subjective measures have been used to assess awareness of stimuli presented under degraded stimulus conditions. In early studies, it was established that rela-tively simple stimuli such as horizontal, vertical, and diagonal lines (e.g. Baker, 1937; Dunlap, 1900), circles, triangles, and squares (e.g. Miller, 1942; Williams, 1938), and letters and digits (e.g. Sidis, 1898; Stroh, Shaw, & Washburn, 1908) are perceived even when there is no awareness of perceiving. In more recent studies, it has been shown that the lexical status of letter strings (e.g. Forster & Davis, 1984;

Forster & Veres, 1998),[1] the meanings of words (e.g. Cheesman & Merikle, 1986; Merikle, Joordens, & Stolz, 1995), and the emotions expressed in faces (e.g. Esteves, Dimberg, & Öhman, 1994; Esteves & Öhman, 1993) are also perceived under conditions that do not lead to the conscious experience of perceiving. In addition, when pictures of faces expressing emotion are presented under conditions that make it impossible for observers to identify the emotional expression, functional magnetic resonance imaging (fMRI) has revealed that fearful faces lead to greater neural activity in the amygdala than happy faces (Whalen et al., 1998), and positron emission tomography (PET) has revealed that angry faces perceived without awareness lead to activation in the right amygdala but not the left amygdala (Morris, Öhman, & Dolan, 1998). Taken together, the results of both the older studies and the more recent studies provide considerable evidence that visual stimuli are perceived even when they are presented under conditions that the observers' conscious experiences lead them to report that they are unaware of the stimuli.

2.1.2. Objective measures of awareness

A widely held view is that objective measures of perceptual discriminations provide a more accurate method for determining whether or not perception is accompanied by an awareness of perceiving than is provided by subjective measures of conscious experiences. When awareness is assessed by subjective measures, there is always the concern that the observers' reports or descriptions of their conscious experiences are influenced by many factors other than their awareness of the critical stimuli (cf. Eriksen, 1960). For example, statements indicating an absence of an awareness of perceiving may reflect preconceived ideas regarding the value of particular conscious experiences for making decisions rather than a true absence of relevant conscious experiences (cf. Merikle, 1984). Given this concern regarding subjective measures of awareness, it has been suggested that awareness should always be assessed using objective measures of perceptual discriminations (e.g. Eriksen, 1960; Holender, 1986). According to this suggestion, successful discriminations between alternative stimulus states, such as the presence or absence of a stimulus, indicate awareness, whereas failures to discriminate between alternative stimulus states indicate an absence of awareness. Therefore, to demonstrate perception without awareness using objective measures, it is necessary to show that critical stimuli are perceived even when the stimulus conditions are such that the observers are unable to discriminate between alternative stimulus states.

Marcel (1974, 1983) was the first investigator to report the results of experiments showing that degraded visual stimuli are perceived even when they are presented below an objectively defined threshold for awareness. In his best known experi-

---

[1] Forster and his colleagues did not directly assess the participants' awareness of the critical stimuli. Rather, based on the results of pilot studies, they selected an exposure duration that did not lead to any significant subjective awareness. It was assumed that the exposure duration selected on the basis of the pilot studies prevented subjective awareness of the critical stimuli in the experiments proper. Thus, the results of the experiments reported by Forster and his colleagues are not based on direct demonstrations of dissociations between measures of awareness and other measures of perception.

ments, Marcel showed that semantic priming was produced by words that were presented under stimulus conditions that made it impossible for the observers to discriminate when a word was present from when a word was absent. These experiments were based on the finding that a target word (e.g. doctor) is responded to faster when it is preceded or 'primed' by a semantically related word (e.g. nurse) than when it is preceded or primed by a semantically unrelated word (e.g. butter) (e.g. Meyer & Schvaneveldt, 1976). The variation that Marcel introduced was that the perceived quality of the primes was degraded to such an extent (a visual mask, presented immediately following each prime) that the observers found it impossible to discriminate between the presence or absence of the primes. However, even though the primes were presented below this objectively defined threshold for awareness, Marcel found that semantic priming still occurred.

Many other investigators have now used Marcel's basic methodology. Not only have there been additional studies demonstrating that words presented below objectively defined thresholds prime subsequent decisions regarding consciously perceived words (e.g. Balota, 1983; Dagenbach, Carr, & Wihelmsen, 1989; Fowler, Wolford, Slade, & Tassinary, 1981; Greenwald, Draine, & Abrams, 1996; Kemp-Wheeler & Hill, 1988), but there are also studies showing that pictures presented below objectively defined thresholds prime subsequent decisions regarding words (McCauley, Parmelee, Sperber, & Carr, 1980) or pictures (Bar & Biederman, 1998). Furthermore, in a recent study in which event-related potentials (ERPs) and fMRI were used to assess neural activity, it was found that semantic analysis of unconsciously perceived primes can involve not only brain areas associated with sensory processing but also brain areas associated with motor programming of responses to the primes (Dehaene et al., 1998). The combined results from these studies based on objectively defined thresholds provide compelling evidence that visual stimuli are perceived, semantically analyzed, and responded to even when they are presented under stimulus conditions that make it difficult if not impossible for observers to discriminate between alternative stimulus states.

2.2. Awareness controlled by the distribution of attention

As an alternative to controlling awareness by varying the stimulus conditions, another method for controlling awareness is to show observers displays containing stimuli at a number of spatial locations and instruct the observers to focus their attention at just one location. Under these conditions, awareness is assessed by subjective measures; the observers are usually aware of the stimuli at the attended location, in the sense that they can correctly report these stimuli, but they are generally unaware of the stimuli at the other locations, in the sense that they report that they do not 'see' these stimuli. Thus, by presenting displays with stimuli at multiple locations and instructing observers on how to distribute their attention, it is possible to vary the observers' awareness of critical stimuli so that they are aware of the stimuli at the focus of attention and unaware of the stimuli at spatial locations outside the focus of attention.

In many respects, studies of the perception of unattended stimuli provide a better experimental analogue of how stimuli are perceived without awareness in natural environments than is provided by studies in which awareness is controlled by varying the stimulus conditions. In studies in which the stimulus conditions are systematically degraded to reduce awareness, the stimulus conditions are so poor that even when observers focus their attention at the spatial location of the critical stimuli, it is not possible for them to become aware of the stimuli. Only in the rarest of circumstances are people ever confronted with such a situation in their natural, everyday environments. However, it is very common for people to be in situations where there are many unattended stimuli outside their immediate focus of attention which are not consciously experienced. In these situations, the unattended stimuli could be consciously experienced if the person's focus of attention changed so that it was directed toward the relevant spatial locations. For this reason, the experimental conditions in studies in which unattended stimuli are presented at spatial locations removed from the current focus of attention more closely resemble the conditions under which visual stimuli are perceived in everyday situations than the experimental conditions in studies in which degraded stimuli are presented within the focus of attention.

The studies by Mack and Rock (1998) of inattentional blindness provide good examples of experiments in which awareness has been controlled by instructing observers on how to focus their attention, and dissociations between the observers' reports of their conscious experiences and behavioral measures of perception are used to demonstrate that unattended stimuli are perceived without awareness. In one series of studies, Mack and Rock assessed the priming produced by unattended words that observers claimed not to see. The general methodology is illustrated in Fig. 2, which shows examples of the types of displays used across the first three trials of these studies. On trials 1 and 2, the observers initially viewed a fixation display for 1500 ms. The fixation display was followed by a 200 ms presentation of a display with a large cross in one quadrant, which in turn was followed by a 500 ms presenta-

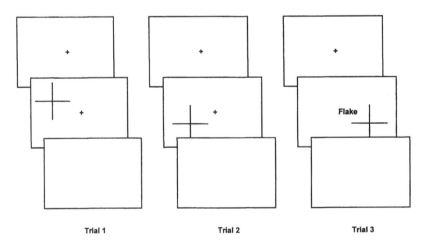

Fig. 2. Examples of the types of visual displays used by Mack and Rock (1998) to study priming.

tion of a blank display. Each cross was constructed so that either the vertical arm was longer than the horizontal arm or vice versa, and on each trial, the observers were required to report whether the horizontal or vertical arm of the cross was longer. Trial 3 was the critical trial in these experiments. On this trial, the sequence of events was the same as had occurred on trials 1 and 2, except that the display with the cross in one quadrant also contained a word located at the center of the display. Following presentation of this display, the observers first reported whether the horizontal or vertical arm of the cross was longer, and they were then asked whether they saw anything on the screen other than the cross. The surprising finding is that approximately 60% of the participants in these studies were 'blind' to the presentation of the word. When asked whether they had seen anything other than the cross, they indicated that they had noticed nothing other than the cross and that the sequence of events seemed similar to the sequence of events on the two preceding trials. Thus, based on these reports of their conscious experiences, it appears that many of the observers were unaware of the word presented at the center of the display.

To assess whether these unattended and unnoticed words were perceived despite the observers' claims that they did not 'see' these words, Mack and Rock (1998) measured whether the words primed performance on subsequent tests of forced-choice recognition and stem completion. For forced-choice recognition, the observers were presented with an array of five words and asked to select the word that had been presented. It was found that approximately 47% of the observers who were 'blind' to the presence of the word actually perceived sufficient information to chose the correct word. For stem completion, Mack and Rock presented the first three letters of the word that the observers claimed not to have seen (e.g. flake) and asked the observers to complete the word stem (e.g. fla) with the first two English words that came to mind. The results indicated that 36% of the 'blind' observers used the presented word (e.g. flake) as one of their two completions, which was considerably higher than the baseline level of performance (i.e. 4%) exhibited by control subjects. These findings clearly show that despite the observers' claims that they were unaware of the unattended words, sufficient information was perceived regarding the words to influence their performance on subsequent tests of forced-choice recognition and stem completion.

The studies conducted by Mack and Rock (1998) provide some of the most compelling evidence to date that unattended words can be perceived without awareness. Although there is a long history of studies investigating the perception of unattended visual stimuli (see Johnson & Dark, 1986 for a review), in the vast majority of these studies no attempt was made to assess the participants' awareness of the unattended stimuli. Thus, it was not possible in these studies to demonstrate a dissociation between a measure of awareness and a measure of performance. In contrast, because Mack and Rock assessed both the perceptual experiences associated with perceiving the unattended words and the priming produced by the unattended words, it was possible for them to demonstrate that the unattended words primed performance on subsequent tasks even when the observers' reports of their perceptual experiences suggested that the unattended words were not perceived. The dissociations found by Mack and Rock are very similar to the dissociations found in studies in which awareness thresholds have been based on subjective measures and awareness has been controlled by varying the stimulus conditions. As such, the findings reported by Mack and Rock provide additional evidence that visual stimuli are perceived even when the observers' perceptual experiences lead them to report that they did not 'see' the stimuli.

2.3. Subjective versus objective measures of awareness

Studies based on subjective and objective measures of awareness assess awareness in what appear to be very different ways. The most striking difference between the two types of studies are the different assumptions regarding performance on forced-choice tasks. In studies based on subjective measures of awareness, correct forced-choice performance is assumed to reflect the perception of stimulus information in the absence of any awareness of perceiving. In contrast, in studies based on objective measures of awareness, correct forced-choice performance is often assumed to reflect the presence of an awareness of perceiving (e.g. Holender, 1986). Despite these very different assumptions regarding correct forced-choice performance, the results from studies based on subjective and objective measures of awareness lead to similar conclusions. These findings raise the issue of how it is possible to reach such similar conclusions when awareness is assessed in such different ways.

The reason that studies based on subjective and objective measures of awareness lead to similar conclusions may be simply that objective measures provide a more conservative estimate than subjective measures of the minimum stimulus conditions needed to perceive a stimulus with awareness.[2] In studies based on objective measures of awareness, it is assumed that a failure to discriminate between alternative stimuli indicates that the observers are unaware of the characteristics that distinguish the stimuli. This is a relatively non-controversial assumption. However, it does not imply, as is often assumed (e.g. Assad, 1999; Holender, 1986), that success in discriminating between alternative stimuli necessarily indicates awareness of the perceptual characteristics that distinguish the stimuli. In other words, the assumption that a failure to discriminate between alternative stimuli indicates an absence of awareness is not necessarily inconsistent with the possibility that correct forced-choice discriminations may also occur even when perception is not accompanied by an awareness of perceiving. In fact, the only direct evidence regarding whether or not correct forced-choice performance occurs when there is no awareness of perceiving comes from studies in which awareness has been assessed using subjective measures. The results of these studies clearly show that correct forced-choice performance can occur even when there is no awareness of perceiving. Viewed in this way, it is not inconsistent to view objective and subjective measures as two different but complementary methods for establishing the minimal stimulus conditions needed to be aware of critical stimuli. The primary difference between

---

[2] For a discussion of other possible reasons why studies based on subjective and objective measures of awareness lead to similar conclusions, see Merikle and Daneman (2000).

the two methods is that the minimal stimulus conditions established with objective measures are typically poorer or more limited than the minimal stimulus conditions established with subjective measures. However, even though objective measures may provide more conservative estimates than subjective measures of the minimal stimulus conditions needed to perceive critical stimuli with awareness, observers may be unaware of critical stimuli presented under the stimulus conditions established using either subjective or objective measures. Thus, there may be no necessary contradiction between using measures of forced-choice performance both to define the minimal stimulus conditions needed to perceive critical stimuli with awareness and to assess perception in the absence of awareness. In many instances, measures of forced-choice performance may simply provide a conservative method for determining whether perception is accompanied by the experience of perceiving.

If the primary difference between objective and subjective measures of awareness is that objective measures provide more conservative estimates than subjective measures of the minimal stimulus conditions necessary to perceive critical stimuli with awareness, the obvious question that arises is which measure is the better measure to use in studies of perception without awareness? The advantage of using objective measures is that by establishing the stimulus conditions that make it impossible for observers to discriminate between alternative stimuli, it is possible to obtain data that provide intuitively compelling demonstrations of perception without awareness. The demonstrations are compelling because it is implausible to assume that observers are aware of critical stimuli when they find it impossible to discriminate between the stimuli. However, as the basis for a general approach to the study of perception without awareness, objective measures have a serious limitation. Unless it is possible to find objective measures that assess perception with awareness exclusively, any approach based on objective measures of awareness will lead to an underestimation of the influence of information perceived without awareness (Merikle & Reingold, 1998). Given that all measures of perception can in principle be influenced both by information perceived with awareness and by information perceived without awareness, the minimal stimulus conditions established using objective measures will not only reduce the likelihood of perception with awareness but will also reduce the likelihood of perception without awareness. For this reason, we suggest that subjective measures should be the preferred means for assessing the presence or absence of awareness. Even though there is a justified uneasiness about using subjective measures of awareness as the basis for distinguishing perception with awareness from perception without awareness, when all things are considered, self-reports of conscious experiences can provide both a direct and an accurate indication of the presence or absence of an awareness of perceiving (cf. Chalmers, 1996; Merikle, 1992).

3. Contrasts between perception with and without awareness

As an alternative to establishing dissociations between measures, it is also possible to demonstrate perception without awareness using a single measure of perception, if there are theoretical/conceptual reasons to believe that the selected measure will reveal qualitatively different results depending on whether information is perceived with or without awareness. The logic underlying this alternative approach is based on the assumption that information perceived with awareness enables a perceiver to act intentionally on the world and to produce effects on the world (cf. Chalmers, 1996; Searle, 1992), whereas information perceived without awareness leads to more automatic reactions that cannot be controlled by the perceiver. Given this assumption, there should be numerous situations in which perceiving with and without awareness will lead to qualitatively different consequences, and by establishing such qualitative differences, it is possible to demonstrate that perception occurs in the absence of an awareness of perceiving.

A good example of the way contrasts between perception with and without awareness have been used to demonstrate perception without awareness comes from a study conducted by Debner and Jacoby (1994). In this study, the likelihood that words were perceived with or without awareness was controlled by varying the stimulus conditions. On each trial, a word was presented and masked, and the interval between the onset of each word and the onset of the mask was either relatively short (i.e. 50 ms) or somewhat longer (i.e. 150 ms). Immediately following the mask, the first three letters of the word were presented again and the participants were told to complete the word stem with the first word that came to mind except the word that had just been presented. For example, if the word presented on the trial was frigid, then immediately following the presentation of frigid, the letter stem fri was presented and the participants were instructed to use any word other than the word that had just been presented to complete the word stem. For example, the participants could complete the word stem with fright, fringe, frites or even Friday but not with frigid.

The general pattern of results found by Debner and Jacoby (1994) is shown at the top of Fig. 3. The figure shows that the participants had difficulty following the instructions when the words that preceded the word stems were presented for the short, 50 ms duration. Despite the explicit instructions not to complete the word stems with the presented words, these words were used to complete the stems much more often than they were used in the baseline condition (i.e. broken line in Fig. 3) in which each word stem was preceded by an unrelated word. However, as is also shown in Fig. 3, when the words were presented for the slightly longer, 150 ms duration, the participants used the presented words much less often to complete the stems than occurred in the baseline condition. Thus, the words presented before the word stems influenced the participants' completions in opposite ways, relative to the baseline condition, depending on whether they were presented for 50 or 150 ms. Given the assumption that perception with awareness enables a perceiver to control actions, whereas perception without awareness leads to more automatic reactions, these results suggest that the participants were generally aware of the words presented for 150 ms and generally unaware of the words presented for 50 ms. As such, the results provide additional evidence that perception can occur in the absence of awareness.

Qualitative differences in the consequences of perception have also been found

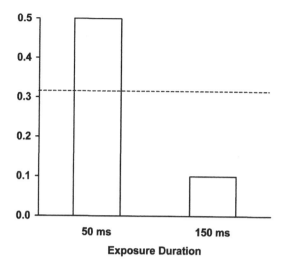

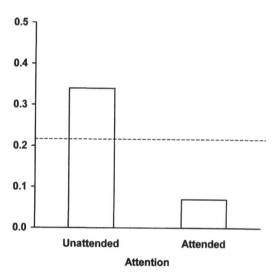

Fig. 3. Probability of NOT following exclusion instructions when awareness is varied via exposure duration (Debner & Jacoby, 1994) and when awareness is varied via attention (Smith & Merikle, 1999). The broken lines indicate baseline performance.

when awareness has been controlled by instructing participants on how to focus their attention. A good example comes from a recent series of studies conducted by Smith and Merikle (1999). In these studies, the stimulus displays were similar to the displays used by Mack and Rock (1998) on trial 3 in their studies of inattentional blindness (see Fig. 2). However, the general methodology differed from the methods used by Mack and Rock in two important ways. First, rather than presenting just one critical display to each participant, a total of 180 displays was presented. Second, the task demands either emphasized the importance of focusing attention on the words in the displays or emphasized the importance of focussing attention on the crosses so that the words were unattended. The consequences of perceiving words with and without attention were assessed using a stem-completion task in conjunction with the same instructions used by Debner and Jacoby (1994). Thus, following each display, the first three letters of the word were presented and the participants were told to complete the word stem with the first word that came to mind except the word that had just been presented. The results are shown at the bottom of Fig. 3. What is immediately apparent when viewing Fig. 3 is that the general pattern of results was similar to the pattern of results reported by Debner and Jacoby (1994). Namely, relative to the baseline level of performance (i.e. broken line in Fig. 3), the attended and unattended words influenced performance in opposite ways. When the words were unattended, the participants had difficulty following the instructions not to use the words in the displays to complete the stems, whereas when the words were attended, the participants were able to exclude most of the words in the displays from their completions of the word stems. These qualitatively different effects of attended and unattended words suggest that the participants were generally unaware of the unattended words and generally aware of the attended words. Thus, these results provide yet another demonstration of perception in the absence of awareness.

Other studies have revealed additional qualitative differences in performance which are consistent with the basic assumption that stimulus information perceived with awareness enables a perceiver to use the perceived information to control actions, whereas stimulus information perceived without awareness leads to more automatic reactions. Awareness in these studies has been controlled either by varying the stimulus conditions (e.g. Jacoby & Whitehouse, 1989; Marcel, 1980; Merikle & Joordens, 1997a; Murphy & Zajonc, 1993) or by instructing observers on how to distribute their attention (e.g. Merikle & Joordens, 1997b). The consistent finding in these studies is that when the stimulus conditions are good and the critical stimuli are attended, observers generally use the perceived stimulus information to control their actions, but when the stimulus conditions are poor or the critical stimuli are outside the immediate focus of attention, observers generally fail to use the perceived information to control their actions. Taken together, the results of these studies, by showing that perception with and without awareness can lead to qualitatively different consequences, provide considerable additional evidence that stimulus information is perceived even when there is no awareness of perceiving.

4. Conscious experience and perception without awareness

Now that it is firmly established that the concept of perception without awareness is valid in the sense that it leads to verifiable predictions, an obvious next step is to examine the functions of perception without awareness. One question that can be asked is how does information that is perceived without awareness influence conscious experience? This question has received relatively little attention in experimental studies to date because the goal of the vast majority of studies has been simply to demonstrate perception without awareness. However, from the limited evidence that is available, it appears that when a visual stimulus is perceived without awareness, it can influence or bias both which stimuli are subsequently perceived with awareness and how subsequent visual stimuli are consciously experienced. Thus, it appears that two important functions of perception without awareness are that it biases what is perceived with awareness and influences how stimuli perceived with awareness are consciously experienced.

An example of how stimuli perceived without awareness can influence or bias what stimuli are perceived with awareness comes from a study reported by McCormick (1997). In this study, a cue was briefly presented to the left or right of a central fixation cross and followed 500 ms later by a target letter (i.e. X or O). The task for the observers was to indicate as fast as possible on each trial whether the target was an X or an O. On 15% of trials, the cue and the target letter appeared on the same side of fixation, whereas on 85% of the trials, the cue and the target letter appeared on opposite sides of fixation. Given that the most likely location of each target letter was to the side of fixation opposite to the location of the cue, the observers were instructed that to optimize performance they should focus their attention to the side of fixation opposite to the cue. The results indicated that when observers were aware of the cues, they were faster at identifying a target letter when it appeared on the side of fixation opposite to the location of the cue than when it appeared on the same side of fixation as the cue. These results clearly show that the observers were able to use the cues to orient their attention to the side of fixation opposite to the location of the cue. However, when the observers were unaware of the cues, the results indicated that the observers were faster at identifying a target letter when it appeared on the same side of fixation as the cue than when it appeared on the opposite side of fixation. These results clearly show that the cues perceived without awareness attracted attention and biased the observers so that they were able to identify a target letter in a cued location more efficiently than a target letter in the opposite location. Thus, the cues that were perceived without awareness influenced what the observers perceived with awareness.

A recent study of how visual cues perceived with and without awareness attract the attention of patients with visual neglect provides another example of how stimuli perceived without awareness can bias what stimuli are subsequently perceived with awareness (Danziger, Kingstone, & Rafal, 1998). For present purposes, the important characteristic of patients with visual neglect is that they typically claim not to see stimuli presented in the visual field contralateral to their lesion whenever stimuli are presented simultaneously to both the left and right visual fields. Danziger et al. (1998) exploited this characteristic by simultaneously presenting one cue in the left visual field and another cue in the right visual field. These cues indicated the two possible locations of a subsequent target stimulus, and because the patients tested in the study had right parietal lesions, the patients neglected the cues presented in the left visual field. Presentation of the cues was always followed by the presentation of a single target stimulus (i.e. a white cross) at the location of one of the cues. The question that Danziger et al. (1998) asked was whether a cue presented to the neglected, left visual field would attract attention despite the fact that the patients were unaware of the cue. The results showed that the patients responded faster to the white cross used as the target stimulus when it appeared in a cued location in the neglected, left visual field than when it appeared in an uncued location in the neglected visual field. These results are entirely consistent with the earlier findings reported by McCormick (1997). They suggest that attention was oriented or attracted to the location of the cues in the neglected field despite the fact that the patients were generally unaware of these cues. As such, the results provide further support for the idea that visual stimuli perceived without awareness can influence or bias what is perceived with awareness.

How a stimulus is consciously experienced can also be influenced by stimuli perceived without awareness. A good example of the way in which a stimuli perceived without awareness can influence how another stimulus is consciously experienced comes from a early study reported by Dunlap (1900). In this study, Dunlap showed that the Müller–Lyer illusion can be induced by stimuli that are "...of such a low intensity as to be imperceptible" (p. 435). The participants in this study were presented with stimuli such as those shown in Fig. 4 and asked to indicate which of the two line segments appeared longer. Not surprisingly, for lines such as the one shown in Fig. 4A, the participants showed no bias in judging either the left or right segments as being longer. However, when faint angular lines such as those shown in Fig. 4B were added to the line segments, the participants were more likely to judge the line segment with the angular lines going away from the line segment (i.e. the left line segment in Fig. 4B) as being longer. Given that the angular lines were presented at stimulus intensities which were below the participant's threshold for reporting aware-ness, Dunlap concluded that "...under certain conditions things of which we are not ... conscious have their immediate effects on consciousness" (p. 436).

More recently, it has been demonstrated that the Müller–Lyer illusion can also be induced by unattended stimuli that are perceived without awareness. In one study, Moore and Egeth (1997) used an adaptation of the procedure developed by Mack and Rock (1998). On the first three trials of this study, two horizontal lines which differed slightly in length were presented against a background of random black and white dots, and the observers reported which line appeared to be longer. On the critical fourth trial, the two lines were equal in length and the background dots were organized so that they formed either inward or outward pointing angular lines at the ends of each line. The results showed that most observers experienced the Müller–Lyer illusion on the fourth trial and judged the line with the outward pointing

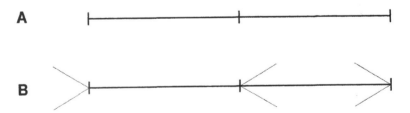

Fig. 4. Examples of the stimuli used by Dunlap (1900).

angular lines as being longer than the line with the inward pointing angular lines. However, the observers appeared to be completely unaware of the organized pattern in the background dots. When asked directly whether they noticed any pattern in the dots, no observer reported noticing a pattern, and when asked to make a forced-choice judgement among four possible patterns, performance did not differ from chance. These findings indicate that how the lines were consciously experienced was influenced by the organized pattern in the unattended background dots which was both unnoticed and perceived without any awareness of perceiving.

Another example of how unattended patterns can influence how stimuli are consciously experienced comes from a study in which the Müller–Lyer illusion was induced in patients with visual neglect by stimulus patterns in the neglected visual field (Mattingley, Bradshaw, & Bradshaw, 1995). These investigators first asked patients with left visuospatial neglect to bisect horizontal line segments. Not surprisingly, the patients bisected the lines with a bias toward the right such that the left portions of the bisected lines were longer than the right portions of the lines. Such findings indicate that the patients were unaware of at least some portion of the lines in the left visual field. To establish whether stimulus information in the neglected left visual field was perceived despite the fact that the patients seemed to be unaware of this information, Mattingley et al. (1995) added either inward or outward pointing angular lines at the left ends of the lines. The results indicated that when inward pointing lines were added, the patients tended to bisect the lines more to the left and that when outward pointing lines were added, the patients tended to bisect the lines more to the right. Thus, the way in which the patients bisected the lines was biased by the angular lines in the neglected left visual field. These findings are entirely consistent with the idea that the patients' conscious percepts of the lines, as indicated by the way in which they bisected the lines, were influenced by information in the neglected left visual field that they were unaware of perceiving. Taken together with the early results reported by Dunlap (1900) and the more recent findings reported by Moore and Egeth (1997), these findings provide considerable support for the idea that stimuli perceived without awareness influence how other stimuli are consciously experienced or perceived.

5. Concluding comments

After more than a century of research studies investigating perception without awareness, it is possible to conclude with considerable confidence that stimulus information can be perceived even when there is no awareness of perceiving. This conclusion is supported both by the results of studies demonstrating dissociations between measures of perception with awareness and measures sensitive to perception without awareness and by the results of studies showing that perception with and without awareness leads to qualitatively different consequences. In addition, the results of these research studies lead to the same conclusion whether awareness has been controlled by varying the stimulus conditions or by instructing observers on how to distribute their attention. Given these findings, the weight of the evidence clearly shows that perception without awareness occurs in numerous situations and under a variety of conditions.

Some may argue that the findings are not convincing because many studies have been based on subjective measures of conscious experiences rather than on objective measures of forced-choice discriminations (e.g. Greenwald et al., 1996; Snodgrass, Shevrin, & Kopka, 1993). Such skepticism, however, is only valid if one makes the dubious assumption that objective measures of forced-choice discriminations provide a more reliable behavioral measure of the subjective conscious state that we call awareness than is provided by observers' reports or descriptions of their conscious mental states. We know of no evidence to support such an assumption. In fact, we suggest that objective measures of performance generally provide conservative indicators of awareness and that verbalizations of subjective conscious experiences generally provide a more direct and accurate indication of the presence or absence of an awareness of perceiving. As long as verbalizations are accepted as a measure of awareness, the only reasonable conclusion that can be reached on the basis of the accumulated evidence is that considerable stimulus information is perceived under conditions that do not lead to the subjective conscious experiences normally associated with perceiving.

Now that the concept of perception without awareness has been shown to have a solid empirical basis, an important direction for future research studies is to explore the ways in which stimulus information perceived without awareness influences conscious experience. The available evidence suggests that information perceived without awareness can influence conscious experience in at least two distinct ways. First, it can bias what stimuli are attended, and second, it can influence how attended stimuli are consciously experienced. In future studies, these and other possible functions of information perceived without awareness need to be further explored. In addition, it will be important to evaluate how any functional differences that are documented may be related to or mediated by different neural pathways. For example, Posner and Rothbart (1992) have made a distinction between a posterior attention network, which mediates the orientation of attention, and an anterior attention network, which mediates consciousness awareness of attended objects. Given this distinction, stimuli perceived without awareness may influence what is attended via the posterior attention network and influence how attended stimuli are consciously experienced via the anterior attention network. With the tools that are now available for assessing perception without awareness, it should be possible to evaluate the role that different neural pathways play in mediating functional differences in the ways that information perceived without awareness influences or biases how other stimuli are consciously perceived and experienced.

Acknowledgements

Preparation of this paper was supported in part by a research grant from the Natural Sciences and Engineering Research Council of Canada (NSERC) to P.M.M. and by a postgraduate scholarship from NSERC to D.S.

References

Adams, J. K. (1957). Laboratory studies of behavior without awareness. Psychological Bulletin, 54, 383–405.

Assad, J. (1999). Now you see it: frontal eye field responses to invisible stimuli. Nature Neuroscience, 2, 205–206.

Baker, L. E. (1937). The influence of subliminal stimuli on verbal behavior. Journal of Experimental Psychology, 20, 84–100.

Balota, D. A. (1983). Automatic semantic activation and episodic memory. Journal of Verbal Learning and Verbal Behavior, 22, 88–104.

Bar, M., & Biederman, I. (1998). Subliminal visual priming. Psychological Science, 9, 464–469.

Chalmers, D. J. (1996). The conscious mind. New York: Oxford University Press.

Cheesman, J., & Merikle, P. M. (1986). Distinguishing conscious from unconscious perceptual processes. Canadian Journal of Psychology, 40, 343–367.

Dagenbach, D., Carr, T. H., & Wihelmsen, A. (1989). Task-induced strategies and near-threshold priming: conscious influences on unconscious perception. Journal of Memory and Language, 28, 412–443.

Danziger, S., Kingstone, A., & Rafal, R. D. (1998). Orienting to extinguished signals in hemispatial neglect. Psychological Science, 9, 119–123.

Debner, J. A., & Jacoby, L. L. (1994). Unconscious perception: attention, awareness, and control. Journal of Experimental Psychology: Learning, Memory, and Cognition, 20, 304–317.

Dehaene, S., Naccache, L., Le Clec'H, G., Koechlin, E., Mueller, M., Dehaene-Lambertz, G., van de Moortele, P.-F., & Le Bihan, D. (1998). Imaging unconscious semantic priming. Nature, 395, 597–600.

Dunlap, K. (1900). The effect of imperceptible shadows on the judgment of distance. Psychological Review, 7, 435–453.

Eriksen, C. W. (1960). Discrimination and learning without awareness: a methodological survey and evaluation. Psychological Review, 67, 279–300.

Esteves, F., Dimberg, U., & Öhman, A. (1994). Automatically elicited fear: conditioned skin conductance responses to masked facial expressions. Cognition and Emotion, 8, 393–413.

Esteves, F., & Öhman, A. (1993). Masking the face: recognition of emotional facial expressions as a function of the parameters of backward masking. Scandinavian Journal of Psychology, 34, 1–18.

Forster, K. I., & Davis, C. (1984). Repetition priming and frequency attenuation in lexical access. Journal of Experimental Psychology: Learning, Memory, and Cognition, 10, 680–698.

Forster, K. I., & Veres, C. (1998). The prime lexicality effect: form-priming as a function of prime awareness, lexical status, and discrimination difficulty. Journal of Experimental Psychology: Learning, Memory, and Cognition, 24, 498–514.

Fowler, C. A., Wolford, G., Slade, R., & Tassinary, L. (1981). Lexical access with and without awareness. Journal of Experimental Psychology: General, 110, 341–362.

Greenwald, A. G., Draine, S. C., & Abrams, R. L. (1996). Three cognitive markers of unconscious semantic activation. Science, 273, 1699–1702.

Holender, D. (1986). Semantic activation without conscious identification in dichotic listening, parafoveal vision, and visual masking: a survey and appraisal. Behavioral and Brain Sciences, 9, 1–23.

Jacoby, L. L., & Whitehouse, K. (1989). An illusion of memory: false recognition influenced by unconscious perception. Journal of Experimental Psychology: General, 118, 126–135.

Johnson, W. A., & Dark, V. J. (1986). Selective attention. Annual Review of Psychology, 37, 43–75.

Kemp-Wheeler, S. M., & Hill, A. B. (1988). Semantic priming without awareness: some methodological considerations and replications. Quarterly Journal of Experimental Psychology, 40A, 671–692.

Mack, A., & Rock, I. (1998). Inattentional blindness. Cambridge, MA: MIT Press.

Marcel, A. J. (1974, July). Perception with and without awareness. Paper presented at the meeting of the Experimental Psychology Society, Stirling, Scotland.

Marcel, A. J. (1980). Conscious and preconscious recognition of polysemous words: locating the selective effects of prior verbal context. In R. S. Nickerson, Attention and performance (Vol. VIII, pp. 435–457). Hillsdale, NJ: Erlbaum.

Marcel, A. J. (1983). Conscious and unconscious perception: experiments on visual masking and word recognition. Cognitive Psychology, 15, 197–237.

Mattingley, J. B., Bradshaw, J. L., & Bradshaw, J. A. (1995). The effects of unilateral visuospatial neglect on perception of Müller–Lyer illusory figures. Perception, 24, 415–433.

McCauley, C., Parmelee, C. M., Sperber, C. D., & Carr, T. H. (1980). Early extraction of meaning from pictures and its relation to conscious identification. Journal of Experimental Psychology: Human Perception and Performance, 6, 265–276.

McCormick, P. A. (1997). Orienting attention without awareness. Journal of Experimental Psychology: Human Perception and Performance, 23, 168–180.

Merikle, P. M. (1984). Toward a definition of awareness. Bulletin of the Psychonomic Society, 22, 449–450.

Merikle, P. M. (1992). Perception without awareness: critical issues. American Psychologist, 47, 792–795.

Merikle, P. M., & Daneman, M. (2000). Conscious vs. unconscious perception. In M. S. Gazzaniga (Ed.), The new cognitive neurosciences (2nd ed., pp. 1295–1303). Cambridge, MA: MIT Press.

Merikle, P. M., & Joordens, S. (1997a). Measuring unconscious influences. In J. D. Cohen, & J. W. Schooler (Eds.), Scientific approaches to consciousness (pp. 109–123). Mahwah, NJ: Erlbaum.

Merikle, P. M., & Joordens, S. (1997b). Parallels between perception without attention and perception without awareness. Consciousness and Cognition, 6, 219–236.

Merikle, P. M., Joordens, S., & Stolz, J. A. (1995). Measuring the relative magnitude of unconscious influences. Consciousness and Cognition, 4, 422–439.

Merikle, P. M., & Reingold, E. M. (1998). On demonstrating unconscious perception. Journal of Experimental Psychology: General, 127, 304–310.

Meyer, D. E., & Schvaneveldt, R. W. (1976). Meaning, memory structure, and mental processes. Science, 192, 27–33.

Miller, J. G. (1942). Unconsciousness. New York: Wiley.

Moore, C. M., & Egeth, H. (1997). Perception without attention: evidence of grouping under conditions of inattention. Journal of Experimental Psychology: Human Perception and Performance, 23, 339–352.

Morris, J. S., Öhman, A., & Dolan, R. J. (1998). Conscious and unconscious emotional learning in the human amygdala. Nature, 393, 467–470.

Murphy, S. T., & Zajonc, R. B. (1993). Affect, cognition, and awareness: affective priming with optimal and suboptimal stimulus exposures. Journal of Personality and Social Psychology, 64, 723–739.

Posner, M. I., & Rothbart, M. K. (1992). Attentional mechanisms and conscious experience. In A. D. Milner, & M. D. Rugg (Eds.), The neuropsychology of consciousness (pp. 91–111). London: Academic Press.

Reingold, E. M., & Merikle, P. M. (1990). On the inter-relatedness of theory and measurement in the study of unconscious processes. Mind & Language, 5, 9–28.

Searle, J. R. (1992). The rediscovery of the mind. Cambridge, MA: MIT Press.

Sidis, B. (1898). The psychology of suggestion. New York: D. Appleton.

Smith, S. D., & Merikle, P. M. (1999, June). Assessing the duration of memory for information perceived without awareness. Poster presented at the 3rd annual meeting of the Association for the Scientific Study of Consciousness, London, Canada.

Snodgrass, M., Shevrin, H., & Kopka, M. (1993). The mediation of intentional judgments by unconscious perception: the influence of task preference, word meaning, and motivation. Consciousness and Cognition, 2, 169–193.

Stroh, M., Shaw, A. M., & Washburn, M. F. (1908). A study of guessing. American Journal of Psychology, 19, 243–245.

Whalen, P. J., Rauch, S. L., Etcoff, N. L., McInerney, S. C., Lee, M. B., & Jenike, M. A. (1998). Masked presentations of emotional facial expressions modulate amygdala activity without explicit knowledge. Journal of Neuroscience, 18, 411–418.

Williams Jr., A. C. (1938). Perception of subliminal visual stimuli. Journal of Psychology, 6, 187–199.

5

Consciousness and the brainstem

Josef Parvizi[1], Antonio Damasio*

Department of Neurology, Division of Behavioral Neurology and Cognitive Neuroscience,
University of Iowa College of Medicine, 200 Hawkins Drive, Iowa city, Iowa 52242, USA

Abstract

In the first part of this article we summarize a theoretical framework and a set of hypotheses aimed at accounting for consciousness in neurobiological terms. The basic form of consciousness, core consciousness is placed in the context of life regulation; it is seen as yet another level of biological processing aimed at ensuring the homeostatic balance of a living organism; and the representation of the current organism state within somato-sensing structures is seen as critical to its development. Core consciousness is conceived as the imaged relationship of the interaction between an object and the changed organism state it causes. In the second part of the article we discuss the functional neuroanatomy of nuclei in the brainstem reticular formation because they constitute the basic set of somato-sensing structures necessary for core consciousness and its core self to emerge. The close relationship between the mechanisms underlying cortical activation and the bioregulatory mechanisms outlined here is entirely compatible with the classical idea that the reticular formation modulates the electrophysiological activity of the cerebral cortex. However, in the perspective presented here, that modulation is placed in the setting of the organism's homeostatic regulation. © 2001 Elsevier Science B.V. All rights reserved.

Keywords: Consciousness; Brainstem; Reticular formation; Cerebral cortex

1. Introduction

The terms consciousness and brainstem have long been associated on the basis of two lines of evidence. The first is the fact that damage to the upper brainstem is a known cause of coma and persistent vegetative state, the disease states in which

---

* Corresponding author. Fax: +1-319-353-6277.

E-mail address: josef-parvizi@uiowa.edu (J. Parvizi).

[1] Co-corresponding author.

consciousness is most severely impaired. The second line of evidence originates from classical experiments which suggested, either through lesions or electrical stimulation, that a part of the brainstem, known as the reticular formation, is associated with the electrophysiological pattern commonly found in wakeful and attentive states. Such evidence supported a general account of the relationship between brainstem and consciousness that can be summarized as follows: (a) the brainstem contains the reticular formation which is the origin of the ascending reticular activating system; (b) the engagement of the ascending reticular activating system activates the cerebral cortex; (c) the process of activating the cortex underlies wakefulness and attention; and (d) wakefulness and attention are indispensable constituents of consciousness, or, as some might say, constitute consciousness.

While there is little doubt that cortical activation due to brainstem engagement is an indispensable part of the conscious state, we believe that the above account is incomplete for a number of reasons. For example, the account dates from a time in which the phenomena of consciousness were conceptualized in exclusively behavioral, third-person terms. Little consideration was given to the cognitive, first-person description of the experience of the subject who is conscious. Moreover, the neuroanatomical view of the brainstem that informs this traditional account does not include recent advances in the description of different nuclei within the reticular formation and of their distinct connections to other brain regions, nor does it include the consequent revision of the concept of reticular formation. No less importantly, the account does not address the functional context in which the brainstem plays its presumed activation role. For example, what drives the brainstem to activate the cerebral cortex in the manner in which it does? Why is the activation system based on brainstem structures as opposed to other structures?

Recently, we have proposed that the role of the brainstem in consciousness can be seen in a new perspective, that of life regulation, and that the new perspective may help explain why and how brainstem nuclei exert their varied influences on structures located rostrally, namely on the cerebral cortex (Damasio, 1998, 1999).

1.1. A brief summary of the new proposal

Some nuclei of the brainstem have long been linked to the regulation of life, along with nuclei in the nearby hypothalamus, but a link between nuclei that regulate life and the process of consciousness has not been proposed before. Likewise, the brainstem nuclei that have long been linked to consciousness, namely those of the reticular formation, have not been linked to the regulation of life. In terms of theoretical background, the critical feature of the proposal is the 3-way connection it proposes for consciousness, for the nuclei involved in homeostasis, and for the nuclei in the reticular formation.

The proposal specifies two closely related but separable problems in the investigation of consciousness. The first is the problem of understanding how the brain engenders the mental patterns we experience as the images of an object. By "object" we mean entities as diverse as a person, a place, a melody, or an emotional state; by "image" we mean a mental pattern in any of the sensory modalities, e.g. a sound image, a tactile image, the image of an aspect of an emotional state as conveyed by visceral senses. Such images convey the physical characteristics of the object as well as the reaction of like or dislike one may have for an object and the plans one may formulate for it, or convey the web of relationships of the object among other objects. This first problem of consciousness is the problem of how we form a temporally and spatially unified "movie-in-the-brain", a metaphorical movie, of course, with as many sensory tracks as the brain's sensory systems. Solving this first problem in neuroscientific terms consists of discovering how the brain makes neural patterns in its neural circuits and turns those neural patterns into the explicit mental patterns of the whole range of possible sensory images, which stand for any object, any relationship, concrete or abstract, any word or any sign.

The second problem of consciousness concerns how, in parallel with creating mental patterns for an object, the brain also creates a sense of self in the act of knowing. The solution for this second problem requires the understanding of how each of us has a sense of "me"; of how we sense that the images in our minds are shaped in our particular perspective and belong to our individual organism. Solving the second problem of consciousness consists of discovering the biological underpinnings for the construction of the mental patterns which automatically convey the sense of a self. Importantly, the solution traditionally proposed for the problem, that of an homunculus creature who is in charge of knowing, is not acceptable. There is no homunculus.

The problem of how the movie in the brain is generated and the problem of how the brain also generates the sense that there is an owner and observer for that movie are so interrelated that the latter problem is nested within the former. The second problem is that of generating the appearance of an owner and observer for the movie, that materializes within the movie.

The new proposal specifies that we first become conscious when, in addition to being awake and capable of making sensory images of an object, our organisms internally construct and internally exhibit a specific kind of wordless knowledge – the knowledge that the organism has been changed by an object – and when such knowledge occurs along with the salient enhancement of the object image caused by attention being allocated to it.

The central question arising from this formulation is how this new knowledge begins to be gathered. The following hypothesis captures the solutions we propose to answer it: core consciousness (the simplest form of consciousness) occurs when the brain's representation devices generate an imaged, nonverbal account of how the organism's own state is affected by the organism's interaction with an object, and when this process leads to the enhancement of the image of the causative object, thus placing the object saliently in a spatial and temporal context. The protagonist of core consciousness is the core self, the simplest form of self.

The hypothesis outlines two component mechanisms: the generation of an imaged nonverbal account of an object-organism relationship, and the enhancement of the images of an object. The hypothesis is grounded on the following premises:

1. That the organism, as a unit, is mapped in the organism's brain, within structures that regulate the organism's life and signal its internal states continuously; that

the object is also mapped within the brain, in the sensory and motor structures activated by the interaction of the organism with the object; that both organism and object are mapped as neural patterns, in first-order maps; and that all of these neural patterns can become mental images.

2. That the neural activity inherent in sensorimotor maps pertaining to the object cause changes in the neural activity of the maps pertaining to the organism.
3. That the activities described in (2) can in turn be conveyed to second-order maps which thus represent the overall relationship of object and organism.
4. That the neural patterns transiently formed in second-order maps can become mental images, just as is the case with the neural patterns in first-order maps, thus producing an image of the relationship between organism and object.

1.2. The proto-self

The organism referred to in the hypothesis is represented in the brain by a coherent collection of neural patterns which map, moment by moment, the state of the organism in its many dimensions. This ceaselessly maintained first-order collection of neural patterns is described in the proposal as the "proto-self". The proto-self occurs not in one brain region but in many, at a multiplicity of levels, from the brainstem and hypothalamus to the cerebral cortex, in structures that are interconnected by neural pathways. These structures are intimately involved in the processes of regulating and representing the state of the organism, two closely tied operations. In short, the proto-self is a coherent collection of neural patterns which map, moment by moment, the state of the physical structure of the organism in its many dimensions.

It should be noted at the outset that the proto-self is not the sense of self in the traditional sense, the sort of self on which our current knowing is centered, that is, the core self (the protagonist of core consciousness), and the autobiographical self (the extended form of self which includes one's identity and is anchored both in our past and anticipated future). The proto-self is the pre-conscious biological precedent of both core and autobiographical self.

The proto-self should also not be confused with the homunculus of classical neurology. The proto-self does not occur in one place only, and it emerges dynamically and continuously from interacting signals originating at multiple levels of the nervous system. The proto-self is not an interpreter; it is a reference.

The structures required to implement the proto-self are as follows:

1. Several brainstem nuclei which regulate body states and map body signals.
2. The hypothalamus and the basal forebrain.
3. The insular cortex, cortices known as S2, and the medial parietal cortices located behind the splenium of the corpus callosum, all of which are part of the somatosensory cortices.

The structures which are not required to implement the proto-self are as follows:

1. Several early sensory cortices, namely those of areas 17, 18, 19, which are

dedicated to vision; 41/42, 22, dedicated to hearing; area 37, which is partly dedicated to vision but is also a higher-order cortex, and the part of S1 concerned with fine touch. These cortices are involved in the making of modality-specific sensory patterns that support the mental images of diverse sensory modalities available in our mind. They play a role in consciousness inasmuch as the images of the object-to-be-known are assembled from these regions, but they play no role in the proto-self.

2. All the inferotemporal cortices, namely areas 20, 21, part of 36, 37, 38. These cortices support many of the autobiographical records on the basis of which the autobiographical self and extended consciousness can be realized, but they play no role in the proto-self.

3. The hippocampus.

4. The hippocampal-related cortices, namely areas 28 and 35.

5. The prefrontal cortices. Some of these cortices participate in high-level working-memory for spatial, temporal, and language functions. Because of their role in working memory, prefrontal cortices are critical for high levels of extended consciousness, but they play no role in proto-self.

6. The cerebellum.

1.3. The basic mechanisms of core consciousness

As the brain forms images of an object and of the organism, and as the images of the object affect the state of the organism, yet another level of brain structure creates a nonverbal account of the events that are taking place in the varied brain regions activated as a consequence of the object-organism interaction. The mapping of the organism and the object occurs in first-order neural maps representing proto-self and object, respectively. On the other hand, the account of the causal relationship between object and organism occurs in second-order neural maps. Examples of second-order structures are the cingulate cortices, the thalamus, and the superior colliculi. The subsequent image enhancement is achieved via modulation from basal forebrain/brainstem nuclei, as well as thalamocortical modulation.

The hypothesis thus pivots on the relationship between the changing organism state and the sensorimotor maps of a given object that causes those changes. As the images of the object affect the state of the organism, another level of brain structures creates a nonverbal account of the events that are taking place as a consequence of the object-organism interaction.

In conclusion, the proposal specifies that the essence of consciousness is a continuously generated image of the act of knowing relative to the mental images of the object to be known. The image of knowing is accompanied by an enhancement of the images of the object. And because the image of knowing originates in neural structures fundamentally associated with the representation of body states, the image of knowing is a feeling.

In its normal and optimal operation, core consciousness is the process of achieving an all encompassing imagetic pattern which brings together the pattern for the object, the pattern for the organism, and the pattern for the relationship between the two. The emergence of each of those patterns and their conjoining in time depends on the contributions of individual brain sites working in close cooperation, and the understanding of the mechanisms of consciousness depends on identifying those individual contributions. But the study of such contributions must be considered in the perspective of an important qualification regarding the relation between brain regions and functions: the functions hypothesized here are not located in one brain region or set of regions, but are, rather, a product of the interaction of neural and chemical signals among a set of regions.

Beyond the mechanisms responsible for core consciousness, there are mechanisms responsible for extended consciousness, the protagonist of which is the autobiographical self. Extended consciousness builds on core consciousness, requires memory, and is enhanced by language. The discussion of these mechanisms is outside the scope of this article (but see Damasio, 1999).

The role of brainstem structures in the generation of consciousness is thus a critical one. This article is dedicated to a review of some of the relevant evidence regarding the functional neuroanatomy of the brainstem, an understanding of which is indispensable to the above account of consciousness.

2. The brainstem and the reticular formation

The brainstem gray matter is organized in nuclei. A brainstem nucleus is a three-dimensional collection of neurons which is usually aligned in parallel to the long axis of the brainstem. Each nucleus has an idiosyncratic cytoarchitecture and tends to have a prevailing neurochemical identity that helps distinguish it from other nuclei; each nucleus has a unique location within the brainstem: each nucleus has connections with a distinct set of other neural structures; and each nucleus tends to have a prevailing function. Cranial nerve nuclei can be identified on the basis of the criteria and are prime examples of brainstem nuclei. For example, each cranial nerve nucleus can be distinguished from other brainstem nuclei based on the fact that it either receives primary afferents from, or sends out primary efferents to, a specific cranial nerve.

The fact that the brainstem has a nuclear organization was established more than a century ago (e.g. Kölliker, 1854; Ramón y Cajal, 1894; Jacobsohn, 1909). However, due to the lack of techniques such as immunohistochemical markers, tracing agents, and novel neurophysiological probes, many brainstem nuclei were defined on the basis of cytoarchitectural features, anatomical connections revealed only by the method of terminal degeneration, or mere appearance. For example, the substantia nigra was so labeled because of the pigmented appearance of its cells, and the periaqueductal gray matter was so named because it occupies the region surrounding the cerebral aqueduct. Similarly, the core region of the brainstem was labeled as the reticular formation because neurons in that region were surrounded by interlacing fibers, which gave the region the appearance of a "reticulum" that is a web. This region occupies most of the central and dorsal part of the brainstem extending from the lower medulla to the level of the upper midbrain (Fig. 1A) (Olszewski & Baxter, 1982; Paxinos & Huang, 1995). It is anatomically continuous with the core regions of the spinal cord and extends rostrally into the thalamus (e.g. Martin, 1996). In short, the term reticular formation was assigned to a region of the brainstem when the nuclear heterogeneity of this region was not yet appreciated because of the limited methods of the time.

The term reticular formation became entrenched in the neuroscientific vocabulary largely because of the classical studies which suggested its involvement in consciousness. As early as the 19th century, there had been evidence that lesions in the brainstem core impair consciousness (e.g. von Economo, 1917), and in a series of classical experiments in the late 1940s, electrical stimulation within the reticular formation in lightly anesthetized non-human mammals, was associated with a desynchronization of the electroencephalogram (EEG) that hallmarks awake and attentive states (Moruzzi & Magoun, 1949; Lindsley, Schreiner, Knowles, Magoun, & Magoun, 1950; French & Magoun, 1952; Magoun, 1952a; Magoun, French, & Von Amerongen, 1952b; French, Verzeano, & Magoun, 1953). It was known by then that the reticular formation projects to the intralaminar nuclei of the thalamus, which are the origin of the so-called diffuse thalamocortical projections, since they are not connected in topographical fashion with specific sensory or motor regions (Morison & Dempsey, 1942). As a consequence, it was proposed that the brainstem reticular formation is the origin of the ascending reticular activating system that

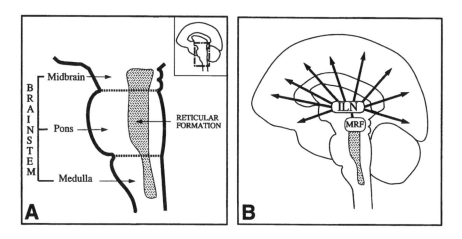

Fig. 1. The brainstem reticular formation and the conventional view of the ascending reticular activating system. (A) The brainstem is located between the spinal cord and the diencephalon. It encompasses the medulla oblongata, the pons, and the midbrain. Earlier histological studies indicated that the central and dorsal part of the brainstem extending from the lower medulla to the level of the upper midbrain had an appearance of a "reticulum". Therefore, this region was labeled as the reticular formation. (B) According to the conventional view, the mesencephalic reticular formation (MRF) is the origin of the ascending reticular activating system that operates through the intralaminar nuclei of the thalamus (ILN) and activates widespread regions of the cortex. As described in the text, this view is incomplete for several reasons.

would operate through the intralaminar nuclei of the thalamus and activate widespread regions of the cortex. Fig. 1B illustrates the conventional view of the brainstem reticular formation and the ascending reticular activating system. Subsequent neuropathological studies suggested that the brainstem areas whose lesions cause coma or persistent vegetative state in humans lie in the central and dorsal regions of the brainstem extending from about the level of the midpons to the level of the upper midbrain, a sizable part of the general region in which the reticular formation is located (Loeb & Stirling Meyer, 1965; Plum & Posner, 1980).

Since then, the conventional view of the reticular formation has been modified based on several lines of evidence. First, it is known that the reticular formation is not a homogeneous mesh of neurons but rather a collection of anatomically and functionally different nuclei (Fig. 2). Thus each component of the reticular formation may have a distinct role to play in modulating the electrophysiological activity of the cerebral cortex. It should be noted that as early as in the 1950s, Olszewski (1954) and Brodal (1959) suggested that the term reticular formation does not refer to a single anatomical unit and may be misleading. Blessing (1997a,b) has even suggested that the term should be avoided. Second, it is known that the heterogeneous collection of nuclei can modulate the activity of the cerebral cortex through routes other than the intralaminar nuclei of thalamus. Some nuclei can influence the entire cortex by making connections with basal forebrain nuclei, from which bilateral and widespread cortical projections originate. Other projections bypass both the thalamus and the basal forebrain and reach large expanses of both cerebral hemispheres directly, thereby inducing a modulatory effect. Moreover, some nuclei can modulate the electrophysiological activity of the cerebral cortex by changing the activity of the reticular nucleus of the thalamus. Jones (1998) has suggested that diffuse projecting thalamic neurons are not confined to the intralaminar nuclei and are present throughout the thalamus. Groenewegen and Berendse (1994) have suggested that each specific region of the intralaminar and midline nuclei of thalamus projects to specific parts of the cerebral cortex and striatum, and therefore, the term diffuse thalamic projections may be misleading. Third, with the advent of histochemical techniques, it has become known that different ascending channels from the reticular formation use different neurotransmitters, thus modulating the electrophysiological activity of the cerebral cortex through different mechanisms. Finally, new evidence suggests that the modulation of the cortex by the brainstem reticular formation is more complex than simply the desynchronization of its electrophysiological rhythm and leads, in effect, to local patterns of synchronization embedded in the global desynchronization (Munk, Roelfsema, König, Engel, & Singer, 1996; Herculano-Houzel, Munk, Neuenschwander, & Singer, 1999). Llinas (Llinas & Paré, 1991; Llinas, Ribary, Contreras, & Pedroarena, 1998) and colleagues have found that the non-specific projections from the thalamus are important for generating a thalamocortical resonance which they suggest is a necessary substrate for consciousness.

In short, although the precise contribution of each reticular nucleus and ascending pathway still remains unclear, it has become apparent that several nuclei and several pathways may be involved in modulating the electrophysiological activity of the

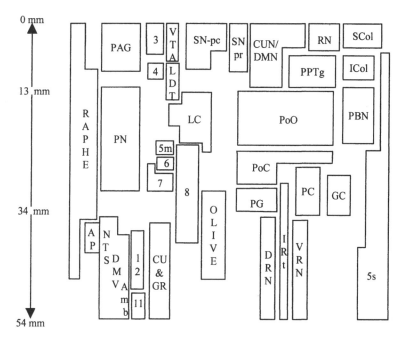

Fig. 2. The heterogeneous collection of brainstem nuclei. The brainstem gray matter, including the region traditionally known as the reticular formation, is organized in nuclei. There are two sets of nuclei, one on each side of the brainstem. Here only the collection of nuclei on one side of the brainstem is shown. A nucleus is a three dimensional collection of neurons which is usually aligned in parallel to the long axis of the brainstem. As this figure illustrates, each nucleus has its own idiosyncratic position within the brainstem. Some extend throughout the entire brainstem (such as the trigeminal nucleus, 5s) whereas some others (such as the area postrema, AP) occupy a small region and extend only a few millimeters or less. The size and the shape of the columns, as shown here, reflect the relative area of the brainstem occupied by the nucleus. Abbreviations: 3: oculomotor; 4: trochlear; 5m: trigeminal motor; 5s: trigeminal sensory; 6: abducens; 7: facial; 8:vestibulochoclear; 12:hypoglossus; Amb: ambiguus; AP: area postrema; CU and GR: cuneate and gracile; CUN/ DMN: cuneiforme and the deep mesencephalic; DMV: dorsal motor nucleus of vagus; DRN: dorsal medullary reticular complex including the region of the subnucleus reticularis dorsalis; EW: Edinger–Westphal; GC: gigantocellularis; ICol: inferior colliculus; IRt: Intermediate reticular zone; LC: locus coeruleus; LDT: laterodorsal tegmental nucleus; NTS: nucleus tractus solitarius; OLIVE: olivary complex; PAG: periaqueductal gray matter; PBN: parabrachial nucleus; PC: parvocellular; PG: paragigantocellular; PoC: pontis caudalis; PoO: pontis oralis; PPTg-pc: pedunculopontine tegmental nucleus pars compacta; PPTg-pd: pedunculopontine tegmental nucleus pars dissipatus; RN: red nucleus; SCol: superior colliculus; SNpc: substantia nigra pars compacta, SN-pr: substantia nigra pars reticulata; and VRN: ventral reticular complex.

cerebral cortex. In the paragraphs ahead, we provide an outline of the anatomical heterogeneity of the reticular formation and of the multiplicity of channels through which the reticular formation influences the activity of the cerebral cortex. We only discuss those components that are, to the best of our knowledge, anatomically capable of modulating the global activity of the cerebral cortex or functionally known to do so. As will be noted, the majority of these components lie in the upper brainstem, and only a few lower brainstem components are mentioned, on the basis of evidence suggesting that they too may influence the activity of the cerebral cortex either directly or via the upper brainstem nuclei. Based on their histochemical features, functional properties, and anatomical connections, we group these components within four families of nuclei:

1.   The classical reticular nuclei which include the nucleus cuneiforme, the deep mesencephalic nucleus, the non-cholinergic portion of the pedunculo-pontine tegmental nucleus, and the pontis oralis nucleus. These nuclei are located in the core of the brainstem in a relatively cell-poor but interlaced region, which first suggested the term reticular formation. They send presumably glutamatergic ascending projections to the basal ganglia and the intralaminar thalamic nuclei which in turn project to various cortical regions (Brodal, 1959; Jones & Leavitt, 1974; Edwards & de Olmos, 1976; Jackson & Crossman, 1983; Kaufman & Rosenquist, 1985; Steriade, Pare, Parent, & Smith, 1988; Lavoie & Parent, 1994; Groenewegen & Berendse, 1994; Newman & Ginsberg, 1994). The deep mesencephalic nucleus and, to a lesser extent, the nucleus pontis oralis project to the basal forebrain, from which widespread cholinergic projections arise aimed at the cerebral cortex (Jones & Yang, 1985).

The classical reticular nuclei mentioned above are located in the upper brainstem. However, some structures in the lower brainstem, well below midbrain and upper pons, may also have the anatomical means to modulate the cerebral cortex either directly or indirectly. Several anatomical tracing studies suggest that there are also neurons projecting to the intralaminar nuclei of the thalamus from classical reticular nuclei located in the lower pons and the medulla, such as the pontis caudalis, paragigantocellularis, parvocellularis, and subnucleus reticular dorsalis (Bernard, Villanueva, Carroué, & Le Bars, 1990b; Royce, Bromley, & Gracco, 1991; Newman & Ginsberg, 1994; Villanueva, Desbois, Le Bars, & Bernard (1998). Yet it should be noted that, as Royce (1991) and colleagues have found, the brainstem afferents to the intralaminar nuclei are most numerous in the upper brainstem and decline gradually at successively caudal levels through the pons and medulla. Finally, there is evidence suggesting that classical reticular nuclei in the lower brainstem can also modulate the activity of the upper brainstem nuclei and thus affect the cerebral cortex indirectly. One such nucleus is the nucleus paragigantocellularis which provides excitatory afferents to the noradrenergic locus coeruleus (Aston-Jones, Ennis, Pieribone, Nickell, & Shipley, 1986; Van Bockstaele & Aston-Jones, 1992, 1995).

2.   The monoaminergic nuclei of the brainstem which encompass noradrenergic, serotonergic, and dopaminergic nuclei (Moore, 1980). There are direct noradrenergic and serotonergic projections from the locus coeruleus and the rostral raphe complex, respectively, to most of the cortical mantle (Moore & Bloom, 1979). The dopaminergic projections from the substantia nigra and the

ventral tegmental area project extensively to the putamen, caudate nucleus, nucleus accumbens, and the thalamus (van Domburg & Ten Donkelaar, 1991). There are also direct dopaminergic projections from the brainstem to many cortical areas with a predominance towards the prefrontal, the cingulate, and the insular cortex (Porrino & Goldman-Rakic, 1982). Moreover, there are projections from brainstem dopaminergic, noradrenergic, and probably serotonergic nuclei to the basal forebrain where, as noted, widespread cortical projections originate (Smiley, Subramanian, & Mesulam, 1999). The physiological involvement of the serotonergic and noradrenergic systems in modulating the global activity of cortex, and in supporting increased attentiveness and behavioral response to environmental stimuli, is well documented (Clark, Geffen, & Geffen, 1987; Jacobs, Wilkinson, & Fornal, 1990; Azmitia & Whitaker-Azmitia, 1991; Aston-Jones, Chiang, & Alexinsky, 1991; Berridge, Arnsten, & Foote, 1993; Geyer, 1996; Bloom, 1997; Cahill & McGaugh, 1998; Rico & Cavada, 1998). The role of dopaminergic nuclei in the same processes is less well understood although their central role in motor control and reward mechanisms underlying motivation is widely accepted (Dunnett & Robbins, 1992; Brown & Gershon, 1993; Schultz, Dayan, & Montague, 1997; Schultz, 1998). The above-mentioned monoaminergic nuclei are located within the upper reticular formation. Monoaminergic nuclei in the lower brainstem reticular formation such as the nuclei in the caudal raphe complex are known to have largely descending rather than ascending projections (Moore, 1980).

3.   The cholinergic nuclei which include the laterodorsal tegmental nucleus and the cholinergic portion of the pedunculopontine tegmental nucleus (Mesulam, Geula, Bothwell, & Hersh, 1989). These cholinergic nuclei are also located in the upper brainstem. They project to several thalamic nuclei including the reticular nucleus of the thalamus (Pare, Smith, Parent, & Steriade, 1988; Steriade, McCormick, & Sejnowski, 1993), and to basal forebrain regions such as the substantia innominata (Muller, Lewandowski, & Singer, 1993). The reticular nucleus of the thalamus projects to other thalamic nuclei (Scheibel & Scheibel, 1966), and inhibits their activity (Steriade & Deschenes, 1984; Barth & MacDonald, 1996), thereby functioning as a pacemaker for the thalamic spindle oscillations which hallmark deep sleep (Steriade & Deschenes, 1984; Steriade, McCormick, & Sejnowski, 1993). The activity of the brainstem cholinergic system blocks the generation of these spindles and thereby initiates the wakeful state (Steriade, 1993).

4.   The autonomic nuclei which include in the upper brainstem the parabrachial nucleus (PBN) and the periaqueductal gray matter (PAG). The PBN and the PAG are known for their involvement in the control of visceral functions, and there is evidence suggesting that they are also involved in modulating the global activity of the cerebral cortex. For instance, both PAG (Jones & Yang, 1985; Kaufman & Rosenquist, 1985; Pare et al., 1988) and the internal lateral

subregion of the PBN (Bester, Bourgeais, Villanueva, Besson, & Bernard, 1999), project to the intralaminar thalamic nuclei. Moreover, there are projections from the PBN (Fulwiler & Saper, 1984; Alden, Besson, & Bernard, 1994) and the PAG (Mantyh, 1983; Beitz, 1990; Parent & Steriade, 1981) to the basal forebrain and other brainstem nuclei such as the classical reticular nuclei involved in activating the cerebral cortex. Thus the PBN and the PAG have the anatomical means to modulate the activity of the cerebral cortex either through the thalamus or the basal forebrain, or through the classical reticular nuclei or monoaminergic and cholinergic nuclei. Interestingly, in a recent study by Munk (1996) and colleagues, the stimulation of the PBN was found to induce maximal changes in the electrophysiological activity of cortex.

In a series of studies by Moruzzi (Moruzzi, Magni, Rossi, & Zanchetti, 1959; Moruzzi, 1963) and others (Batini, Moruzzi, Palestini, Rossi, & Zanchetti, 1959) it was found that another component of the brainstem autonomic system, the nucleus tractus solitarius (NTS) in the medulla, can strongly modulate the global activity of the cerebral cortex. In these experiments, both synchronized and desynchronized states of the EEG were elicited depending on the frequency and the power of electrical stimulation in the NTS. Recently, the stimulation of the vagus nerve, which is the major source of afferents to the NTS, has been shown to be effective in the treatment of epilepsy by changing the pathologically synchronized electrophysiological activity of the cortex (Schachter & Saper, 1998).

Altogether, the above discussion indicates that first, the principal nuclei involved in modulating the electrophysiological activity of the cerebral cortex lie in the upper pons and in the midbrain, but this does not exclude the possible involvement of some lower brainstem structures. Second, it indicates that cortical activation is not likely to depend on one single brainstem nucleus or one single family of nuclei, but rather on a network formed by several families of nuclei (Fig. 3). Accordingly, several studies have confirmed that bilateral single lesions to some of the brainstem nuclei mentioned above are not sufficient to cause coma (Jones et al., 1973; Kitsikis & Steriade, 1981; Webster & Jones, 1988; Lai, Shalita, Hajnik, Wu, Kuo, Chia, & Siegel, 1999). Third, it also indicates that the notion of "mesencephalic" reticular formation as the sole platform for modulating the global activity of the cerebral cortex is incorrect because many of the relevant nuclei are located in the pons rather than in the midbrain (Fig. 2). Bremer's (1935) discovery that transecting the brainstem of cats at the pontomesencephalic junction, which he referred to as cerveau isolé preparation led to irreversible synchronization of the EEG is in keeping with this view. In a recent study, it was shown that a cell specific lesion in the core of the midbrain – that spared both ascending pathways originated below the midbrain and local connections within the midbrain – did not cause alterations in the EEG pattern (Denoyer, Sallanon, Kitahama, & Jouvet, 1991).

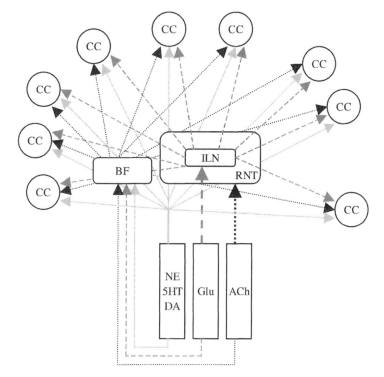

Fig. 3. The modern view of the ascending reticular activating system. There is evidence that the activation of the cerebral cortex (CC) by the brainstem is mediated through several channels, each of which originates from a different set of nuclei. Each set is distinguished on the basis of neurotransmitter of its component nuclei or the neural structures they target. Some nuclei send glutamatergic projections (Glu, dashed red lines) to the intralaminar nuclei of the thalamus (ILN) or to the basal forebrain (BF), from which widespread projections to the cerebral cortex originate. Other nuclei serve as the source of cholinergic (Ach, dotted white lines) projections to the BF or to the reticular nucleus of the thalamus (RNT). The RNT inhibits (black arrows) the activity of the other thalamic nuclei. There are also direct monoaminergic projections (solid blue lines) from noradrenergic (NE), serotonergic (5HT), and dopaminergic (DA) nuclei to the BF or to the cerebral cortex.

3. A functional context for the ascending reticular activating system

In the introduction to this article, we noted that it is important to understand the context in which the ascending reticular activating system operates, an issue which includes, among others, the consideration of why the system is located in the brainstem, and of which functional influences drive its operation. A possible answer to such questions can be gleaned in part from the pattern of afferent connections of the brainstem nuclei discussed above. These afferents are grouped based on the source of the signals they carry (Fig. 4).

1.   One of the major sources of afferents originates from (a) the lamina I of the superficial dorsal horn of the spinal cord located continuously throughout

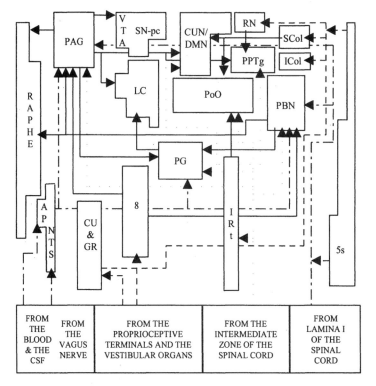

Fig. 4. The afferents to brainstem reticular nuclei. The brainstem reticular nuclei receive afferents from various sources. The state of the organism is portrayed in its multiple dimensions via incoming afferents each of which signals the current state of the internal milieu and the viscera – including the afferents to the vagal complex, and the introceptive afferents from the lamina I of the spinal cord (green dashed and dotted lines). There are also afferents from the vestibular organs and the musculoskeletal frame (yellow dashed lines); The deeper zones of the spinal cord convey signals about ongoing changes in the state of the organism as it interacts with an object (purple dotted lines). White solid lines represent the local connections within the brainstem nuclei. For abbreviations see Fig. 2.

the vertical extent of the cord, at the level of all its segments, and (b) the caudal spinal trigeminal subnucleus of the medulla, which is the rostral extension of the superficial dorsal horn. Both the superficial dorsal horn and the caudal spinal trigeminal subnucleus receive primary afferents through unmyelinated C-fibers and lightly myelinated $A\delta$ fibers which convey signals related to pain and temperature. The phylogenetically old C- and $A\delta$ fibers have free endings, unlike other sensory fibers which have specialized sensory receptors (Cervero & Iggo, 1980; Brown, 1982; Willis & Coggeshall, 1991: pp. 13–45).

Among the brainstem nuclei that receive the majority of these C- and $A\delta$ fiber-related inputs are the PBN and the PAG (Wiberg & Blomqvist, 1984; Bernard & Besson, 1990a; Blomqvist & Berkley, 1992; Barnett et al., 1995; Craig,

1995; Willis and Westlund, 1997). In fact it is estimated that the lamina I projects three times more densely to the PAG than to the thalamus (Mouton & Holstege, 1998). The noradrenergic nuclei such as the locus coeruleus, and the classical reticular nuclei such as the nucleus cuneiforme are examples of other nuclei that receive this kind of spinal afferents (Wiberg & Blomqvist, 1984; Blomqvist & Berkley, 1992; Barnett et al., 1995; Craig, 1995; Willis and Westlund, 1997). Projections from the superficial dorsal horn of the spinal cord and the caudal spinal trigeminal subnucleus provide the anatomical means for relaying to the upper brainstem information about potentially harmful stimuli. In addition to their role in detecting noxious stimuli, recent evidence suggests that C-fibers are also involved in detecting changes in pH, pCO_2, pO_2, glucose concentration, osmolarity and in signaling the presence of inflammatory agents (Moskowitz, 1991; MacIver & Tanelian, 1992; Burnstock & Wood, 1996; see Craig, 1997, for more references). Thus these fibers carry signals related to the internal state of the organism. Contrary to the traditional view, not all C-fibers are silent in the absence of noxious stimuli (e.g. Schaible and Schmidt, 1983). Moreover, only a portion of cells in the superficial dorsal horn of the spinal cord are specific to noxious stimuli (Zhang, Han, & Craig, 1993; Han, Zhang, & Craig, 1998). Other studies have confirmed that there are both nociceptive and non-nociceptive C-fibers (e.g. Vallbo et al., 1993; or see Lawson, 1996, for more references). As Craig has suggested, the ascending pathways from lamina I and the caudal spinal trigeminal subnucleus should be considered introceptive rather than only nociceptive (Craig, 1996, 1997).

Interestingly, the PAG and the PBN are also major endpoints for projections from the NTS and the area postrema (Beckstead, Morse, & Norgren, 1980; Mantyh, 1982; Fulwiler & Saper, 1984; Herbert, Moga, & Saper, 1990; Ito & Seki, 1998). As mentioned, the NTS receives afferents through cranial nerves such as the vagus, which carry signals pertaining to the visceral state. While the NTS constructs a neural map of the viscera, the area postrema, which is one of the periventricular organs lacking a blood brain barrier and is located in the vicinity of the NTS, receives signals pertaining to the chemical profile of the organism (Ito & Seki, 1998).

2.   The brainstem also receives major projections from the intermediate zone of the spinal cord. Many neurons in this part of the spinal cord, such as the so-called "wide dynamic range" neurons, receive convergent input from several sensory laminae and thus function as an integrative pool for several somatosensory submodalities (Willis & Coggeshall, 1991). Some neurons in the intermediate zone are also able to act as interneurons, coupling sensory and motor neurons. The intermediate zone is a major recipient of descending projections from the motor regions of the brainstem, cerebellum, and cerebral cortex. Thus the projections from the intermediate zone to the brainstem are well suited to signal the presence of interactions between an object and the

organism without signaling the sort of specific information about the object. Interestingly, the nuclei that receive most of the projections from the intermediate zone are many classical reticular nuclei such as the subnucleus reticularis dorsalis (Villanueva, Cliffer, Sorkin, Le, & Willis, 1990), the nucleus paragigantocellularis, the nuclei pontis caudalis and oralis (Willis & Westlund, 1997), which together constitute, in anatomical terms, the rostral extension of the intermediate zone.

3. The brainstem also receives signals from the vestibular system. The vestibular nuclei are located at the level of the upper medulla and lower pons, and receive their afferents from the vestibular organs in the inner ear which are involved in detecting changes in the position and the movement of the head in space. There are major projections from the vestibular nuclei to other brainstem nuclei such as the PBN in the upper brainstem (Balaban, 1996; Balaban & Porter, 1998). These projections are involved in mediating adjustments in cardiovascular, respiratory, and gastroenteric functions needed when the position of the body is changed in space.

4. The state of the musculoskeletal frame is also represented in the brainstem. The proprioceptive afferents from muscles and tendons ascend in the dorsal column of the spinal cord along with afferents conveying signals from primary cutaneous receptors or some visceral nociceptors (Willis & Coggeshall, 1991: pp. 265–295; Willis & Westlund, 1997). They terminate in the gracile and cuneate nuclei of the medulla (known as the dorsal column nuclei). There is evidence that different modalities of afferents terminate in distinct groups of neurons within these nuclei. Anatomical and physiological studies indicate that some clusters of neurons receive ascending input almost exclusively via primary afferent fibers from cutaneous origin whereas other regions within these nuclei receive primary muscle afferents and non-primary afferents from deep structures or cutaneous receptors with large receptive fields (see Willis and Coggeshall, 1991: pp. 265–306). In turn, there are distinct projections from the dorsal column nuclei to rostral regions such as in the midbrain, thalamus, zona incerta, and cerebellum (Berkley, Budell, Blomqvist, & Bull, 1986). Interestingly, the regions that receive primary cutaneous afferents project, in somatotopical order, to the thalamic relay nuclei whereas the upper brainstem receives projections from neurons that receive nonprimary or muscle afferents (Berkley et al., 1986; Wiberg, Westman, & Blomqvist, 1987). In the midbrain, the tectum is among the recipients of these projections (Berkley & Hand, 1978; Berkley et al., 1986; Wiberg & Blomqvist, 1984; Wiberg et al., 1987). In turn the tectum projects to the nuclei of the pons and midbrain (Shammah-Lagnado, Negrao, Silva, & Ricardo, 1987; Cornwall, Cooper, & Phillipson, 1990). Another motor-related channel to the upper brainstem is via the cerebellum (Brodal, 1959; Boivie, 1988; Rathelot & Padel, 1997). Some other nuclei in the brainstem, such as the

lateral reticular nucleus, also receive motor related projections directly from
the spinal cord (Brodal, 1959).

The picture we are drawing of a context for the operation of brainstem nuclei is
completed by evidence that the brainstem nuclei receive major afferents from rostral
brain structures. For instance, the classical reticular nuclei receive major afferents
from the zona incerta, the hypothalamus, and the medial thalamic nuclei (Parent &
Steriade, 1981; Steriade, Parent, Ropert, & Kitsikis, 1982; Shammah-Lagnado et al.,
1987; Cornwall et al., 1990). These rostral structures and the extended amygdala,
cingulate gyrus, insula, and prefrontal cortex are also known to project to the PAG
and the PBN (Hardy & Leichnetz, 1981a,b; Holstege, Meiners, & Tan, 1985; Moga,
Herbert, Hurley, Yasui, Gray, & Saper, 1990; Beitz, 1990; Buchanan, Thompson,
Maxwell, & Well, 1994; An, Bandler, Ongur, & Price, 1998; Moga et al., 1990). In a
recent study, R.J. Morecraft has traced direct projections from the cingulate cortex to
the locus coeruleus (personal communication).

In conclusion, the state of the organism is continuously portrayed in its multiple
dimensions by incoming afferents to several brainstem nuclei. These diverse afferents relay signals related to the current state of the internal milieu, the viscera, the
vestibular system, and the musculoskeletal frame. There are also afferents relaying
signals which describe ongoing changes in the state of the organism as it interacts
with an object. There is little doubt that the fundamental function of these brainstem
nuclei is the regulation of the state of the organism based on the representation of its
current state along several dimensions. It is reasonable to suggest, however, that
there are other closely related functions, namely (a) the modulation of the electrophysiological state of the cerebral cortex as influenced by the current state of the
organism with the goal of supporting mental processes and behaviors conducive to
further homeostatic regulation; and (b) the generation of a composite representation
of organism states available to rostral brain structures.

In effect, evidence that the nuclei within the brainstem reticular formation are
involved in functions other than modulating the electrophysiological activity of the
cerebral cortex is already available. For instance, the serotonergic system is involved
in the modulation of autonomic activities, hunger and body weight regulation,
neuroendocrine functions, reproductive behavior, aggression and suicidality (for
extensive review see Feldman, Meyer, & Quenzer, 1997: Chapter 9, pp. 380–9);
the noradrenergic system is involved in mechanisms underlying attention and learning (Aston-Jones & Bloom, 1981a,Aston-Jones and Bloom, 1981b; Aston-Jones,
Rajkowski, Kubiak, Valentino, & Shipley, 1996; Cahill and McGaugh, 1998); the
dopaminergic system is involved in motor control and reward mechanisms underlying motivation (Dunnett & Robbins, 1992; Brown & Gershon, 1993; Schultz et al.,
1997; Schultz, 1998). Furthermore, classical reticular nuclei such as the nucleus
cuneiforme and the pedunculopontine tegmental nucleus are also involved in loco-
motion (Allen, Inglis, & Winn, 1996). The pedunculopontine tegmental nucleus also
plays an important role in mechanisms underlying attention and learning (Allen et
al., 1996), and in subserving the rewarding effect of opiates (Bechara & van der
Kooy, 1989). As already noted, the PBN and the PAG are essential for homeostatic

control. The PBN and the PAG have extensive reciprocal connections with rostral and caudal regions involved in cardiovascular, respiratory and gastroenteric control. These are structures appropriate for integrating signals related to the body proper and coordinating distinct innate behavioral strategies for coping with environmental demands. In keeping with this view, it has been shown that the stimulation of the lateral column of the PAG brings about an active coping strategy with vocalization, confrontation, hypertension, tachycardia, and aggression, whereas stimulation of ventrolateral columns of the PAG, on the other hand, produces a passive coping strategy with hyporeactivity, hypotension, bradycardia, freezing, and immobility (Bandler & Shipley, 1994).

Evidence from functional imaging studies also supports the notion that the upper brainstem nuclei are involved in a broad range of functions. For instance, Maquet and colleagues (Maquet, Dive, Salmon, Sadzot, Franco, Poirrier, von Frenckell, & Franck, 1990; Maquet, Peters, Aerts, Delfiore, Degueldre, Luxen, & Franck, 1996) found that the regional blood flow in pontine tegmentum was increased during rapid-eye-movement sleep and decreased during deep sleep; Kinomura, Larsson, Gulyás, and Roland (1996) found a significant blood flow increase in mesencephalic nuclei when subjects performed tests requiring attention; and recently, we found a significant blood flow increase in the upper pons and midbrain when subjects reenacted past emotional events (Damasio, Grabowski, Bechara, Damasio, Parvizi, Ponto, & Hichwa, 2000).

The remarkable overlap of functions thus revealed might be a fortuitous combination of anatomical units, but we see it instead as indicative of a meaningful anatomical and functional integration engendered by evolution. In fact, these functions – wakefulness, basic attention, and emotion – are interrelated and all aim, in one way or another, at achieving homeostatic balance. The close proximity of structures governing wakefulness and attention and structures involved in processing emotion would enhance their functional and anatomical interdependence.

The close relationship between the mechanisms underlying cortical activation and bioregulatory mechanisms, as outlined here, is entirely compatible with the classical idea about the role of the reticular formation in modulating the electrophysiological activity of the cerebral cortex. But it places that modulation in the setting of the organism's homeostatic regulation.

4. Concluding remarks

The multiple dimensions which describe the overall current state of the organism are mapped in several groups of brainstem nuclei. We believe that this comprehensive and continually changing map of the organism state creates a functional context for the brainstem nuclei whose activity can modulate the operation of rostral brain structures, namely those in the cerebral cortex. In addition, the map of the organism state, along with the fact that such a state is being changed as a result of an interaction with an object, can be signaled to rostrally located structures and be remapped. We see the remapping of the changing organism state in relation to a causative object as the basis for the experience of knowing, the very core of the process of consciousness and self.

The brainstem is the source of several ascending neural pathways, each of which originates in distinct sets of nuclei. These pathways, which reach widespread regions of the cortex either directly or via the thalamus and the basal forebrain, affect the operations of the cerebral cortex both by modulating aspects of its overall activity (and leading to wakefulness and attention) and by conveying to specific regions the contents with which a subjective sense can be created.

In the framework outlined at the outset of this article, consciousness is grounded in both of these brainstem roles: providing an organism-based context for the modulation of rostral brain structures; and conveying signals necessary to represent the "caused changed state" of the organism within rostral structures.

The intriguing overlap of functions attributable to the several families of brainstem nuclei – emotion, wakefulness and sleep, basic attention, and of course consciousness itself – becomes less intriguing when it is seen in the perspective of homeostasis, the ultimate physiological role of all the operations in which these nuclei are involved.

Acknowledgements

Supported in part by a grant from the Mathers Foundation.

References

Alden, M., Besson, J. M., & Bernard, J. F. (1994). Organizations of the efferent projections from the pontine parabrachial area to the bed nucleus of the stria terminalis and neighboring regions: a PHA-L study in the rat. The Journal of Comparative Neurology, 341, 289–314.

Allen, L., Inglis, W. L., & Winn, P. (1996). Is the cuneiform nucleus a critical component of the mesencephalic locomotor region? Brain Research Bulletin, 41 (4), 201–210.

An, X., Bandler, R., Ongur, D., & Price, J. L. (1998). Prefrontal cortical projections to longitudinal columns in the midbrain periaqueductal gray in macaque monkeys. Journal of Comparative Neurology, 401 (4), 455–479.

Aston-Jones, G., & Bloom, F. E. (1981a). Activity of norepinephrine-containing locus coeruleus neurons in behaving rats anticipates fluctuations in the sleep-waking cycle. Journal of Neuroscience, 1 (8), 876–886.

Aston-Jones, G., & Bloom, F. E. (1981b). Norepinephrine-containing locus coeruleus neurons in behaving rats exhibit pronounced responses to non-noxious environmental stimuli. Journal of Neuroscience, 1 (8), 887–900.

Aston-Jones, G., Ennis, M., Pieribone, V. A., Nickell, W. T., & Shipley, M. T. (1986). The brain nucleus locus coeruleus: restricted afferent control of a broad efferent network. Science, 234 (4777), 734–737.

Aston-Jones, G., Chiang, C., & Alexinsky, T. (1991). Discharge of noradrenergic locus coeruleus neurons in behaving rats and monkeys suggests a role in vigilance. Progress in Brain Research, 88, 501–520.

Aston-Jones, G., Rajkowski, J., Kubiak, P., Valentino, R. J., & Shipley, M. T. (1996). Role of the locus coeruleus in emotional activation. Progress in Brain Research, 107, 379–402.

Azmitia, E. C., & Whitaker-Azmitia, P. M. (1991). Awakening the sleeping giant: anatomy and plasticity of the brain serotonergic system. Journal of Clinical Psychiatry, 52, 4–16.

Balaban, C. D. (1996). Vestibular nucleus projections to the parabrachial nucleus in rabbits: implications for vestibular influences on the autonomic nervous system. Experimental Brain Research, 108 (3), 367–381.

Balaban, C. D., & Porter, J. D. (1998). Neuroanatomic substrates for vestibulo-autonomic interactions. Journal of Vestibular Research, 8 (1), 7–16.

Bandler, R., & Shipley, M. T. (1994). Columnar organization in the rat midbrain periaqueductal gray: modules for emotional expression? Trends in Neurosciences, 17 (9), 379–389.

Batini, C., Moruzzi, G., Palestini, M., Rossi, G. F., & Zanchetti, A. (1959). Effects of complete pontine transections on the sleep-wakefulness rhythm: the midpontine pretrigeminal preparation. Archives Italiennes de Biologie, 97, 1–12.

Barnett, E. M., Evans, G. D., Sun, N., Perlman, S., & Cassell, M. D. (1995). Anterograde tracing of trigeminal afferent pathways from the murine tooth pulp to cortex using herpes simplex virus type 1. Journal of Neuroscience, 15 (4), 2972–2984.

Barth, D. S., & MacDonald, K. D. (1996). Thalamic modulation of high-frequency oscillating potentials in auditory cortex. Nature, 383, 78–81.

Bechara, A., & van der Kooy, D. (1989). The tegmental pedunculopontine nucleus: a brain-stem output of the limbic system critical for the conditioned place preferences produced by morphine and amphetamine. Journal of Neuroscience, 9 (10), 3400–3409.

Beckstead, R. M., Morse, J. R., & Norgren, R. (1980). The nucleus of the solitary tract in the monkey: projections to the thalamus and brainstem nuclei. The Journal of Comparative Neurology, 190, 259–282.

Beitz, A. J. (1990). Central gray. In G. Paxinos (Ed.), The human nervous system (pp. 307–320). New York: Academic Press.

Berkley, K. J., & Hand, P. J. (1978). Efferent projections of the gracile nucleus in the cat. Brain Research, 153 (2), 263–283.

Berkley, K. J., Budell, R. J., Blomqvist, A., & Bull, M. (1986). Output systems of the dorsal column nuclei in the cat. Brain Research, 396 (3), 199–225.

Bernard, J. F., & Besson, J. M. (1990a). The spino(trigemino)pontoamygdaloid pathway: electrophysiological evidence for an involvement in pain processes. Journal of Neurophysiology, 63 (3), 473–490.

Bernard, J. F., Villanueva, L., Carroué, J., & Le Bars, D. (1990b). Efferent projections from the subnucleus reticularis dorsalis (SRD): a phaseolus vulgaris leucoagglutinin study in the rat. Neuroscience Letters, 116, 257–262.

Berridge, C. W., Arnsten, A. F., & Foote, S. L. (1993). Noradrenergic modulation of cognitive function: clinical implications of anatomical, electrophysiological and behavioural studies in animal models. Psychological Medicine, 23 (3), 557–564.

Bester, H., Bourgeais, L., Villanueva, L., Besson, J. M., & Bernard, J. F. (1999). Differential projections to the intralaminar and gustatory thalamus from the parabrachial area: a PHA-L study in the rat. Journal of Comparative Neurology, 405 (4), 421–449.

Blessing, W. W. (1997a). Inadequate frameworks for understanding bodily homeostasis. Trends in Neurosciences, 20 (6), 235–239.

Blessing, W. W. (1997b). The lower brainstem and bodily homeostasis (1st ed.) New York: Oxford University Press.

Blomqvist, A., & Berkley, K. J. (1992). A re-examination of the spino-reticulo-diencephalic pathway in the cat. Brain Research, 579 (1), 17–31.

Bloom, F. E. (1997). What is the role of general activating systems in cortical function? In P. Rakic, & W. Singer (Eds.), Neurobiology of neocortex (pp. 407–421). New York: Wiley.

Boivie, J. (1988). Projections from the dorsal column nuclei and the spinal cord to the red nucleus in cat. Behavioural Brain Research, 28 (1-2), 75–79.

Bremer, F. (1935). Cerveau "isolé" et physiologie du sommeil. Comptes Rendus de la Societé Biologie, 118, 1235–1241.

Brodal, A. (1959). The reticular formation of the brainstem: anatomical aspect and functional correlation. Edinburgh: The William Ramsay Henderon Trust.

Brown, A. G. (1982). The dorsal horn of the spinal cord. Quarterly Journal of Experimental Physiology, 67, 193–212.

Brown, A. S., & Gershon, S. (1993). Dopamine and depression. Journal of Neural Transmission – General Section, 91 (2-3), 75–109.

Buchanan, S. L., Thompson, R. H., Maxwell, B. L., & Well, D. A. (1994). Efferent connections of the medial prefrontal cortex in the rabbit. Experimental Brain Research, 100 (3), 469–483.

Burnstock, G., & Wood, J. N. (1996). Puringergic receptors: their role in nociception and primary afferent neurotransmission. Current Opinion in Neurobiology, 6 (4), 526–532.

Cahill, L., & McGaugh, J. L. (1998). Mechanisms of emotional arousal and lasting declarative memory. Trends in Neurosciences, 21 (7), 294–299.

Cervero, F., & Iggo, A. (1980). The substantia gelatinosa of the spinal cord. Brain, 103, 717–772.

Clark, C. R., Geffen, G. M., & Geffen, L. B. (1987). Catecholamines and attention. I: Animal and clinical studies. Neuroscience and Biobehavioral Reviews, 11 (4), 341–352.

Cornwall, J., Cooper, J. D., & Phillipson, O. T. (1990). Afferent and efferent connections of the later-odorsal tegmental nucleus in the rat. Brain Research Bulletin, 25 (2), 271–284.

Craig, A. D. (1995). Distribution of brainstem projections from spinal lamina I neurons in the cat and the monkey. Journal of Comparative Neurology, 361 (2), 225–248.

Craig, A. D. (1996). An ascending general homeostatic afferent pathway originating in lamina I. Progress in Brain Research, 107, 225–242.

Craig, A. D. (1997). Pain, temperature and the sense of the body. In O. Franzen, R. Johansson, & L. Terenius (Eds.), Proceedings of the 1994 Wenner-Gren Symposium on somatosensation Birkhauser: Basel.

Damasio, A. R. (1998). Investigating the biology of consciousness. Philosophical Transactions of the Royal Society of London – Series B: Biological Sciences, 353 (1377), 1879–1882.

Damasio, A. R. (1999). The feeling of what happens: body and emotion in the making of consciousness, New York: Harcourt Brace.

Damasio, A. R., Grabowski, T. J., Bechara, A., Damasio, H., Ponto, L.L., Parvizi, J., & Hichwa, R. D. (2000). Distinctive patterns of subcortical and cortical brain activation associated with self-generated emotions and feelings. Nature Neuroscience, 3 (10), 1049–1056.

Denoyer, M., Sallanon, M., Kitahama, K., & Jouvet, M. (1991). Neurotoxic lesion of the mesencephalic reticular formation and/or the posterior hypothalamus does not alter waking n the cat. Brain Research, 539 (2), 287–303.

Dunnett, S. B., & Robbins, T. W. (1992). The functional role of mesotelencephalic dopamine systems. Biological Reviews of the Cambridge Philosophical Society, 67 (4), 491–518.

Edwards, S. B., & de Olmos, J. S. (1976). Autoradiographic studies of the projections of the midbrain reticular formation: ascending projections of nucleus cuneiformis. Journal of Comparative Neurology, 165 (4), 417–431.

Feldman, R. S., Meyer, J. S., & Quenzer, L. F. (1997). Principles of neuropsychopharmacology (1st ed.). Sunderland, MA: Sinauer Associates.

French, J. D., & Magoun, H. W. (1952). Effect of chronic lesions in central cephalic brainstem of monkeys. Archives of Neurology and Psychiatry, 68, 591–604.

French, J. D., Verzeano, M., & Magoun, H. W. (1953). An extralemniscal sensory system in the brain. Archives of Neurology and Psychiatry, 69, 505–519.

Fulwiler, C., & Saper, C. B. (1984). Subnuclear organization of the efferent connections of the parabrachial nucleus in the rat. Brain Research Reviews, 7, 229–259.

Geyer, M. A. (1996). Serotonergic functions in arousal and motor activity. Behavioural Brain Research, 73 (1-2), 31–35.

Groenewegen, H. J., & Berendse, H. W. (1994). The specificity of the 'nonspecific' midline and intra-laminar thalamic nuclei. Trends in Neurosciences, 17 (2), 52–57.

Han, Z. S., Zhang, E.-T., & Craig, A. D. (1998). Nociceptive and thermoceptive lamina I neurons are anatomically distinct. Nature Neuroscience, 1 (3), 218–225.

Hardy, S. G. P., & Leichnetz, G. R. (1981a). Cortical projections to the periaqueductal gray in the monkey: a retrograde and orthograde horseradish peroxidase study. Neuroscience Letters, 22, 97–101.

Hardy, S. G. P., & Leichnetz, G. R. (1981b). Frontal cortical projections to the periaqueductal gray in the rat: a retrograde and orthograde horseradish peroxidase study. Neuroscience Letters, 23, 13–17.

Herbert, H., Moga, M. M., & Saper, C. B. (1990). Connections of the parabrachial nucleus with the nucleus of the solitary tract and the medullary reticular formation in the rat. The Journal of Comparative Neurology, 293, 540–580.

Herculano-Houzel, S., Munk, M. H., Neuenschwander, S., & Singer, W. (1999). Precisely synchronized oscillatory firing patterns require electroencephalographic activation. Journal of Neuroscience, 19 (10), 3992–4010.

Holstege, G., Meiners, L., & Tan, K. (1985). Projections of the bed nucleus of the stria terminalis to the mesencephalon, pons, and medulla oblongata in the cat. Experimental Brain Research, 58 (2), 379–391.

Ito, H., & Seki, M. (1998). Ascending projections from the area postrema and the nucleus of the solitary tract of Suncus murinus: anterograde tracing study using Phaseolus vulgaris leucoagglutinin. Okajimas Folia Anatomica Japonica, 75 (1), 9–31.

Jackson, A., & Crossman, A. R. (1983). Nucleus tegmenti pedunculopontinus: efferent connections with special reference to the basal ganglia, studied in the rat by anterograde and retrograde transport of horseradish peroxidase. Neuroscience, 10 (3), 725–765.

Jacobsohn, L. (1909). Über die Kerne des menschlichen Hirnstammes (der medulla oblongata, des pons und des pedunculus). Vorlautige Mitteilung Neurol Centralblad, xxviii, 674–679.

Jacobs, B. L., Wilkinson, L. O., & Fornal, C. A. (1990). The role of brain serotonin. A neurophysiologic perspective. Neuropsychopharmacology, 3 (5–6), 473–479.

Jones, E. G. (1998). Viewpoint-the core and matrix of thalamic organization. Neuroscience, 85 (2), 331–345.

Jones, B. E., Bobillier, P., Pin, C., & Jouvet, M. (1973). The effect of lesions of catecholamine-containing neurons upon monoamine content of the brain and EEG and behavioral waking in the cat. Brain Research, 58 (1), 157–177.

Jones, E. G., & Leavitt, R. Y. (1974). Retrograde axonal transport and the demonstration of non-specific projections to the cerebral cortex and striatum from thalamic intralaminar nuclei in the rat, cat and monkey. Journal of Comparative Neurology, 154 (4), 349–377.

Jones, B. E., & Yang, T. Z. (1985). The efferent projections from the reticular formation and the locus coeruleus studied by anterograde and retrograde axonal transport in the rat. Journal of Comparative Neurology, 242 (1), 56–92.

Kaufman, E. F., & Rosenquist, A. C. (1985). Afferent connections of the thalamic intralaminar nuclei in the cat. Brain Research, 335 (2), 281–296.

Kinomura, S., Larsson, J., Gulyás, B., & Roland, P. (1996). Activation by attention of the human reticular formation and thalamic intralaminar nuclei. Science, 271, 512–515.

Kitsikis, A., & Steriade, M. (1981). Immediate behavioral effects of kainic acid injections into the midbrain reticular core. Behavioural Brain Research, 3 (3), 361–380.

Kölliker, A. (1854). Manual of human histology. London: Sydenham Society.

Lai, Y. Y., Shalita, T., Hajnik, T., Wu, J. P., Kuo, J. S., Chia, L. G., & Siegel, J. M. (1999). Neurotoxic N-methyl-D-aspartate lesion of the ventral midbrain and mesopontine junction alters sleep-wake organization. Neuroscience, 90 (2), 469–483.

Lavoie, B., & Parent, A. (1994). Pedunculopontine nucleus in the squirrel monkey: projections to the basal ganglia as revealed by anterograde tract-tracing methods. Journal of Comparative Neurology, 344 (2), 210–231.

Lawson, S. N. (1996). Neurochemistry of cutaneous nociceptors. In C. Belmonte, & F. Cervero (Eds.), Neurobiology of nociceptors (p. 85). New York: Oxford University Press.

Llinas, R. R., & Paré, D. (1991). Of dreaming and wakefulness. Neuroscience, 44 (3), 521–535.

Llinas, R., Ribary, U., Contreras, D., & Pedroarena, C. (1998). The neuronal basis for consciousness. Philosophical Transactions of the Royal Society of London – Series B: Biological Sciences, 353 (1377), 1841–1849.

Lindsley, D. B., Schreiner, L. H., Knowles, W. B., Magoun, M. S., & Magoun, H. W. (1950). Behavorial and EEG changes following chronic brainstem lesions in the cat. Electroencephalography and Clinical Neurophysiology, 2, 483–498.

Loeb, C., & Stirling Meyer, J. (1965). Strokes due to vertebro-basilar disease: infarction, vascular insufficiency and hemorrhage of the brainstem and cerebellum. Springfield, IL: Charles C. Thomas.

MacIver, M. B., & Tanelian, D. L. (1992). Activation of C fibers by metabolic perturbations associated with tourniquet ischemia. Anesthesiology, 76, 617–623.

Magoun, H. W. (1952a). Ascending reticular activating system in the brainstem. Archives of Neurology and Psychiatry, 67 (145), 154.

Magoun, H. W., French, J. D., & Von Amerongen, F. K. (1952b). An activating system in brainstem of monkey. Archives of Neurology and Psychiatry, 68 (5), 577–590.

Mantyh, P. W. (1982). The ascending input to the midbrain periaqueductal gray of the primate. Journal of Comparative Neurology, 211 (1), 50–64.

Mantyh, P. W. (1983). Connections of midbrain periaqueductal gray in the monkey. I. Ascending efferent projections. Journal of Neurophysiology, 49 (3), 567–581.

Maquet, P., Dive, D., Salmon, E., Sadzot, B., Franco, G., Poirrier, R., von Frenckell, R., & Franck, G. (1990). Cerebral glucose utilization during sleep-wake cycle in man determined by positron emission tomography and [18F]2-fluoro-2-deoxy-D-glucose method. Brain Research, 513 (1), 136–143.

Maquet, P., Peters, J., Aerts, J., Delfiore, G., Degueldre, C., Luxen, A., & Franck, G. (1996). Functional neuroanatomy of human rapid-eye-movement sleep and dreaming. Nature, 383 (6596), 163–166.

Martin, J. H. (1996). Neuroanatomy, Text and Atlas. New York: A Simon and Schuster Company.

Mesulam, M. M., Geula, C., Bothwell, M. A., & Hersh, L. B. (1989). Human reticular formation: cholinergic neurons of the pedunculopontine and laterodorsal tegmental nuclei and some cytochemical comparisons to forebrain cholinergic neurons. The Journal of Comparative Neurology, 283 (4), 611–633.

Moga, M. M., Herbert, H., Hurley, K., Yasui, Y., Gray, T. S., & Saper, C. B. (1990). Organizations of cortical, basal forebrain, and hypothalamic afferents to the parabrachial nucleus in the rat. The Journal of Comparative Neurology, 295, 624–661.

Moore, R. Y., & Bloom, F. E. (1979). Central catecholamine neuron systems: anatomy and physiology of the norepinephrine and epinephrine systems. Annual Review of Neuroscience, 2, 113–168.

Moore, R. Y. (1980). The reticular formation: monoamine neuron systems. In J. A. Hobson, & M. A. B. Brazier (Eds.), The reticular formation revisited (pp. 67–81). New York: Raven Press.

Morison, R. S., & Dempsey, E. W. (1942). A study of thalamo-cortical relations. American Journal of Physiology, 135, 281–292.

Moruzzi, G. (1963). Active process in the brainstem during sleep. Harvey Lectures (pp. 233–297). .

Moruzzi, G., Magni, F., Rossi, G. F., & Zanchetti, A. (1959). EEG arousal following inactivation of the lower brainstem by selective injection of barbiturate into the vertebral circulation. Archives Italiennes de Biologie, 97, 33–46.

Moruzzi, G., & Magoun, H. W. (1949). Brain stem reticular formation and activation of the EEG. Electroencephalography and Clinical Neurophysiology, 1, 455–473.

Moskowitz, M. A. (1991). The visceral organ brain: implications for the pathophysiology of vascular head pain. Neurology, 41, 182–196.

Mouton, L. J., & Holstege, G. (1998). Three times as many lamina I neurons project to the periaqueductal gray than to the thalamus – a retrograde tracing study in the cat. Neuroscience Letters, 255 (2), 107–110.

Muller, C. M., Lewandowski, M. H., & Singer, W. (1993). Structures mediating cholinergic reticular facilitation of cortical responses in the cat: effects of lesions in immunocytochemically characterized projections. Experimental Brain Research, 96 (1), 8–18.

Munk, M. H. J., Roelfsema, P. R., König, P., Engel, A., & Singer, W. (1996). Role of reticular activation in the modulation of intracortical synchronization. Science, 272, 271–274.

Newman, D. B., & Ginsberg, C. Y. (1994). Brainstem reticular nuclei that project to the thalamus in rats: a retrograde tracer study. Brain, Behavior and Evolution, 44 (1), 1–39.

Olszewski, J. (1954). Cytoarchitecture of the human reticular formation. In J. F. Delafresnaye (Ed.), Brain mechanisms and consciousness (pp. 54–80). Springfield, Il: Charles C. Thomas.

Olszewski, J., & Baxter, D. (1982). Cytoarchitecture of the human brainstem (2nd ed.). New York: Karger.

Pare, D., Smith, Y., Parent, A., & Steriade, M. (1988). Projections of brainstem core cholinergic and non-cholinergic neurons of cat to intralaminar and reticular thalamic nuclei. Neuroscience, 25 (1), 69–86.

Parent, A., & Steriade, M. (1981). Afferents from the periaqueductal gray, medial hypothalamus and medial thalamus to the midbrain reticular core. Brain Research Bulletin, 7 (4), 411–418.

Paxinos, G., & Huang, X. F. (1995). Atlas of the human brainstem (1st ed.). New York: Academic Press.

Plum, F., & Posner, J. B. (1980). The Diagnosis of Stupor and Coma (3rd ed.). Philadelphia, PA: F.A. Davis Company.

Porrino, L. J., & Goldman-Rakic, P. S. (1982). Brainstem innervation of prefrontal and anterior cingulate cortex in the rhesus monkey revealed by retrograde transport of HRP. Journal of Comparative Neurology, 205 (1), 63–76.

Ramón y Cajal, S. (1894). Estructura del ganglio habénula de los mamíferos. Anales de la Sociedad Española de Historia Natural (Tomo 23).

Rathelot, J. A., & Padel, Y. (1997). Ascending spinal influences on rubrospinal cells in the cat. Experimental Brain Research, 116 (2), 326–340.

Rico, B., & Cavada, C. (1998). Adrenergic innervation of the monkey thalamus: an immunohistochemical study. Neuroscience, 84 (3), 839–847.

Royce, G. J., Bromley, S., & Gracco, C. (1991). Subcortical projections to the centromedian and parafascicular thalamic nuclei in the cat. Journal of Comparative Neurology, 306 (1), 129–155.

Schachter, S. C., & Saper, C. B. (1998). Vagus nerve stimulation. Epilepsia, 39 (7), 677–686.

Schaible, H. G., & Schmidt, R. F. (1983). Activation of groups III and IV sensory units in medial articular nerve by local mechanical stimulation of knee joint. Journal of Neurophysiology, 49 (1), 35–45.

Scheibel, M. E., & Scheibel, A. B. (1966). The organization of the nucleus reticularis thalami: a Golgi study. Brain Research, 1 (1), 43–62.

Schultz, W., Dayan, P., & Montague, P. R. (1997). A neural substrate of prediction and reward. Science, 275 (5306), 1593–1599.

Schultz, W. (1998). Predictive reward signal of dopamine neurons. Journal of Neurophysiology, 80 (1), 1–27.

Shammah-Lagnado, S. J., Negrao, N., Silva, B. A., & Ricardo, J. A. (1987). Afferent connections of the nuclei reticularis pontis oralis and caudalis: a horseradish peroxidase study in the rat. Neuroscience, 20 (3), 961–989.

Smiley, J. F., Subramanian, M., & Mesulam, A. M. (1999). Monoaminergic-cholinergic interactions in the primate basal forebrain. Neuroscience, 93 (3), 817–829.

Steriade, M. (1993). Central core modulation of spontaneous oscillations and sensory transmission in thalamocortical systems. Current Opinion in Neurobiology, 3 (4), 619–625.

Steriade, M., & Deschenes, M. (1984). The thalamus as a neuronal oscillator. Brain Research, 320 (1), 1–63.

Steriade, M., McCormick, D. A., & Sejnowski, T. J. (1993). Thalamocortical oscillations in the sleeping and aroused brain. Science, 262 (5134), 679–685.

Steriade, M., Pare, D., Parent, A., & Smith, Y. (1988). Projections of cholinergic and non-cholinergic neurons of the brainstem core to relay and associational thalamic nuclei in the cat and macaque monkey. Neuroscience, 25 (1), 47–67.

Steriade, M., Parent, A., Ropert, N., & Kitsikis, A. (1982). Zona incerta and lateral hypothalamic afferents to the midbrain reticular core of cat–HRP and electrophysiological study. Brain Research, 238 (1), 13–28.

Vallbo, A., Olausson, H., Wessberg, J., & Norrsell, U. (1993). A system of unmyelinated afferents for innocuous mechanoreception in the human skin. Brain Research, 628 (1–2), 301–304.

Van Bockstaele, E. J., & Aston-Jones, G. (1992). Collateralized projectionis from neurons in the rostral medulla to the nucleus locus coeruleus, the nucleus of the solitary tract and the periaqueductal gray. Neuroscience, 49 (3), 653–668.

Van Bockstaele, E. J., & Aston-Jones, G. (1995). Integration in the ventral medulla and coordination of sympathetic, pain and arousal functions. Clinical and Experimental Hypertension, 17 (1-2), 153–165.

van Domburg, P. H., & Ten Donkelaar, H. J. (1991). The human substantia nigra and ventral tegmental area. A neuroanatomical study with notes on aging and aging diseases. Advances in Anatomy, Embryology and Cell Biology, 121, 1–132.

Villanueva, L., Cliffer, K. D., Sorkin, L. S., Le, B. D., & Willis Jr. W. D. (1990). Convergence of heterotopic nociceptive information onto neurons of caudal medullary reticular formation in monkey (Macaca fascicularis). Journal of Neurophysiology, 63 (5), 1118–1127.

Villanueva, L., Desbois, C., Le Bars, D., & Bernard, J. F. (1998). Organization of diencephalic projections from the medullary subnucleus reticularis dorsalis and the adjacent cuneate nucleus: a retrograde and anterograde tracer study in the rat. Journal of Comparative Neurology, 390 (1), 133–160.

Von Economo, C. F. (1917). Encephalitis lethargica. Wien: W. Braumuller.

Webster, H. H., & Jones, B. E. (1988). Neurotoxic lesions of the dorsolateral pontomesencephalic tegmentum-cholinergic cell area in the cat. II. Effects upon sleep-waking states. Brain Research, 458 (2), 285–302.

Wiberg, M., & Blomqvist, A. (1984). The spinomesencephalic tract in the cat: its cells of origin and termination pattern as demonstrated by the intra-axonal transport method. Brain Research, 291 (1), 1–18.

Wiberg, M., Westman, J., & Blomqvist, A. (1987). Somatosensory projection to the mesencephalon: an anatomical study in the monkey. Journal of Comparative Neurology, 264 (1), 92–117.

Willis, W. D., & Coggeshall, R. E. (1991). Peripheral nerves and sensory receptors. Sensory Mechanisms of the spinal cord. New York: Plenum Press.

Willis, W. D., & Westlund, K. N. (1997). Neuroanatomy of the pain system and the pathways that modulate pain. Journal of Clinical Neurophysiology, 14 (1), 2–31.

Zhang, E. -T., Han, Z. S., & Craig, A. D. (1993). Morphological classes of spinothalamic lamina I neurons in the cat. Journal of Comparative Neurology, 367 (4), 537–549.

6

Introspective physicalism as an approach to the science of consciousness

Anthony I. Jack*, Tim Shallice

Department of Psychology, Institute of Cognitive Neuroscience, University College London,
Alexandra House, 17 Queen Square, London WC1N 3AR, UK

Abstract

Most 'theories of consciousness' are based on vague speculations about the properties of conscious experience. We aim to provide a more solid basis for a science of consciousness. We argue that a theory of consciousness should provide an account of the very processes that allow us to acquire and use information about our own mental states – the processes underlying introspection. This can be achieved through the construction of information-processing models that can account for 'Type-C' processes. Type-C processes can be specified experimentally by identifying paradigms in which awareness of the stimulus is necessary for an intentional action. The Shallice (1988b) framework is put forward as providing an initial account of Type-C processes, which can relate perceptual consciousness to consciously performed actions. Further, we suggest that this framework may be refined through the investigation of the functions of prefrontal cortex. The formulation of our approach requires us to consider fundamental conceptual and methodological issues associated with consciousness. The most significant of these issues concerns the scientific use of introspective evidence. We outline and justify a conservative methodological approach to the use of introspective evidence, with attention to the difficulties historically associated with its use in psychology.
© 2001 Elsevier Science B.V. All rights reserved.

Keywords: Consciousness; Awareness; Executive control; Intentional action; Subjective reports; Introspection; Prefrontal cortex

1. Problems with the science of consciousness

Thirty years ago the attempt to produce scientific accounts of consciousness was a

---

* Corresponding author. Fax: +44-20-7813-2835.
  E-mail address: a.jack@ucl.ac.uk (A.I. Jack).

somewhat disreputable exercise indulged in by just a few (Mandler, 1975; Posner & Klein, 1973; Shallice, 1972). Yet, the last few decades have seen a burgeoning of scientific interest in consciousness. Commentaries on consciousness arise from a bewildering variety of scientific and philosophical traditions. New journals have been created to accommodate the 'interdisciplinary' literature. More significantly, articles on consciousness have begun to appear in the flagship journals of mainstream science (e.g. Tononi & Edelman, 1998). Nonetheless, it will not have escaped the notice of those interested in the topic that we have, at present, nothing resembling a science of consciousness (see Section 2.1).

It is no simple matter to define what makes a field of enquiry a science. However, it is tempting to believe that it is possible to get some indication of what is involved by looking at cases which are generally acknowledged to constitute successful science. The discovery of the double-helix structure of DNA provides a classical example of a scientific identification between a physical entity and a theoretical entity: as Watson and Crick (1953) pointed out, the structure proposed suggested a mechanism for replication, a property clearly essential for the gene. Many scientific theories of consciousness (e.g. Baars, 1988; Crick, 1994; Hameroff & Penrose, 1996; Tononi & Edelman, 1998) seem attractive because they appear to follow a similar model. A physical structure or process is proposed (e.g. global workspace, 40 Hz oscillations, collapse of the quantum wave equation, dynamic core) which is thought to account for some essential properties of consciousness (e.g. availability of information to multiple processes, unity of perceptual experience, non-determinism and non-locality, 'integration' and 'differentiation' of conscious states). There is a gross flaw in the analogy. The basic properties of the gene were already clear. In contrast, the essential properties of conscious experience remain undecided. The very diversity of proposed solutions indicates a problem. And, for each of the theories mentioned, either the claimed properties of conscious experience, or the existence of the physical process which is postulated to account for it, may be called into question. Even when consensus emerges – in this volume there is some convergence on a global workspace model (see Dehaene & Naccache and Dennett) – there is ample room to doubt that it is built on a solid foundation (e.g. Chalmers, 1996).

The theoretical and methodological difficulties facing a science of consciousness run deep. From time to time, a precarious consensus may emerge and cause these difficulties to fade from view. At such times, there is a temptation to forge ahead with experimental and theoretical work – to take advantage of the temporary suspension of critical impediments. Yet, there are eminently practical reasons for attending to the difficulties. Unless they are dealt with explicitly, they are likely to resurface, throwing much previous work into doubt.

2. A history of controversy

A boom and bust cycle of consensus and controversy is evident throughout the history of scientific investigations of consciousness. At the turn of the last century, the founding schools of psychology were confident in the conviction that experience should form the basic subject matter of a scientific psychology. Then intractable disagreements emerged between schools over the measurement and fundamental nature of experience (for a review, see Humphrey, 1951). These paved the way for a very different conception of psychology. Behaviourism (Watson, 1913) determinedly separated scientific accounts from the mental world seemingly known through experience (Wilkes, 1988). Even after the arrival of information processing (e.g. Broadbent, 1958; Miller, 1956), and the subsequent increase in confidence that those mistakes have been placed behind us, there has been a "widespread underestimation of the legacy of behaviourism" (Bisiach, 1988, p. 101). In the last half-century experimental psychology has dogmatically resisted any widespread use of verbal reports as data (Ericsson & Simon, 1993).

The persistence of unresolved difficulties throughout the last 50 years is evident from another boom and bust cycle. Dixon (1971) provides an early history of research in perception without awareness. He shows that belief in the hypothesis of perception without awareness was widespread prior to the influential critique of Ericksen (1960), after which confidence in the hypothesis was slow to recover. He did not foresee that shortly after the publication of his second book on subliminal perception (Dixon, 1981), similar concerns would again throw the field into controversy (Campion, Latto, & Smith, 1983; Holender, 1986; Merikle, 1984; Schacter, 1989; Shanks & St. John, 1994). A third wave of confidence has arrived. It seems very clear to the contributors to this volume that there is good evidence for perception without awareness (e.g. see Dehaene & Naccache, Kanwisher and Merikle, Smilek, & Eastwood). Yet, this confidence does not derive from a theoretical resolution of earlier difficulties. For instance, the Merikle (1984) critique of subjective measures of awareness introduced the influential notion of discrimination as an 'objective' or 'bias-free' measure of awareness. Merikle et al. argue that "subjective measures should be the preferred means for assessing the presence or absence of awareness". Yet, they do not attempt to elucidate the conditions, if any, under which subjective measures might suffer from the problem of bias. If, as we argue, introspective evidence is essential for the investigation of subjective phenomena, then it must be a priority to clearly establish its methodological limitations.[1]

It seems unlikely that there will be yet another collapse of confidence in the hypothesis of perception without awareness, in part because of the influential contribution of neuropsychological evidence from blindsight (Weiskrantz, 1986), as well as other syndromes (Driver & Mattingley, 1998; Milner & Goodale, 1995; Shallice, 1988a). Similarly, the rigorous methodological treatment of verbal protocol procedures given by Ericsson and Simon (1993) is likely to ensure that verbal reports are increasingly recognized as a valuable source of evidence (e.g. Goel, Grafman, Tajik, Gana, & Danto, 1997). Still, these important advances provide only the very first steps towards the formulation of a method for studying consciousness. Numerous conceptual difficulties remain (see Section 1).

---

[1] In fact, we have argued that the charge of 'bias' is misconceived, arising from a misunderstanding about the relevance of Signal Detection Theory to measurements of awareness (Jack, 1998, Ch. 2). Other methodological issues are addressed in Section 5.

2.1. Do we already have a method for studying consciousness?

Much attention has centred recently on the search for the 'neural correlates of consciousness' or NCC. Can this approach of looking for neural activity associated with conscious mental representations elucidate the mechanisms of consciousness? It cannot, but it can still provide useful data.

Crick and Koch (1998) are strong proponents of the NCC approach, boldly stating its motivating assumptions and reviewing relevant experimental research. For them, the strongest experimental model comes from the pioneering work of Logothetis and colleagues (Leopold & Logothetis, 1996; Logothetis & Schall, 1989; Sheinberg & Logothetis, 1997) using binocular rivalry. Two distinct stimuli are presented to each eye. Although the input remains constant, the conscious percept gradually alternates between the two images. Sheinberg and Logothetis (1997) demonstrate a close association between the conscious percept and the activity of 90% of single neurones (sensitive to one of the stimuli when presented alone but not the other) in inferior temporal cortex (IT) and superior temporal sulcus (STS). Many fewer neurones (~35% or less) in earlier visual areas (e.g. V1/V2, V4, V5/MT) show this close association with awareness (Leopold & Logothetis, 1996; Logothetis & Schall, 1989). These experiments suggest a special role for the processing accomplished by neurones in IT and STS in the formation of a conscious percept. Plausibly, this processing is necessary for awareness. However, the NCC approach offers little insight into the nature of this processing. Furthermore, it is implausible that this processing alone could be sufficient for awareness. Crick and Koch (1998) put forward the hypothesis that consciousness arises from an exchange of information between prefrontal cortex and other areas. The NCC approach neither suggested nor is capable of testing this hypothesis.

Frith, Perry, and Lumer (1999) propose extending the NCC approach to include cases such as when the stimulus changes yet subjective experience remains constant. This may provide evidence about the anatomical location of the neural processing sufficient for awareness. Yet, it is again clear that this correlational method can offer little insight into the mechanisms operating in those areas. Frith et al. (1999) note that the approach can only address "the association between consciousness and neural activity and not the more difficult question of how consciousness arises from neural activity". This is well illustrated in Kanwisher's clear discussion of research using the NCC. She uses these findings to argue that neural activity associated with the contents of consciousness is located in modality specific regions of the brain. Yet, she is forced to turn elsewhere in search of an answer to the question of what further activity or processing, over and above mere strength of activation, would be sufficient for awareness.

Most other experimental research has only addressed the question of consciousness indirectly. Psychological and neuropsychological investigations have tended to be concerned with processes that can occur in the absence of awareness (Dehaene et al., 1998; Driver & Mattingley, 1998; Marcel, 1983; Reber, 1997; Weiskrantz, 1986). This work can give us important data about the processes that are not associated with awareness – the functions that are not specific to consciousness. Yet, it does not address the processes that make a particular representation conscious – nor identify the function of consciousness.

3. The function of consciousness

The essential properties of the gene were clear because its function was clear. The gene was posited to explain the inheritance of biological characteristics from one generation to the next. To perform that function, the gene needed (a) to encode a large amount of information and (b) to replicate that information in order to pass it on during reproduction. The function of consciousness is not clear (e.g. Block, 1995). This provides room for the diverging views about its essential properties mentioned in Section 2.

One reason why we do not know the function of consciousness is that there is no clear agreement about what needs to be explained. In other words, there is no coherent body of established empirical data on the phenomenon – equivalent to the findings that existed on inherited characteristics. This paper aims to resolve that problem by outlining a strategy for the collection of data relevant to consciousness (the focus of Sections 4 and 5). In addition, we will suggest methods for advancing our understanding of how these findings can be explained (see Sections 6 and 7).

First, we need to know what we are looking for. We take the view that in trying to locate or find some grounding for the concept of 'consciousness', there is little point in considering organisms, mechanisms or mental processes whose status is a matter of dispute. In the absence of a strong theory, the attribution of 'consciousness' to such borderline cases remains entirely speculative. Instead, a good place to start is with folk-psychological attributions that we use in everyday conversation to describe our own mental states (see Section 8). The term 'conscious' is usually applied in two ways that appear to convey meaningful information. We may say that we are 'conscious of' something, or that we have 'consciously' performed an action.[2]

The question about the function of consciousness can be understood as one about the functional difference between the cases in which we describe ourselves as conscious, and those in which we do not. First, consider the case of being 'conscious of' some information. Driver and Vuilleumier (this volume) are concerned with investigating the processes that determine whether we are 'conscious of' a perceptual stimulus – in other words, the processes underlying attentional selection (see also Merikle et al.). The question of function is different – it is 'What does attention

---

[2] We will attempt to avoid confusion about these two senses of 'conscious' by referring to (perceptual) awareness and intentional action. We regard these as synonyms for the two senses. Are 'consciously' performed actions just actions that we are 'conscious of'? We do not believe so. The phenomenology of perception and action have long been thought of as distinct (e.g. James, 1890). For example, one can be 'conscious of' performing a non-intentional or automatic action. There also appear to be some unusual cases in which subjects lack 'consciousness of' distinctly intentional actions (see Section 5, which discusses Siegler & Stern, 1998).

select for?' In other words, what processes are carried out on this information, which differ from the processes carried out on non-conscious information, and over and above the processes responsible for selection itself? In order to answer this question, we need to focus on characterizing the ways in which conscious information influences thought and behaviour.

Second, consider the case where we perform an action 'consciously' (also 'deliberately' or 'intentionally', or referred to as 'volitional' or 'willed' action) as opposed to 'non-consciously' ('automatically' or in an 'ideo-motor' fashion). The phenomenological distinction between these two cases has been argued to be relevant to the understanding of impairments caused by injury to prefrontal cortex (Norman & Shallice, 1986; Shallice, 1988a). The investigation of the processes underlying consciously performed action, such as those involved in planning, problem solving, inhibition of pre-potent response, and response to novelty, has become a major topic of research. This is variously described as research into 'executive function' and 'control processes'. Whilst the exact characterization of control processes remains a topic for further investigation (see Section 7), it is generally agreed that intentional actions engage processes different to those engaged by less effortful automatic actions.

We will now argue that there is a close conceptual linkage between these two senses of 'conscious', which is highly relevant to the question of the function of consciousness.

There is a fundamental principle that pervades work on perceptual awareness. This is the principle that awareness is necessary for intentional action. In some cases, this principle is explicitly stated in one of a variety of different forms. For instance, Van Gulick (1994) writes "Information needs to be presented to us phenomenally for it to play a role in the choice, initiation, or direction of the intentional action." Crick and Koch (1995, 1998) claim that the function of visual consciousness is "to produce the best current interpretation of the visual scene ... and to make this interpretation directly available ... to the parts of the brain that contemplate and plan voluntary motor output". In other cases, experimental evidence is interpreted as directly supporting this principle (e.g. Merikle et al.). However, by far the most significant role of this principle has been as an assumption underlying methodological approaches to the investigation of awareness. In particular, it is the foundation of the Process Dissociation Procedure (Jacoby, 1991, 1998), on which a large amount of empirical work on perception, memory and learning with and without awareness is now based. The details of this procedure are not relevant here. However, an important point is its use of tasks that place two processes in opposition: a 'conscious' and an 'automatic' process. An example of this sort of task is the Jacoby exclusion task, discussed by Merikle et al. (see also Dehaene & Naccache and Dennett). In the task, subjects are first shown a masked stimulus (e.g. 'table'), and then they are asked to complete a stem (e.g. 'tab...') with any word other than the stimulus. Awareness of a stimulus is inferred from the ability to 'consciously' avoid giving that stimulus as a completion of the stem, whereas non-conscious processing of the stimulus is evidenced by the 'automatic' tendency to repeat the stimulus presented.

We view the principle that awareness is necessary for intentional action as a contingent claim that is broadly[3] supported by a large and growing body of empirical work (e.g. see Dehaene & Naccache, this volume; Jacoby, 1998; Weiskrantz, 1997). Similarly to others, we adopt the principle as a working hypothesis. This principle motivates the approach we suggest for the collection of data on the function of consciousness. However, we do not use this principle in the manner suggested by Jacoby and others. We do not assume that the principle holds and use it as a basis for the measurement of conscious and unconscious information. Nor do we regard the statement of this principle, as it stands, to constitute an adequate specification of the function of consciousness. Instead, we view the principle itself as the focus of investigation. The aim of our investigation is to provide a thorough scientific characterization of this principle, or (as the philosophers might say) to 'cash it out' in information-processing terms.

That a scientific characterization of the principle is essential can be seen by examining the problems that have plagued research in perception without awareness (see Section 2). Here we believe the principle has been misapplied (Jack, 1998). For many years, research in perception without awareness has been hindered by disagreement over the measurement of awareness. It has long been known that subjects are affected by stimuli which they claim not to see (e.g. Ericksen, 1960). However, doubt has been cast on this evidence on the grounds that subjective measures are prone to a number of methodological difficulties. Two methodological issues have been of particular importance. Firstly, there has been a concern that it is not clear what subjects mean when they claim not to be aware of stimuli. Watson (1920) drew attention to this when he wrote about 'the problem of reference'. More recently it has been referred to as the problem of establishing a 'criterion for awareness' (Ericksen, 1960; Reingold & Merikle, 1990). Heavy masking of stimuli can give rise to anomalous visual impressions, which are difficult to characterize (e.g. see Kanwisher). Perhaps subjects say they are not aware of stimuli even when they are aware of partial information which is sufficient to allow them to identify the stimulus (Fuhrer & Ericksen, 1960). Secondly, subjects may not report being aware because, although they have a fleeting visual impression of the stimulus, they lack confidence that this impression is veridical (Merikle, 1984; Shanks & St. John, 1994).

These methodological problems are important (see Section 5). However, they are only problems in principle for experiments purporting to show perception without awareness – there is no empirical evidence indicating that they actually occurred (see Merikle et al.). Furthermore, they might be avoided by the adoption of more

---

[3] As mentioned previously, a great deal of work has simply assumed that this principle holds, and used it as a basis for deciding either that the subject lacks awareness or that a particular sort of action is intentional. Experimental findings may only be read as supporting the principle when there are independent sources of evidence establishing (a) that the subject is perceptually aware (or unaware) and (b) that the action is intentional (or automatic). In general, only evidence relevant to (a) is collected. However, enough is known about the qualitative differences between different types of action in terms of their behavioural properties (e.g. susceptibility to dual task interference) to infer whether an action is intentional or automatic, and thus provide broad support for the principle (see Section 6).

rigorous methods for questioning subjects (e.g. see Dixon, 1971, 1981). By themselves, these possible methodological problems should not have been sufficient to
cast doubt on the large number of studies showing perception without awareness. In
fact, the most influential critiques of perception without awareness (Ericksen, 1960;
Holender, 1986; Merikle, 1984) all contained an extra element. All of these reviews
gave bite to their methodological criticisms by using evidence from other, objective,
measures that appeared to indicate that when subjects said they were not aware of
the stimuli, they actually were aware of them (e.g. discrimination performance in
Ericksen, 1960; Merikle, 1984; as well as other measures in Holender, 1986).

   Why was this objective evidence interpreted as providing evidence about the
subjective state of awareness? The answer is explicit in the original critique of
Ericksen (1960). He assumed that discrimination performance provided a measure
of awareness because the task appeared to involve an intentional response directly
concerning the identity of the stimulus. In summary, the history of perception without awareness shows that methodological concerns about subjective evidence were
lent weight because of the overly crude application of the principle that awareness is
necessary for intentional action. By employing the principle, experimenters
attempted to collect objective rather than subjective evidence of awareness. Yet,
subjects viewed themselves as 'guessing' (e.g. Marcel, 1983), which is clearly
phenomenologically distinct from full intentional action. Evidently, subjective
measures of awareness are more reliable than experimenters' intuitions about
whether an action is intentional or not. It is a mistake, historically motivated by
behaviourism, to suppose that objective evidence is needed to validate subjective
measures of awareness (e.g. as argued by Merikle, 1992; Merikle, Joordens, & Stolz,
1995). Rather, subjective evidence is needed to validate the claim that an objective
measure serves as a measure of awareness. If the principle (that awareness is
necessary for intentional action) is correct, then the fact that subjects report no
awareness of stimuli that they can discriminate at above chance levels must indicate
that discrimination is not an intentional act. Accordingly, we believe that the task of
discriminating between a small set of known stimulus alternatives – a fast low-effort
task involving a one-to-one stimulus-response mapping – can be carried out largely
automatically.

   If the principle that awareness is necessary for intentional action is to be
preserved, and to be of practical use, it needs to be made more precise. We identify
three ways in which this principle needs be better characterized. Progress in all three
is, we believe, essential for a scientific understanding of the function of consciousness. In order to understand why this principle needs further clarification, it is
important to realize that it is not, in the first instance, a principle couched in information-processing terms. This should be clear, since there is at present no definitive
information-processing account of intentional action, and no account had even been
attempted when Ericksen (1960) explicitly appealed to the principle and mistakenly
assumed that awareness is necessary for discrimination.

   We regard this principle as being based primarily on introspective evidence. In
other words, the terms used in the principle (i.e. 'awareness' and 'intentional') are
terms which we come to understand through consideration of, and abstraction from,

the phenomenology associated with our own mental states (see Section 8). A scientific specification of the function of consciousness requires a restatement of this principle in information-processing terms. However, in order that this restatement should count as a scientific specification of the function of consciousness, it is essential that we formulate the information-processing account in such a way that it coheres with our phenomenological understanding of the principle. Therefore, we proceed in two directions. Firstly, we attempt to provide an account of how the principle should be grounded in phenomenology. Secondly, we suggest two ways in which we may generate and/or refine an understanding of the principle in information-processing terms: (i) by providing a more precise specification of the relation between perceptual awareness and intentional action; and (ii) through the search for concepts which can be used to explain intentional action. We discuss next the grounding of the principle in phenomenology, and implications for the collection of data on consciousness. The relation between awareness and intentional action (i) is further discussed in Section 6. There we introduce the Supervisory Attentional System model (Norman & Shallice, 1986; Shallice, 1988a). This model also provides a framework for understanding intentional action (ii). Section 7 discusses how this framework may be further refined.

How can our phenomenological understanding of 'awareness' and 'intentional action' be used to guide the search for the scientific formulation of the principle? This issue touches on a deep and long-standing methodological problem for psychology. Namely, how can we use introspective evidence to inform scientific accounts of mental processes? This issue is discussed in greater depth in Section 5. This discussion is central to the project we outline here, since we regard introspective evidence as essential for the generation of solid empirical results on the function of consciousness. In our proposal, introspective evidence is necessary to identify certain processes, which we shall call Type-C processes, that can only operate on information available for report. In addition, introspective evidence may help in the search for tasks involving intentional action. In our framework, the principle that awareness is necessary for intentional action can be more precisely stated as the hypothesis that tasks involving intentional action recruit Type-C processes, whereas automatic actions do not.[4]

We regard the use of introspective evidence to measure perceptual awareness as largely unproblematic, provided certain methodological precautions are taken. The reason that introspective reports concerning states of perceptual awareness are unproblematic is that these reports are closely related to objective judgements

---

[4] Could there be cases in which Type-C processes operate, and yet where there are no 'conscious contents'? We would allow such cases. Our claim is that the operation of a Type-C process on information is a necessary and sufficient condition for awareness of that information. However, there may be cases in which a Type-C process operates without operating on any information. In other words, there may be special types of 'unguided' intentional action for which perceptual awareness is not necessary (for an analogous concept, see Humphrey, 1951). This would be our interpretation of cases where subjects are asked to select an action (from a range of possible actions) without having any information on which to base the selection (as reviewed by Frith, 2000). For a related discussion of awareness and executive control see Badgaiyan (2000).

concerning stimuli presented. For instance, a judgement of awareness may be equivalent to a judgement about the presence of a stimulus (Cowey & Stoerig, 1995). Thus, judgements of perceptual awareness are well grounded – it is relatively easy to establish what subjects mean by their reports. The use of introspective evidence to identify instances of intentional action is much less straightforward – it is much harder to establish what subjects mean by the claim that an action was intentional (see Section 5). Nonetheless, we believe it is important to attempt to 'anchor' our understanding of intentional action, by identifying what we regard as the paradigm example of a conscious act. This is the act of introspection itself, i.e. the act of reflecting upon, imagining, or comparing between one's own mental states. Some acts of introspection involve making a judgement about one's own mental state, and result in the production of a response that indicates the judgement made (e.g. 'the coffee tastes more bitter than I remember the last time I tried it'; see Dennett, 1988). We regard this as the paradigm case in which awareness is necessary for intentional action. For in this case, it is clear that the phenomenology associated with the perceptual experience plays a causal role in the production of response. In our view, we will have a theory of consciousness when, and only when, we can provide a detailed information-processing account of all[5] the processes involved in making judgements of this sort.

At present, we are a long way from providing any such account. How are we going to get there? Our approach rests on the assumption that mental states that appear, introspectively, to be related are likely to be functionally related (see Section 8).

Some 'Higher Order Thought' theorists hold that mental states are conscious just if we are introspecting, i.e. only when we are having thoughts about that state (Rosenthal, 1986). However, Ryle (1949, p. 164) remarks that "introspection is an attentive operation and one which is only occasionally performed, whereas consciousness is supposed to be a constant element of all mental processes". Whilst we agree on the special theoretical status given to introspection, our view is different from Rosenthal's. We explain the impression that we are virtually constantly conscious by positing that the processes that underlie introspection are closely functionally related to the processes that operate during the performance of other intentional mental operations. According to our view, to be conscious of information, it is sufficient for any Type-C process to be effectively operating on that information.[6] As will become clear in Section 4, Type-C processes are involved in many judgements that only explicitly concern the world outside the subject (e.g. fine discriminations of colour shade). Thus, on our view, there is no requirement for

---

[5] It is important to appreciate that an account that merely serves to explain the origin of the difference in perceptual appearance, i.e. why the coffee seems more bitter, is not going to be sufficient. Critically, what we want is an account of the more general processes responsible for comparing any current experience with any past experience, and translating the resulting information into a form capable of guiding response. For some preliminary remarks, see Section 6.

[6] Note that it becomes meaningless to discuss the temporal aspects of phenomenal processes at a finer grain than the operation of individual Type-C processes (see Dennett, 1991).

the subject to be making a judgement 'about' their own mental state in order to be conscious.[7]

It is important to note that introspection, as understood here, cannot be defined purely behaviourally – for instance, as occurring whenever subjects make reports about their own mental states. Along with Ryle (see above), we regard introspection as an attentive activity, requiring mental effort and resources. We follow Ericsson and Simon (1993) in their claim that some forms of concurrent verbal protocol can be carried out largely automatically. This may occur (e.g. whilst solving an arithmetic problem) when subjects are simply required to verbalize their conscious contents as they naturally occur, and where the reported contents (e.g. numbers) are of a form that can easily be converted into language. Whilst these reports constitute a form of subjective evidence, in the sense that there is no direct method of verifying their accuracy, their production (after practice) does not appear to require subjects to make introspective judgements (for a closely related claim, see Weiskrantz, 1997, p. 75).

4. Type-C processes

In this section we provide an outline for a cognitive research project. As mentioned in Section 3, the aim of this project is to provide data in need of explanation by a theory of consciousness. Type-C processes are defined as processes that can only operate effectively on information when normal subjects report awareness of that information. The aim is to identify these Type-C processes by providing examples of tasks which are well specified in two senses: (i) the Type-C process should play a role in the production of responses which can be experimentally isolated; and (ii) the task should reliably recruit the Type-C process (i.e. it should not be possible to perform the task accurately except by recruiting the Type-C process). Candidate processes may be identified, and then tested, by applying the principle that there must be no situations in which a Type-C process can occur in the absence of reported awareness of the relevant content.[8] Later in the section, we provide an initial list of seven Type-C processes. Only four of these, listed as 'experimentally characterized Type-C processes' (Section 4.2), are well specified in the two senses outlined above. The other three 'pre-experimentally characterized

---

[7] It may turn out, on closer inspection, that all Type-C processes do in fact involve the subject making a judgement about their own mental state. According to Rosenthal, we might overlook this because we can fail to notice that we are having a thought about our own mental state. On his scheme, noticing that we have these thoughts would require us to have a thought about a thought about our own mental state. We allow for Rosenthal's position, but we do not assume it is correct.

[8] In theory, it may be possible to interfere specifically with the Type-C processes underlying introspective report but not with other Type-C processes. Thus, the finding that a process can operate when subjects are unable to report the relevant content does not logically entail that the process is not Type-C. In practice, any such finding in normal subjects must be taken to indicate the process is not Type-C unless a strong a priori case can be made for the interference being specific to report. Otherwise, the hypothesis that a process is Type-C would be unfalsifiable.

Type-C processes' (Section 4.1) are included because of their central theoretical importance.

Although often overlooked, it is self-evident that a full theory of consciousness should give an account of the processes which specifically operate on reportable information, and underlie its various behavioural effects – in particular the processes involved in the actual production of reports (see also Dennett, 1991, p. 255; where he calls this the 'Hard Question'). However, opinions differ as to the theoretical status of such an account. Some theorists (e.g. Crick & Koch, 1990) regard these processes as subsidiary to the processes that actually give rise to or constitute a state of awareness. In the terminology of Weiskrantz (1997, p. 203), this would be the same as the view that Type-C processes merely enable the subject to use or communicate conscious information. The alternative view would be that Type-C processes themselves endow awareness. Weiskrantz (1997, p. 76) suggests that "it is the very achieving of the ability to make a commentary of any particular event that is what gives rise to awareness". Similarly, our view is that all Type-C processes (including, of course, those involved in making commentaries or introspective reports) share some basic information-processing operations, and that those operations actually give rise to awareness. Consequently, we regard the project of identifying Type-C processes as essential for the collection of further empirical data on consciousness. Through further investigations of Type-C processes, we aim to get a 'fix' on these basic information-processing operations. Nonetheless, the 'endowing' view is not assumed by the project outlined in this section. This view would need to be abandoned if, for instance, it is shown that there is no single functional distinction that distinguishes between Type-C processes and other processes (for a related possibility, see Allport, 1988).

A theoretically important subset of Type-C processes are those that actually involve making an introspective judgement. One way of attempting to identify tasks of this sort is by looking for tasks that appear, introspectively, to involve thoughts about one's own mental states. However, how can objective evidence be used to identify tasks involving an introspective judgement? In certain cases, a type of task may already have been extensively investigated behaviourally. In this case, the hypothesis that the task involves an introspective judgement may be supported because it helps to explain patterns of behavioural data in a number of experiments. A strong example of this sort is provided by Koriat and Goldsmith (1996). They present an argument for the existence of and importance of recognizing metamemory processes in free recall. Koriat and Goldsmith's claim, which they support empirically, is that, in free recall tasks as opposed to forced-choice recognition tasks, subjects control the production of items on the basis of judgements they make concerning their own recall accuracy. Experiments involving attributions of perceptual fluency (Jacoby & Whitehouse, 1989; Mandler, Nakamura, & Van Zandt, 1987; Whittlesea, 1993) provide a second example where the hypothesis that some tasks involve an introspective judgement helps to explain patterns of data across many experiments (Bornstein & D'Agostino, 1992; Jack, 1998).

Even where evidence from a large number of behavioural experiments is not available, it is sometimes possible to make a strong case for the claim that a task involves an introspective judgement. Consider the Jacoby exclusion task discussed in Section 3. It is possible to make a case, supported by objective evidence, that subjects typically understand the instructions for this task as involving a judgement about their own state of awareness. In other words, subjects understand the instructions to be 'If you are aware of the masked word, do not give it as a completion to the stem. Otherwise, give the first word that comes to mind.' (Jack, 1998).[9]

We now provide an initial list of Type-C processes.

4.1. Pre-experimentally characterized Type-C processes

1. 'Conscious reflection' – the process which occurs when we reflect upon the nature of an experience, and which underlies the ability to make judgements based on the nature of that experience (e.g. judgements of familiarity and perceptual clarity; Whittlesea, Jacoby, & Girard, 1990). This process is held to underlie the ability to discriminate between mental states, as well as discriminations concerning the world external to the subject which require a careful consideration of the phenomenology associated with perception (e.g. fine discriminations of colour). A subset of cases will further involve 'meta-awareness' – the process that occurs when we have the thought that we have experienced a particular conscious mental state (e.g. the thought 'I was aware of x'). This process is held to underlie the ability to categorize one's own states of awareness.
2. The process which underlies the ability to freely report the identity of an unanticipated but known stimulus at the time of presentation, and which occurs when we have the subjective sense of spontaneously recognizing or 'noticing' (Bowers, 1984) a stimulus. We take this to be a pre-experimental process as it is presumed to be the same process whatever type of stimulus is being recognized.
3. The process underlying the re-experiencing of a past event held in memory. This is a process of 'autonoetic consciousness' involving 'ecphory', in the terminology of Tulving (1983), and is held to be the basis of 'remember' as opposed to 'know' judgements (Gardiner, Ramponi, & Richardson-Klavehn, 1998). In addition, the processes underlying the use of information from episodic memory for the strategic regulation of performance (Koriat & Goldsmith, 1996), checking the veridicality of recalled information (Burgess & Shallice, 1996a), or for the planning of action (Schank, 1982).

---

[9] Jack (1998) shows that when subjects are given instructions that stress the need to avoid repeating the word presented, regardless of whether or not they consciously see it, they adopt additional strategies. For instance, when they cannot see the masked word, they complete the stem with unusually long and infrequent words that are unlikely to match the high-frequency words presented. This illustrates a distinction between understanding the task instructions as purely objective (always try to avoid giving the masked word), as opposed to understanding them as having a subjective component (only avoid repeating the masked word if you are aware of it).

4.2. Experimentally characterized Type-C processes

4. The process involved in encoding material into episodic memory – the process, occurring at the time of stimulus presentation, which enables the later process of retrieval to occur, in which we have the subjective sense of recollecting the perceptual event (autonoetic consciousness; Tulving, 1983). This process is held to underlie the ability to retrospectively report the identity of the earlier stimulus in, say, a free recall task. This process is also a prerequisite for above chance performance on some recognition tasks (e.g. Mandler et al., 1987), although it is not for others. On the two-process theory of recognition (Mandler, 1980), the critical factor would be whether the subject is willing to make their response purely on a feeling of familiarity. Familiarity can be evoked by perceptual fluency (see process 6 below and Merikle & Reingold, 1991).
5. The process of 'exclusion' involved in the Jacoby exclusion task, discussed in previous sections (see also Merikle et al.).
6. The process underlying the discounting of perceptual fluency due to prior exposure of a stimulus. This process is held to underlie the abolition of various 'perceptual fluency' effects, which have been shown to influence judgements of familiarity, preference, perceptual clarity, brightness and darkness (e.g. Mandler et al., 1987; Whittlesea et al., 1990). For instance, Jacoby and White-house (1989) show that subjects are more likely to judge that a word has been presented in a previous study episode if it is presented, heavily masked, just prior to the judgement being made. Subjects do not show the same bias when the stimulus is lightly masked and clearly visible. In the second case, awareness of the word presented allows them to discount the effect of fluency on their familiarity judgement. Bornstein and D'Agostino (1994) and Whittlesea (1993) provide experimental evidence for the generalization of this effect to other task contexts.
7. The process underlying the addition of stimuli to a discriminatory response set. Jack (1998) investigated the situation where subjects have to identify single letters in a perceptual masking experiment. Subjects were told that four different stimuli were to be presented; however, they were only familiar with the identity of three of these stimuli. The fourth stimulus was initially presented only heavy masked, but later in the experiment it was also presented under light masking conditions. Subjects were able to discriminate the three familiar stimuli well above chance under all masking conditions throughout the experiment. However, they were only able to discriminate the fourth unanticipated stimulus once it had been consciously identified in the lightly masked condition. Incorporation of the stimulus into the response set required conscious identification.

If the current approach is correct, the tasks listed above must all involve at least one component process, such that awareness of a particular content is necessary for the operation of the process. For each of the seven examples, there are no situations known where the Type-C process can occur without the relevant content being available for report. This is critical. A basic assumption underlying the approach is: if on some occasions subjects carry out a task in the absence of awareness of particular information (e.g. the identity of a masked word), then we conclude that Type-C processes are not necessary for processing the information in that manner (e.g. semantic priming); any awareness of the relevant content on other occasions is taken to be due to the operation, on those occasions, of one or more additional processes. Awareness of a word involves processes over and above those mediating semantic priming effects, as shown for instance by Marcel (1983).

We have not included in our list one process hypothesized by Merikle et al. (this volume) (see also Cheesman & Merikle, 1986; Merikle et al., 1995) to require awareness. This is the process held responsible for the facilitation of reaction time due to stimulus redundancy in their modified Stroop task. Other experiments indicate that closely related effects occur in the absence of awareness (Jack, 1998; Miller, 1987; Shanks & Johnstone, 1997). Clearly, it is important to make an effort to investigate any suggestion that a candidate process can operate when the relevant information is not available for report. The historical example of discrimination indicates that tasks that initially appear to involve an intentional action may still not qualify as Type-C processes (see Section 3).

The division between experimental and pre-experimental Type-C processes is not simply a division between processes that are and are not engaged in common experimental paradigms. The three pre-experimental processes listed, and their variations, occur frequently whilst subjects are carrying out a wide range of experimental paradigms. In many cases, the operation of these pre-experimental processes may be the immediate precursor of response (e.g. process 1 in the experiments of Mandler et al., 1987). However, it is only for the tasks listed under experimental Type-C processes (Section 4.2) that an experimental manipulation affects whether or not the Type-C process operates, and where the operation of the Type-C process is clearly reflected in performance. Thus, the analysis of tasks that meet the criteria for experimental Type-C processes may inform hypotheses concerning the processes involved in introspection. An initial goal of our proposed project would be to extend the list of experimental Type-C processes through the identification of tasks that similarly isolate the pre-experimental Type-C processes (Section 4.1). In addition, it may be possible to isolate other Type-C processes using tasks that involve problem solving, planning, reasoning, rule generation and verification,[10] inhibition of pre-potent responses, correction of action slips, following instructions, and response to novel situations.

5. Introspective evidence

In Section 4, we distinguished between our belief that Type-C processes endow consciousness and the view that Type-C processes merely enable the communica-

---

[10] Explicit, as opposed to implicit, learning may be accounted for by the operation of these processes, and the subsequent use of inferred information in the creation of schemas for action (see also Shanks & St. John, 1994; St. John & Shanks, 1997).

tion and/or use of information that has already reached consciousness. In either case, introspective evidence is needed to identify types of behaviour that can only occur when information is available for introspective report. Nonetheless, according to the 'endowing' view the primary goal of a theory of consciousness should be to account for particular sorts of objectively observable behaviour. More specifically, the theoretical framework we outline in Section 6 aims to provide an initial account of the processes that distinguish one set of objectively observable behaviours (which can only be carried out when information is available for report) from another (which can be carried out when information is not available for report).

In contrast, most theorists tend to assume the 'enabling' view, and adopt a strategy that relies on introspective evidence in a different way. This strategy involves the identification of a very limited set of specific properties of experience. A theory of consciousness is then proposed in which particular mechanisms or processes are claimed to account for these subjective properties. The scientific theories of consciousness listed in Section 1 all adopt this approach. For example, Tononi and Edelman (1998) put forward their dynamic core hypothesis partly on the basis that it accounts for the observation that "each conscious state comprises a single "scene" that cannot be decomposed into independent components".

Philosophers have also argued that experience has peculiar properties, although they frequently do so in order to argue that consciousness presents a special problem for scientific accounts. For example, Block (1995) argues that scientific attempts to account for the functional role of conscious information ('access-consciousness') do not address the phenomenological properties of conscious experience ('phenomenological-consciousness').

We are sceptical of accounts that place such a heavy burden on analyses of such individual properties of conscious experience. Our concern is that these properties are highly abstract and based on the consideration of introspective evidence alone. It is hazardous to place any reliance on generalizations derived from experience unless they can be validated by objective evidence. This is because the principal problem with the use of introspective evidence is that it is prone to misinterpretation. This is dramatically illustrated by the history of psychophysics.

In an important book, Laming (1997) reviews the history of the measurement of sensation, beginning with Fechner. He finds that unjustified interpretations of subjects' reports have caused the field to be mired in controversy right up to the present day. It was Fechner's conception of a 'physics of the mind' and search for psychophysical laws (relating physical dimensions of the stimulus to subjective dimensions) which led to the emergence of experimental psychology in the middle of the nineteenth century. Nonetheless, Laming argues that Fechner was fundamentally mistaken in "the implicit assumption that sensation admitted measurement on any kind of continuum at all". In a thorough analysis, Laming outlines where each of a series of psychophysical laws breaks down, from the Weber–Fechner law (which accounts for comparisons between stimuli) to Stevens' power law (which attempts to describe judgements of absolute magnitude). He concludes: "The evidence so far to hand does not support any intermediate continuum at the psychological level of description which might reasonably be labelled 'sensation'. While the underlying pattern of sensory neural activity is obviously germane to the perceptual process, not even that can be identified as 'sensation', essentially because there is no corresponding psychological entity. Although this rejoinder might seem no more than a philosophical quibble, it does matter in practice. Experiments by different investigators, seeking to measure the perception of that neural activity as sensation by different methods, have found no basis for agreement."

Laming advises scientists as follows, "...without independent corroboration, introspective evidence should not be taken at face value. Psychologists who disregard this dictum are liable to involve themselves in artificial arguments... [T]he seeming impossibility of such corroboration does not mean that scientists should proceed without it; it means, instead, that the question addressed lacks the empirical basis needed for an answer to be agreed and that scientists should not proceed at all."[11]

The philosopher David Chalmers has argued that conscious experience cannot be captured by the 'third-person' language of science (Chalmers, 1996; also see Dennett in this volume). He proposes instead that a different sort of language should be developed – one that captures our 'first-person' experience. According to Chalmers, these authentic first-person accounts might then be related to physical states, which he believes have a one-to-one correspondence with conscious states. Yet, the project that Chalmers proposes anew appears to be identical to Fechner's.

There is a simple and fundamental reason why all attempts to get at the 'raw data' of experience fail: introspective evidence always arrives already interpreted. In other words, all descriptions of experience, no matter how basic, carry implicit theoretical commitments of one sort or another. In order to understand and describe an experience, subjects need to employ concepts and categories (i.e. mental state concepts, see Section 7.1). Thus, introspective reports may be seen as the product of two factors: firstly the 'raw data', which the subject has access to via introspection, and secondly the conceptual framework, or 'model', which the subject uses to interpret that data. The extent to which subjects are correct depends on the validity of their model for interpreting the 'raw data'. As the history of psychophysics illustrates, introspective reports may be highly misleading if the self-reflective concepts used by subjects rely on the wrong implicit assumptions about brain organization and function.

The use of objective evidence to inform scientific accounts also depends on interpretation. Kuhn (1996) eloquently argues that the observations that are used to support theories in physics are always theory-laden. Similarly, objective behavioural data, for example from a perceptual discrimination task, are of little use unless they can be interpreted as representing a genuine attempt by the subject to comply with the task instructions. Only then can percent correct or reaction time

---

[11] See Laming (1997, pp. 208–209). This needs some clarification. The point is not that, in practice, it should be simple to find objective evidence to corroborate valid hypotheses based on introspective evidence. It is often hard to find evidence for scientific theories. However, there is an onus to establish that any given interpretation can be corroborated in principle by objective evidence. If this cannot be convincingly established then the interpretation must be regarded as questionable.

measures inform hypotheses about the information processing taking place. The critical difference between introspective and objective evidence is that with objective evidence it is possible to go back to the raw data. For instance, a closer examination of subjects' responses may support or invalidate the assumption that they were following the task instructions. This makes it easier to resolve disputes over the interpretation of objective data. In the absence of this safeguard, great care is needed to ensure that interpretations of introspective evidence are well grounded.

How, then, can introspective evidence be used to inform scientific accounts? Essentially, there are two areas for investigation. First, we may attempt to use introspective evidence to examine the self-reflective subsystems – the processes responsible for the 'model' subjects have for understanding their own mental states – and the effect these processes have on thought and behaviour. Second, we may attempt to use introspective evidence to distinguish between mental states – by using the information that is made available to reflective subsystems when subjects introspect.

The processes involved in reflection remain poorly understood. However, an initial attempt to examine the operation of the self-reflective subsystems can be seen in a recent experiment on self-reports of strategy use in children (Siegler & Stern, 1998). In this study, children (around 9 years old) are given arithmetic problems of the form 'Y + X − X ='. Initially the children solve this problem by first adding 'X' to 'Y', and then subtracting 'X' from the result. However, with experience the children stop performing any arithmetic calculations and simply state the answer as 'Y'. The experimenter can reliably discern the strategy used from the response time. The interesting finding arises from children's reports when they are asked how they solved the problem. Once the strategy is well established, children reliably report its use. However, for the first few trials on which they use the strategy, children report counting just as they had before. In other words, the children appeared to lack awareness of their own discovery and use of the strategy. This study shows that, at least during development, repeated experience of a mental state or process is necessary before the model is updated to allow accurate introspective identification of that state or process. This is surprising, since slow and deliberate processes such as arithmetic calculation and strategy application are usually thought of as directly available for report (Ericsson & Simon, 1993). We take it to support our broad distinction between the information available to introspective processes and the model used to interpret that information.

How can introspective evidence be used to distinguish between mental states? According to the view presented here, introspective processes have access to information concerning limited functional aspects of mental states. However, we do not (usually) interpret this information as information about our functional states. Instead, we interpret this information using our own implicit folk-psychological theories. These conceptual frameworks may be developed through consideration of one's own experiential states and attempts to relate this information to observations of behaviour, as well as through conversation with others. Moreover, there will be interpersonal differences in the conceptual frameworks or 'models' used by subjects, even to the extent that subjects may mean different things when they use the same mental state terms (Watson, 1920). In other words, different subjects may use different criteria for response in introspective report tasks (Ericksen, 1960; Kahneman, 1968; Reingold & Merikle, 1990). The resulting 'self-portrait' of the subject's mental state will remain obscure, due to difficulties in understanding their 'palette' of self-reflective concepts.

We propose that the critical process necessary for the productive scientific use of introspective reports is that of replacing or refining the subject's model for understanding their own mental states. There are two ways of doing this. The first involves providing the subject with a well specified model for interpreting their own experience. The second involves re-interpreting the subject's reports in terms of a testable functional theory. The first of these methods can be productively used to yield quantifiable empirical data. The second can be used in exploratory studies, which are concerned with the generation and refinement of theoretical accounts.

In some situations, it is a conceptually simple matter to ensure that subjects are using a well specified model for interpreting their reports, provided the relevant states can be reliably elicited. This is well illustrated by the pioneering work of Logothetis and colleagues on bistable percepts, involving the collection of introspective reports from primates (Leopold & Logothetis, 1996; Logothetis & Schall, 1989; Sheinberg & Logothetis, 1997). All that it is necessary to do is to elicit the relevant states, and teach subjects to respond accordingly. This procedure provides subjects with reference points that serve to guide their responses, thus ensuring that subject and experimenter have a common understanding of what is meant by the report response. Thus, Logothetis and colleagues trained primates to respond to visual stimuli presented in isolation. Once the primates could reliably discriminate between the two stimuli, the responses could be used to infer the contents of awareness during binocular rivalry – when the two stimuli were presented simultaneously, one to each eye.

In practice, two sorts of difficulties arise with this procedure. Firstly, anomalous conscious states may arise that are hard to categorize (see Kanwisher). Secondly, the criterion for response may change with time and/or experience. The first of these difficulties can be tackled by employing an initial development phase, in which subjects give free reports of the phenomenology involved in the task. This allows the generation of a range of relevant categories. In binocular rivalry, parts of both images can sometimes be seen simultaneously during an intermediate phase when neither image is dominant. Logothetis and colleagues circumvented this problem by creating images which, when presented alone, were indistinguishable from this experience. The primates were also trained using these images. The solution to the second problem is also illustrated in the experiments of Logothetis and colleagues. During testing, they occasionally used 'catch trials' in which the non-rivalrous images used in training were presented. This allowed them to check that the primates were maintaining the intended criterion for response.

It should be clear from the example above that rigorous methods can be available for specifying the model that subjects use to categorize states of awareness, if two conditions apply. The first is that the relevant conscious states can be reliably elicited by varying the stimulus and/or experimental conditions. The second is that the introspective reports, concerning the subject's state of awareness, are closely related to objective judgements, concerning the world outside the subject. Thus, in the example above, the introspective report concerning the contents of consciousness was effectively equivalent to an objective judgement concerning the stimulus presented. Two other examples of equivalence are given. The introspective judgement of being 'aware of something' is effectively equivalent to an objective judgement of presence or absence. The introspective judgement of being 'aware of a word' is effectively equivalent to an objective judgement of whether a word or a non-word (letter string) was presented.[12] Introspective reports concerning states of perceptual awareness are not generally problematic, since these two conditions can usually be met.

It is also clear historically that verbal reports obtained from 'think aloud' protocols can be a valuable source of evidence in other cases (Ericsson & Simon, 1993). This use of introspective evidence appears to be successful for two reasons. Firstly, the instructions for 'think aloud' protocols discourage subjects from providing elaborate interpretations of the mental states they report, thus helping to ameliorate the difficulties associated with rationalization (Gazzaniga, 1985; Nisbett & Wilson, 1977). Secondly, these verbal protocols are used in the development of functional accounts of the processing that the subject is carrying out in the situation. Accounts of this sort may be tested by standard scientific means. For example, in a study of autobiographical memory, Burgess and Shallice (1996a) used a complex retrospective commentary procedure in which subjects produced short descriptions, or even single words, for each experience as they attempted to recall. The tape was then replayed and the subject elaborated on the introspective responses they had produced a minute or two before. The reports were then categorized by the experimenters into 25 types of thought element selected on the basis of pilot studies. A model – a development of that of Norman and Bobrow (1976) – was produced to account for both qualitative and quantitative aspects of the memory retrieval protocols. The model was then applied to a number of findings from objective neuropsychological investigations (Burgess & Shallice, 1996a; Dab, Claes, Morais, & Shallice, 1999; see also the related position of Schacter, Curran, Galluccio, Milberg, & Bates, 1996) and cognitive neuroscience (Fletcher, Shallice, Frith, Frackowiak, & Dolan, 1998; Henson, Shallice, & Dolan, 1999).

In other cases, for example involving neuropsychological and psychiatric disorders, introspective evidence can only be used to inform scientific accounts when the experimenter adopts a different interpretation to the patient. Critically, these cases require the experimenter to do considerable work eliciting reports in order to understand and avoid the erroneous interpretations arrived at by patients. Cytowic illustrates this point very well in his discussion of the work of Heinrich Kluver, who

---

[12] These examples are chosen because they have been confused in some accounts of perception without awareness. For instance, Holender (1986) interprets evidence of the ability to detect the presence of word stimuli as evidence that subjects are aware of the identity of the words. In doing so he ignores earlier work showing that subjects can base presence/absence responses on perceived duration of the stimulus sequence (Fehrer & Biederman, 1962) and/or apparent motion (Kahneman, 1967).

carried out extensive work attempting to understand the experience of hallucinators. Cytowic (1997) reports that Kluver was initially "frustrated by the vagueness with which subjects described their experience, their eagerness to yield uncritically to cosmic or religious interpretations, to 'interpret' or poetically embroider the experience in lieu of straightforward but concrete description, and their tendency to be overwhelmed and awed by the 'indescribableness' of their visions". Yet, Kluver (1966) eventually identified three classes of visual pathology: (i) 'form' constants, which describe hallucinated patterns, e.g. grating, lattice, honeycomb or chessboard patterns; (ii) alterations in the number, size and shape of perceived objects; and (iii) alterations in spatiotemporal relations between objects. Ffytche and Howard (1999) have further extended this work, illustrating the consistency of these and other pathological reports across a range of clinical conditions, and reviewing neuroscience research that may be relevant to their explanation. For the case of synaesthesia, Cytowic (1997, p. 24) summarizes the attitude that is required in order to reduce introspective reports to scientifically useful descriptions as follows: "Though synaesthetes are often dismissed as being poetic, it is we who must be cautious about unjustifiably interpreting their comments." We regard abstract properties of awareness, derived solely from introspective evidence, as a dangerous base for a science of consciousness. Nonetheless, when introspective evidence is carefully collected and interpreted in specific experimental situations, then it can be of considerable scientific value.

6. A framework for understanding conscious processes

In the information-processing accounts of consciousness developed in the 1970s the unitary nature and control functions of consciousness were explained in terms of the involvement of a limited capacity higher-level processing system (Mandler, 1975; Posner & Klein, 1973). With the diversification of processing systems that cognitive psychology, cognitive neuropsychology and cognitive neuroscience have produced and the realization that processing systems are often informationally encapsulated (Fodor, 1983), it became less plausible to associate the unitary characteristics of consciousness with the operation of any single processing system. In Shallice (1988b) an alternative approach was put forward. It was argued that a number of high-level systems have a set of characteristics in common which distinguish them from the run of cognitive systems which realize routine informationally encapsulated processes. It was held that the contrast between the effective operation of these systems and those realizing informationally encapsulated processes corresponded in phenomenological terms to that between conscious and non-conscious processes.

This approach to consciousness was based on the model of Norman and Shallice (1986) which was originally introduced to explain results from experimental psychological studies on attention and the impairments of patients with prefrontal lesions, the domain to which it has primarily been applied (Della Malva, Stuss, D'Alton, & Willmer, 1993; Shallice, 1988a; Shallice & Burgess, 1996). The

Norman–Shallice model is concerned with action selection. It has three main processing levels. The lowest is that of special-purpose processing subsystems, each specialized for particular types of operation, such as translating from orthographic to phonological representations. Second, there are held to be a large number of action and thought schemas, one for each level of each well learned routine task or subtask. Schemas are selected for operation through a process involving mutually inhibitory competition (contention scheduling). The operation of schemas in a particular situation is dependent on the way their arguments are filled, which is done using representations from other systems, e.g. the perceptual systems. (See Cooper and Shallice (2000) for technical details and simulations of relevant neuropsychological disorders, and Dehaene and Changeux (1997) for a closely related simulation.) Third, to cope with non-routine situations, an additional system – the Supervisory Attentional System (SAS) – provides modulating activating input to schema in contention scheduling.

How does this model relate to consciousness? On the current approach Type-C processes have the following characteristics. (1) They involve the Supervisory System. (2) They lead directly to the selection in contention scheduling of a schema for thought or action, plus its arguments. This selection leads to action and/or to a qualitative change in the operation of lower-level special-purpose processing systems. By contrast, a non-conscious process is one which does not directly involve output from the Supervisory System and where its effects lead to only quantitative changes in the on-line processing systems. On this view, awareness of a particular content will involve either the triggering of a schema, or the modification of a pre-existing schema. However, once a schema is selected, and provided that schema does not conflict with a strongly established schema for action (as in cases requiring inhibition of pre-potent response), then action may proceed without any transfer of information from the SAS.

For some of the Type-C processes discussed previously, the relation to the SAS model is straightforward. An excellent example of the involvement of the Supervisory System is the Jacoby exclusion task (process 5). This case appears to involve the inhibition of a strong pre-potent response, namely the tendency to repeat the word previously presented. In this respect, the task is closely analogous to the Hayling B task (Burgess & Shallice, 1996b), originally used as a neuropsychological test of frontal function. However, the Jacoby task operates in the orthographic lexical domain while the Hayling B task requires the subject to give a completion to a sentence frame that makes no sense in the context of the frame. Tasks involving the inhibition of a strong pre-potent response do not appear to become automated with practice. Therefore, this sort of Type-C process is relatively easy to operationalize in an experimental setting (Jacoby, 1991).

Other Type-C processes are more complex. Some examples require a more precise specification of the relation between perceptual awareness and intentional action (as discussed in Section 3). Take the apparently direct perception of an external stimulus. The first case we consider illustrates the need to distinguish what the subject is 'aware of' – for instance, the presence of a stimulus, as opposed to its location or identity. Studies on blindsight show that awareness of the location of the stimulus is not necessary for accurate performance on a simple pointing task when subjects are asked to guess. Nonetheless, in this case, awareness of the presence of the stimulus, which has to be provided by an auditory cue, is necessary for the initiation of the pointing action (Weiskrantz, 1997). On the model the blindsight subject requires input via the SAS to initiate a pre-existing schema for pointing; however, once that schema is initiated, non-conscious information held in special-purpose processing systems can serve to guide the action.

A second case, the experiment by Jack (1998) involving the discrimination of masked letters (process 7 in the list of Type-C processes), illustrates the critical role of prior experience. In that experiment, subjects were initially unable to discriminate a heavily masked stimulus which was not initially specified to be a member of the response set. However, as soon as the stimulus had been presented under lighter masking conditions, and consciously seen, subjects were immediately able to discriminate the stimulus under heavy masking conditions. Awareness of the identity of the stimulus on one occasion allowed subjects to discriminate the stimulus without awareness thereafter. On the model modification of the response set requires top-down change from the SAS, which alters the arguments of the schema controlling discrimination performance. Once the schema and the response set are established then the operation of lower-level processing systems is sufficient for above-chance performance, even for perceptually degraded stimuli (for a related simulation where above-chance forced-choice performance occurs without explicit identification, see Hinton & Shallice, 1991).

Then there are anomalous cases in which an apparently intentional action is initiated in the absence of full awareness, for instance whilst we are in a distracted state or engaged in another task. Examples include reaching for and drinking from a glass whilst talking (Norman & Shallice, 1986), slips of highly routine actions which involve action lapses of the 'capture' error type (Norman, 1981; Reason, 1984), and changing gear or braking whilst driving (this issue is discussed in relation to awareness in Shallice, 1988b). It is not clear that we would wish to speak, in everyday language, of these actions as completely unconscious. Instead, they fit well with the phenomenological distinction between the foreground and background of consciousness (Shallice, 1988b). We explain these anomalous cases by distinguishing between the influence of the stimulus on contention scheduling, and the influence on the SAS. On the model, the selection of well learnt and relatively undemanding schema need not require SAS involvement. For instance, selection may be facilitated because the relevant schema are child-schemas of a larger parent-schema for action. According to this suggestion, the parent-schema for action (i.e. starting the car and beginning to drive) will be selected consciously via the SAS, but the parent-schema may itself include contingencies for the triggering of child-schemas (e.g. braking) without SAS intervention.

Since these anomalous cases do not require focal awareness, and are hypothesized not to involve the SAS, they cannot be classified as involving Type-C processes. However, they are obviously partially analogous to conscious processes, since they do involve schema selection. This suggestion would account for the apparent context sensitivity of anomalous cases (e.g. we don't instantly move our right foot to brake when riding a bicycle). If something like this analysis is correct, then whether or not an action can be classified as involving a Type-C process may depend on the larger task context. We would predict that the action of reaching for a glass and taking a drink would require awareness of the glass in some contexts, for instance if the subject is in an unfamiliar situation and has not already had a chance to look at the glass and mentally rehearse the action of drinking from it. When the action is familiar to the context, awareness may not be necessary to initiate the action. On our approach, objects or thoughts in the 'background of consciousness' would correspond to representations that are rapidly accessible for use by a Type-C process. This would include perceptual stimuli available to be selected by the parietal visuo-spatial attention system discussed by Driver and Vuilleumier.

What account can we offer of conscious reflection (process 1), which we have identified as the prototypically conscious process? For instance, consider the case in which a subject makes a fine discrimination of perceptual quality (e.g. taste or colour) and then responds via a simple two-choice key press. The details of the processes required to accomplish this remain obscure. Nonetheless, the framework offered here would appear to contrast with at least one aspect of that offered by Baars (1988). According to Baars, conscious perceptual information is made 'globally available' for the guidance of response. However, it is not clear that the 'broadcasting' of information encoded in sensory areas to the subsystems controlling movement would be necessary, or indeed possible. In our view, the representational codes would not be compatible. Rather, the critical conscious processes would appear to be as follows: (i) that of modulating the relevant perceptual subsystem, so that it can accomplish the computations necessary to make the appropriate comparison and return information on the result; (ii) the selection of the relevant motor subsystem to make a response contingent on the returned result; (iii) the mediation of the minimal information transfer required between the two subsystems (in this case, a single 'bit' of information).

We will consider just one more example from the list of Type-C processes presented earlier. This is the process underlying encoding of information into episodic memory (process 4). This is of central theoretical importance, for the following reason: the ability to remember a stimulus or thought is the principal criterion for the self-ascription that we were conscious of that stimulus or thought (Allport, 1988). Thus, in our view any putative theory that fails to account for the encoding of conscious information in episodic memory must be considered incomplete.

In our framework, we view episodic memory encoding as a process that results whenever Supervisory System modulation of lower-level processes occurs. This explains why a semantic orienting task is sufficient to give adequate memory encoding even when no instruction to remember is given (Hyde & Jenkins, 1969). It also fits with the computationally based claim that episodic memory encoding processes occur when novel operations are being carried out but not when routine processing is occurring (Sussman, 1975). Thus, episodic encoding may be seen as a by-product of the operation of any Type-C process. It is frequently the case that the only observable consequence of the operation of Type-C processes is the ability of the subject to later recall information about their perceptions and thoughts. How can this fit with our emphasis on understanding the function of consciousness? Schank (1982) argues that a key evolutionary function of episodic memory is that of reminding the subject of relevant autobiographical episodes in order to provide relevant material for strategy development in non-routine situations. On this perspective the subsystems involved in controlling episodic memory retrieval should also be seen as a part of the Supervisory System as their overall function is to assist in coping with non-routine situations.

The aim of this discussion is to indicate the utility of the Shallice (1988a) model as a framework for the description of conscious or Type-C processes, and initial theorizing about those processes. In this discussion, we have attempted to illustrate that the framework can both accommodate various aspects of phenomenology, and coheres with empirical evidence and theorizing in cognitive psychology. Nonetheless, we stress the point that the model only provides a conceptual framework capable of characterizing consciousness in broad information-processing terms. This framework may help to identify some of the computations involved, yet it is a long way from an account of consciousness embedded in neurally plausible computational models of the precise information-processing operations involved. Section 7 aims to illustrate how we may get closer to this goal.

7. Localization of function: specifying conscious operations

In Section 6 some of the Type-C processes listed – and in particular the operationally more critical experimental Type-C processes (Section 4.2) – relate to individual tasks and therefore come from a very large, if not infinite, set. Can one produce a more basic set of such processes? Secondly, in later versions of the Supervisory System model, the Supervisory System is held to contain a variety of special-purpose subsystems localized in different parts of prefrontal cortex (Shallice & Burgess, 1996). Should the relation between a Type-C process and effective operation of the 'Supervisory System' not then be capable of being specified further?

Work on localization of function in prefrontal cortex can potentially allow us to specify a more basic set of Type-C processes relating to different Supervisory System operations localized in different parts of cortex. There is evidence that functions carried out in prefrontal cortex are compatible with our general view of conscious processing. We claim that supervisory operations are not informationally encapsulated, and thus are not specific to particular modalities of input. This is consistent with one position in a recent debate concerning the lack of material-specificity in operations carried out in regions of left dorsolateral prefrontal cortex (Owen, 1997). We have also characterized conscious processing as an attentive operation (see Section 2). In our view, different conscious processes operating in the same short interval of time must have the same effective input. To judge from psychological refractory period and attentional blink phenomena the short interval of time is of the order of several hundred milliseconds. This view is consistent with a suggestion of Moscovitch (pers. commun.) concerning processes located in prefrontal cortex. He argued that these processes would not be able to be carried out at the same time as a structurally unrelated but demanding task. Support for this position is provided by the functional imaging dual-task study of Shallice et al. (1994), where a demanding but structurally unrelated additional task led to a significant reduction in activation in left dorsolateral prefrontal cortex. On this view, a demanding additional task should lead to the primary task being carried by means of lower-level processing systems alone. It follows from the model that there should not be full awareness of the relevant stimuli, as discussed in Section 6.

It is known experimentally that reading aloud and repeating or writing of a continuous sequence of words can be carried out in parallel to other tasks (Allport, Antonis, & Reynolds, 1972; Shallice, McLeod, & Lewis, 1985). That this is possible fits with work showing that naming, say in word reading or repeating, can be modelled in terms of feed-forward networks (e.g. Plaut, McClelland, Seidenberg, & Patterson, 1996) – suggesting that it can be carried out by lower-level processes alone. More critically, and as the model predicts, in these situations subjects lack full consciousness of the task and stimuli (Spelke, Hirst, & Neisser, 1976). Full awareness of a word would still be necessary for repeating or reading aloud when words are presented alone (i.e. cases involving 'spontaneous recognition', process 2 in the list of Type-C processes). This situation is known to be different, since processing is not properly automated for the first word in a rapidly presented sequence (see Allport & Wylie, 2000; Treisman & Davies, 1973).

What of the specific information-processing operations we have discussed in Section 6? A recent review by Frith (2000) provides excellent evidence that the key operation of modulation of lower-level schemas by the Supervisory System can be localized. Frith (2000) reviews a number of functional imaging tasks, where he argues that "sculpting the response space" is the key process that distinguished experimental and control conditions. The experiments considered involve carrying out a willed action compared with a choice response (Frith, 1992), the generation of a response when there are no strong pre-existing pre-potent responses compared with when such strong tendencies exist, e.g. the Nathaniel-James, Fletcher, and Frith (1997) study using the Hayling task (Burgess & Shallice, 1996b), and random number generation (Jahanshahi et al., see Frith, 2000) which involves the avoidance of responding using routine sets (Baddeley, Emslie, Kolodny, & Duncan, 1998; Jahanshahi & Dirnberger, 1999). The tasks Frith reviews all activate a region of left dorsolateral prefrontal cortex involving the middle and inferior frontal gyri. Further, imaging studies of memory encoding may be interpreted as supporting our claim that episodic encoding results from the operation of this process. Studies of encoding, for instance requiring the active organization of material, activate the same swathe of cortex identified by Frith (Fletcher, Shallice, & Dolan, 1998; Shallice et al., 1994). It has also been shown that carrying out novel operations – requiring schema generation on the model – activates left dorsolateral prefrontal cortex (Dolan & Fletcher, 1997; Tulving, Markowitsch, Kapur, Habib, & Houle, 1994). Now that a plausible anatomical location has been found for this critical executive function, further investigations may serve to give a more precise picture of the information-processing operations involved.

In addition to refining the model as discussed above, evidence from localization of function can extend it. We give two examples. Based on functional imaging evidence, it has been argued that the anterior cingulate cortex plays an essential role in conscious processing (Posner & Rothbart, 1998). The anterior cingulate is a structure activated in many task comparisons but is especially likely to be more activated in more difficult task situations (Paus, Koski, Caramanos, & Westbury, 1998). There is not yet complete agreement in its function. However, it would appear to be the more activated the more concentration is required (Posner & Petersen, 1990) and a meta-analysis has shown that the anterior cingulate tends to be highly active when there is conflict between competing inputs and/or responses (Carter, Botvinick, & Cohen, 1999). Indeed Posner and DiGirolamo (1998) have argued that any Supervisory System operation necessarily involves activation of the anterior cingulate. One possibility which fits with evidence on how its activation is affected by dopaminergic agonists in schizophrenics (Fletcher, Frith, Grasby, Friston, & Dolan, 1996) is that it is involved in top-down supervisory modulation of which processing systems are to be involved in on-line processing. The anterior cingulate therefore appears to complement the left dorsolateral region – involved in the top-down control of content as discussed earlier. On this view, the prefrontal cortex and the anterior cingulate would have complementary roles in conscious processing. A distinction might be made between different aspects of conscious processing with the concentration/mental effort aspects having a separate but linked material basis from those related to conscious content.

Second, imaging investigations inform our view of episodic memory retrieval (listed as pre-experimental process 3 in Section 4.1, but only mentioned in passing in the previous section). It is now well known that memory retrieval tasks activate predominantly right prefrontal cortex (Shallice et al., 1994; Tulving, Kapur, Craik, Moscovitch, & Houle, 1994; but see also Nolde, Johnson, & Raye, 1998). However, a number of different processes and regions appear to be involved (Lepage, Ghaffar, Nyberg, & Tulving, 2000). One process located in right dorsolateral prefrontal cortex appears to be linked to checking the retrieved memory (Henson et al., 1999). Checking retrieved memories may be a special case of a more general process responsible for the monitoring of on-going cognitive operations (Fink et al., 1999; Stuss & Alexander, 1994). Monitoring requires the matching of an overt or covert action with pre-specified criteria. If there is a match then there is no interruption of on-going behaviour. However, if a mismatch occurs a process of correction or more systematic checking takes place. This will involve top-down modulation of schema, somewhat analogous to that occurring with inhibition of a pre-potent response. Since the smooth operation of on-line processing systems is only interrupted in this case, it would follow from the theory given here that there is consciousness of a mismatch but not of a match.

In this section we argued that Type-C processes have two general characteristics – they are not informationally encapsulated and they are resource demanding. We have suggested three basic types of Type-C processes: (i) top-down schema modulation, also giving rise to episodic encoding; (ii) retrieval from episodic memory; and (iii) interruption of on-going operations through mismatch detection. Intention realization (Burgess, Quale, & Frith, 2000; Shallice & Burgess, 1991) would be a further possibility. We believe that cognitive neuroscience now has the potential to extend this list further.

8. *Rene

It is now widely accepted in cognitive science that the cognitive subsystems which are concerned with operating on knowledge about ourselves and other minds differ at least in part from the cognitive subsystems concerned with knowledge about physical mechanisms and causation (e.g. Baron-Cohen, Leslie, & Frith, 1985; Brothers, 1995; Frith & Frith, 1999). Consider an artificial intelligence, we shall call '*Rene', whose categories for understanding itself are completely unrelated to those for understanding its external material world, with the same applying to the abstractions it has developed from those categories. By assumption, *Rene's artificial mental states are just functional states. Yet, *Rene would not be able to use its physical or mechanical concepts to categorize its own artificial mental states. Without being told, or conducting its own investigations, *Rene would therefore have no way of knowing what functional state it is in at any particular moment in time.

Nonetheless, if *Rene's self-reflective capacities are to be useful to it – for instance, it could know that a particular type of pain would grow less with time – then its subjective concepts should map, at least broadly, onto functional distinctions between its cognitive states. Thus, another system could use *Rene's introspective reports as a guide to *Rene's functional organization, as well as providing data on the operation of *Rene's self-reflective cognitive subsystems. Similarly, at least some of the subjective concepts we use to differentiate between mental states promise to map directly onto information-processing distinctions between those states (e.g. aware or unaware, intentional or automatic, dream sleep or dreamless sleep). Furthermore, unlike *Rene, the different conceptual systems that humans use to describe themselves are not forced to remain distinct above the level of basic categories. The methods of cognitive science allow us to identify and distinguish between the different functional states involved in different cognitive activities. Through experiencing 'what it is like to' do well specified tasks, we may learn to relate our subjective understanding of our own mental states to such objective specifications of those states.

Would *Rene believe in dualism? There is no determinate answer. Presumably, *Rene could imagine a highly complex mechanism capable of producing the same behaviours as itself. Consequently, *Rene might entertain the possibility that its mental states are just physical states. Yet, crucially, *Rene's understanding of this equivalence could only be highly abstract. *Rene can't simply collapse and simplify his two conceptual systems into a unified whole. Thus, *Rene's understanding of the world (including itself) would remain equally complex, regardless of whether it believed in this equivalence or not. Indeed, in order for *Rene to begin imagining the highly complex mechanism as experiencing the same mental states as itself, *Rene would have to make a complete shift of mental set, bringing a wholly new set of concepts into play. *Rene's new train of thought would be so disjointed from the last, it might seem to *Rene that it was thinking about a completely different sort of thing.

*Rene would find no contradiction in imagining an entity that does all the same information processing as itself, yet which lacks its mental states. There would only be a contradiction if there were overlap in the criteria *Rene uses for applying mental and physical concepts. This may explain why we can imagine (in the abstract) an entity that does all the same information processing as us, yet lacks experiential states – the philosopher's zombie (see Dennett). There is no reason to suppose that there could be any actual difference between an entity doing all the same processing as us and a 'conscious' being (as supposed, for example, by Block, 1978; Chalmers, 1996; Kripke, 1972; Searle, 1992). The only difference is the 'attitude', 'stance', or 'mental set' we adopt when we are encouraged to think in different ways about the same thing (Dennett, 1987, 1991, 1996; Papineau, 1998).[13]

9. Summary and conclusion

In this paper we have placed our emphasis on the development of a scientific program for studying consciousness, rather than on a particular account of the neural or computational processes involved. This reflects our belief that the science of consciousness remains in its infancy, and that substantial progress will require a clarification of the deep conceptual and methodological difficulties that surround scientific attempts to understand human experience. In our view, most scientific proposals to date have attempted to bridge the gap between the physical and the experiential too quickly. In his discussion of biological psychiatry and its attempts to account for subjective phenomena (i.e. psychotic symptoms such as hallucinations), Frith (1992, see discussion pp. 25–30) notes that "The history of biological psychiatry is full of 'elephant footprints in the mud' (Lancet, 1978); findings which have made a big impact at the time, but have then faded away." As Frith argues, this has occurred precisely because of a failure to provide an adequate theoretical framework linking physical phenomena to mental phenomena, causing researchers to over-interpret "spurious and irrelevant associations".

In contrast, our approach is to present a theoretical framework to guide further investigation. The principal goal of this approach is the elucidation of the function of consciousness – the question of how conscious information, as opposed to non-conscious information, influences thought and behaviour, and in particular its role in the production of introspective reports. Our strategy for explaining the function of consciousness consists of two distinct components. First, in Section 4 we outline a method for the identification of tasks that provide a handle on relevant psychological

---

[13] Whilst we credit Dennett with this insight, he does not adopt the same position on philosophical zombies. He claims that we can't properly conceive of zombies, because he doesn't believe that there is a separation between the categories used – Dennett believes that mental state terms only refer to functional concepts or 'dispositions to behave'. We dispute this point (see also Loar, 1996). Ultimately, the issue should be resolved empirically. The view of Papineau (1998) is consistent with ours.

phenomena. This component of the strategy is geared to the production of empirical phenomena that are both suitable for further investigation and in need of explanation, so providing basic data for a theory of consciousness. As the second component, we adopted a particular theoretical framework and used it to understand conscious and non-conscious processes (see Section 6). The basic theoretical elements of this framework, originally put forward to describe the executive functions of prefrontal cortex, are not precisely specified in neural or computational terms. However, they allow an initial grasp of the relevant psychological phenomena using concepts that also link to information processing and/or systems neuroscience descriptions of brain function (see Section 7). Thus, this framework provides a broad structural outline for putative theories of consciousness, and serves to guide experimental work.

More generally, the presentation (and, to a much greater extent, the generation) of this approach has required us to consider some fundamental conceptual and methodological issues relating to consciousness. The term 'Introspective Physicalism' reflects the conclusions we have reached in three ways. Our first step is to adopt, and defend, a form of physicalism[14] (see Section 8). The goal of a theory of consciousness cannot be to tell us 'what it is like to be' in a mental state (as supposed by Jackson, 1995; McGinn, 1989; Nagel, 1974). Nor should we naively suppose that every subjective concept, however 'self-evident', accurately describes some aspect of the mind. Subjective concepts can only be acquired through consideration of our own experience (Lewis, 1990). Inevitably, some of these concepts will 'carve nature at its joints', whilst others will simply serve to mislead. Misleading concepts will not map onto functional distinctions between mental states. However, science may still study them from a distance by investigating the self-reflective processes that give rise to them. The closest that science can come to accounting for subjectivity is through elucidating the mechanisms that allow us to understand ourselves from our own point of view. Thus, our second step is to argue that a theory of consciousness must account for the processes underlying introspection.

Our third step is to emphasize the role of introspective evidence in the formulation of scientific accounts. As physicalists, we reject meta-physical dualism. Yet, we support methodological dualism, and attempt to address the specific methodological issues that arise concerning the use of introspective evidence. Although frequently overlooked, the history of psychology provides important lessons about the subtle complexities and difficulties associated with introspective evidence. Ultimately, it should be possible to account for all 'phenomenal appearances'. However, in so far as introspective observations are taken to reflect properties of the mental states under consideration, it is not yet clear which observations will ultimately be considered veridical, which will need to be re-described in order to cohere with a scientific understanding of the mind, and which will be explained as outright illusions. Thus,

---

[14] More specifically we are 'token' physicalists and 'type' functionalists (see Davidson, 1980). Every instance, or instantiation, of a mental state is identical with a physical state (physicalism). However, the type of mental state is determined solely by the causal relationships that the token mental state has with other mental states (functionalism).

we argue that obtaining valid introspective evidence is a complex craft. In our discussion, we have stressed the need to take a sceptical approach to observations based solely on introspective evidence, pending the collection of objective evidence that can validate the interpretation placed on that evidence. Nonetheless, introspective evidence can and should play both a major and an explicit role in the development of information-processing theories. Introspective evidence is an essential component of our research proposal for the identification of the processes necessary and sufficient for awareness, 'Type-C' processes. It also informs the theoretical framework we propose for understanding those processes.

From a philosophical perspective, this view of the use of introspective evidence in cognitive psychology relies on an inversion of the argument of Nagel (1974). Nagel argues that it is our knowledge of 'what it is like to be' in certain mental states that presents a barrier to the science of the mind. The argument here is the converse: it is precisely because we know what it is like to be in certain mental states that we are able to bring this evidence to bear on functional theories in general, and on theories of consciousness in particular. Scientific theories that are informed by introspective evidence in this way can justifiably claim to provide an account that links the mental and the physical.

Acknowledgements

The preparation of this paper was supported by a research grant from the Welcome Trust (053288/Z/98/Z/JRS/JP/JAT). We would like to thank Ned Block, David Papineau, Stanislas Dehaene, Michael Martin, Patrick Haggard, Vinod Goel and two anonymous reviewers for comments on previous versions of this work.

References

Allport, A. (1988). What concept of consciousness? In A. J. Marcel, & E. Bisiach (Eds.), Consciousness in contemporary science (pp. 159–182). Oxford: Clarendon Press/Oxford University Press.

Allport, A., & Wylie, G. (2000). Selection-for-action in competing (Stroop) tasks: 'task-switching', stimulus-response bindings, and negative priming. In S. Monsell, & J. S. Driver (Eds.), Control of cognitive processes: attention and performance, Vol. XVIII. Cambridge, MA: MIT Press.

Allport, D. A., Antonis, B., & Reynolds, P. (1972). On the division of attention: a disproof of the single channel hypothesis. Quarterly Journal of Experimental Psychology, 24 (2), 225–235.

Baars, B. J. (1988). A cognitive theory of consciousness. Cambridge: Cambridge University Press.

Baddeley, A., Emslie, H., Kolodny, J., & Duncan, J. (1998). Random generation and the executive control of working memory. Quarterly Journal of Experimental Psychology A, 51 (4), 819–852.

Badgaiyan, R. D. (2000). Executive control, willed actions, and nonconscious processing. Human Brain Mapping, 9 (1), 38–41.

Baron-Cohen, S., Leslie, A. M., & Frith, U. (1985). Does the autistic child have a "theory of mind"? Cognition, 21 (1), 37–46.

Bisiach, E. (1988). The (haunted) brain and consciousness. In A. J. Marcel, & E. Bisiach (Eds.), Consciousness in contemporary science (pp. 101–120). Oxford: Clarendon Press/Oxford University Press.

Block, N. (1978). Troubles with functionalism. In C. W. Savage (Ed.), Perception and cognition: issues in the foundation of psychology. Minneapolis, MN: University of Minnesota Press.

Block, N. (1995). On a confusion about a function of consciousness. Behavioral and Brain Sciences, 18, 227–287.

Bornstein, R. F., & D'Agostino, P. R. (1992). Stimulus recognition and the mere exposure effect. Journal of Personality and Social Psychology, 63 (4), 545–552.

Bornstein, R. F., & D'Agostino, P. R. (1994). The attribution and discounting of perceptual fluency: preliminary tests of a perceptual fluency/attributional model of the mere exposure effect. Social Cognition, 12 (2), 103–128.

Bowers, K. S. (1984). On being unconsciously influenced and informed. In K. S. Bowers, & D. Meichenbaum (Eds.), The unconscious reconsidered (pp. 227–272). New York: Wiley.

Broadbent, D. E. (1958). Perception and communication. London: Pergamon.

Brothers, L. (1995). Neurophysiology of the perception of intentions by primates. In M. S. Gazzaniga (Ed.), The cognitive neurosciences (pp. 1107–1115). Cambridge, MA: MIT Press.

Burgess, P. W., Quale, A., & Frith, C. D. (2000). Brain regions involved in prospective memory according to positron emission tomography. Manuscript submitted for publication.

Burgess, P. W., & Shallice, T. (1996a). Confabulation and the control of recollection. Memory, 4 (4), 359–411.

Burgess, P. W., & Shallice, T. (1996b). Response suppression, initiation and strategy use following frontal lobe lesions. Neuropsychologia, 34 (4), 263–272.

Campion, J., Latto, R., & Smith, Y. M. (1983). Is blindsight an effect of scattered light, spared cortex, and near-threshold vision? Behavioural and Brain Sciences, 6, 423–448.

Carter, C. S., Botvinick, M. M., & Cohen, J. D. (1999). The contribution of the anterior cingulate cortex to executive processes in cognition. Annual Review of Neuroscience, 10 (1), 49–57.

Chalmers, D. J. (1996). The conscious mind. New York: Oxford University Press.

Cheesman, J., & Merikle, P. M. (1986). Distinguishing conscious from unconscious perceptual processes. Canadian Journal of Psychology, 40 (4), 343–367.

Cooper, R., & Shallice, T. (2000). Contention scheduling and the control of routine activities. Cognitive Neuropsychology, 17, 297–338.

Cowey, A., & Stoerig, P. (1995). Blindsight in monkeys. Nature, 373, 247–249.

Crick, F. H. C. (1994). The astonishing hypothesis: the scientific search for the soul. New York: Charles Scribner's Sons.

Crick, F., & Koch, C. (1990). Some reflections on visual awareness. Cold Spring Harbor Symposia on Quantitative Biology, 55, 953–962.

Crick, F., & Koch, C. (1995). Are we aware of neural activity in primary visual cortex? Nature, 375 (6527), 121–123.

Crick, F., & Koch, C. (1998). Consciousness and neuroscience. Cerebral Cortex, 8, 97–107.

Cytowic, R. E. (1997). Synaesthesia: phenomenology and neuropsychology. In S. Baron-Cohen, & J. E. Harrison (Eds.), Synaesthesia (pp. 17–42). Oxford: Blackwell.

Dab, S., Claes, T., Morais, J., & Shallice, T. (1999). Confabulation with a selective descriptor process impairment. Cognitive Neuropsychology, 16, 215–242.

Davidson, D. (1980). Essays on actions and events. Oxford: Oxford University Press.

Dehaene, S., & Changeux, J. P. (1997). A hierarchical neuronal network for planning behavior. Proceedings of the National Academy of Sciences USA, 94 (24), 13293–13298.

Dehaene, S., Naccache, L., Le Clec, H. G., Koechlin, E., Mueller, M., Dehaene-Lambertz, G., van de Moortele, P. F., & Le Bihan, D. (1998). Imaging unconscious semantic priming. Nature, 395 (6702), 597–600.

Della Malva, C. L., Stuss, D. T., D'Alton, J., & Willmer, J. (1993). Capture errors and sequencing after frontal brain lesions. Neuropsychologia, 31, 363–372.

Dennett, D. C. (1987). The intentional stance. Cambridge, MA: MIT Press/A Bradford Book.

Dennett, D. C. (1988). Quining qualia. In A. J. Marcel, & E. Bisiach (Eds.), Consciousness in contemporary science (pp. 42–77). Oxford: Clarendon Press/Oxford University Press.

Dennett, D. C. (1991). Consciousness explained. London: Penguin.

Dennett, D. C. (1996). Facing backwards on the problem of consciousness. Journal of Consciousness Studies, 3 (1), 4–6.

Dixon, N. F. (1971). Subliminal perception: the nature of a controversy. London: McGraw-Hill.

Dixon, N. F. (1981). Preconscious processing. Chichester: Wiley.

Dolan, R. J., & Fletcher, P. C. (1997). Dissociating prefrontal and hippocampal function in episodic memory encoding. Nature, 388 (6642), 582–585.

Driver, J., & Mattingley, J. B. (1998). Parietal neglect and visual awareness. Nature Neuroscience, 1 (1), 17–22.

Ericksen, C. W. (1960). Discrimination and learning without awareness: a methodological survey and evaluation. Psychological Review, 67, 279–300.

Ericsson, K. A., & Simon, H. A. (1993). Protocol analysis: verbal reports as data (Rev. ed.). Cambridge, MA: MIT Press.

Fehrer, E., & Biederman, I. (1962). A comparison of reaction and verbal report in the detection of masked stimuli. Journal of Experimental Psychology, 64, 126–130.

Ffytche, D. H., & Howard, R. J. (1999). The perceptual consequences of visual loss: 'positive' pathologies of vision. Brain, 122 (Pt. 7), 1247–1260.

Fink, G. R., Marshall, J. C., Halligan, P. W., Frith, C. D., Driver, J., Frackowiak, R. S., & Dolan, R. J. (1999). The neural consequences of conflict between intention and the senses. Brain, 122 (Pt. 3), 497–512.

Fletcher, P. C., Frith, C. D., Grasby, P. M., Friston, K. J., & Dolan, R. J. (1996). Local and distributed effects of apomorphine on fronto-temporal function in acute unmedicated schizophrenia. Journal of Neuroscience, 16 (21), 7055–7062.

Fletcher, P. C., Shallice, T., & Dolan, R. J. (1998). The functional roles of prefrontal cortex in episodic memory. I. Encoding. Brain, 121, 1239–1248.

Fletcher, P. C., Shallice, T., Frith, C. D., Frackowiak, R. S., & Dolan, R. J. (1998). The functional roles of prefrontal cortex in episodic memory. II. Retrieval. Brain, 121, 1249–1256.

Fodor, J. A. (1983). The modularity of mind. Cambridge, MA: MIT Press.

Frith, C. D. (1992). The cognitive neuropsychology of schizophrenia. Hove: Lawrence Erlbaum Associates.

Frith, C. D. (2000). The role of dorsolateral prefrontal cortex in the selection of action, as revealed by functional imaging. In S. Monsell, & J. Driver (Eds.), Control of cognitive processes: attention and performance, Vol. XVIII. Cambridge, MA: MIT Press.

Frith, C. D., & Frith, U. (1999). Interacting minds – a biological basis. Science, 286 (5445), 1692–1695.

Frith, C., Perry, R., & Lumer, E. (1999). The neural correlates of conscious experience: an experimental framework. Trends in Cognitive Sciences, 3 (3), 105–114.

Fuhrer, M. J., & Ericksen, C. W. (1960). The unconscious perception of the meaning of verbal stimuli. Journal of Abnormal and Social Psychology, 62, 432–439.

Gardiner, J. M., Ramponi, C., & Richardson-Klavehn, A. (1998). Experiences of remembering, knowing, and guessing. Consciousness and Cognition, 7, 1–26.

Gazzaniga, M. S. (1985). The social brain. New York: Basic Books.

Goel, V., Grafman, J., Tajik, J., Gana, S., & Danto, D. (1997). A study of the performance of patients with frontal lobe lesions in a financial planning task. Brain, 120 (Pt. 10), 1805–1822.

Hameroff, S., & Penrose, R. (1996). Conscious events as orchestrated space-time selections. Journal of Consciousness Studies, 3 (1), 36–53.

Henson, R. N., Shallice, T., & Dolan, R. J. (1999). Right prefrontal cortex and episodic memory retrieval: a functional MRI test of the monitoring hypothesis. Brain, 122 (Pt. 7), 1367–1381.

Hinton, G. E., & Shallice, T. (1991). Lesioning an attractor network: investigations of acquired dyslexia. Psychological Review, 98 (1), 74–95.

Holender, D. (1986). Semantic activation without conscious identification in dichotic listening, parafoveal vision, and visual masking: a survey and appraisal. Behavioral and Brain Sciences, 9 (1), 1–66.

Humphrey, G. (1951). Thinking: an introduction to its experimental psychology. London: Methuen.

Hyde, T. S., & Jenkins, J. J. (1969). Differential effects of incidental tasks on the organization of recall of a list of highly associated words. Journal of Experimental Psychology, 82, 472–481.

Jack, A. I. (1998). Perceptual awareness in visual masking. Unpublished doctoral dissertation, University College London.

Jackson, F. (1995). What Mary didn't know. In P. K. Moser, & J. D. Trout (Eds.), Contemporary materialism. London: Routledge.

Jacoby, L. L. (1991). A process dissociation framework: separating automatic from intentional uses of memory. Journal of Memory and Language, 30 (5), 513–541.

Jacoby, L. L. (1998). Invariance in automatic influences of memory: toward a user's guide for the process-dissociation procedure. Journal of Experimental Psychology: Learning, Memory and Cognition, 24 (1), 3–26.

Jacoby, L. L., & Whitehouse, K. (1989). An illusion of memory: false recognition influenced by unconscious perception. Journal of Experimental Psychology: General, 118 (2), 126–135.

Jahanshahi, M., & Dirnberger, G. (1999). The left dorsolateral prefrontal cortex and random generation of responses: studies with transcranial magnetic stimulation. Neuropsychologia, 37 (2), 181–190.

James, W. (1890). The principles of psychology. New York: Holt.

Kahneman, D. (1967). An onset-onset law for one case of apparent motion and metacontrast. Perception and Psychophysics, 2, 577–584.

Kahneman, D. (1968). Method, findings, and theory in studies of visual masking. Psychological Bulletin, 70 (6), 404–425.

Kluver, H. (1966). Mescal and mechanisms of hallucinations. Chicago, IL: University of Chicago Press.

Koriat, A., & Goldsmith, M. (1996). Monitoring and control processes in the strategic regulation of memory accuracy. Psychological Review, 103 (3), 490–517.

Kripke, S. A. (1972). Naming and necessity. Cambridge, MA: Harvard University Press.

Kuhn, T. S. (1996). The structure of scientific revolutions (3rd ed.). Chicago, IL: University of Chicago Press.

Laming, D. R. J. (1997). The measurement of sensation, Oxford: Oxford University Press.

Leopold, D. A., & Logothetis, N. K. (1996). Activity changes in early visual cortex reflect monkeys' percepts during binocular rivalry. Nature, 379, 549–553.

Lepage, M., Ghaffar, O., Nyberg, L., & Tulving, E. (2000). Prefrontal cortex and episodic memory retrieval mode. Proceedings of the National Academy of Sciences USA, 97 (1), 506–511.

Lewis, D. (1990). What experience teaches. In W. C. Lycan (Ed.), Mind and cognition: a reader (pp. 499–519). Oxford: Blackwell.

Loar, B. (1996). Phenomenal states. In N. Block, O. Flanagan, & G. Guzeldere (Eds.), The nature of consciousness. Cambridge, MA: MIT Press.

Logothetis, N., & Schall, J. (1989). Neuronal correlates of subjective visual perception. Science, 245, 761–763.

Mandler, G. (1975). Mind and emotion. New York: Wiley.

Mandler, G. (1980). Recognising: the judgment of previous occurrence. Psychological Review, 87, 252–271.

Mandler, G., Nakamura, Y., & Van Zandt, B. J. (1987). Nonspecific effects of exposure on stimuli that cannot be recognized. Journal of Experimental Psychology: Learning, Memory, and Cognition, 13 (4), 646–648.

Marcel, A. J. (1983). Conscious and unconscious perception: experiments on visual masking and word recognition. Cognitive Psychology, 15 (2), 197–237.

McGinn, C. (1989). Can we solve the mind-body problem? Mind, 98, 349–366.

Merikle, P. M. (1984). Toward a definition of awareness. Bulletin of the Psychonomic Society, 22 (5), 449–450.

Merikle, P. M. (1992). Perception without awareness: critical issues. American Psychologist, 47 (6), 792–795.

Merikle, P. M., Joordens, S., & Stolz, J. A. (1995). Measuring the relative magnitude of unconscious influences. Consciousness and Cognition: an International Journal, 4 (4), 422–439.

Merikle, P. M., & Reingold, E. M. (1991). Comparing direct (explicit) and indirect (implicit) measures to study unconscious memory. Journal of Experimental Psychology: Learning, Memory, and Cognition, 17 (2), 224–233.

Miller, G. A. (1956). The magical number seven, plus or minus two: some limits on our capacity for processing information. Psychological Review, 63 (2), 81–97.

Miller, J. (1987). Priming is not necessary for selective-attention failures: semantic effects of unattended, unprimed letters. Perception and Psychophysics, 41 (5), 419–434.

Milner, D., & Goodale, M. (1995). The visual brain in action. Oxford: Oxford University Press.

Nagel, T. (1974). What is it like to be a bat? Philosophical Review, 83, 435–450.

Nathaniel-James, D. A., Fletcher, P., & Frith, C. D. (1997). The functional anatomy of verbal initiation and suppression using the Hayling test. Neuropsychologia, 35 (4), 559–566.

Nisbett, R. E., & Wilson, T. D. (1977). Telling more than we can know: verbal reports on mental processes. Psychological Review, 75, 522–536.

Nolde, S. F., Johnson, M. K., & Raye, C. L. (1998). The role of prefrontal cortex during tests of episodic memory. Trends in Cognitive Sciences, 2 (10), 399–406.

Norman, D. A. (1981). Categorisation of action slips. Psychological Review, 88, 1–15.

Norman, D. A., & Bobrow, D. G. (1976). On the role of active memory processes in perception and cognition. In C. N. Cofer (Ed.), The structure of human memory (pp. 114–132). San Francisco, CA: Freeman.

Norman, D. A., & Shallice, T. (1986). Attention to action: willed and automatic control of behavior (Rev. ed.). In R. J. Davidson, G. E. Schwartz, & D. Shapiro (Eds.), Consciousness and self-regulation (Vol. 4). New York: Plenum Press.

Owen, A. M. (1997). The functional organization of working memory processes within human lateral frontal cortex: the contribution of functional neuroimaging. European Journal of Neuroscience, 9 (7), 1329–1339.

Papineau, D. (1998). Mind the gap. In J. Tomberlin (Ed.), Language, mind and ontology. Philosophical perspectives (Vol. 12, pp. 373–388). Oxford: Blackwell.

Paus, T., Koski, L., Caramanos, Z., & Westbury, C. (1998). Regional differences in the effects of task difficulty and motor output on blood flow response in the human anterior cingulate cortex: a review of 107 PET activation studies. NeuroReport, 9 (9), 37–47.

Plaut, D. C., McClelland, J. L., Seidenberg, M. S., & Patterson, K. (1996). Understanding normal and impaired word reading: computational principles in quasi-regular domains. Psychological Review, 103, 56–115.

Posner, M. I., & DiGirolamo, G. J. (1998). Executive attention: conflict, target detection, and cognitive control. In R. Parasuraman (Ed.), The attentive brain. Cambridge, MA: MIT Press.

Posner, M. I., & Klein, R. M. (1973). On the functions of consciousness. In S. Kornblum (Ed.), Attention and performance (Vol. IV, pp. 21–35). New York: Academic Press.

Posner, M. I., & Petersen, S. E. (1990). The attentional system of the human brain. Annual Review of Neuroscience, 13, 25–42.

Posner, M. I., & Rothbart, M. K. (1998). Attention, self-regulation and consciousness. Philosophical Transactions of the Royal Society of London, Series B, Biological Sciences, 353 (1377), 1915–1927.

Reason, J. T. (1984). Lapses of attention. In R. Parasuraman, R. Davies, & J. Beatty (Eds.), Varieties of attention. Orlando, FL: Academic Press.

Reber, A. S. (1997). Implicit ruminations. Psychonomic Bulletin and Review, 4 (1), 49–55.

Reingold, E. M., & Merikle, P. M. (1990). On the inter-relatedness of theory and measurement in the study of unconscious processes. Mind and Language, 5, 9–28.

Rosenthal, D. M. (1986). Two concepts of consciousness. Philosophical Studies, 94 (3), 329–359.

Ryle, G. (1949). The concept of mind. London: Hutchinson.

Schacter, D. L. (1989). On the relation between memory and consciousness: dissociable interactions and conscious experience. In H. L. Roediger, & F. I. M. Craik (Eds.), Varieties of memory and consciousness: essays in honour of Endel Tulving (pp. 355–389). Hillsdale, NJ: Erlbaum.

Schacter, D. L., Curran, T., Galluccio, L., Milberg, W. P., & Bates, J. F. (1996). False recognition and the right frontal lobe: a case study. Neuropsychologia, 34 (8), 793–808.

Schank, R. C. (1982). Dynamic memory. Cambridge: Cambridge University Press.

Searle, J. R. (1992). The rediscovery of the mind. Cambridge, MA: MIT Press.

Shallice, T. (1972). Dual functions of consciousness. Psychological Review, 79, 383–393.

Shallice, T. (1988a). From neuropsychology to mental structure. New York: Cambridge University Press.

Shallice, T. (1988b). Information-processing models of consciousness: possibilities and problems. In A. J. Marcel, & E. Bisiach (Eds.), Consciousness in contemporary science (pp. 305–333). Oxford: Clarendon Press/Oxford University Press.

Shallice, T., & Burgess, P. W. (1991). Deficits in strategy application following frontal lobe damage in man. Brain, 114 (Pt 2), 727–741.

Shallice, T., & Burgess, P. (1996). The domain of supervisory processes and temporal organization of behaviour. Philosophical Transactions of the Royal Society of London, Series B, 351 (1346), 1405–1412.

Shallice, T., Fletcher, P., Frith, C. D., Grasby, P., Frackowiak, R. S., & Dolan, R. J. (1994). Brain regions associated with acquisition and retrieval of verbal episodic memory. Nature, 368 (6472), 633–635.

Shallice, T., McLeod, P., & Lewis, K. (1985). Isolating cognitive modules with the dual-task paradigm: are speech perception and production separate processes? Quarterly Journal of Experimental Psychology A, 37 (4), 507–532.

Shanks, D. R., & Johnstone, T. (1997). Implicit knowledge in sequential learning tasks. In M. A. Stadler, & P. A. Frensch (Eds.), Handbook of implicit learning. London: Sage.

Shanks, D. R., & St. John, M. F. (1994). Characteristics of dissociable human learning systems. Behavioral and Brain Sciences, 17 (3), 367–447.

Sheinberg, D. L., & Logothetis, N. K. (1997). The role of temporal cortical areas in perceptual organisation. Proceedings of the National Academy of Sciences USA, 94, 3408–3413.

Siegler, R. S., & Stern, E. (1998). Conscious and unconscious strategy discoveries: a microgenetic analysis. Journal of Experimental Psychology: General, 127 (4), 377–397.

Spelke, E., Hirst, W., & Neisser, U. (1976). Skills of divided attention. Cognition, 4 (3), 215–230.

St. John, M. F., & Shanks, D. R. (1997). Implicit learning from an information processing standpoint. In D. C. Berry (Ed.), How implicit is implicit learning? (pp. 162–194). Oxford: Oxford University Press.

Stuss, D. T., & Alexander, M. P. (1994). Functional and anatomical specificity of frontal lobe functions. In L. S. Cermak (Ed.), Neuropsychological explorations of memory and cognition: essays in honor of Nelson Butters (pp. 191–200). New York: Plenum Press.

Sussman, G. J. (1975). A computational model of skill acquisition. New York: American Elsevier.

Tononi, G., & Edelman, G. M. (1998). Consciousness and complexity. Science, 282 (5395), 1846–1851.

Treisman, A. M., & Davies, A. (1973). Divided attention to ear and eye. In S. Kornblum (Ed.), Attention and performance (Vol. IV). London: Academic Press.

Tulving, E. (1983). Elements of episodic memory. Oxford: Oxford University Press.

Tulving, E., Kapur, S., Craik, F. I., Moscovitch, M., & Houle, S. (1994). Hemispheric encoding/retrieval asymmetry in episodic memory: positron emission tomography findings. Proceedings of the National Academy of Sciences USA, 91 (6), 2016–2020.

Tulving, E., Markowitsch, H. J., Kapur, S., Habib, R., & Houle, S. (1994). Novelty encoding networks in the human brain: positron emission tomography data. NeuroReport, 5 (18), 2525–2528.

Van Gulick, R. (1994). Deficit studies and the function of phenomenal consciousness. In G. Graham, & L. Stephens (Eds.), Philosophical psychology (pp. 25–50). Cambridge, MA: MIT Press.

Watson, J. B. (1913). Psychology as the behaviorist views it. Psychological Review, 20, 158–177.

Watson, J. B. (1920). Is thinking merely the action of language mechanisms? British Journal of Psychology, 11, 87–104.

Watson, J. D., & Crick, F. H. (1953). Molecular structure of nucleic acids: a structure for deoxyribose nucleic acid. Nature, 171 (4356), 737–738.

Weiskrantz, L. (1986). Blindsight. New York: Oxford University Press.

Weiskrantz, L. (1997). Consciousness lost and found: a neuropsychological exploration. New York: Oxford University Press.

Whittlesea, B. W. A. (1993). Illusions of familiarity. Journal of Experimental Psychology: Learning, Memory, and Cognition, 19 (6), 1235–1253.

Whittlesea, B. W., Jacoby, L. L., & Girard, K. (1990). Illusions of immediate memory: evidence of an attributional basis for feelings of familiarity and perceptual quality. Journal of Memory and Language, 29 (6), 716–732.

Wilkes, K. V. (1988). —, yishi, duh, um, and consciousness. In A. J. Marcel, & E. Bisiach (Eds.), Consciousness in contemporary science (pp. 16–41). Oxford: Clarendon Press/Oxford University Press.

7

Paradox and cross purposes in recent work on consciousness

Ned Block[*]

Philosophy Department, Main Building, Room 503E, New York University, 100 Washington Square East, New York, NY 10003, USA

Abstract

Functionalists about consciousness identify consciousness with a role; physicalists identify consciousness with an implementer of that role. The global workspace theory of consciousness fits the functionalist perspective, but the physicalist sees consciousness as a biological phenomenon that implements global accessibility. © 2001 Elsevier Science B.V. All rights reserved.

Keywords: Paradox; Cross purposes; Consciousness

1. Introduction

Dehaene and Naccache, Dennett and Jack and Shallice (this volume) "see convergence coming from many different quarters on a version of the neuronal global workspace model" (Dennett). On the contrary, even within this volume, there are commitments to very different perspectives on consciousness. And these differing perspectives are based on tacit differences in philosophical starting places that should be made explicit. Indeed, it is not clear that different uses of 'consciousness' and 'awareness' in this volume can be taken to refer to the same phenomenon. More specifically, I think there are three different concepts of consciousness in play in this issue. The global workspace model makes much more sense on one of these than on the others.

---

[*] Fax: +1-212-995-4179.
E-mail address: nb21@is5.nyu.edu (N. Block).

Part of the point of this comment is that 'consciousness' and 'awareness' are ambiguous terms, and I often follow the usage of authors being discussed in using these terms without specifying a sense.

2. The paradox of recent findings about consciousness

The most exciting and puzzling results described in this issue appear in a linked set of experiments reported by Kanwisher, Driver and Vuilleumier and Dehaene and Naccache (this volume). Kanwisher notes that "...neural correlates of perceptual experience, an exotic and elusive quarry just a few years ago, have suddenly become almost commonplace findings". And she backs this up with impressive correlations between neural activation on the one hand and indications of perceptual experiences of faces, houses, motion, letters, objects, words and speech on the other. Conscious perception of faces whether rivalrous or not correlates with activity in the fusiform face area (FFA) but not the parahippocampal place area (PPA). And conversely for perception of places. This work is especially extensive in vision, where what I will refer to as the ventral stream, a set of occipital-temporal pathways, is strongly implicated in visual experience. Apparently, the further into the temporal cortex, the more dominant the correlation with the percept. (The precise pathway depends on the subject matter, the different areas determining the different contents of consciousness.)

As Kanwisher notes, the FFA and PPA were selected for scrutiny in these experiments, not because of any association with consciousness but because it was known that they specialize in these sorts of stimuli. These areas are not activated by most other stimuli that are not places or faces. Thus, the neural basis of consciousness is not localized in one set of cells, but rather in the very areas that do the perceptual analysis. Nonetheless, in a broader sense, this work does suggest a single neural basis for visual consciousness, because all visual stimuli affect areas of a single stream of processing, albeit different parts of that stream. Although finding the neural basis for visual consciousness would be exciting, it would be foolish to suppose it would immediately yield an understanding of why it is the neural basis. That understanding will no doubt require major ideas of which we now have no glimmer.

So we apparently have an amazing success: identification of the neural basis of visual consciousness in the ventral stream. Paradoxically, what has also become commonplace is activation of the very same ventral stream pathways without awareness. Damage to the inferior parietal lobes has long been known to cause visual extinction, in which, for example, subjects appear to lose subjective experience of stimuli on one side when there are stimuli on both sides, yet show signs of perception of the stimuli, e.g. the extinguished stimuli often facilitate responses to non-extinguished stimuli. (Extinction is associated with visual neglect in which subjects don't notice stimuli on one side. For example, neglect patients often don't eat the food on one side of the plate.) Driver and Vuilleumier point out that the ventral stream is activated for extinguished stimuli (i.e. which the subject claims not to see).

Rees et al. (in press) report studies of a left-sided neglect and extinction patient on face and house stimuli. Stimuli presented only on the left side are clearly seen by the patient, but when there are stimuli on both sides, the subject acknowledges just the stimulus on the right. However, the 'unseen' stimuli show activation of the ventral pathway that is the same in location and temporal course as the seen stimuli. Further, studies in monkeys have shown that a classic 'blindness' syndrome is caused by massive cortical ablation that spares most of the ventral stream but not inferior parietal and frontal lobes (Nakamura & Mishkin, 1980, 1986, as cited in Lumer & Rees, 1999). Kanwisher notes that dynamic visual gratings alternating with a gray field – both very faint stimuli – showed greater activation for the gratings in V1, V2, V3A, V4v and MT/MST despite the subjects saying they saw only a uniform gray field. Dehaene and Naccache note that processing of a masked number word proceeds all the way through the occipital-temporal pathway to a motor response even though subjects were at chance in discriminating presence from absence and in discriminating words from non-words: "…an entire stream of perceptual, semantic and motor processes, specified by giving arbitrary verbal instructions to a normal subject, can occur outside of consciousness."

Is the difference between conscious and unconscious activation of the ventral pathway just a matter of the degree of activation? As Kanwisher notes, Rees et al. (in press) found activations for extinguished face stimuli that were as strong as for conscious stimuli. And evidence from ERP studies using the attentional blink paradigm shows that neural activation of meaning is no less when the word is blinked and therefore not consciously perceived than when it isn't, suggesting that it is not lower neural activation strength that accounts for lack of awareness. Further, in a study of neglect patients, McGlinchey-Berroth, Milberg, Verfaellie, Alexander, and Kilduff (1993) showed that there is the same amount of semantic priming from both hemifields, despite the lack of awareness of stimuli in the left field, again suggesting that it is not activation strength that makes the difference. The upshot is that something in addition to activation strength must be playing a role.

Driver and Vuilleumier put the paradox as follows: "How then can the patient remain unaware of a contralesional stimulus, even when it can still activate the pathways that are most often considered to support conscious experience?" The paradox then is that our amazing success in identifying the neural correlate of visual experience in normal vision has led to the peculiar result that in masking and neglect that very neural correlate occurs without, apparently, subjective experience.

What is the missing ingredient, X, which, added to ventral activation (of sufficient strength), constitutes conscious experience? Kanwisher and Driver and Vuilleumier, despite differences of emphasis, offer pretty much the same proposal as to the nature of X: (1) activation of the ventral stream supplies the contents of consciousness; (2) X is what makes those ventral contents conscious; (3) X is the binding of perceptual attributes with a time and a place, a token event; and (4) the neural basis of X is centered in the parietal cortex. If this is true, it is extremely significant, suggesting that the causal basis of all experience is spatiotemporal experience.

But I have a number of doubts about this proposal.

1. The proposal is wrong if there can be unbound but nonetheless conscious experiences, for example, experienced shape and color not attached to one another. When a person has a visual experience of a ganzfeld, in which a color fills the subject's whole field of vision, that visual experience is apparently unbound and yet conscious. (I am indebted to correspondence with Ann Treisman on this matter.) Friedman-Hill, Robertson, and Treisman (1995) and Wojciulik and Kanwisher (1998) discuss a patient (RM) with bilateral parietal damage who has binding problems. In many tasks, RM's level of illusory conjunctions (e.g. reporting a blue X and a red O when seeing a red X and a blue O) are high. Wojciulik and Kanwisher (1998) discuss a number of tasks in which RM is at chance, e.g. reporting which of two words is colored (rather than white). Perhaps RM has bound but illusory experiences, e.g. if the stimulus is a green 'short' and white 'ready', he experiences a green 'ready' and a white 'short'. Or perhaps RM experiences green, white, 'short' and 'ready' but without colors bound to words. (I haven't been able to tell which from the published literature.) The binding hypothesis may withstand this putative disconfirmation, however, since as Wojciulik and Kanwisher (1998) report, he appears to be binding 'implicitly' as indicated by his normal interference in a Stroop-like task. (It takes him longer to name the colored word if he is presented with a green 'brown' and a white (i.e. non-colored) 'green' than a green 'green' and a white 'brown'.)

2. Weiskrantz and his colleagues (Kentridge, Heywood, & Weiskrantz, 1999) have reported that attention can be guided to a flashed dot in the blind field by an arrow in the blind field. Further, the patient, GY, learns when the contingencies are changed so that the arrow is misleading about where the dot will appear. A straightforward conjunction experiment requires a choice between four options, but the usual blindsight choice is between two, which may introduce skepticism about whether binding can be detected in blindsight. However, GY can choose among four options (DeGelder, Vroomen, Pourtois, & Weiskrantz, 1999). Can a demonstration of binding in the blind field be far off?

3. Why take X to be binding rather than just attention? (This would only be a viable suggestion if lack of consciousness in blindsight could be blamed on, e.g. insufficient ventral actibation). Tipper and Behrman (1996) show a neglect patient a 'barbell' consisting of two circles joined by a line, with target words flashed in both circles. The patient doesn't recognize the target words on the left. But if the barbell is rotated so that the circle that was on the left is now on the right, the subject doesn't recognize the words on the right. (Caramazza and Hillis (1990) obtained similar results.) The usual explanation is that the subject's attention travels with the object that was initially on the left. So it seems attention is crucial to whether a stimulus is extinguished. Perhaps attention determines binding, and binding determines consciousness (in the presence of the right kind of activation). But anyone who pursues this hypothesis should investigate whether we need the middleman. (Milner and Goodale (1995) propose that consciousness is ventral stream activity plus attention and a similar view is advocated by Prinz (2000).)

Rees et al. (in press) make two suggestions as to (in my terms) what X is. One is that the difference between conscious and unconscious activation is a matter of neural synchrony at fine time-scales. The finding that ERP components P1 and N1 revealed differences between left-sided 'unseen' stimuli and left-sided seen stimuli supports this idea. Driver and Vuilleumier mention preliminary data to the same effect. As Driver and Vuilleumier note, ERP is probably more dependent on synchrony than fMRI. Their second suggestion is that the difference between seen and 'unseen' stimuli might be a matter of interaction between the classic visual stream and the areas of parietal and frontal cortex that control attention. Since both of these proposals concern hypothetical mechanisms of attention, there may be no difference between them and the attention hypothesis.

Whether or not any of these proposals are right, the search for X seems to me the most exciting current direction for consciousness research. The search for X is a diagnostic for the main difference of opinion in this volume. Kanwisher, Driver and Vuilleumier and I give it prominence. Dehaene and Naccache, Dennett and Jack and Shallice do not. (Parvizi and Damasio (this volume) are engaging different issues.) More on what the sides represent is given below.

Surprisingly, given her proposal that X = binding, Kanwisher also gives a second answer: that "awareness of a particular element of perceptual information must entail not just a strong enough neural representation of that information, but also access to that information by most of the rest of the mind/brain". What's going on here? Why two solutions to one problem? Are these meant as exclusive alternatives? Or are they both supposed to be true?

The answer is found in the rationale given by Kanwisher for the access condition. She appeals to a "common intuition about perceptual awareness (e.g. Baars, 1988), if you perceive something, then you can report on it through any output system [in my terms, the information is globally available – NB]... Perceptual information that could be reported through only one output system and not through another just would not fit with most people's concept of a true conscious percept ... it seems that a core part of the idea of awareness is that not only effector systems, but indeed most parts of the mind have access to the information in question." Common intuition gives us access to the meanings of our words and our concepts but not necessarily to what they are concepts of. The rationale for saying that the concept of consciousness does not apply in the absence of global availability is like the rationale for calling a darkening of the skin 'sunburn' only if the sun causes it. The identical skin change – spelled out in molecular terms – could fail to fit the concept of sunburn if it had a different cause. The suggestion is that the concept of consciousness only applies to states that are globally accessible.

But that leads to a question: could there be ventral stream activation plus X (whatever X turns out to be) that is not widely broadcast and therefore doesn't deserve to be called 'consciousness' in this 'access' sense that Kanwisher is invoking? Kanwisher mentions that the neural synchrony that is involved in binding might also play a role in broadcasting. But the hypothesis serves to make salient the opposite idea. Whatever the role synchrony plays in making a representation phenomenal is unlikely to be exactly the same as the role it plays in subserving broadcasting. And even if it is the same, what would prevent the causal path to broadcasting from being blocked? Even if we make it a condition on X that X cause the reliable broadcast of the contents of the activated area, any reliable mechanism can fail or be damaged, in which case we would have activation plus X without broadcasting. If such a thing happened, no doubt one concept of 'awareness' (e.g. global accessibility) would not apply to it. But maybe another concept – phenomenality – would. (What is phenomenality? What it is like to have an experience. When you enjoy the taste of wine, you are enjoying gustatory phenomenality.)

Any appeal to evidence to back a theory of consciousness depends on a pretheoretic concept of consciousness to supply a starting point. We have now seen two such concepts, phenomenality and global accessibility.[1]

Dehaene and Naccache state the global accessibility view as follows: "An information becomes conscious ... if the neural population that represents it is mobilized by top-down attentional amplification into a brain-scale state of coherent activity that involves many neurons distributed throughout the brain. The long-distance connectivity of these "workspace neurons" can, when they are active for a minimal duration, make the information available to a variety of processes including perceptual categorization, long-term memorization, evaluation and intentional action." Or for short, consciousness is being broadcast in a global neuronal workspace. Dennett, advocating a similar view, takes consciousness to be cerebral celebrity, fame in the brain.

The proposal that consciousness is ventral activation plus X (e.g. neural synchrony) is based on a different starting point, a different concept of consciousness than the proposal that consciousness is cerebral celebrity or global neuronal broadcasting. (I will ignore one difference, namely that the first is a theory of visual consciousness and the second is a theory of consciousness simpliciter.) We could see the two types of proposals as responses to different questions. The question that motivates the ventral activation plus X type of proposal is: what is the neural basis of phenomenality? The question that motivates the global neuronal broadcasting type of proposal is: what makes neuronal representations available for thought, decision, reporting and control of action, the main types of access? We can try to force a unity by postulating that it is a condition on X that it promote access, but that is a verbal maneuver that only throws smoke over the difference between the concepts and questions. Alternatively, we could hypothesize rather than postulate that X plus ventral stream activation as a matter of fact is the neural basis of global neuronal broadcasting. Note, however, that the neural basis of global neuronal broadcasting may exist but the normal channels of broadcasting nonetheless may be blocked or cut, again opening daylight between phenomenality and global accessibility, and showing that we cannot think of the two as one. (An analogy: rest mass and relativistic mass are importantly different from a theoretical point of view despite

---

[1] Block (1997) says a representation is access conscious if it is poised for global control. Block (1995) adopts a more cumbersome formulation which lists various types of control. (The advantage of the cumbersome formulation is that it avoids ascribing consciousness to simple devices which nonetheless have global control.) Since consciousness is best thought of as an occurrence, actively poised for global control would be better. (See Burge (1997), which criticizes Block (1995).)

coinciding for all practical purposes at terrestrial velocities. Failure of coincidence even if rare is theoretical dynamite if what you are after is the scientific nature of consciousness.)

I imagine that someone will suggest that X just is global broadcasting itself. That is, consciousness = ventral stream activation + global broadcasting. First, this thesis doesn't tell us what it is that makes ventral stream activity cerebrally famous. Second, the upshot is that consciousness is not global broadcasting, since consciousness is global broadcasting plus something else, ventral stream activation. Thus, the proposal raises the unwelcome possibility of global broadcasting without consciousness (e.g. a 'zombie') if something other than {ventral stream activation + whatever it is that makes ventral activity cerebrally famous} could produce global broadcasting.

Driver and Vuilleumier suggest that we should see X in part in terms of winner-take-all functions. But this hypothesis is more of a different way of putting the question than an answer to it if winner-takes-all means 'winner gets broadcast'.

Many of us have had the experience of suddenly noticing a sound (say a jackhammer during an intense conversation) at the same time realizing that the sound has been going on for some time even though one was not attending to it. If the subject did have a phenomenal state before the sound was noticed, that state was not broadcast in the global neuronal workspace until it was noticed. If this is right, there was a period of **phenomenality without broadcasting**. Of course, this is merely anecdotal evidence. And the appearance of having heard the sound all along may be a false memory. But the starting point for work on consciousness is introspection and we would be foolish to ignore it.

If we take seriously the idea of phenomenality without access, there is a theoretical option that should be on the table, one that I think is worth investigating – that ventral stream activation is visual phenomenality and the search for X is the search for the neural basis of what makes visual phenomenality accessible. The idea would be that the claims of extinction patients not to see extinguished stimuli are in a sense wrong – they really do have phenomenal experience of these stimuli without knowing it. A similar issue will arise in the section to follow in which I will focus on the relation between phenomenality and a special case of global accessibility, reflexive or introspective consciousness, in which the subject not only has a phenomenal state but also has another state that is about the phenomenal state, say a thought to the effect that he has a phenomenal state.

The theory that consciousness is ventral stream activation plus, for example, neural synchrony, and the theory that consciousness is broadcasting in the global neuronal workspace are instances of the two major rival approaches to consciousness in the philosophical literature, physicalism and functionalism. The key to the difference is that functionalism identifies consciousness with a role, whereas physicalism identifies consciousness with a physical or biological property that fills or implements or realizes that role in humans. Global availability could be implemented in many ways but the human biological implementation involves specific electrical and chemical quantities, which, according to the physicalist, are necessary for consciousness. By contrast, functionalism in its pure form is implementation-independent. As Dennett says, "The proposed consensual thesis is ... that this global availability ... is, all by itself, a conscious state." Consciousness is defined as global accessibility, and although its human implementation depends on biochemical properties specific to us, the functionalist says that artificial creatures without our biochemistry could implement the same computational relations. Thus, functionalism and physicalism are incompatible doctrines since silicon implementations of the functional organization of consciousness would not share our biological nature. The rationale is expressed in Dennett's statement that "handsome is as handsome does, that matter matters only because of what matter can do". He says "Functionalism in this broad sense is so ubiquitous in science that it is tantamount to a reigning presumption of all science." I disagree. The big question for functionalists is this: How do you know that it is broadcasting in the global workspace that makes a representation conscious as opposed to something about the human biological realization of that broadcasting that makes it conscious? There is a real issue here with two legitimate sides. The biological point of view is represented here by the hypothesis of ventral stream activation plus, for example, neural synchrony, which on one natural way of filling in the details requires a specific biological realization.[2]

This section has concerned two concepts of consciousness, phenomenality and global accessibility. In the next section, we add a third.

3. What are experiments 'about consciousness' really about?

Merikle, Smilek and Eastwood (this volume) describe the Debner and Jacoby (1994) 'exclusion' paradigm, in which subjects follow instructions not to complete a word stem with the end of a masked word just presented to them only if the word is presented consciously (lightly masked). If the word is presented unconsciously (heavily masked), the subjects are more likely than baseline to disobey the instructions, completing the stem with the very word that was presented.

But what is the 'conscious/unconscious' difference in this experiment? Perhaps in the case of the conscious presentation, the subject says to himself something on the order of (though maybe not this explicitly) 'I just saw 'reason', so I'd better complete the stem 'rea' with something else, say 'reader'.' (I'm not saying the

---

[2] The problem for functionalists could be put like this: the specifically human realization of global availability may be necessary to consciousness – other realizations of global availability being 'ersatz' realizations. Dennett responds to this point by arguing in effect that we can preserve functionalism by simply characterizing global availability in a more detailed way – at the level of biochemistry. But the utility of this technique runs out as one descends the hierarchy of sciences, because the lowest level of all, that of basic level physics, is vulnerable to the same point. Putting the point for simplicity in terms of the physics of 40 years ago, the causal role of electrons is the same as that of anti-electrons. If you formulate a functional role for an electron, an anti-electron will realize it. Thus, an anti-electron is an ersatz realizer of the functional definition of electron. Physics is characterized by symmetries that allow ersatz realizations. For an introduction to issues about functionalism, the reader could consult the entries on consciousness or on functionalism in any of the truly excellent philosophy reference works that have been published in the last 5 years, The Routledge Encyclopedia of Philosophy, The Oxford Companion to Philosophy, The Cambridge Companion to Philosophy, Blackwell's Companion to Philosophy of Mind or the supplement to Macmillan's The Encyclopedia of Philosophy.

monologue has to be experienced by the subject on every trial. Perhaps it could be automatized if there are enough trials.) And in the case of the unconscious presentation, there is no internal monologue of this sort. If so, the sense of the 'conscious/ unconscious' difference that is relevant to this experiment has something to do with the presence or absence of whatever is required for an internal monologue, perhaps something to do with introspection. Tony Jack tells me that many of his subjects in this paradigm complained about how much effort was required to follow the exclusion instructions, further motivating the hypothesis of an internal monologue.

We get some illumination by attention to another experimental paradigm described by Merikle and Joordens (1997), the 'false recognition' paradigm of Jacoby and Whitehouse (1989). Subjects are given a study list of 126 words presented for half a second each. They are then presented with a masked word, $word_1$, and an unmasked word, $word_2$. Their task is to report whether $word_2$ was old (i.e. on the study list) or new (not on the study list). The variable was whether $word_1$ was lightly or heavily masked, the former presentations being thought of as 'conscious' and the latter as 'unconscious'. The result, confining our attention just to cases in which $word_1 = word_2$, is that subjects were much more likely to mistakenly report $word_2$ as old when $word_1$ was unconsciously presented than when $word_1$ was consciously presented. (When $word_1$ was consciously presented, they were less likely than baseline to mistakenly report $word_2$ as old; when $word_1$ was unconsciously presented, they were more likely than baseline to err in this way.) As before, the explanation would appear to be that when $word_1$ was consciously presented, the subjects were able to use an internal monologue of the following sort (though perhaps not as explicit): 'Here's why 'reason' ($word_2$) looks familiar – because I just saw it (as $word_1$)', thereby explaining away the familiarity of $word_2$. But when $word_1$ was unconsciously presented, the subjects were not able to indulge in this monologue and consequently mistakenly blamed the familiarity of $word_2$ on its appearance in the original study list.

Any reasoning that can reasonably be attributed to the subject in this paradigm concerns the subject thinking about why a word ($word_2$) looks familiar to the subject. For it is only by explaining away the familiarity of $word_2$ that the subject is able to decide that $word_2$ was not on the study list. (If you have a hypothesis about what is going on in this experiment that doesn't appeal to the subject's explaining away the familiarity, I'd like to hear it. Of course, I would allow that the monologue could be automatized. I suppose a skeptic might think it has already been automatized even before the experiment starts by natural versions of the experiment.) Thus, in the 'conscious' case, the subject must have a state that is about the subject's own perceptual experience (looking familiar) and thus the sense of 'conscious' that is relevant here is what might be termed a 'reflexive' sense. An experience is conscious in this sense just in case it is the object of another of the subject's states, for example one has a thought to the effect that one has that experience.[3] The reflexive sense of 'consciousness' contrasts with phenomenality, which perhaps attaches to some states which are not the objects of other mental states. Reflexivity is phenomenality

---

[3] This definition is overly simple but complications won't matter here.

plus something else (reflection) and that opens up the possibility in principle for phenomenality without reflexivity. For example, it is at least conceptually possible for there to be two people in pain, one of whom is introspecting the pain, the other not. (Perhaps infants or animals can have pain but don't introspect it.) The first is reflexively conscious of the pain, but both have phenomenally conscious states, since pain is by its very nature a phenomenally conscious state. Reflexivity (of the sort we are considering) involves phenomenality plus another state, one that is about the phenomenal state. Note that reflexivity might occur but be unconscious (in the phenomenal sense). (Perhaps this could occur in blindsight or in a Freudian process.) There is clearly a conceptual distinction between phenomenality and reflexivity, even if one or the other does not deserve to be called 'consciousness'. (Oddly, I find some interlocutors want to bar one, some the other; we would be better off not using words like 'consciousness' and 'awareness' since there is so little terminological agreement about them. I would rather use 'phenomenality' and 'reflexivity'.) In any case, the salient empirical question is whether phenomenality and reflexivity come to the same thing in the brain?

What is the relation between reflexivity and the notion of global accessibility discussed in the last section? Global accessibility does not logically require reflexivity, since global accessibility only requires access to the response modes that the organism actually has. Perhaps a dog or a cat does not have the capacity for reflection.[4] Reflexivity is a special kind of access, one that requires intellectual resources that may not be available to every being that can have conscious experience.

There is another aspect to both experimental paradigms just discussed, which motivates taking seriously the hypothesis that the reflexively unconscious case might possibly be phenomenally conscious. In another variant of the exclusion paradigm reported by Debner and Jacoby (1994), heavy masking was replaced by divided attention. Subjects were presented with pairs of words flanked by digits, for example '4reason5', and then given stems consisting of the first three letters of the word ('rea___') to complete. There were two conditions. In the 'conscious' condition, they were told to ignore the digits. In the 'unconscious' condition, they were told to report the sum of the digits before completing the stem. The results were the same as before both qualitatively and quantitatively: in the 'conscious' condition, the subjects were much more likely than baseline to follow the instructions and complete the stem with a word other than 'reason', whereas with 'unconscious' presentations, subjects were much more likely than baseline to violate the exclusion instructions, completing the stem with 'reason'. Merikle and Joordens (this volume) report corresponding results for the false recognition paradigm with divided attention substituted for heavy masking. The added significance of this variant is that it makes one wonder whether there was a fleeting phenomenal consciousness of 'reason' as the subject's eyes moved from the '4' to the '5' in '4reason5'.

---

[4] To avoid over-attributing access consciousness, we have to specify the machinery instead of using the catchall 'global'. For a specific brain architecture that provides flexibility in the choices of devices the conscious information is passed to, see Dehaene, Kerszberg, and Changeux (1998).

What is the status of the 'unconscious' percepts in these experiments? Two theoretical options come to the fore.

1. The 'unconscious perceptions' are both phenomenally and reflexively unconscious. (In this case, the exclusion and false recognition paradigms are about consciousness in both senses.)
2. The 'unconscious perceptions' are phenomenally conscious but reflexively unconscious.

A third option, that they are phenomenally unconscious but 'reflexively conscious', seems less likely because the reflective consciousness would be 'false' – that is, subjects would have a state 'about' a phenomenal state without the phenomenal state itself. That hypothesis would require some extra causal factor that produced the false recognition and would thus be less simple. As between options 1 and 2, I see no reason to think one is more probable than the other. Some critics have disparaged the idea of fleeting phenomenal consciousness in this paradigm. But what they owe us is evidence for 1 or else a reason to think that 1 is the default view.

What about the fact, detailed in the first half of Dehaene and Naccache, that reportable phenomenal experience of a stimulus is systematically correlated with the ability to perform a vast variety of operations with the stimulus, while non-reportable stimulus presentation is associated with a limited, encapsulated set of processing options. This certainly is evidence for a correlation between reflexivity and accessibility. But what does it tell us about phenomenality? First, consider whether it provides evidence that phenomenality and reflexivity go together. It would be question-begging to take the evidence provided by Dehaene and Naccache as evidence of a correlation of phenomenality itself (as opposed to reports of phenomenality) with reflexivity. For the very issue we are considering is whether some of those cases of limited encapsulated processing might involve a brief flash of phenomenality. Of course, the cases of phenomenality that subjects report are reflexively conscious. The issue is whether there are cases of phenomenality that are not reported. Broadening our focus, the same point applies to the supposition that this evidence supports a correlation between phenomenality and accessibility. (In addition, though the considerations presented by Dehaene and Naccache do show a correlation between reflexivity and accessibility in alert adult humans, we cannot generalize to infants or dazed adults or non-humans.)

It may be said that although there is no evidence for preferring 1 to 2, 1 is preferable on methodological grounds. Here is a way of putting the point: 'How are we going to do experiments on consciousness without taking at face value what people say about whether or not they saw something? For example, if we gave up this methodology, we would have to reject blindsight work.' But I am not suggesting abandoning that methodology. We can hold onto the methodology because it is the best we have while at the same time figuring out ways to test it. No one promised us that work on consciousness was going to be easy! In the next section, I will suggest a methodological principle that will help in thinking about how to get evidence on this issue.

Let me tie the issue of this section in with that of the last – the issue stemming from the fact that the classic ventral stream can be activated without reports of awareness. There are three options about the ventral stream in, say, extinction that deserve further consideration.

1. The ventral stream is not activated enough for either phenomenality or reflexivity. (As I mentioned, this one seems disconfirmed.)
2. The ventral stream is activated enough for phenomenality but not enough or in the right way for reflexivity (and more generally, for accessibility). Something else, X, is required (possibly not exactly the same extra ingredient for both).
3. There is no phenomenality or reflexive consciousness of the extinguished stimuli, but what is missing is not activation level but something else, X.

Again, what reason do we have for regarding option 2 (phenomenality without reflexivity) as less likely than 1 or 3?

Dehaene and Naccache argue that durable and explicit information maintenance is one of the functions of consciousness. One of their items of evidence is the Sperling (1960) experiment on iconic memory. Sperling flashed arrays of letters (e.g. 3×3) to subjects for brief periods (e.g. 50 ms). Subjects typically said that they could see all or most of the letters, but they could report only about half of them. Were the subjects right in saying that they could see all the letters? Sperling tried signaling the subjects with a tone. A high tone meant the subject was to report the top row, a medium tone indicated the middle row, etc. If the tone was given immediately after the stimulus, the subjects could usually get all the letters in the row, whatever row was indicated. But once they had named those letters, they usually could name no others. Why did the information decay? One possibility is that the subjects had phenomenal images of all (or almost all) of the letters, and what they lacked was access consciousness and reflexive consciousness of their identities. Subjects report that they see all the letters (Baars, 1988, p. 15; Sperling, 1960), suggesting phenomenal experience of all of them. If so, durable and explicit information maintenance may be a function of reflexive consciousness (or access consciousness) without being a function of phenomenality.

Dehaene and Naccache suggest that the introspective judgments that fuel my phenomenal/access distinction can be accounted for by postulating three levels of accessibility. The two extremes are I_1, total inaccessibility, and I_3, global accessibility. Set I_2 consists of representations that are connected to the global workspace and that can be ushered into it by the application of attention. They suggest that the letters in the Sperling phenomenon are in I_2 until attention is applied to only some of them, at which point those representations enter I_3.

But where does phenomenality come into this system? One option is that both I_2 and I_3 are phenomenal, in which case I_2 representations are phenomenal without being globally accessible, as I argued. Another option – the one favored by Dehaene and Naccache – is that only representations in the global workspace (I_3) are phenomenal. Their proposal is geared towards explaining away the appearance that the subjects saw each letter, claiming that the source of the subjects' judgment is that they could potentially see each letter by focusing on its location. In other words, their proposal is that the subjects mistake potential phenomenality for actual phenomenality, and this yields the appearance of phenomenality without access. Let us call this the Refrigerator Light illusion, the allusion being to the possibility that a technologically naive person might have the illusion that the refrigerator light is always on because it is always on when he looks.

Note, however, that phenomenally active location is not enough to capture the experience of Sperling's subjects. Subjects do not report seeing an array of blobs at locations that turn into letters when they attend to them. Subjects report seeing an array of letters. Subjects in a related masking experiment (to be discussed below) were able to give judgments of brightness, sharpness and contrast for letters that they could not report and they also seemed aware that the stimuli were letters. Speaking as a subject in the Sperling experiment, I am entirely confident that subjects could give such judgments.

The natural way for Dehaene and Naccache to respond would be to say that both the phenomenal and reflexive contents of the subjects in the Sperling experiment include features such as letter-like and features of degrees of sharpness, brightness, and contrast. Thus, they would say, early vision gives subjects experience of these features, which are both phenomenally and reflexively conscious, so there is no discrepancy. Hence, my disagreement with them focuses on the shapes. I say the subjects have phenomenal experience of the shapes, whereas the functionalists say the appearance that the subjects have phenomenal experience of shapes is a case of the Refrigerator Light illusion fostered by the fact that the subjects could potentially access the shapes. (Rather than imputing views to Dehaene and Naccache that they don't actually state, I'll refer to the position that I see as developing out of their view as the functionalist position.)

At this point, the reader may feel that there is little to choose between the two points of view. But there are two considerations that I believe tip the balance in favor of phenomenality without access. The first is that the functionalist position does not accommodate what it is like for the subjects as well as does phenomenality without access. Speaking as a subject, what it is like for the subjects is experiencing all or most of the letter shapes. An analogy: suppose you are one of a group of subjects who report definitely seeing red. The hypothesis that you and the other subjects have an experience as of red accommodates what it is like for the subjects better than the hypothesis that all of you are under the illusion that you have an experience as of red but are really experiencing green. Postulating an illusion is an extreme measure.

Second and more impressive, there is another hypothesis that applies in this case that also applies in the case of some other phenomena (to be discussed). The functionalist appeal to the Refrigerator Light illusion by contrast does not apply so well or not at all in these other cases. Thus, the phenomenality without access hypothesis has the advantage of more generality, whereas the functionalist has the disadvantage of ad hoc postulation.

Let me fill in the phenomenality without access idea a bit. The picture is that the subjects in the Sperling experiment are phenomenally conscious of the letter shapes, but don't have the attentional resources to apply letter concepts or even shape concepts of the sort one applies to unfamiliar shapes when one has plenty of time. Phenomenal experience of shapes does not require shape concepts but reflexive consciousness being an intentional state does require shape concepts, concepts that the subjects seem unable to access in these meager attentional circumstances.

Liss (1968) contrasted subjects' responses to brief unmasked stimuli (one to four letters) with their responses to longer lightly masked stimuli. He asked for judgments of brightness, sharpness and contrast as well as what letters they saw. He found that lightly masked 40 ms stimuli were judged as brighter and sharper than unmasked 9 ms stimuli, even though the subjects could report three of four of the letters in the unmasked stimuli and only one of four in the masked cases. He says: "The Ss commented spontaneously that, despite the high contrast of the letters presented under backward masking, they seemed to appear for such brief duration that there was very little time to identify them before the mask appeared. Although letters presented for only 7 msec with no masking appeared weak and fuzzy, their duration seemed longer than letters presented for 70 msec followed by a mask." (p. 329).

As in the Sperling phenomenon, my hypothesis is that the subjects were phenomenally conscious of all the masked letter shapes, but could not apply the letter concepts required for reflexive consciousness of all of them. And as before, there is an alternative hypothesis – that the contents of both the subject's phenomenal states and their reflexive states are the same and include the features sharp, high contrast, bright and letter-like without any specific shape representation. The key difference between Sperling and Liss is that in the Liss experiment, there is no evidence that the subjects were able to access any letter they chose. Sperling asked them to report an indicated row, whereas Liss did not. In the Liss experiment, subjects were trying to grab all the letters they could, and they could get only about one of four when masked. Thus, the Refrigerator Light illusion hypothesis applied by Dehaene and Naccache to the Sperling phenomenon gets no foothold in the Liss phenomenon. The subjects' conviction that they saw all four of the masked letters would have to be explained in some other way, and that makes the functionalist position ad hoc compared with the hypothesis of phenomenality without reflexivity. The third and final stage of this argument will be presented in the next section in the discussion of the grain of vision where I will mention a third experimental paradigm, one that is completely different from that of either Sperling or Liss which also does not fit the Refrigerator Light illusion hypothesis but does suggest phenomenality without access.

Dennett takes a stand similar to that of Dehaene and Naccache, arguing that potential and actual fame in the brain are all that are needed to handle such phenomena. The Liss experiment just described suggests phenomenality without fame or even potential fame. In addition, potential fame without any hint of phenomenality is often reported. Many people have representations of direction (which way is North) and time without (apparently) phenomenality or the illusion of phenomenality. As soon as they ask themselves the question of what time it is or which way is North, they 'just know'. Before the knowledge popped into mind, it was potentially famous but with no phenomenality or illusion of phenomenality.

Moving back to the main subject of this section, we have seen three concepts of consciousness, phenomenality, reflexive consciousness and access consciousness. Can we blame the disagreements among our authors on different concepts of consciousness?

This ecumenical stance is especially helpful in reading Parvizi and Damasio and Jack and Shallice. Parvizi and Damasio characterize consciousness as follows: "core consciousness occurs when the brain's representation devices generate an imaged, nonverbal account of how the organism's own state is affected by the organism's interaction with an object, and when this process leads to the enhancement of the image of the causative object, thus placing the object saliently in a spatial and temporal context". This would be a mysterious account of phenomenality, since the images mentioned in it presumably already have phenomenality, making the non-verbal account unnecessary. And the account would make little sense as an account of access consciousness, since a thought can be access conscious without involving such images much less images of a causative object or the enhancement of them. The account is best construed as a characterization of reflexive consciousness, since it emphasizes the knowledge of the subject of how that subject has been affected by an interaction, and thus involves reflection.

Jack and Shallice propose that a conscious process is one in which a supervisory system directly selects one of a number of competing schemata plus its arguments. But they do not give us any evidence against the possibility of either phenomenality or global access without supervisory selection, or supervisory selection without phenomenality or global access. Phenomenality might be a matter of activation plus binding, which, as far as we know, could occur in an organism that does not have a supervisory system, or even in an organism that has a supervisory system, without its activity, or even with its activity, without its selecting one of a number of competing schemata. Access might be a matter of broadcasting in a system that contains no supervisor. Conversely, it would appear at first glance that there could be supervisory selection of the sort they suggest without phenomenality or global access. They do give evidence that supervisory selection among schemata does lead to encoding of specific episodes, but they don't argue that this encoding requires either phenomenality or global accessibility. If Jack and Shallice were advancing a theory of phenomenality or of access consciousness, there would be a heavy burden on them to justify it, a burden that they give no hint of acknowledging. But as a theory of reflexive consciousness it makes much more sense. Reflexive consciousness involves one aspect of the mind monitoring another aspect, for example a sensory state, so in one sense of 'supervisory', reflexive consciousness necessarily involves a supervisory system. (They make a similar point.) Jack and Shallice would still owe us an account of why there can't be reflexive consciousness where the supervisory system focuses on a sensory state without choosing among competing schemata. But at least with reflexive consciousness they are in the right ballpark.

Jack and Shallice may be skeptical about the global workplace account. Shallice (1975) argued that there is reason to think that there is more than one 'workplace' for different functions, and no global one. He was criticizing the Atkinson and Shiffrin (1971) idea that "in some sense consciousness can be 'equated' with the short-term store" (Shallice, 1975, p. 270). And Jack and Shallice note that it is unlikely that representational codes in different modules match. But the version of the global workspace model advocated by Dehaene and Naccache does not extend to broadcasting within modules. They are not committed to the idea that conscious experiences of, say, color are available to the phonology module, nor do Jack and Shallice suggest any such thing.

Perhaps Jack and Shallice think that representations that have been selected by a supervisory system of a certain sort are as a matter of fact globally accessible in an appropriately qualified sense, but that does not address the issue of why their definition characterizes a necessary condition for global accessibility (of an appropriately limited sort). Could a machine be made which has globally accessible representations that are not the result of selection of competing schemata by a supervisory system? They don't say why not.

Though Jack and Shallice give an account that makes sense as a theory of reflexive consciousness (and maybe as an account of access consciousness restricted to humans), they have ambitions for its application to any process that is **phenomenally** the same. They say "Tasks involving Type-C processes should either actually require the subject to make an introspective judgment, or be phenomenologically similar to tasks that do." Also, Dehaene and Naccache make it clear that they see their stance as applying to (as I would put it) phenomenality. Just after the words quoted earlier, they say "We postulate that this global availability of information through the workspace is what we subjectively experience as a conscious state." Someone (like myself) who believes in phenomenality as distinct from its function would naturally think that phenomenality causes the global availability of information, not that phenomenality is the global availability of information (although, given our ignorance about the fundamental nature of phenomenality, I am not prepared to rule that option out a priori). In sum, these theories are best seen as theories of reflexivity or global accessibility rather than as theories of phenomenality but their advocates claim phenomenality nevertheless.

4. Is it impossible in principle to empirically distinguish phenomenality from reflexivity?

Some objectors think that the distinction between phenomenality and reflexivity has no real empirical significance. Here is a version of that view: 'In order to ascertain empirically whether a phenomenal state is present or absent or what its content is, we require the subject's testimony. But when a subject says that he did or didn't see something, or that his state did or didn't have a certain content, he is exhibiting presence or absence of the relevant reflexive consciousness too. So how can there ever be an empirical wedge between phenomenality and reflexivity or between phenomenal content and reflexive content?' Further, if the contents of phenomenal states are non-conceptual, how can we ever find out what they are by attention to what a subject says? (A similar but more difficult issue arises about the relation between phenomenality and global accessibility that I won't have the space to discuss.)

Here are some considerations that should loosen the grip of this pessimistic point of view. First, consider the common experience, mentioned earlier, of suddenly noticing that one has been hearing a noise for some time. Testimony at time t_2 can be evidence for phenomenality at time t_1 even though the subject did not notice the phenomenal experience at time t_1. That is, a phenomenal state does not have to be accompanied simultaneously by a reflection on it for there to be testimony about it. How do we know there wasn't also a brief flash of reflexivity about the phenomenality at t_1? There is no reason to believe there is any principled problem of discovering such a thing, since reflexivity is a kind of thought. (For example, if we discover a language of thought hypothesis to characterize thought in other circumstances, we could apply it here.)

Second, note that reflexivity involves phenomenality plus more – reflection on the phenomenality.[5] If this is right, we can see that whatever processes produce the reflection will – like all physical processes – sometimes misfire and we will have phenomenality without reflexivity. Therefore, the prior probability of phenomenality without reflexivity is considerable. Jack and Shallice may think otherwise – their theory certainly presupposes otherwise – but they do not present a single empirical result that points in this direction. To the extent that they supply a case against phenomenality without reflexivity, it is entirely philosophical.

We can guess that phenomenality without reflexivity will happen when the machinery of reflection is damped down – perhaps in infants whose reflection machinery is undeveloped or in adults where it is permanently or temporarily damaged, or in animals where it is minimal to begin with. When we know that something very likely occurs and we have an idea of what makes it occur, we should not be pessimistic about our ability to find a reliable way of experimentally exploring it.

The best way to silence the pessimistic point of view is to canvas some empirical approaches. One line of evidence emerges from work by Cavanagh and his colleagues that shows that the resolution of visual attention is five to ten times coarser than the resolution of vision itself (Cavanagh, He, & Intriligator, 1998; He, Cavanagh, & Intriligator, 1996; Intriligator & Cavanagh, in press). The grain of visual attention is about 5–10 arc min (1 arc min is a 60th of a degree) at the fovea (the densest area of the retina), whereas the grain of vision is about 1 arc min at the fovea. What is meant by 'grain' and 'resolution'? In the experiments by Cavanagh and his colleagues, the resolution of vision is measured by such procedures as whether a subject can verbally distinguish a set of lines from a uniform gray field, and whether the subject can report the orientation of the lines. The resolution of visual attention can be measured by whether the subject can count the items to be resolved, but a better measure is a 'stepping' procedure that is illustrated in Fig. 1. First, fixate on the dot in the middle. (This is necessary to avoid eye movements, and consequent complication in interpretation; whether subjects succeed in fixating can be checked with eye-tracking

---

[5] I am ignoring the possibility that reflexivity might occur without the experience it is normally about.

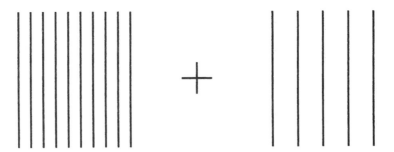

Fig. 1. Fixate on the dot at the center and attend to the lines on the right, with the page held at arm's length. (Distance is not very important with this display.) Subjects are capable of 'stepping' (described in the text) from one line to another on the right (though with trouble on line 3) but not on the left. From Cavanagh et al. (1998).

devices.) One line lights up; the subject is asked to focus on that one, then move, for example, one to the right, another to the right, one to the left, or one to the right. Success is determined by checking which line the subject is focused on at the end. In the set of four lines on the right in Fig. 1, most subjects can step through the first, second and fourth lines from the left, but the third tends to cause trouble. Most subjects cannot step through the lines on the left even though the lines on the left are visually resolvable. Attentional resolution can also be measured by a tracking task developed by Pylyshyn and his colleagues (Pylyshyn and Storm, 1988).

How are these findings relevant to the distinction between phenomenality and reflexivity? Landolt (1891) – who apparently was the first to publish an observation of the phenomenon – asked observers to count finely spaced dots or stripes. As Intriligator and Cavanagh (in press) note, Landolt's observers could not count the stripes or dots if their spacing was less than about 5 arc min, even though they could still see them. Landolt says "You get to a point where you can no longer count them at all, even though they remain perfectly and distinctly visible."[6] (Landolt's subjects looked right at them instead of fixating to a single spot to the side, but it turns out that that the eye movements didn't matter much for his stimuli.) The individual lines remain "purely and distinctly visible" – in my terms, one is phenomenally conscious of them. And one can say roughly how many there are. But, to the extent that one cannot attend to them, one cannot apply concepts to them, e.g. shape concepts. True, one has an impression of lines of a certain length (as on the left of Fig. 1), but to the extent that one cannot attend to individual items, one cannot distinguish the shape of one from another. If the items are gratings rather than lines, one cannot say what the orientation is, and if they are letters, one can see that they are letters but not which letters they are. My suggestion is the same as the one I made in the case of Sperling and Liss, namely that the subjects may have phenomenal awareness of the individual

---

[6] "on arrive à un point où l'on ne peut plus les compter d'aucune façon, alors qu'ils demeurent encore parfaitement et distinctement visibles" (p. 385).

shapes without the attentional resources to apply shape concepts to them and thus without reflexive awareness of them.

There is an alternative hypothesis – that the contents of both the subject's phenomenal states and their reflexive states are the same and include the feature 'letter-like' without any specific shape. Cavanagh speaks of seeing a 'texture'. There is a reason for preferring my hypothesis – namely that subjects find the individual items "perfectly and distinctly visible" in Landolt's phrase. (Look at Fig. 1. Doesn't it seem to you that you see each line, rather than just a texture of a sort one has learned is produced by lines?) But perhaps subjects are under an illusion of some sort? Perhaps, but if so, it is not the same as the 'Refrigerator Light' illusion postulated by Dehaene and Naccache in the case of the Sperling phenomenon. You will recall that they supposed that the sense of subjects in the Sperling experiment that they saw all the letters derived from the fact that they could attend to any small number of their locations and be aware of the identity of the letter. But there is no such thing here. No matter how hard subjects try, they cannot ascertain the identity of stimuli that are crowded to the point of being below the grain of attention. This hypothesis, then, has more generality than the Refrigerator Light illusion hypothesis of Dehaene and Naccache.

Interestingly, adaptation to the orientation of gratings that the subject cannot report affects the detection of other gratings as much as uncrowded gratings whose orientation the subjects can report. He et al. (1996) note that V1 is the first site of orientation processing, so the attentional effect of crowding must occur later in processing than V1. They conclude that activation of neurons in V1 is "insufficient for conscious perception" (p. 335), but although this result shows V1 is insufficient for reflexive consciousness, it is less effective in showing that activation in V1 is insufficient for phenomenality (Block, 1996). Don't get me wrong. I'm not saying activation in V1 is sufficient for phenomenality. I'm making a logical point about comparative strength of evidence, the upshot of which is that an empirical wedge between phenomenality and reflexivity is possible. More generally, I agree that it could be discovered that, contrary to what I've been arguing, one is phenomenally aware of exactly the same features that one is reflexively aware of. I do not say that there is strong evidence for phenomenality without reflexivity. My point is that for stimuli that are below the level of attentional resolution but above the level of visual resolution, there is a better case for phenomenal awareness than for reflexive awareness.

If my picture of the attentional phenomena is accepted, it can also avoid the conclusion that many have drawn from the change blindness and inattentional blindness literature (Simons, 2000), that there is an 'illusion' of rich visual awareness of the world. As Cavanagh (1999) puts it, "But what of our feeling that we piece together our world in multiple glances, building up a reasonably complete model of a stable world around us? This concept of a rich model of the world does not hold up." Vision, he says give us a "false sense of "knowing what is out there"". (This view, a version of the Refrigerator Light hypothesis, is strongly defended in O'Regan (1992).) We can avoid the idea that vision creates an illusion if our perception of the world is phenomenally rich but attentively (and therefore conceptually) sparse.

That is, our phenomenal impression is accurate, but only the attended aspects of it are available for the tasks tapped in the change blindness literature.[7]

Turning to something completely different. I will mention an old somewhat anecdotal result, not because it is itself serious evidence for anything, but because it illustrates some methodological points.

I have in mind the strange phenomenon of aerodontalgia (Melzack & Wall, 1988; Nathan, 1985). Two American dentists in Britain in World War II noticed that pilots who went up in the unpressurized planes of the time often complained of pains that seemed to be recreations of pains of previous dental work, even though the dental work had been done under anesthesia. They hypothesized that the recreated pains all derived from dental work done under general anesthesia rather than local anesthesia and they put this hypothesis to the test by doing extractions under combinations of local and general anesthesia. The result was that they only got recreated pains for general anesthesia. For example, if they gave a pilot general anesthesia and also local anesthetic on the left side and then extracted teeth from both sides, they got recreated pains from the right side only. (They used a substitute for the unpressurized planes – stimulation of the nasal mucosa – since it turned out that the effect of the unpressurized cabins was mediated by sinus stimulation.)

My point is not that this is serious evidence for phenomenal states under general anesthesia. This is old work that was not done by behavioral scientists. I don't know of any replication. Further, even if replicated, there would be a problem since maybe what happened was that traces were laid down under general anesthesia without any phenomenal event, and then those traces later produced a phenomenal event. This would be representation of pain under general anesthesia rather than pain under general anesthesia. My points about this experiment are these:

1. Though the evidence is flawed, it is better evidence for phenomenality under general anesthesia than it is for reflexive consciousness under general anesthesia, since a reflexively conscious pain is a phenomenal event (pain is necessarily phenomenal) plus something else – reflection on it. That is, we are on better ground postulating a pain under general anesthesia than a pain plus reflection on it.
2. The methodological point is that the reflexively conscious second pain can be evidence for the first pain even though the first pain isn't reflexively conscious – we don't need the subject's testimony about the first pain itself. It is this feature of the aerodontalgia case that makes it methodologically interesting despite the obvious flaws and despite the fact that it is not in itself serious evidence for phenomenality without reflexivity. To see the interest of this methodological item, consider the following objection: 'If you think of phenomenality as a purely

---

[7] Wolfe (1999) advocates 'inattentional amnesia' rather than inattentional blindness, which comports with the view I am advocating. Simons (2000) quotes Wolfe as suggesting that we might think of subject's failure to notice in the change and inattentional 'blindness' literature as 'inattentional agnosia'. Since agnosia involves failure of application of concepts to stimuli, there is another overlap between my view and that of Wolfe.

subjective phenomenon – something only the subject can tell you about – how can you possibly get evidence for phenomenality which the subject can't report?' Answer: the sense of subjectivity in the objection is faulty. Subjectivity does not entail that only the subject can tell us about it.

Objection: 'But you have admitted that this is far from conclusive evidence for phenomenality without reflexivity. Doesn't the principled problem arise again when you try to go from highly flawed evidence of the sort you are presenting to conclusive evidence of the sort that the scientific community would be compelled to believe? How could we ever get more than a glimmer of evidence for phenomenality without reflexivity?' The answer is that if we can get many convergent though flawed sources of evidence – so long as the flaws are of different sorts and uncorrelated – we will have a convincing case. (Note that I am not saying that a lot of weak evidence adds up to strong evidence.) For example, there are different methods of dating rocks and artifacts based on isotopes. Those based on counting the products of radioactive decay, 'daughter' isotopes (e.g. potassium-argon dating), have different flaws from those based on counting decay of the parent substance (e.g. carbon-14 dating), and other methods such as the fission track method have still different flaws, but if a number of measures with different flaws agree, that is very convincing.

5. Conclusion

The papers in this volume deploy three different concepts of consciousness.

1. Phenomenality: experience. This is the concept of consciousness that is most directly the subject of the hypothesis discussed by Driver and Vuilleumier and Kanwisher that visual consciousness is ventral stream activation plus X.
2. Access consciousness: global accessibility. This is the concept of consciousness most directly related to Dehaene and Naccache's account of consciousness as being broadcast in a global neuronal workspace and Dennett's account of consciousness as cerebral celebrity.
3. Reflexive consciousness: a special kind of access; a state is introspectively conscious just in case (roughly) it is the object of another state. This is the concept of consciousness most clearly involved in reasoning about the false recognition and exclusion experiments (Merikle et al.) and is most appropriate to Jack and Shallice.

Some of the disagreements among the contributors to the volume can be explained by interpreting them as talking about different things.

Are the three kinds of consciousness aspects of a single thing? There are a number of ways of interpreting this question. One is the sense of aspects of a single thing in which the solid, liquid and gaseous phase are aspects of a single substance. In this sense, being an aspect of a single thing requires that for any solid substance there be some conditions under which it would be gaseous. In this sense, I think it is a wide-open empirical question whether phenomenality and access consciousness are aspects of a single thing. But I suspect that it is less likely that reflexivity can be included with these two. If a lizard has phenomenality, must there be conditions in which it would have reflexive consciousness of that phenomenality? If you are doubtful, then you are doubtful whether all three kinds of consciousness are aspects of a single thing.

Acknowledgements

I am grateful to Susan Carey, Nancy Kanwisher, Georges Rey and Jesse Prinz for comments on an earlier version, and I am especially grateful to Stan Dehaene and Tony Jack for many rounds of debate on key issues on which we disagree. The paper has been much improved as a result of these controversies.

References

Atkinson, & Shiffrin (1971). The control of short-term memory. Scientific American, 225, 82–90.

Baars, B. J. (1988). A cognitive theory of consciousness. Cambridge University Press: Cambridge.

Block, N. (1995). On a confusion about a function of consciousness. Behavioral and Brain Sciences, 18, 2. Reprinted in N. Block, O. Flanagan, & G. Güzeldere (Eds.), Consciousness. Cambridge, MA: MIT Press, 1997.

Block, N. (1996). How can we find the neural correlate of consciousness? Trends in Neuroscience, 19, 456–459.

Block, N. (1997). Biology vs. computation in the study of consciousness. Behavioral and Brain Sciences, 20, 1.

Burge, T. (1997). Two kinds of consciousness. In N. Block, O. Flanagan, & G. Güzeldere (Eds.), Consciousness. Cambridge, MA: MIT Press.

Caramazza, A., & Hillis, A. E. (1990). Levels of representation, coordinate frames, and unilateral neglect. Cognitive Neuropsychology, 7 (5/6), 391–445.

Cavanagh, P. (1999). Attention: exporting vision to the mind. In C. Taddei-Ferretti, & C. Musio (Eds.), Neuronal basis and psychological aspects of consciousness (pp. 129–143). Singapore: World Scientific.

Cavanagh, P., He, S., & Intriligator, J. (1998). Attentional resolution: the grain and locus of visual awareness. In C. Taddei-Ferretti (Ed.), Neuronal basis and psychological aspects of consciousness. Singapore: World Scientific.

Debner, J. A., & Jacoby, L. L. (1994). Unconscious perception: attention, awareness and control. Journal of Experimental Psychology: Learning, Memory and Cognition, 20, 304–317.

DeGelder, B., Vroomen, J., Pourtois, G., & Weiskrantz, L. (1999). Non-conscious recognition of affect in the absence of striate cortex. NeuroReport, 10, 3759–3763.

Dehaene, S., Kerszberg, M., & Changeux, J. P. (1998). A neuronal model of a global workspace in effortful cognitive tasks. Proceedings of the National Academy of Sciences USA, 95, 14529–14534.

Friedman-Hill, S., Robertson, L., & Treisman, A. (1995). Parietal contributions to visual feature binding: evidence from a patient with bilateral lesions. Science, 269, 853–855.

He, S., Cavanagh, P., & Intriligator, J. (1996). Attentional resolution and the locus of visual awareness. Nature, 383, 334–337.

Intriligator, J., & Cavanagh, P. (in press). The spatial resolution of visual attention. Cognitive Psychology.

Jacoby, L. L., & Whitehouse, K. (1989). An illusion of memory: false recognition influenced by unconscious perception. Journal of Experimental Psychology: General, 118, 126–135.

Kentridge, R. W., Heywood, C. A., & Weiskrantz, L. (1999). Attention without awareness in blindsight. Proceedings of the Royal Society of London, Series B, Biological Science, 266 (1430), 1805–1811.

Landolt, E. (1891). Nouvelles recherches sur la physiologie des mouvements des yeux. Archives d'Ophthalmologie, 11, 385–395.

Liss, P. (1968). Does backward masking by visual noise stop stimulus processing? Perception & Psychophysics, 4, 328–330.

Lumer, E., & Rees, G. (1999). Covariation of activity in visual and prefrontal cortex associated with subjective visual perception. Proceedings of the National Academy of Sciences USA, 96, 1669–1673.

McGlinchey-Berroth, R., Milberg, W. P., Verfaellie, M., Alexander, M., & Kilduff, P. (1993). Semantic priming in the neglected field: evidence from a lexical decision task. Cognitive Neuropsychology, 10, 79–108.

Melzack, R., & Wall, P. (1988). The challenge of pain (2nd ed.). London: Penguin.

Merikle, P., & Joordens, S. (1997). Parallels between perception without attention and perception without awareness. Consciousness and Cognition, 6, 219–236.

Milner, A. D., & Goodale, M. A. (1995). The visual brain in action. Oxford: Oxford University Press.

Nathan, P. (1985). Pain and nociception in the clinical context. Philosophical Transactions of the Royal Society of London, Series B, 308, 219–226.

O'Regan, J. K. (1992). Solving the 'real' mysteries of visual perception: the world as an outside memory. Canadian Journal of Psychology, 46, 461–488.

Prinz, J. J. (2000). A neurofunctional theory of visual consciousness. Consciousness and Cognition, 9 (2), 243–259.

Pylyshyn, Z., & Storm, R. (1988). Tracking multiple independent targets: evidence for a parallel tracking mechanism. Spatial Vision, 3, 179–197.

Rees, G., Wojciulik, E., Clarke, K., Husain, M., Frith, C., & Driver, J. (in press). Unconscious activation of visual cortex in the damaged right hemisphere of a parietal patient with extinction. Brain.

Shallice, T. (1975). On the contents of primary memory. In P. M. A. Rabbit, & S. Dornic (Eds.), Attention and performance, V. London: Academic Press.

Simons, D. (2000). Attentional capture and inattentional blindness. Trends in Cognitive Science, 4 (4), 147–155.

Sperling, G. (1960). The information available in brief visual presentations. Psychological Monographs, 74 (11), 1–29.

Tipper, S. P., & Behrman, M. (1996). Object-centered not scene based visual neglect. Journal of Experimental Psychology: Human Perception and Performance, 22, 1261–1278.

Wojciulik, E., & Kanwisher, N. (1998). Implicit visual attribute binding following bilateral parietal damage. Visual Cognition, 5, 157–181.

Wolfe, J. M. (1999). Inattentional amnesia. In V. Coltheart (Ed.), Fleeting memories. Cambridge, MA: MIT Press.

8

Are we explaining consciousness yet?

Daniel Dennett

Center for Cognitive Studies, Tufts University, Medford, MA 02155, USA

Abstract

Theorists are converging from quite different quarters on a version of the global neuronal workspace model of consciousness, but there are residual confusions to be dissolved. In particular, theorists must resist the temptation to see global accessibility as the cause of consciousness (as if consciousness were some other, further condition); rather, it is consciousness. A useful metaphor for keeping this elusive idea in focus is that consciousness is rather like fame in the brain. It is not a privileged medium of representation, or an added property some states have; it is the very mutual accessibility that gives some informational states the powers that come with a subject's consciousness of that information. Like fame, consciousness is not a momentary condition, or a purely dispositional state, but rather a matter of actual influence over time. Theorists who take on the task of accounting for the aftermath that is critical for consciousness often appear to be leaving out the Subject of consciousness, when in fact they are providing an analysis of the Subject, a necessary component in any serious theory of consciousness. © 2001 Elsevier Science B.V. All rights reserved.

Keywords: Consciousness; Fame; Explaining

1. Clawing our way towards consensus

As the Decade of the Brain (declared by President Bush in 1990) comes to a close, we are beginning to discern how the human brain achieves consciousness. Dehaene and Naccache (in this volume) see convergence coming from quite different quarters on a version of the global neuronal workspace model. There are still many differences of emphasis to negotiate, and, no doubt, some errors of detail to correct, but there is enough common ground to build on. I agree, and will attempt to re-articulate

E-mail address: ddennett@tufts.edu (D. Dennett).

this emerging view in slightly different terms, emphasizing a few key points that are often resisted, in hopes of precipitating further consolidation. (On the eve of the Decade of the Brain, Baars (1988) had already described a 'gathering consensus' in much the same terms: consciousness, he said, is accomplished by a "distributed society of specialists that is equipped with a working memory, called a global workspace, whose contents can be broadcast to the system as a whole" (p. 42). If, as Jack and Shallice (this volume) point out, Baars' functional neuroanatomy has been superceded, this shows some of the progress we've made in the intervening years.)

A consensus may be emerging, but the seductiveness of the paths not taken is still potent, and part of my task here will be to diagnose some instances of backsliding and suggest therapeutic countermeasures. Of course those who still vehemently oppose this consensus will think it is I who needs therapy. These are difficult questions. Here is Dehaene and Naccache's (this volume) short summary of the global neuronal workspace model, to which I have attached some amplificatory notes on key terms, intended as friendly amendments to be elaborated in the rest of the paper:

At any given time, many modular (1) cerebral networks are active in parallel and process information in an unconscious manner. An information (2) becomes conscious, however, if the neural population that represents it is mobilized by top-down (3) attentional amplification into a brain-scale state of coherent activity that involves many neurons distributed throughout the brain. The long distance connectivity of these "workplace neurons" can, when they are active for a minimal duration (4), make the information available to a variety of processes including perceptual categorization, long-term memorization, evaluation, and intentional action. We postulate that this global availability of information through the workplace is (5) what we subjectively experience as a conscious state. (from the Abstract)

(1) Modularity comes in degrees and kinds; what is being stressed here is only that these are specialist networks with limited powers of information processing.

(2) There is no standard term for an event in the brain that carries information or content on some topic (e.g. information about color at a retinal location, information about a phoneme heard, information about the familiarity or novelty of other information currently being carried, etc.). Whenever some specialist network or smaller structure makes a discrimination, fixes some element of content, 'an information' in their sense comes into existence. 'Signal', 'content-fixation' (Dennett, 1991), 'micro-taking' (Dennett & Kinsbourne, 1992), 'wordless narrative' (Damasio, 1999), and 'representation' (see Jack and Shallice in this volume) are among the near-synonyms in use.

(3) We should be careful not to take the term 'top-down' too literally. Since there is no single organizational summit to the brain, it means only that such attentional amplification is not just modulated 'bottom-up' by features internal to the processing stream in which it rides, but also by sideways influences, from competitive, cooperative, collateral activities whose emergent net result is what we may lump together

and call top-down influence. In an arena of opponent processes (as in a democracy) the 'top' is distributed, not localized. Nevertheless, among the various competitive processes, there are important bifurcations or thresholds that can lead to strikingly different sequels, and it is these differences that best account for our pre-theoretical intuitions about the difference between conscious and unconscious events in the mind. If we are careful, we can use 'top-down' as an innocent allusion, exploiting a vivid fossil trace of a discarded Cartesian theory to mark the real differences that that theory mis-described. (This will be elaborated in my discussion of Jack and Shallice (this volume) below.)

(4) How long must this minimal duration be? Long enough to make the information available to a variety of processes – that's all. One should resist the temptation to imagine some other effect that needs to build up over time, because...

(5) The proposed consensual thesis is not that this global availability causes some further effect or a different sort altogether – igniting the glow of conscious qualia, gaining entrance to the Cartesian Theater, or something like that – but that it is, all by itself, a conscious state. This is the hardest part of the thesis to understand and embrace. In fact, some who favor the rest of the consensus balk at this point and want to suppose that global availability must somehow kindle some special effect over and above the merely computational or functional competences such global availability ensures. Those who harbor this hunch are surrendering just when victory is at hand, I will argue, for these 'merely functional' competences are the very competences that consciousness was supposed to enable.

Here is where scientists have been tempted – or blackmailed – into defending unmistakably philosophical theses about consciousness, on both sides of the issue. Some have taken up the philosophical issues with relish, and others with reluctance and foreboding, with uneven results for both types. In this paper I will highlight a few of the points made and attempted, supporting some and criticizing others, but mainly trying to show how relatively minor decisions about word choice and emphasis can conspire to mislead the theoretician's imagination. Is there a 'Hard Problem' (Chalmers, 1995, 1996) and if so what is it, and what could possibly count as progress towards solving it? Although I have staunchly defended – and will defend here again – the verdict that Chalmers' 'Hard Problem' is a theorist's illusion (Dennett, 1996b, 1998a), something inviting therapy, and not a real problem to be solved with revolutionary new science, I view my task here to be dispelling confusion first, and taking sides second. Let us see, as clearly as we can, what the question is, and is not, before we declare any allegiances.

Dehaene and Naccache (this volume) provide a good survey of the recent evidence in favor of this consensus, much of it analyzed in greater deal in the other papers in this volume, and I would first like to supplement their survey with a few anticipations drawn from farther afield. The central ideas are not new, though they have often been overlooked or underestimated. In 1959, the mathematician (and coiner of the term, 'artificial intelligence') John McCarthy, commenting on Oliver Selfridge's pioneering Pandemonium, the first model of a competitive, non-hierarchical computational architecture, clearly articulated the fundamental idea of the global workspace hypothesis:

I would like to speak briefly about some of the advantages of the pandemonium model as an actual model of conscious behaviour. In observing a brain,
one should make a distinction between that aspect of the behaviour which is
available consciously, and those behaviours, no doubt equally important, but
which proceed unconsciously. If one conceives of the brain as a pandemonium
– a collection of demons – perhaps what is going on within the demons can be
regarded as the unconscious part of thought, and what the demons are publicly
shouting for each other to hear, as the conscious part of thought. (McCarthy,
1959, p. 147)

And in a classic paper, the psychologist Paul Rozin (1976), argued that

specializations... form the building blocks for higher level intelligence... At
the time of their origin, these specializations are tightly wired into the functional system they were designed to serve and are thus inaccessible to other
programs or systems of the brain. I suggest that in the course of evolution these
programs become more accessible to other systems and, in the extreme, may
rise to the level of consciousness and be applied over the full realm of behavior
or mental function. (p. 246)

The key point, for both McCarthy and Rozin, is that it is the specialist demons'
accessibility to each other (and not to some imagined higher Executive or central
Ego) that could in principle explain the dramatic increases in cognitive competence
that we associate with consciousness: the availability to deliberate reflection, the
non-automaticity, in short, the open-mindedness that permits a conscious agent to
consider anything in its purview in any way it chooses. This idea was also central to
what I called the Multiple Drafts Model (Dennett, 1991), which was offered as an
alternative to the traditional, and still popular, Cartesian Theater Model, which
supposes there is a place in the brain to which all the unconscious modules send
their results for ultimate conscious appreciation by the Audience. The Multiple
Drafts Model did not provide, however, a sufficiently vivid and imagination-friendly
antidote to the Cartesian imagery we have all grown up with, so more recently I have
proposed what I consider to be a more useful guiding metaphor: 'fame in the brain'
or 'cerebral celebrity' (Dennett, 1994a, 1996a, 1998a).

2. Competition for clout

The basic idea is that consciousness is more like fame than television; it is not a
special 'medium of representation' in the brain into which content-bearing events
must be transduced in order to become conscious. As Kanwisher (this volume) aptly
emphasizes: "the neural correlates of awareness of a given perceptual attribute are
found in the very neural structure that perceptually analyzes that attribute". Instead
of switching media or going somewhere in order to become conscious, heretofore
unconscious contents, staying right where they are, can achieve something rather
like fame in competition with other fame-seeking (or just potentially fame-finding)
contents. And, according to this view, that is what consciousness is.

Of course consciousness couldn't be fame, exactly, in the brain, since to be famous is to be a shared intentional object in the conscious minds of many folk, and although the brain is usefully seen as composed of hordes of demons (or homunculi), if we were to imagine them to be au courant in the ways they would need to be to elevate some of their brethren to cerebral celebrity, we would be endowing these subhuman components with too much human psychology – and, of course, installing a patent infinite regress in the model as a theory of consciousness. The looming infinite regress can be stopped the way such threats are often happily stopped, not by abandoning the basic idea but by softening it. As long as your homunculi are more stupid and ignorant than the intelligent agent they compose, the nesting of homunculi within homunculi can be finite, bottoming out, eventually, with agents so unimpressive that they can be replaced by machines (Dennett, 1978). So consciousness is not so much fame, then, as political influence – a good slang term is clout. When processes compete for ongoing control of the body, the one with the greatest clout dominates the scene until a process with even greater clout displaces it. In some oligarchies, perhaps, the only way to have clout is to be known by the King, dispenser of all powers and privileges. Our brains are more democratic, indeed somewhat anarchic. In the brain there is no King, no Official Viewer of the State Television Program, no Cartesian Theater, but there are still plenty of quite sharp differences in political clout exercised by contents over time. In Dehaene and Naccache's (this volume) terms, this political difference is achieved by 'reverberation' in a 'sustained amplification loop', while the losing competitors soon fade into oblivion, unable to recruit enough specialist attention to achieve self-sustaining reverberation.

What a theory of consciousness needs to explain is how some relatively few contents become elevated to this political power, with all the ensuing aftermath, while most others evaporate into oblivion after doing their modest deeds in the ongoing projects of the brain. Why is this the task of a theory of consciousness? Because that is what conscious events do. They hang around, monopolizing time 'in the limelight'. We cannot settle for putting it that way, however. There is no literal searchlight of attention, so we need to explain away this seductive metaphor by explaining the functional powers of attention-grabbing without presupposing a single attention-giving source. This means we need to address two questions. Not just (1) How is this fame in the brain achieved? but also (2) – which I have called the Hard Question – And Then What Happens? (Dennett, 1991, p. 255). One may postulate activity in one neural structure or another as the necessary and sufficient condition for consciousness, but one must then take on the burden of the explaining why that activity ensures the political power of the events it involves – and this means taking a good hard look at how the relevant differences in competence might be enabled by changes in status in the brain.

Hurley (1998) makes a persuasive case for taking the Hard Question seriously in somewhat different terms: the Self (and its surrogates, the Cartesian res cogitans, the Kantian transcendental ego, among others) is not to be located by subtraction, by peeling off the various layers of perceptual and motor 'interface' between Self and World. We must reject the traditional 'sandwich' in which the Self is isolated from the outside world by layers of 'input' and 'output'. On the contrary, the Self is large, concrete, and visible in the world, not just 'distributed' in the brain but spread out into the world. Where we act and where we perceive is not funneled through a bottleneck, physical or metaphysical, in spite of the utility of such notions as 'point of view'. As she notes, the very content of perception can change, while keeping input constant, by changes in output (p. 289).

This interpenetration of effects and contents can be fruitfully studied, and several avenues for future research are opened up by papers in this volume. What particularly impresses me about them is that the authors are all, in their various ways, more alert to the obligation to address the Hard Question than many previous theorists have been, and the result is a clearer, better focused picture of consciousness in the brain, with no leftover ghosts lurking. If we set aside our philosophical doubts (settled or not) about consciousness as global fame or clout, we can explore in a relatively undistorted way the empirical questions regarding the mechanisms and pathways that are necessary, or just normal, for achieving this interesting functional status (we can call it a Type-C status, following Jack and Shallice (this volume), if we want to remind ourselves of what we are setting aside, while remaining noncommittal). For example, Parvizi and Damasio (this volume) claim that a midbrain panel of specialist proto-self evaluators accomplish a normal, but not necessary, evaluation process that amounts to a sort of triage, which can boost a content into reverberant fame or consign it to oblivion; these proto-self evaluators thereby tend to secure fame for those contents that are most relevant to current needs of the body. Driver and Vuilleumier (this volume) concentrate on the 'fate of extinguished stimuli', exploring some of the ways that multiple competitions – e.g. as proposed by the Desimone and Duncan (1995) Winner-Take-All Model of multiple competition – leave not only single winners, but lots of quite powerful semi-finalists or also-rans, whose influences can be traced even when they don't achieve the canonical – indeed, operationalized – badge of fame: subsequent reportability (more on that, below). Kanwisher (this volume) points out that sheer 'activation strength' is no mark of consciousness until we see to what use that strength is put ('And then what happens?') and proposes that "the neural correlates of the contents of visual awareness are represented in the ventral pathway, whereas the neural correlates of more general-purpose content-independent processes associated with awareness (attention, binding, etc.) are found primarily in the dorsal pathway", which suggests (if I understand her claim rightly) that, just as in the wider world, whether or not you become famous can depend on what is going on elsewhere at the same time. Jack and Shallice (this volume) propose a complementary balance between prefrontal cortex and anterior cingulate, a sort of high-road versus low-road dual path, with particular attention to the Hard Question: what can happen, what must happen, what may happen when Type-C processes occur, or put otherwise, what Type-C-processes are necessary for, normal for, not necessary for. Particularly important are the ways in which successive winners dramatically alter the prospects (for fame, for influence) of their successors, creating nonce-structures that temporarily govern the competition. Such effects, described at the level of competition between 'informations', can begin to explain how one (one agent, one subject) can 'sculpt the response space' (Frith, 2000, discussed in Jack and Shallice in this volume). This downstream capacity of one information to change the competitive context for whatever informations succeed it is indeed a fame-like competence, a hugely heightened influence that not only retrospectively distinguishes it from its competitors at the time but also, just as importantly, contributes to the creation of a relatively long-lasting Executive, not a place in the brain but a sort of political coalition that can be seen to be in control over the subsequent competitions for some period of time. Such differences in aftermath can be striking, perhaps never more so than those recently demonstrated effects that show, as Dehaene and Naccache (this volume) note, "the impossibility for subjects [i.e. Executives] to strategically use the unconscious information", in such examples as Debner and Jacoby (1994) and Smith and Merikle (1999) (discussed in Merikle, Smilek, & Eastwood in this volume).

Consciousness, like fame, is not an intrinsic property, and not even just a dispositional property; it is a phenomenon that requires some actualization of the potential – and this is why you cannot make any progress on it until you address the Hard Question and look at the aftermath. Consider the following tale. Jim has written a remarkable first novel that has been enthusiastically read by some of the cognoscenti. His picture is all set to go on the cover of Time Magazine, and Oprah has lined him up for her television show. A national book tour is planned and Hollywood has already expressed interest in his book. That's all true on Tuesday. Wednesday morning San Francisco is destroyed in an earthquake, and the world's attention can hold nothing else for a month. Is Jim famous? He would have been, if it weren't for that darn earthquake. Maybe next month, if things return to normal, he'll become famous for deeds done earlier. But fame eluded him this week, in spite of the fact that the Time Magazine cover story had been typeset and sent to the printer, to be yanked at the last moment, and in spite of the fact that his name was already in TV Guide as Oprah's guest, and in spite of the fact that stacks of his novel could be found in the windows of most bookstores. All the dispositional properties normally sufficient for fame were in place, but their normal effects didn't get triggered, so no fame resulted. The same (I have held) is true of consciousness. The idea of some information being conscious for a few milliseconds, with none of the normal aftermath, is as covertly incoherent as the idea of somebody being famous for a few minutes, with none of the normal aftermath. Jim was potentially famous but didn't quite achieve fame, and he certainly didn't have any other property (an eerie glow, an aura of charisma, a threefold increase in 'animal magnetism' or whatever) that distinguished him from the equally anonymous people around him. Real fame is not the cause of all the normal aftermath; it is the normal aftermath.

The same point needs to be appreciated about consciousness, for this is where theorists' imaginations are often led astray: it is a mistake to go looking for an extra will-of-the-wisp property of consciousness that might be enjoyed by some events in the brain in spite of their not enjoying the fruits of fame in the brain. Just such a quest is attempted by Block (this volume), who tries to isolate 'phenomenality' as something distinct from fame ('global accessibility') but still worthy of being called a variety of consciousness. "Phenomenality is experience", he announces, but what does this mean? He recognizes that in order to keep phenomenality distinct from global accessibility, he needs to postulate, and find evidence for, what he calls "phenomenality without reflexivity" – experiences that you don't know you're having.

> If we want to use brain imaging to find the neural correlates of phenomenality, we have to pin down the phenomenal side of the equation and to do that we must make a decision on whether the subjects who say they don't see anything do or do not have phenomenal experiences.

But what then is left of the claim that phenomenality is experience? What is **experiential** (as contrasted with what?) about a discrimination that is not globally accessible? As the convolutions of Block's odyssey reveal, there is always the simpler hypothesis to fend off: there is potential fame in the brain (analogous to the dispositional status of poor Jim, the novelist) and then there is fame in the brain, and these two categories suffice to handle the variety of phenomena we encounter. Fame in the brain is enough.

3. Is there also a Hard Problem?

The most natural reaction in the world to this proposal is frank incredulity: it seems to be leaving out the most important element – the Subject! People are inclined to object: "There may indeed be fierce competition between 'informations' for political clout in the brain, but you have left out the First Person, who entertains the winners." The mistake behind this misbegotten objection is not noticing that the First Person has in fact already been incorporated into the multifarious further effects of all the political influence achievable in the competitions. Some theorists in the past have encouraged this mistake by simply stopping short of addressing the Hard Question. Damasio (1999) has addressed our two questions in terms of two intimately related problems: how the brain "generates the movie in the brain" and how the brain generates "the appearance of an owner and observer for the movie within the movie", and has noted that some theorists, notably Crick (1994) and Penrose (1989), have made the tactical error of concentrating almost exclusively on the first of these problems, postponing the second problem indefinitely. Oddly enough, this tactic is reassuring to some observers, who are relieved to see that these models are not, apparently, denying the existence of the Subject but just not yet tackling that mystery. Better to postpone than to deny, it seems.

A model that, on the contrary, undertakes from the outset to address the Hard Question, assumes the obligation of accounting for the Subject in terms of "a collective dynamic phenomenon that does not require any supervision", as Dehaene and Naccache (this volume) put it. This risks seeming to leave out the Subject, precisely because all the work the Subject would presumably have done, once it had enjoyed the show, has already been parceled out to various agencies in the brain, leaving the Subject with nothing to do. We haven't really solved the problem of consciousness until that Executive is itself broken down into subcomponents that are themselves clearly just unconscious underlaborers which themselves work (compete, interfere, dawdle, ...) without supervision. Contrary to appearances, then, those who work on answers to the Hard Question are not leaving consciousness out, they are explaining consciousness by leaving it behind. That is to say, the only way to explain consciousness is to move beyond consciousness, accounting for the effects consciousness has when it is achieved. It is hard to avoid the nagging feeling, however, that there must be something that such an approach leaves out, something that lies somehow in between the causes of consciousness and its effects.

Your body is made up of some trillions of cells, each one utterly ignorant of all the things you know. If we are to explain the conscious Subject, one way or another the transition from clueless cells to knowing organizations of cells must be made without any magic ingredients. This requirement presents theorists with what some see as a nasty dilemma (e.g. Andrew Brook, in press). If you propose a theory of the knowing Subject that describes whatever it describes as like the workings of a vacant automated factory – not a Subject in sight – you will seem to many observers to have changed the subject or missed the point. On the other hand, if your theory still has tasks for a Subject to perform, still has a need for the Subject as Witness, then although you can be falsely comforted by the sense that there is still somebody at home in the brain, you have actually postponed the task of explaining what needs explaining. To me one of the most fascinating bifurcations in the intellectual world today is between those to whom it is obvious – obvious – that a theory that leaves out the Subject is thereby disqualified as a theory of consciousness (in Chalmers' terms, it evades the Hard Problem), and those to whom it is just as obvious that any theory that doesn't leave out the Subject is disqualified. I submit that the former have to be wrong, but they certainly don't lack for conviction, as these recent declarations eloquently attest.

> If, in short, there is a community of computers living in my head, there had also better be somebody who is in charge; and, by God, it had better be me. (Fodor, 1998, p. 207)

> Of course the problem here is with the claim that consciousness is 'identical' to physical brain states. The more Dennett et al. try to explain to me what they mean by this, the more convinced I become that what they really mean is that consciousness doesn't exist. (Wright, 2000, fn. 14, Ch. 21)

> Daniel Dennett is the Devil... There is no internal witness, no central recognizer of meaning, and no self other than an abstract 'Center of Narrative Gravity' which is itself nothing but a convenient fiction... For Dennett, it is not a case of the Emperor having no clothes. It is rather that the clothes have no Emperor. (Voorhees, 2000, pp. 55–56)

This is not just my problem; it confronts anybody attempting to construct and defend a properly naturalistic, materialistic theory of consciousness. Damasio (1999) is one who has attempted to solve this pedagogical (or perhaps diplomatic) problem by appearing to split the difference, writing eloquently about the Self, proclaiming that he is taking the Subject very seriously, even restoring the Subject to its rightful place in the theory of consciousness – while quietly dismantling the Self, breaking it into 'proto-selves' and identifying these in functional, neuroanatomic terms as a network of brain-stem nuclei (see Parvizi and Damasio in this volume). This effort at winsome redescription, which I applaud, includes some artfully couched phrases that might easily be misread, however, as conceding too much to those who fear that the Subject is being overlooked. One passage in particular goes to the heart of current controversy. They disparage an earlier account that "...dates from a time in which the phenomena of consciousness were conceptualized in exclusively behavioral, third-person terms. Little consideration was given to the cognitive, first-person description of the phenomena, that is, to the experience of the subject who is conscious." Notice that they do not say that they are now adopting a first-person perspective; they say that they are now giving more consideration to the 'first-person description' that subjects give. In fact, they are strictly adhering to the canons and assumptions of what I have called heterophenomenology, which is specifically designed to be a third-person approach to consciousness (Dennett, 1991, Ch. 4, p. 98). How does one take subjectivity seriously from a third-person perspective? By taking the reports of subjects seriously as reports of their subjective experience. This practice does not limit us to the study of human subjectivity; as numerous authors have noted, non-verbal animals can be put into circumstances in which some of their behavior can be interpreted, as Weiskrantz (1998) has put it, as 'commentaries', and Kanwisher (this volume) points out that in Newsome's experiments, for instance, the monkey's behavior is "a reasonable proxy for such a report".

It has always been good practice for scientists to put themselves in their own experimental apparatus as informal subjects, to confirm their hunches about what it feels like, and to check for any overlooked or underestimated features of the circumstances that could interfere with their interpretations of their experiments. (Kanwisher in this volume gives a fine example of this, inviting the reader into the role of the subject in rapid serial visual display (RSVP), and noting from the inside, as it were, the strangeness of the forced choice task: you find yourself thinking that 'tiger' would be as good a word as any, etc.) But scientists have always recognized the need to confirm the insights they have gained from self-administered pilot studies by conducting properly controlled experiments with naive subjects. As long as this obligation is met, whatever insights one may garner from 'first-person' investigations fall happily into place in 'third-person' heterophenomenology. Purported discoveries that cannot meet this obligation may inspire, guide, motivate, illuminate one's scientific theory, but they are not data – the beliefs of subjects about them are the data. Thus, if some phenomenologist becomes convinced by her own (first-) personal experience, however encountered, transformed, reflected upon, of the existence of a feature of consciousness in need of explanation and accommodation within her theory, her conviction that this is so is itself a fine datum in need of explanation, by her or by others, but the truth of her conviction must not be presupposed by science. There is no such thing as first-person science, so if you want to have a science of consciousness, it will have to be a third-person science of consciousness, and none the worse for it, as the many results discussed in this volume show.

Since there has been wholesale misreading of this moral in the controversies raging about the 'first person point of view', let me take this opportunity to point out that every study reported in every article in this volume has been conducted according to the tenets of heterophenomenology. Are the researchers represented here needlessly tying their own hands? Are there other, deeper ways of studying consciousness scientifically? This has recently been claimed by Petitot, Varela, Pachoud, and Roy (1999), who envision a 'naturalized phenomenology' that somehow goes beyond heterophenomenology and derives something from a first-person point of view that cannot be incorporated in the manner followed here, but while their anthology includes some very interesting work, it is not clear that any of it finds a mode of scientific investigation that in any way even purports to transcend this third-person obligation. The one essay that makes such a claim specifically, Thompson, Noë, and Pessoa's essay on perceptual completion or 'filling in' (cf. Pessoa, Thompson, & Noë, 1998), corrects some errors in my heterophenomenological treatment of the same phenomena, but is itself a worthy piece of heterophenomenology, in spite of the authors declarations to the contrary (see Dennett, 1998b, and their reply, same issue). Chalmers (1999) has made the same unsupported claim:

> I also take it that first-person data can't be expressed wholly in terms of third-person data about brain processes and the like. [my italics]... That's to say, no purely third-person description of brain processes and behavior [my italics] will express precisely the data we want to explain, though it may play a central role in the explanation. So 'as data', the first-person data are irreducible to third-person data. (p. 8)

This swift passage manages to overlook the prospects of heterophenomenology altogether. Heterophenomenology is explicitly not a first-person methodology (as its name makes clear) but it is also not directly about 'brain processes and the like'; it is a reasoned, objective extrapolation from patterns discernible in the behavior of subjects, including especially their text-producing or communicative behavior, and as such it is about precisely the higher-level dispositions, both cognitive and emotional, that convince us that our fellow human beings are conscious. By sliding from the first italicized phrase to the second (in the quotation above), Chalmers executes a (perhaps unintended) sleight-of-hand, whisking heterophenomenology off the stage without a hearing. His conclusion is a non sequitur. He has not shown that first-person data are irreducible to third-person data because he has not even considered the only serious attempt to show how first-person data can be 'reduced' to third-person data (though I wouldn't use that term).

The third-person approach is not antithetical to, or eager to ignore, the subjective nuances of experience; it simply insists on anchoring those subjective nuances to something – anything, really – that can be detected and confirmed in replicable experiments. For instance, Merikle et al. (this volume), having adopted the position that "with subjective measures, awareness is assessed on the basis of the observer's self-reports", note that one of the assumptions of this approach is that "information perceived with awareness enables a perceiver to act on the world and to produce effects on the world". As contrasted to what? As contrasted to a view, such as that of Chalmers (1996) and Searle (1992), that concludes that consciousness might have no such enabling role – since a 'zombie' might be able to do everything a conscious person does, passing every test, reporting every effect, without being conscious. One of the inescapable implications of heterophenomenology, or of any third-person approach to subjectivity, is that one must dismiss as a chimera the prospect of a philosopher's zombie, a being that is behaviorally, objectively indistinguishable from a conscious person but not conscious. (For a survey of this unfortunate topic, see Journal of Consciousness Studies, 2, 1995, "Zombie Earth: a symposium", including short pieces by many authors.)

I find that some people are cured of their attraction for this chimera by the observation that all the functional distinctions described in the essays in this volume would be exhibited by philosophers' zombies. The only difference between zombies and regular folks, according to those who take the distinction seriously, is that zombies have streams of unconsciousness where the normals have streams of consciousness! Consider, in this regard, the word stem completion task of Debner and Jacoby (1994) discussed by Merikle et al. (this volume). If subjects are instructed to complete a word stem with a word other than the word briefly presented as a prime (and then masked), they can follow this instruction only if they are aware of the priming word; they actually favor the priming word as a completion if it is presented so briefly that they are not aware of it. Zombies would exhibit the same effect, of course – being able to follow the exclusion policy only in those instances in which the priming word made it through the competition into their streams of unconsciousness.

4. But what about 'qualia'?

As Dehaene and Naccache note,

[T]he flux of neuronal workspace states associated with a perceptual experience is vastly beyond accurate verbal description or long-term memory storage. Furthermore, although the major organization of this repertoire is shared by all members of the species, its details result from a developmental process of epigenesis and are therefore specific to each individual. Thus the contents of perceptual awareness are complex, dynamic, multi-faceted neural states that cannot be memorized or transmitted to others in their entirety. These biological properties seem potentially capable of substantiating philosophers' intuitions about the "qualia" of conscious experience, although considerable neuroscientific research will be needed before they are thoroughly understood.

It is this informational superabundance, also noted by Damasio (1999) (see especially p. 93), that has lured philosophers into a definitional trap. As one sets out to answer the Hard Question ('And then what happens?'), one can be sure that no practical, finite set of answers will exhaust the richness of effects and potential effects. The subtle individual differences wrought by epigenesis and a thousand chance encounters create a unique manifold of functional (including dysfunctional) dispositions that outruns any short catalog of effects. These dispositions may be dramatic – ever since that yellow car crashed into her, one shade of yellow sets off her neuromodulator alarm floods (Dennett, 1991) – or minuscule – an ever so slight relaxation evoked by a nostalgic whiff of childhood comfort food. So one will always be 'leaving something out'. If one dubs this inevitable residue qualia, then qualia are guaranteed to exist, but they are just more of the same, dispositional properties that have not yet been entered in the catalog (perhaps because they are the most subtle, least amenable to approximate definition). Alternatively, if one defines qualia as whatever is neither the downstream effects of experiences (reactions to particular colors, verbal reports, effects on memory...) nor the upstream causal progenitors of experiences (activity in one cortical region or another), then qualia are, by definitional fiat, intrinsic properties of experiences considered in isolation from all their causes and effects, logically independent of all dispositional properties. Defined thus, they are logically guaranteed to elude all broad functional analysis – but it's an empty victory, since there is no reason to believe such properties exist! To see this, compare the qualia of experience to the value of money. Some naive Americans cannot get it out of their heads that dollars, unlike francs and marks and yen, have intrinsic value ('How much is that in real money?'). They are quite content to 'reduce' the value of other currencies in dispositional terms to their exchange rate with dollars (or goods and services), but they have a hunch that dollars are different. Every dollar, they declare, has something logically independent of its functionalistic exchange powers, which we might call its vis. So defined, the vis of each dollar is guaranteed to elude the theories of economists forever, but we have no reason to believe in it – aside from their heartfelt hunches, which can be explained without being honored. It is just such an account of philosophers' intuitions that Dehaene and Naccache (this volume) propose.

It is unfortunate that the term qualia has been adopted – in spite of my warnings (Dennett, 1988, 1991, 1994b) – by some cognitive neuroscientists who have been unwilling or unable to believe that philosophers intend that term to occupy a peculiar logical role in arguments about functionalism that cognitive neuroscience could not resolve. A review of recent history (drawn, with revisions, from Dennett, in press) will perhaps clarify this source of confusion and return us to the real issues.

Functionalism is the idea enshrined in the old proverb: handsome is as handsome does. Matter matters only because of what matter can do. Functionalism in this broadest sense is so ubiquitous in science that it is tantamount to a reigning presumption of all of science. And since science is always looking for simplifications, looking for the greatest generality it can muster, functionalism in practice has a bias in favor of minimalism, of saying that less matters than one might have thought. The law of gravity says that it doesn't matter what stuff a thing is made of – only its mass matters (and its density, except in a vacuum). The trajectory of cannonballs of equal mass and density is not affected by whether they are made of iron, copper or gold. It might have mattered, one imagines, but in fact it doesn't. And wings don't

have to have feathers on them in order to power flight, and eyes don't have to be blue
or brown in order to see. Every eye has many more properties than are needed for
sight, and it is science's job to find the maximally general, maximally non-committal
– hence minimal – characterization of whatever power or capacity is under consideration. Not surprisingly, then, many of the disputes in normal science concern the
issue of whether or not one school of thought has reached too far in its quest for
generality.

Since the earliest days of cognitive science, there has been a particularly bold
brand of functionalistic minimalism in contention, the idea that just as a heart is
basically a pump, and could in principle be made of anything so long as it did the
requisite pumping without damaging the blood, so a mind is fundamentally a control
system, implemented in fact by the organic brain, but anything else that could
compute the same control functions would serve as well. The actual matter of the
brain – the chemistry of synapses, the role of calcium in the depolarization of nerve
fibers, and so forth – is roughly as irrelevant as the chemical composition of those
cannonballs. According to this tempting proposal, even the underlying micro-archi-
tecture of the brain's connections can be ignored for many purposes, at least for the
time being, since it has been proven by computer scientists that any function that can
be computed by one specific computational architecture can also be computed
(perhaps much less efficiently) by another architecture. If all that matters is the
computation, we can ignore the brain's wiring diagram, and its chemistry, and
just worry about the 'software' that runs on it. In short – and now we arrive at the
provocative version that has caused so much misunderstanding – in principle you
could replace your wet, organic brain with a bunch of silicon chips and wires and go
right on thinking (and being conscious, and so forth).

This bold vision, computationalism or 'strong AI' (Searle, 1980), is composed of
two parts: the broad creed of functionalism – handsome is as handsome does – and a
specific set of minimalist empirical wagers: neuroanatomy doesn't matter; chemistry
doesn't matter. This second theme excused many would-be cognitive scientists from
educating themselves in these fields, for the same reason that economists are
excused from knowing anything about the metallurgy of coinage, or the chemistry
of the ink and paper used in bills of sale. This has been a good idea in many ways, but
for fairly obvious reasons it has not been a politically astute ideology, since it has
threatened to relegate those scientists who devote their lives to functional neuroanatomy and neurochemistry, for instance, to relatively minor roles as electricians
and plumbers in the grand project of explaining consciousness. Resenting this
proposed demotion, they have fought back vigorously. The recent history of
neuroscience can be seen as a series of triumphs for the lovers of detail. Yes, the
specific geometry of the connectivity matters; yes, the location of specific neuromodulators and their effects matter; yes, the architecture matters; yes, the fine
temporal rhythms of the spiking patterns matter, and so on. Many of the fond
hopes of opportunistic minimalists have been dashed: they had hoped they could
leave out various things, and they have learned that no, if you leave out x, or y, or z,
you can't explain how the mind works.

This has left the mistaken impression in some quarters that the underlying idea of functionalism has been taking its lumps. Far from it. On the contrary, the reasons for accepting these new claims are precisely the reasons of functionalism. Neurochemistry matters because – and only because – we have discovered that the many different neuromodulators and other chemical messengers that diffuse through the brain have functional roles that make important differences. What those molecules do turns out to be important to the computational roles played by the neurons, so we have to pay attention to them after all.

This correction of overoptimistic minimalism has nothing to do with philosophers' imagined qualia. Some neuroscientists have thus muddied the waters by befriending qualia, confident that this was a term for the sort of functionally characterizable complication that confounds oversimplified versions of computationalism. (Others have thought that when philosophers were comparing zombies with conscious people, they were noting the importance of emotional state, or neuromodulator imbalance.) I have spent more time than I would like explaining to various scientists that their controversies and the philosophers' controversies are not translations of each other as they had thought but false friends, mutually irrelevant to each other. The principle of charity continues to bedevil this issue, however, and many scientists generously persist in refusing to believe that philosophers can be making a fuss about such a narrow and fantastical division of opinion. Meanwhile, some philosophers have misappropriated those same controversies within cognitive science to support their claim that the tide is turning against functionalism, in favor of qualia, in favor of the irreducibility of the 'first-person point of view' and so forth. This widespread conviction is an artifact of interdisciplinary miscommunication and nothing else. A particularly vivid exposure of the miscommunication can be found in the critics' discussion of Humphrey (2000). In his rejoinder Humphrey says

> I took it for granted that everyone would recognise that my account of sensations was indeed meant to be a functional one through and through – so much so that I actually deleted the following sentences from an earlier draft of the paper, believing them redundant: "Thus [with this account] we are well on our way to doing the very thing it seemed we would not be able to do, namely giving the mind term of the identity, the phantasm, a functional description – even if a rather unexpected and peculiar one. And, as we have already seen, once we have a functional description we're home and dry, because the same description can quite well fit a brain state."But perhaps I should not be amazed. Functionalism is a wonderfully – even absurdly – bold hypothesis, about which few of us are entirely comfortable.

5. Conclusion

A neuroscientific theory of consciousness must be a theory of the Subject of consciousness, one that analyzes this imagined central Executive into component parts, none of which can itself be a proper Subject. The apparent properties of consciousness that only make sense as features enjoyed by the Subject must thus also be decomposed and distributed, and this inevitably creates a pressure on the imagination of the theorist. No sooner do such properties get functionalistically analyzed into complex dispositional traits distributed in space and time in the brain, than their ghosts come knocking on the door, demanding entrance disguised as qualia, or phenomenality or the imaginable difference between us and zombies. One of the hardest tasks thus facing those who would explain consciousness is recognizing when some feature has already been explained (in sketch, in outline) and hence does not need to be explained again.

References

Brook, A. (in press). Judgments and drafts eight years later. In D. Ross, & A. Brook (Eds.), Dennett's philosophy: a comprehensive assessment. Cambridge, MA: MIT Press.

Chalmers, D. (1995). Facing up to the problem of consciousness. Journal of Consciousness Studies, 2, 200–219.

Chalmers, D. (1996). The conscious mind. Oxford: Oxford University Press.

Chalmers, D. (1999). First-person methods in the science of consciousness. Consciousness Bulletin, Fall, 8–11.

Crick, F. (1994). The astonishing hypothesis: the scientific search for the soul. New York: Scribner.

Damasio, A. (1999). The feeling of what happens: body and emotion in the making of consciousness, New York: Harcourt Brace.

Debner, J. A., & Jacoby, L.L. (1994). Unconscious perception: attention, awareness and control. Journal of Experimental Psychology: Learning, Memory and Cognition, 20, 304–317.

Dennett, D. (1988). Quining qualia. In A. Marcel, & E. Bisiach (Eds.), Consciousness in modern science (pp. 42–77). Oxford: Oxford University Press.

Dennett, D. (1991). Consciousness explained. Boston, MA: Little, Brown.

Dennett, D. (1994a). Real consciousness. In A. Revonsuo, & M. Kamppinen (Eds.), Consciousness in philosophy and cognitive neuroscience (pp. 55–63). Hillsdale, NJ: Lawrence Erlbaum.

Dennett, D. (1994b). Instead of qualia. In A. Revonsuo, & M. Kamppinen (Eds.), Consciousness in philosophy and cognitive neuroscience (pp. 129–139). Hillsdale, NJ: Lawrence Erlbaum.

Dennett, D. (1996a). Consciousness: more like fame than television [Bewusstsein hat mehr mit Ruhm als mit Fernsehen zu tun]. In C. Maar, E. Pöppel, & T. Christaller (Eds.), Die Technik auf dem Weg zur SeeleMunich: Rowohlt.

Dennett, D. (1996b). Facing backwards on the problem of consciousness, commentary on Chalmers for Journal of Consciousness Studies, 3 (1) (special issue, part 2), 4–6. Reprinted in J. Shear (Ed.), Explaining consciousness – the 'Hard Problem'. Cambridge, MA: MIT Press/Bradford Book, 1997.

Dennett, D. (1998a). The myth of double transduction. In S. Hameroff, A. W. Kaszniak, & A. C. Scott (Eds.), International consciousness conference. Towards a science of consciousness II: the second Tucson discussions and debates (pp. 97–107). Cambridge, MA: MIT Press.

Dennett, D., et al. (1998b). No bridge over the stream of consciousness, commentary on Pessoa et al. Behavioral and Brain Sciences, 21, 753–754.

Dennett, D. (in press). The zombic hunch: the extinction of an illusion? Philosophy (special issue on philosophy at the Millennium).

Dennett, D., & Kinsbourne, M. (1992). Time and the observer: the where and when of consciousness in the brain. Behavioral and Brain Sciences, 15, 183–247.

Fodor, J. (1998). Review of Steven Pinker's How the mind works, and Henry Plotkin's Evolution in mind. London Review of Books, Jan 22, 1998. Reprinted in Fodor, In Critical Condition. Cambridge, MA: MIT Press/Bradford Book, 1998.

Humphrey, N. (2000). How to solve the mind-body problem (with commentaries and a reply by the author). Journal of Consciousness Studies, 7, 5–20.

Hurley, S. (1998). Consciousness in action. Cambridge, MA: Harvard University Press.

McCarthy, J. (1959). Symposium on the mechanization of thought processes. London: HMSO.

Penrose, R. (1989). The emperors new mind: concerning computers, minds and the laws of physics, Oxford: Oxford University Press.

Pessoa, L., Thompson, E., & Noë, A. (1998). Finding out about filling in: a guide to perceptual completion for visual science and the philosophy of perception. Behavioral and Brain Sciences, 21, 723–802.

Petitot, J., Varela, F., Pachoud, B., & Roy, J.-M. (1999). Naturalizing phenomenology: issues in contemporary phenomenology and cognitive science. Stanford, CA: Stanford University Press.

Rozin, P. (1976). The evolution of intelligence and access to the cognitive unconscious. Progress in psychobiology and physiological psychology (Vol. 6, pp. 245–280). New York: Academic Press.

Searle, J. (1980). Minds, brains, and programs. Behavioral and Brain Sciences, 3, 417–458.

Voorhees, B. (2000). Dennett and the deep blue sea. Journal of Consciousness Studies, 7, 53–69.

Weiskrantz, L. (1998). Consciousness and commentaries. In S. R. Hameroff, A. W. Kaszniak, & A. C. Scott (Eds.), Towards a science of consciousness II: the second Tucson discussions and debates (pp. 11–25). Cambridge, MA: MIT Press.

Wright, R. (2000). Nonzero: the logic of human destiny. New York: Pantheon.

Index